THE
IMPOSSIBLE
CLIMB

Alex Honnold,
El Capitan, and
the Climbing Life

MARK SYNNOTT

DUTTON

DUTTON

An imprint of Penguin Random House LLC
penguinrandomhouse.com

Title page artwork by Clay Waldman, climbingmaps.com
Photograph on page 5 of Cathedral Ledge © Peter Doucette
Photograph on page 83 of Great Trango © Mark Synnott
Photograph on page 223 of El Capitan © Christian George
DUTTON and the D colophon are registered trademarks of
Penguin Random House LLC.

LIBRARY OF CONGRESS CATALOGING-IN-PUBLICATION DATA
Names: Synnott, Mark, author.
Title: The impossible climb : Alex Honnold, El Capitan, and the Climbing Life /
Mark Synnott.
Description: New York, New York : Dutton, [2018]
Identifiers: LCCN 2018007271| ISBN 9781101986646 (hardcover) |
    ISBN 9781101986653 (ebook)
Subjects: LCSH: Honnold, Alex. | Mountaineers—United States—Biography. |
    Free climbing—California—El Capitan.
Classification: LCC GV199.92.H67 S96 2018 | DDC 796.522092 [B] —dc23
LC record available at https://lccn.loc.gov/2018007271

Printed in the United States of America
10 9 8 7 6 5 4 3 2

Set in Adobe Garamond Pro
Designed by Cassandra Garruzzo

For
Tommy,
Lilla,
Matt,
Will, and
Hampton

CONTENTS

CONTENTS

THE
IMPOSSIBLE
CLIMB

| Prologue

The Ditch, as climbers sometimes call Yosemite Valley, typically remains summer hot well into September, but a rogue cold front had blown in overnight. A wan sun slouched low to the east, barely discernible through a thick, overcast sky. Tiny droplets of water saturated the air. Alex wondered, *Is the rock getting slippery?* The friction still felt okay, probably because a stiff breeze was drying the stone as quickly as the moisture-laden air was wetting it. But the rock had absorbed the raw gray cold, and that was starting to bother his feet. His toes were a little numb, and the size 42 shoes felt sloppy on the glacier-polished granite. He wished he'd worn the 41s.

Years earlier, when he first contemplated free soloing El Capitan, Alex had made a list of all the crux sections on Freerider, the parts that would require careful study and extensive rehearsal. The traverse to Round Table Ledge, the Enduro Corner, the Boulder Problem, the downclimb into the Monster, and the slab section on pitch 6, six hundred feet off the deck, which he now confronted. Of all the various cruxes on the 3,000-foot-high route, this one haunted him most, and for a simple reason: It's a friction climb that is entirely devoid of grips on which to pull or stand. *Like walking up glass,* thought Alex.

1

He couldn't help thinking about the fact that it had spit him off before. It's only rated 5.11, which, while still expert-level climbing, is three grades below Alex's maximum of 5.14. But unlike the overhanging limestone routes in Morocco that Alex could bully into submission by cracking his knuckles on the positively shaped holds, the crux here required trusting everything to a type of foothold called a smear. As the name implies, a smear involves pasting the sticky-rubber shoe sole against the rock. Whether the shoe sticks depends on many factors, including, critically, the angle at which it presses the rock. The best angle is found by canting one's body out away from the wall as far as possible without toppling over backward. This weights the foot more perpendicular to the stone, generating the most friction available. The more a climber can relax, the better a smear feels. Conversely, a tense or timid climber instinctively leans in toward the rock, questing for a non-existent purchase with the hands. To rely solely on such a delicate balance between the necessary adhesion and teetering past the tipping point in a high-consequence situation is perhaps the most dreaded move a rock climber can encounter.

Alex had climbed this section of El Cap twenty times and fallen once on this move. A guy who keeps numerical records of every climb he has done since high school, he had noted to himself in recent days that 5 percent of his attempts at this move had gone awry. And those were low-consequence situations; he had worn a rope clipped to a bolt two feet below his waist.

He had obsessed about free soloing El Capitan for nine years, nearly a third of his life. By now he had analyzed every possible angle. "Some things are so cool, they're worth risking it all," he had told me in Morocco. This was the last big free solo on his list, and if he could pull it off, perhaps he might start winding things down, maybe get married, start a family, spend more time working on his foundation. He loved life and had no intention of dying young, going out in a blaze of glory. And so one in twenty wasn't going to cut it. He needed to get this move, along with the other crux sections, as close to 100 percent as possible.

But Alex wasn't thinking any of this. He had trained himself not to let his mind wander when he was on the rock. He was famous, after all, for his ability to put fear in a box and set it on an out-of-the-way shelf in the back of his mind. The life questions, the analyses—he saved that stuff for when he was hanging out in his van, hiking, or riding his bike. At that moment, he was just having fun and not thinking about anything except climbing and climbing well.

Details, whether they rose to the surface of his mind or not, did factor into the climbing equation he was in the midst of solving: how he wasn't sure how his right foot felt because his big toe was slightly numb, or how the callus on the tip of his left index finger seemed glassy on the cold rock, or that his peripheral vision, key for picking up all the subtle ripples and depressions in the rock, diminished when he had his hood up, as he did now.

Back in the 1960s, when this section of El Cap was pioneered, the first ascensionist drilled a quarter-inch hole in the rock here, hammered in an expansion bolt, clipped an *étrier* to it, and stood up in this stirrup to reach past the blankness. That bolt (since replaced with a much beefier three-eighths-inch stainless steel version) was still right here, next to Alex's ankle.

Balancing on his left foot, Alex lifted his right leg high and squeegeed his toe onto the blank seventy-five-degree-angle rock. Trusting more than feeling the friction, he rocked the full weight of his body onto this smear.

It held. But only for a second.

Oftentimes, a foot slip can be checked by bearing down on the handholds. But Alex's palms were laid flat against the smooth, holdless slab; nothing counteracted the pitiless pull of gravity. Alex was weightless and picking up speed when the heel of his right foot hit a bulge in the wall, snapping his ankle over hard. But before he could register any pain, the rope tied to his harness came taut and he skidded to a stop. It could have been a short, routine fall like the other time he'd slipped, but Alex had chosen not to clip to the bolt protecting the crux, because he wanted to feel out, and perhaps ease into, being ropeless on this section of Freerider. He dangled some thirty feet below where he had come off.

"Ow, ow," whimpered Sanni, who was now only ten feet down and to the right of Alex. While he was in the air, Sanni had tried to reel in a handful of rope to shorten the fall. She was pulling with her left arm, her right down by her hip. When Alex's 160 pounds hit the end of the rope, the force of the fall pulled Sanni up violently, snapping her against the tether that connected her to the anchor and slamming her left arm against the cold granite.

"Are you okay?" Alex asked his girlfriend.

"I'm okay, it's just a bruise," she called up, her breaths coming fast and ragged. "Are you?"

"I think I'm okay, but my ankle really hurts." Alex looked down and saw his right ankle swelling. Bright red blood was splotched across the wall around him. He pressed his fingers into his knee. It felt spongy and full of fluid, like something had burst inside of it.

"I'm gonna try to weight it," he said. He put down his foot on a small shelf and tried to step up. Lightning bolts of pain shot up his leg. "Okay, that feels really bad, sickeningly bad."

Alex's first foray onto Freerider for the season could have been worse. Had this been his free solo attempt, he'd be dead at the base of the wall.

CATHEDRAL LEDGE, NEW HAMPSHIRE

PART ONE

Youth

CHAPTER ONE

"The Hon Is Going to Solo El Cap"

Jimmy Chin took a deep breath, puffed out his cheeks, and exhaled slowly. "There's something I need to tell you," he whispered. "Can you keep a secret?" We stood chest to chest in the Jackson Hole aerial tramway, crammed in with about a hundred other ruddy-faced skiers. It was February 2016, and I was in the Tetons with two of my sons, ages seventeen and fourteen, for their February school vacation. They huddled a few feet away, ignoring me and trying to catch a glimpse of the mountain through a foggy plexiglass window. We had run into Jimmy a few minutes earlier in the line for the tram. I hadn't seen him in almost a year.

"Of course," I whispered back. "What's up?"

Jimmy leaned in until his face was a few inches from mine. His eyes grew wide. "The Hon is going to solo El Cap this fall," he said.

"What? You're messing with me, right?"

"I swear."

I looked around to see if anyone had overheard, but everyone was grooving to AC/DC's "Back in Black," which pumped from a speaker overhead. Jimmy stared back at me, his mouth hanging open.

"He told you?" I asked.

"Yeah. Chai and I are making a film about it. The only people who know about this have all signed NDAs, so please keep it on the down low." Elizabeth Chai Vasarhelyi is Jimmy's wife, and, like him, she's an award-winning documentary filmmaker.

"Is he doing Freerider?"

"Yep."

"When?"

"Probably in early November."

As the reality of what I had just been told sank in, the core of my body quivered. *El Capitan. Without a rope. Whoa.*

I had climbed Freerider. Or, I should say, I had attempted it. I got to the top after several days of brutal effort, but not before the climb spit me off numerous times along the way, ropes and protective equipment arresting each fall. On a few of the hardest parts, the cruxes, I simply couldn't hang on to the fingertip jams and the flaring cracks where my hands wouldn't stick. So I had been forced to use "aid," meaning I hung on mechanical devices I slotted into cracks in the rock. I cheated. Freerider is so named because it's a "free" climb, which means it can be ascended with nothing more than your hands and feet, the rope acting only as a safety net, in case you slip off. The very best climbers can scale Freerider without aid, but I couldn't think of a single person who hadn't fallen at least once on the way up.

So what in the world was Alex Honnold thinking? El Capitan is 3,000 feet of sheer, gleaming, glacier-polished wall. And he planned to attempt it alone. Untethered. With no equipment. No fail-safe. Hoping for precision in each grab, in each step. One slip, a toe placed a centimeter too high, a shoe canted off a few degrees, a hold grabbed with the wrong hand—and Alex would plummet through the air, possibly screaming, as the ground rushed upward at 120 miles per hour. If he fell off the Boulder

Problem, which is the crux of the route, 2,100 feet up the side of the wall, he could be in the air for as long as fourteen seconds— about the time it would take me to run the length of a football field.

I knew it was Alex's dream to be the first to free solo El Capitan— I just never thought it would actually happen. When I took him on his first international expedition to Borneo in 2009, he confided to me that he was thinking about it. In the ensuing years, Alex joined me on more climbing expeditions, to Chad, Newfoundland, and Oman. Along the way, I experienced many classic "Alexisms," like him explaining at the base of the wall in Borneo why he didn't climb with a helmet, even on dangerously loose rock (he didn't own one); or the time in Chad's Ennedi Desert that he sat yawning and examining his cuticles while Jimmy Chin and I faced down four knife-wielding bandits (he thought they were little kids). Perhaps the most classic Alexism of all occurred below a 2,500-foot sea cliff in Oman, when he strapped our rope to his back and told me that he'd stop when he thought it was "appropriate to rope up" (the appropriate place never appeared). But Alex and I also spent countless hours talking about philosophy, religion, science, literature, the environment, and his dream to free solo a certain cliff.

I often played his foil, especially when it came to the subject of risk. It's not that I'm against the idea of free soloing—I do it myself on occasion. I just wanted Alex to think about how close he was treading to the edge. Like most climbers, I had an unwritten list of the people who seemed to be pushing it too hard—and Alex Honnold was at the top. By the time I met him, most of the other folks on my list had already met an early demise (and the rest weren't far behind). I liked Alex, and it didn't seem like there were many people willing to call him out, so I felt okay playing the role of father figure. And Alex didn't seem to mind. In fact, it seemed as though he enjoyed engaging me on the topic of risk, and he climbed over my arguments with the same skill and flair with which he dispatched finger cracks and overhangs. What it all came down to was that for Alex Honnold, a life lived less than fully is a fate worse than dying young.

I looked over at my two sons, still peering through the tram window, eager to ski. Alex was only twenty-nine years old. If he allowed himself to make it to my age, he might have more things outside of himself to live for; presumably his desire for risk would diminish in kind—as it had for me.

But most of all, I wondered, now that Jimmy had burdened me with the knowledge that this was happening, what I should do about it. Should I try to talk Alex out of it? Could I? Or should I support this mad enterprise and help him achieve his dream?

"COME WITH US," I said to Jimmy, when we off-loaded from the tram. "We're heading into Rock Springs. There's a ton of good snow back there."

"I want to," he replied, "but I can't. I have a lot on my plate right now. I just came up to clean out the pipes. I have to get back to work."

He fist-bumped Will and Matt, then leaned in to get me.

"I think I want to write about this," I said, as our gloved fists connected. I had quickly decided that it wasn't my place to try to stop Alex. And if it had been one of my sons or my daughter committing to a challenge like this, I'd try to have the same respect for their decision. It would be hard, but I'd try.

"Yeah, I figured. I'll call you," said Jimmy, jabbing his poles into the snow and pushing off. A few seconds later, he disappeared into the gloom.

JIMMY AND I SPOKE FREQUENTLY over the next few months. It had been a year since he and Chai had debuted *Meru,* the first film they co-directed. *Meru* tells the story of a last great problem of Himalayan climbing, called the Shark's Fin, which Jimmy, Conrad Anker, and Renan Ozturk finally solved in 2011. Well-made mountaineering films usually have their moment within the climbing community; then they fade into obscurity. But Jimmy, with Chai's help, had turned *Meru* into a smash hit. It won the Audience Award at the Sundance Film Festival, was shortlisted for an Oscar, and finished out as the highest-grossing documentary in 2015.

Hollywood had discovered Jimmy and Chai. Companies like Sony, Universal, and 21st Century Fox wanted to know what they were doing next. Jimmy told me that one day he was cold-called by a guy named Evan Hayes, the president of a production company called Parkes+MacDonald. Walter Parkes and Laurie MacDonald are legendary Hollywood producers. In 1994, they helped start DreamWorks SKG motion picture studio, where they went on to produce three Oscar-winning films in a row—*American Beauty, Gladiator,* and *A Beautiful Mind.* Hayes had just finished producing the film *Everest,* a drama inspired by the 1996 Everest tragedy that formed the basis of Jon Krakauer's book *Into Thin Air.* Hayes loved the climbing genre and wanted to make another film in the same space. And he had been in the audience at Sundance when *Meru* got a five-minute standing ovation.

Hayes tossed out some ideas he had for mountaineering-related films, but none of them captured Jimmy's imagination. They were about to hang up when Jimmy decided to share a half-formed notion that had been floating in his mind for the past few months.

"Well, there is this one idea I've been playing with," he said.

And then he told Hayes about Alex Honnold, the world's greatest free soloist. He didn't mention El Capitan, because at that moment he had no idea Alex was thinking about the free solo. In all the years he had known Alex, he had never once asked him about it. And Alex hadn't yet told a soul that he was seriously considering it.

"That's it," said Hayes. "That's the film."

Jimmy backtracked. "Well, um, yeah, but I'm not really sure I actually want to make that film. I need to think about it."

Later, he talked it over with Chai, and they decided she should call Alex to size him up, ascertain if he had enough depth to hold together a feature-length documentary. It was during the call with Chai that Alex mentioned, ever so casually, that he might want to free solo El Capitan. Chai isn't a climber, so the significance of what Alex had just dropped didn't immediately register.

"When Chai told me about El Cap, I backed right off," Jimmy told me. "That's when I knew that I really didn't want to make the film. When you live in this world and you see the aftermath . . . dying isn't that glorious." For the next two months, Jimmy avoided Hayes. And he hardly slept.

Jimmy needed advice and direction, but he hadn't bounced the idea off any of his mentors because he worried they would judge him harshly for even considering it. Then he found himself in Manhattan at the same time as his old friend Jon Krakauer. As they strolled down an avenue on the Upper East Side, Jimmy told Krakauer about his idea for the documentary. He said it was a story about "following your dreams" and the choices that one makes when faced with life-or-death decisions. Then he mentioned that Alex had said he was thinking he might free solo El Cap as part of the project.

According to Jimmy, Krakauer replied, "Oh, so that's really what it's about."

"Yeah, I guess so," replied Jimmy.

"Well, he's going to do it with or without you, and if he wants it filmed, you're the people to do it."

"So? Should I do it?" asked Jimmy.

"I'll watch it," said Krakauer.

A lot had to happen. A lot had already happened. This story is about what led up to an impossible climb. To understand what Alex would soon attempt, you need to know some things about how he lived and the world in which he became the man he is. It's a climbing world. Not everyone lives in it. But I'm happy, even proud, to say I still do. I guess you could say that I've been lucky that my path in life happened to intersect with Alex Honnold's and Jimmy Chin's, and with those of a whole bunch of other people who helped lay the foundation for what was going to happen.

Alex was going to climb beyond himself, beyond all of us.

CHAPTER TWO

Crazy Kids of America

"What happens when you die?" I asked my dad one day, as he sat reading *The New York Times* in the sunroom of our family's brick colonial.

My father lowered his paper and looked me in the eyes. "You're worm food, Mark." Snapping his paper back into place, he went back to his reading, just like that, as I stood there dumbfounded.

That night, while lying in bed, I turned the brief conversation over and over in my ten-year-old mind. If there's nothing on the other side, I reasoned, if heaven and hell are figments of our collective imaginations, then death must be absolute—an eternal void from which there is no return. Worm food. Forever.

From then on, contemplation of my own nonexistence consumed me. How does one become reconciled, I wondered, to the idea that at some unknown future date one will cease to exist? What was I supposed to do with my limited time on earth? I tried to rationalize my way out of this existential conundrum, but the thoughts began to loop endlessly inside my head—and I couldn't find the off switch.

MY IDOL AT THE TIME was Evel Knievel. My dad bought me a windup Evel on his stunt bike, and I spent hours launching the plastic superhero off elaborate ramps built with discarded shoe boxes and shingles. I loved the spectacular wipeouts when he failed to clear the Matchbox cars and toy soldiers I'd line up underneath him. I turned to the real thing with no hesitation. On a long, unused dirt driveway behind the home of some senior citizens, my friends and I used two-by-fours and plywood to build a ten-foot-high ramp-to-ramp jump. The ramps were about twice our height and prone to collapsing when we hit them at high speed on our bikes. I crashed so many times, and required so many stitches, that authorities at the Newton-Wellesley Hospital questioned my father on suspicion of child abuse.

At night I would wait for my parents to fall asleep, and then I'd sneak out of the house through the window of my third-floor room. I'd slide down the slate shingles, hang off the gutter, and quietly jump down onto the flat copper roof above my dad's study. A quick shimmy down a drainpipe and I was free. Sometimes, I would strip myself naked, save for shoes and socks, and streak through the neighborhood playing ding-dong ditch. I'd ring a house's doorbell, retreating to a nearby bush to hide. When my bleary-eyed neighbors opened their front doors to see who had rung the doorbell in the middle of the night, I'd shoot them with bottle rockets accurately launched from the end of a Wiffle ball bat that I'd sawed in half and glued back together into the shape of a tommy gun.

My discovery of risk taking as an existential salve guided me to long friendships with people who more or less shared this habit, but my young friends often lacked motivation for my style of daredevilry. One day, while I was rooting around in my father's den, I found a box of fancy wooden matches with gold tips that he must have picked up on one of his business trips. I had a clandestine site in the woods behind my house where I set afire all manner of things, from candles and birch bark to bottle rockets and Black Snakes novelty fireworks, so I pocketed the matches.

On the way to the bus stop the next morning, I decided the matches were too precious to burn. As I held up one of my new treasures between my fingers, the other kids in my neighborhood gazed in awe.

"Is that real gold?" asked one of them.

"It is indeed," I replied.

"Can I have one?" he asked.

The bus stop was next to a small, shallow, scum-filled pond. It was early winter, and a thin veneer of ice covered the black muddy water. Bobbing in the ice about fifty yards from shore was a foam takeout coffee cup.

"Retrieve that cup," I told him, "and this thing is yours."

Seconds later, he was off, breaking the ice with his fists as he half swam, half waded through the freezing swampy water. He never made it to school that day, but he got the match—and became the first of the "Golden Fellows."

FOR THE NEXT couple of weeks, the gold-tipped matches kept my friends motivated as we worked our way through an important mission I laid out for the Golden Fellows—to dance on the chimney of every house in the neighborhood. As each of my friends, from the scrawniest to the beefiest, found his route up a typically snowy roof and did his *Solid Gold* moves on or above its ridge, we'd laugh and whoop. The boy would scramble down, a grin splashed across his face, burning with the adventure, awaiting his prize. I'd make a ceremony of the presentation of the Golden Match in the middle of the icy night.

When I handed out the final gold-tipped match, it was like the Once-ler felling the last Truffula Tree in *The Lorax*—everyone packed up and went home. There were still several houses left on the list, so I persevered alone, scaling drainpipes, friction climbing up slate roofs, and going hand over hand across gutters, but it just wasn't the same dancing my little jigs on top of people's houses without anybody watching and cheering me on.

EVERY FRIDAY AFTERNOON my mom would push us kids into the back of our lemon-colored Chrysler station wagon and pick my dad up in the parking garage below the Bank of Boston. There, my dad would assume the wheel for the three-hour drive up to our vacation house in New Hampshire's White Mountains. My mom sat next to him, her primary job to keep him plied with cans of Coors and to act as a sounding board as my dad vented about the irritations and venal corruptions of the world of banking in which he lived much of his life.

My sister and I slid around the back seat, seat belt–less, bored, annoying each other however we could. I learned that if I developed what my dad called "diarrhea of the mouth"—a common tactic was to chant the slogan for Coca-Cola, which at the time was "Coke is it!," but add an "sh" to "it"—my parents would offer me money to shut up. The pay was only twenty-five cents, but with this I could play a game of Pac-Man at an inn near our house, or I could get a Charleston Chew at the candy store. My parents, I'm sure, had no idea how carefully I followed their conversations during these silent contests or how deeply they resonated. All these years later I can still remember the names of all the people who were trying to undermine my dad, who was a senior vice president. My obsession with the black eternal void of death that was coming down the pike made me vitally aware that how you spent your time alive mattered. Banking, or anything like it, certainly didn't sound like time well spent. Years later, when my dad would ask me what I planned to do with myself after graduating from college with a philosophy degree, I'd tell him in all seriousness, "I've decided not to have a career."

IN NEW HAMPSHIRE, I used the Golden Fellows model to start a new club that I called Crazy Kids of America, which quickly drew in my ski-racing buddies. The club included some noteworthy characters, including Tyler Hamilton, a compact ball of energy who always had a sly sparkle in his eyes, and who'd go on to become Lance Armstrong's right-hand man in the Tour de France, and Rob Frost, who was small for his age but scrappier than a junkyard dog, and who is now a high-angle cameraman and filmmaker. Even Chris Davenport, today a legendary extreme skier, joined us occasionally for Crazy Kid missions, his catlike athletic ability and rambunctious daredevil spirit making him a perfect fit for our crew.

I had learned from the Golden Fellows that the reward for completing a stunt shouldn't be something in finite supply, so for Crazy Kids of America, I created ranks. But instead of captain, sergeant, lieutenant, and so forth, I used the various superheroes—Spider-Man, Batman, Robin, Superman, Aquaman, Wonder Woman—and when I ran out of superheroes, I added on Tom Sawyer and Huck Finn. Each rank was further divided into junior, middle, and senior. Depending on how dangerous the mission was, you could gain a certain number of ranks.

Our specialty was pole-vaulting across ice-choked rivers with bamboo ski gates that we'd filch from our ski team lodge at Wildcat Mountain. A few of my top lieutenants—including a senior Aquaman and a junior Batman—and I became highly skilled vaulters, propelling ourselves across fifteen-foot spans of water. Of course, we had picked the sturdiest gates from the supply, leaving the rest of the kids to choose from the leftover bamboo poles, which were flimsy and prone to snapping in half at the very worst times.

Every mission followed a similar routine. A top-ranking Crazy Kid and I would find a jump across the small river that ran past the Wildcat Base Lodge. We'd pull off the feat by the skin of our teeth; then I'd offer up a few ranks, and my senior superheroes and I would apply intense peer pressure to the lower-ranked kids to follow suit. "You've totally got this, dude," I'd call to a junior Wonder Woman from the far side of the river, rubbing my hands together in anticipation of a spectacular failure.

Many a fledgling Crazy Kid took what we called the Nestea Plunge. A new recruit once showed up wearing his ski boots (rather than the Moon Boots the rest of us wore) and then proceeded to attempt a varsity-level pole vault from an ice-slicked rock over the most turbulent section of the river. We knew it was sheer folly to shoot for Spider-Man rank without some practice first, but who were we to stop him if he wanted to try? He missed badly and completely disappeared underwater. He resurfaced a short distance downstream and, like the good Crazy Kid that he was, scrapped his way back to shore.

Our ski coaches pretended they were unaware of their team's extracurricular activities, but they must have noticed the rapidly dwindling supply of ski gates and our banter about who had risen to which rank. And in a show of tacit approval at the end-of-the-season banquet, they let me give out my own Crazy Kids of America awards. Each Crazy Kid got a cardboard Burger King crown on which I had pasted our logo—a hand-drawn pencil rendering of a kid pole-vaulting over a river. The top-ranked kids got parachute men, which we saved to launch off the top of Cathedral Ledge, a five-hundred-foot cliff in nearby North Conway.

Most of the parents appreciated my contribution to New Hampshire youth culture, "Live free or die" and all that, but a few of them thought I was reckless and a bad influence. At least one kid, after taking the Nestea Plunge and going home nearly hypothermic, was forbidden from further engagement in our club's activities.

FROM WHERE MY DAD was sitting in his station wagon, he could clearly see the vertical wall of granite through an opening in the towering pine trees that lined the base of Cathedral Ledge. In the foreground stood two fifteen-year-old boys. One of them was yours truly, his hyperactive son, who had stayed back in kindergarten because he was a biter—and couldn't count, do his ABCs, or tie his shoes.

Perhaps it was the tightly laced Converse Chuck Taylors on my feet, or the hardware-store white utility rope neatly coiled over my shoulder, or the fact that my buddy Jeff Chapman, a top Crazy Kids lieutenant and a frequent partner in crime, stood by my side, but for once, my dad—who had an uncanny knack for failing to observe much of anything—realized that something was up.

"Hey," he called over, his arm hanging out the window of the K-car. "What exactly are you guys planning to do here?"

"Oh, nothing much," I replied. "Don't worry about us. Just come back in a few hours to pick us up."

My dad gave the scene a good hard look, then delivered the wood-paneled door two hard slaps. "Okay," he said. "You boys have fun."

EVERYTHING I KNEW about rock climbing had been gleaned from a poster my dad had hung on the wall in my bedroom. It pictured a craggy-jawed man hanging by his fingertips from the lip of an overhang, suspended in thin air with nothing but a skinny rope tied around his waist. Why my dad bought me that poster never occurred to me; he was a boring banker who enjoyed outdoor pursuits like skiing and hiking, but he wasn't one to push boundaries. No one had told me that it was a vintage poster from the earliest days of the sport, before the invention of harnesses and kernmantle ropes. And I didn't ask.

With the poster as our sole how-to manual, Jeff and I established our cardinal rule: The leader must not fall. But we decided whoever followed behind should have the security of the rope being held from above. This way, only one person had to risk his life.

For our first rock climb we chose a mossy gully in the center of the wall. With its ample supply of trees and vegetation, it appeared an ideal route to the summit. We took turns clawing our way up through the loose rock and vegetation, and when the rope ran out, we would untie, give it a couple of loops around a tree, then use the friction against the bark to provide security for the second climber. The higher we climbed, the steeper the wall became, until we stood on either side of a stout hemlock growing from a matrix of hard-packed dirt, moss, and rusty beer cans. Above us loomed the crux pitch, a vertical wall of loose blocks stacked on top of one another like a life-size game of Jenga.

It was Jeff's lead, but he wasn't sure he was up for it. I certainly wanted nothing to do with the crumbling wall that hung above us, so I offered up a few Crazy Kids ranks. By this point I had become a bit of a master at persuading kids to do dangerous things, and Jeff was not immune to my charms; plus, I very rarely gave anyone the opportunity to achieve junior Tom Sawyer status. A few minutes later, he was several body lengths above me, clinging to a mossy house of cards. When he reached over his head for a grip in a horizontal crack, a television-size flake shifted, raining pebbles and dirt down the wall onto my head. "I think I'm going to fall," he cried out.

"Hold on a second," I called up, untying from the rope and then using it to lash myself to the hemlock like someone about to be burned at the stake. After several turns around the tree, I locked the end off with a series of half hitches, knots I'd learned how to tie by trial and error. Satisfied there was no way I was going anywhere should he come hurtling down, I called up to Jeff something obnoxious like, "Okay, you can fall now."

Jeff looked down between his legs and saw me lashed to the tree. Two things were clear: He was going to die (or at least be badly mangled) if he fell—and I wasn't. Something about this situation seemed to violate our honor code, and the injustice of me not bleeding and broken by his side at the base of the cliff inspired him to pull it together and climb back down.

As we scrabbled our way down the gully, still determined to ascend the cliff, I noticed a horizontal break that offered a potential traverse out onto the main face. We followed it, scrambling sideways, clawing our way hand over hand through bushes to reach a small ledge about two hundred feet above the deck, with sweeping walls of clean granite surrounding it in every direction. Still tied together with the clothesline, each with some extra coils over our shoulders, we sat side by side, taking in the bird's-eye view of the valley far below us. We gave each other a knowing look. We had taken Crazy Kids of America to a whole new level, and it felt so right.

Our reverie was cut short by a jangly metallic sound, and a few seconds later a hand appeared at the lip below our feet, followed by a man who hauled himself onto our ledge. What followed was a moment of mutual disbelief as the two climbing parties took each other in. He was probably in his twenties, bearded, with calloused fingers and taut arms all muscle and sinew. I stared at his collection of space-age-looking gadgets, which hung from snap links on a bandolier over his shoulder. His rope—unlike ours, which was comprised of three lumpy braids—had a smooth sheath decorated in an Indian print of yellow and black geometric patterns.

"Wow, that's some nice-looking gear you've got," I said.

The fit man stared back at us, his face all surprise, and said something like, "How the hell did you two jackasses get up here?"

Jeff and I scooted out of his way and observed with rapt attention as he secured himself to some bolts in the wall with a couple of snap links he unhooked from his harness. "We should get our hands on some of those for next time," I said to Jeff.

When the climber's partner arrived and saw us sitting side by side next to his friend, he was equally bewildered. But the climbers wasted no time feeding their ropes through some rings in the wall and setting up what I would learn was a rappel. I keenly observed their every move, secretly hoping that our new friends might have a word of advice for our descent or, better, help us get down. Lowering yourself down on a rope looked like a great option, but as I observed them set up their gear, it was obvious that it would be tricky without harnesses, their snap links, or those fancy figure-eight thingies they were now feeding their ropes into. At the very least I wanted some props from them, a word or two acknowledging that we men were all cut from the same cloth.

But instead, as nonchalant about our fate as my dad had been that morning, they stepped off the edge onto the steep, smooth rock wall below. They slid down their ropes, leaving us kids alone on the ledge to figure out our own way down.

After they hit the ground below, they pulled their ropes out of the anchor by our heads, leaving them empty. So we fed our clothesline through the rings, just like we'd seen them do. Since we didn't have any gear other than the rope, the only option was a Batman-style bare-handed rappel, which worked for me until I reached the end of the rope and found myself dangling in the middle of a blank wall, still a hundred feet above the ground. Thankfully, using my feet to push off, I was able to pendulum swing over into the gully. Jeff followed suit. From there it was an easy climb back to terra firma.

I WAS A CLIMBER NOW, which meant it was time to begin a proper apprenticeship. So I was thrilled to discover that the Wellesley Free Library had a climbing and mountaineering section. I'd been rooting around in this library since I was a little kid, and all those years this treasure trove had been sitting right under my nose: *The Vertical World of Yosemite* by Galen Rowell, *Mountaineering: The Freedom of the Hills* by the Mountaineers, *Climbing Ice* by Yvon Chouinard, *The White Spider* by Heinrich Harrer, *Blank on the Map* by Eric Shipton, *Annapurna* by Maurice Herzog, and *The Shining Mountain* by Peter Boardman. I signed them out and greedily read them in quick succession. These books and others opened my eyes to a hitherto unknown world of high adventure, to a time frame the authors referred to as "the golden age" of climbing and exploration. The golden age, from what I read, was a time when there were still blanks on the map, when all the great mountains of the world were unclimbed, and any man or woman who had the courage, the resolve, the tenacity, could go stick a flag in a place on planet Earth where no person had ever been.

In the photo insert of *The Shining Mountain* was a picture of a bearded Joe Tasker hanging in a hammock suspended on the side of a frozen vertical wall of white Himalayan granite called Changabang, a glacier thousands of dizzying feet below. I stared at that picture for days until I could just about feel the cold granite against my back, the nylon pinching my shoulders, a cold wind frosting my face. Far more than the summit, I became enthralled with the idea of the bivouac, the part of these epic climbs when you get to relax, when maybe you'd had a decent meal and were warmly ensconced in your sleeping bag, comfy and secure in the midst of a thin-aired, cold, cold world of rock and ice.

There was one mountain that stood out like a beacon among all the rest—the Trango Tower. I first gazed upon its otherworldliness while ensconced at a carrel desk in a back room of the library. This ethereal spire rising into the mist knitted perfectly with my vision of what a mountain should be. One day . . .

While my new heroes may not have come right out and said it in so many words, I knew that the golden age of mountaineering was the greatest time in human history. And I had missed it. Here I was, a hyperactive kid, desperate to find something that could give meaning and direction to my life. Then, just as I discovered heroes to lead the way, they quashed my delusions of grandeur. Why couldn't I have been born a generation sooner?

I sulked about it for a week or so, until it struck me: What if the golden age wasn't completely over? What if there still were some obscure blanks on the map that hadn't yet been filled in? What if I could find some random mountain that no one had ever heard of, a mountain that my heroes had overlooked?

And there, in the musty reading room of the local library, a trajectory was firmly set.

CHAPTER THREE

A Vision of the Stonemasters' Lightning

Alex Honnold was screwed.

He had climbed hundreds of feet up the frozen gully, lured in by the initial low angle and the softness of the snow. But as he ascended, kicking steps with the REI snowshoes he had found in his dad's closet the day before, the gully had gradually narrowed and steepened until he found himself clawing the boilerplate ice in front of him with his bare fingers. If he'd had any idea how to climb snow and ice, the snowshoes would have long been stowed away on his pack in favor of crampons with steel toe spikes. But Alex didn't own crampons or an ice ax. It was his first winter hike. And he was alone.

A more experienced mountaineer might still have saved himself by retreating down the staircase of tiny toeholds the same way one descends a ladder. Instead, when Alex realized he had no choice but to retreat, he turned around to get an eye on the steep slope below him, like a skier sizing up his run. A second later, he was on his back, careening down the mountain. As he picked up speed, Alex looked down and saw a field of angular granite blocks at the bottom of the slope. His last thought before he slammed into the talus was *I'm going to die.*

———————

DIERDRE WAS MAKING TEA at the kitchen counter when the phone rang.

"Hello?"

"Hello, Mother."

"Alexandre?" It sounded like Alex, but something wasn't right. His voice was muffled, like his mouth was stuffed with cotton balls.

"Where am I? Why am I all covered in blood?"

Dierdre rushed into the bedroom in back; woke up her daughter, Stasia, who is two years older than Alex; and handed her the phone. "Keep him talking," she said. "I'm going to call 911."

The dispatcher at the El Dorado County Sheriff's Office told Dierdre to ask Alex what he could see. Were there any landmarks they could use to determine where he was? She grabbed the phone back from Stasia.

"What do you see?"

Silence. *Did he pass out?* "Alex, Alex, are you there? Are you awake?"

"Who is this?"

"This is Mom."

"Well, what are you speaking English for?" replied Alex, sounding annoyed. "I thought you were somebody else."

Indeed, it was the first time in nineteen years since Alex's birth that Dierdre, a professor who taught French, Spanish, and English as a second language, had spoken to her son in English. She wanted to raise her children in a bilingual household. Alex mostly replied in English, his way of letting his mom know he thought the whole thing was kind of stupid.

"Ne bouge pas, les secours arrivent" (Sit tight, help is on its way), she said, switching to French.

HE'D OWNED THE CELL PHONE for less than twenty-four hours. His mom had given it to him for Christmas. She had almost returned it because Verizon had given her the wrong one, the fancy model with the built-in camera. But it was the camera that had made Alex think to bring it with him that day. Luckily, it survived his tumble down the hill.

He faded in and out of consciousness. In his more lucid moments, he gazed to the north toward Lake Tahoe, which he vaguely recognized. But he still didn't know why he was lying in a pile of rocks at the base of a snowfield. There was a streak of blood on the slope above him. He looked down at his shredded hands. His right thumb had been degloved and felt broken. The side of his head was raw and swollen. There was a hole in his cheek, and his chest hurt like hell whenever he breathed in. His puffy jacket looked as though a tiger had attacked it. Down stuck to the blood all over his body, as if he'd been tarred and feathered. The more he probed his body, the more hurt parts he found.

The first helicopter, an Airbus H135, located Alex but couldn't land due to high winds. The pilot radioed his position back to the sheriff's office, which told Dierdre they would have to send in a team on foot. This was going to take hours, and a powerful storm was developing over the Sierra Nevada. *He's going to freeze to death,* thought Dierdre. Then she got some good news. A smaller chopper operated by the California Highway Patrol had made a gutsy landing at the base of the southeast chute. As they packaged Alex for the evacuation, he lost consciousness again.

Alex's mom took him home from the hospital in Reno late that night. He had stitches in his hand and face, a punctured sinus, chipped teeth, a broken right hand, and a serious concussion. The next day, lying in bed, his eyes nearly swollen shut, Alex recorded the ordeal in the diary he had started a month earlier. With his left hand (he was a righty), he neatly scribed the following:

Tallac

Fell, broke hand. . . . airlifted.

Should have stayed more calm and walked off. Pussy

FOR THE NEXT SEVERAL MONTHS, Alex recuperated at home in Carmichael, a suburb of Sacramento. A new video game had just come out called *World of Warcraft*, set in an alien world called Azeroth inhabited by zombies, werewolves, and gryphons. The object of the game is to complete quests that reward the player with points and currency that can be used to buy weapons and superpowers. Alex escaped to Azeroth for hours every day. In the game, he could lose himself in a fantasy world and forget about his own life, which hadn't been going so well lately.

His grandfather, with whom he was close, had died the year before. The route Alex used to ride his bike to the climbing gym went past his grandfather's house, so he would often stop by to play cribbage and chess with the old man. Several months later, after Alex graduated from high school, his parents announced they were divorcing, though Alex and his sister already knew, because they'd been reading their mom's e-mails on the family computer. Charlie Honnold moved out of the family home that summer. Not long afterward, Alex enrolled at UC Berkeley, thinking he might major in civil engineering. He lived off campus in the apartment of a family friend. Alex skulked around in sweatpants and an oversize sweatshirt, usually with the hood up. He had always been socially reserved, but now, without the support of his childhood best friend Ben Smalley or his girlfriend, Elizabeth, he withdrew into his own private world, a place with which he was already deeply acquainted.

According to Ben, Alex had a lot of social anxiety in high school. He never went to a single party or made the slightest effort to try to fit in and be popular. At lunch, while the cool crowd gathered in their exclusive section of the cafeteria, Alex retreated to the algebra room to "hang out with all the losers."

"If something made him uncomfortable or he was nervous about it, he would just avoid it," says Smalley. "He would sometimes make offhanded comments about the shiny, happy people, but it was never like, 'Oh, I wish I was one of them, I wish they liked me.' It was more like an acknowledgment that they exist, and he wasn't one of them. He was so far from being like them that he decided he wasn't going to bother even trying to get there."

But although Alex was a confirmed geek, people still respected him, says Ben, because he was so intelligent. He was a top student in the school's International Baccalaureate program, despite having no real passion for academics. He did the bare minimum to get by. Alex's mom was a member of Mensa, a society for people with high IQs. Alex also took their test and passed. According to Mensa, his intelligence puts him in at least the top two percent of the general population.

At UC Berkeley, Alex was surrounded by more shiny people than he'd ever seen in his life, but he was so shy and socially timid that he sometimes went months without communicating face-to-face with anyone. He claims that he never made a single friend that entire year. His second semester he started cutting classes to go rock climbing. His favorite spot was Indian Rock in the Berkeley Hills, two miles north of campus. He'd ride up there on his bike and spend hours traversing back and forth on the volcanic outcropping. Between climbs he'd sit on top of the rocks next to the acorn-grinding pits carved by Native Americans, eat plain bread, and stare out past the houses toward campus to the south. To the north, he could see

San Francisco Bay, which was often blanketed in fog, only the towers of the Golden Gate Bridge rising above the mist.

Climbing was his one salvation, and he hardly ever missed a day. When he wasn't hitting the gym, Indian Rock, or the stone-clad buildings on campus, he sat around in his boxers playing video games and doing pull-ups on the doorframe of his room. His classmates, who had little to no awareness of his existence, had no way of knowing that the quiet genius who was flying under everyone's radar was slowly transforming himself into a climber the likes of which the world had never seen.

THE FIRST HONNOLD blip on the climbing world's radar was in July 2004, after his first year at Berkeley, at the National Climbing Championships. The competition was held at Pipeworks in Sacramento, a gym where Alex had been training since it opened in 2000. Feeding off the energy of the hometown crowd, Alex delivered an inspired performance and took second place in the youth division (ages fourteen to nineteen). This qualified him for the world championships in Scotland, which would take place two months later. Shortly after the nationals, Alex's father, who had served as his one-man support crew over the past eight years, driving him to competitions all over California and holding his rope for countless hours, died from a heart attack while hustling to catch a flight at the Phoenix airport. He was fifty-five years old.

At the world championships in September, Alex couldn't muster any motivation or enthusiasm for the event. He placed thirty-ninth.

The thought of another year at UC Berkeley filled Alex with dread, so he asked his mom if he could drop out. Knowing how miserable he had been—he had described the college experience as "heinous"—she agreed. Then, the day after Christmas 2004, Alex nearly killed himself on Mount Tallac.

For several months after the accident, Alex sat around his mom's house feeling sorry for himself. He would later call it his "blue period." He describes himself during this time as a "ganglylooking" dude with a bad complexion who was "just not cool at all, with, like, no real prospects, no real future." Smalley visited Alex that winter and grew concerned about the way his friend was handling the death of his father, which was to act as though nothing had happened.

"I remember explicitly asking him, 'Why aren't you grieving more?'" says Smalley.

Alex explained it away, telling Smalley, "Dad and I weren't super close. All he really did was take me climbing—it's all we shared. We didn't talk. He just sort of ghosted through the house. It's hard to miss someone who wasn't really there."

When Smalley pressed, explaining to Alex that it was important for his emotional health to go through the grieving process, Alex replied, "You don't understand. Your family is normal and wholesome, and my family is weird and fucked up."

Alex would later tell me that his dad's death had been somewhat surreal. One day, he came home and found his mom sitting on the edge of their pool with her legs dangling in the water. She was crying. "Your dad died," she said.

"I never actually saw the body or went to a funeral or anything like that," said Alex. "There was no closure. And I remember thinking that there was no real verification that he was actually dead." Alex also told me, in retrospect, that his father's death was especially tragic because Charlie had been in the process of transforming himself after the divorce. It was like a weight had been lifted off his shoulders, and the taciturn, reserved man who hardly spoke was showing a whole new side to his personality. He started traveling again, which had been his passion before Stasia and Alex had come along. He had plans to see the world. He would go to all the countries still on his list and buy more souvenir masks to add to his collection. Alex had heard about this alter ego from members of his dad's family, but now he was seeing it for the first time. He was excited to get to know this new person. Then suddenly he was gone.

In the aftermath of his father's passing, Alex became, in his words, "a born-again atheist." Dierdre had been raised Catholic and had taken Alex and Stasia to mass a few times, but Alex knew that neither of his parents believed in God, and neither did he. Years later, when I asked him about his spirituality, he said, "All this talk about intelligent design—'Like, wow, look how incredibly well designed the eyeball is'—that's all bullshit. I'm totally happy ascribing it all to chance. You just need enough bits and random events and eventually crazy things happen."

That winter, when he wasn't getting lost in video-game fantasy worlds, Alex thought about what might constitute a good life. It all boiled down to a few simple facts. He did not believe in an afterlife, which meant the most precious commodity he possessed was time. So how to spend his capital? Climbing was the one thing in his life that lit his fire. Nothing else inspired him, no other interests, not friends or girls, certainly not school. Climbing allowed him to get lost in the joy of the moment. And he was good at it. When he climbed, people noticed him.

After only a week on the couch, he rode his bike to the climbing gym, where he tentatively tested how it felt to pull on his broken hand. Only his pinky and ring finger stuck out of the cast. It hurt when he pulled himself up the plastic holds with his two weakest fingers, but not enough to stop him. "Should you really be doing that?" people asked. "It's no big deal," Alex would reply. His wrist took months longer to heal than it should have.

He was still climbing indoors on plywood walls covered in textured paint, a medium as far removed from the real world as the landscapes of Azeroth. But the books and magazines by his bedside showed a whole world beyond indoor climbing where a man could leave his mark. Alex devoured every new issue of *Climbing* and *Rock and Ice* and, like every other climber, saw that among all of the sport's various disciplines, from indoor climbing to bouldering to high-altitude mountaineering, it was the free soloists like Henry Barber, John Bachar, Peter Croft, and Dean Potter who were lauded as climbing's heroes. Alex watched videos like *Masters of Stone,* over and over, in which these guys climbed into the stratosphere on fairy-tale cliffs, clinging to existence with nothing but a few fingers and a sliver of boot rubber.

One image in particular captured Alex's imagination: a photo of John Bachar, sans rope, high off the deck on a steep and slippery Yosemite crack called New Dimensions. The photo was taken in 1982, six years after Bachar made history when he free soloed it for the first time—Yosemite's first 5.11-rated free solo. The fingers on Bachar's left hand are sunk into a crack that splits a soaring, vertical open book, three hundred feet above the ground. He leans into the left page of the book with his shoulder while his right hand tucks behind his back into his chalk bag. His left toe is boxed in the crack while the right is pasted against the opposite wall, blank but for a peppering of black lichen. He wears a pair of white track shorts with blue stripes on the hip and a red long-sleeve collared shirt. His wavy blond hair sticks out from under a backward-facing pinstriped train engineer's cap. A thin mustache traces his firmly closed lips, which are neither smiling nor frowning. Piercing blue eyes look directly into the camera. He appears utterly relaxed and nonchalant, with more than a hint of arrogance in his expression; he stares you down like a street hooligan lounging against a lamppost on his home turf. It's a photo that inspired a generation of climbers. A picture of a man unchained.

JOHN BACHAR GREW UP a few miles from Los Angeles International Airport in Westchester, California, in the 1960s and early '70s. He was a precocious boy who excelled in both academics and sports. In high school he played baseball and tennis and was an all-conference pole-vaulter. Bachar dreamed of being an Olympian and trained for a few years under Joe Douglas, whose Santa Monica Track Club would go on to produce world record holders like Carl Lewis. But Bachar soon became disillusioned with the rigid structure of traditional sports, and while casting about for something new into which he could pour himself, he found his way to the graffiti-covered boulders at Stoney Point, a small climbing area in the hills north of Hollywood. On these rocks, Bachar, having no idea what he was doing, tested himself on the same short but strenuous boulder problems that iconic climbers like Royal Robbins and Yvon Chouinard had used as their training ground back in the 1950s and early '60s.

When he got his driver's license, Bachar headed for Joshua Tree National Park, where he fell in with a group of hard-core climbers that included Rick Accomazzo, Richard Harrison, and a boisterous, muscle-bound high school senior named John Long. A few months before Bachar first arrived on the scene, these three ruffians were passing around a joint in Harrison's basement in the foothills of the San Gabriel Mountains, when one of them gave voice to an idea that had been marinating in the stew of their collective unconscious. *The Stonemaster.* No one remembers who said it, but "just mentioning the name was to conjure The Stonemaster himself and his lightning struck us right between the eyes," wrote Long, in an essay describing that fateful night. The Stonemasters, a group of climbers that would forever change the trajectory of the sport of rock climbing, had just been born.

Months later, Long was showing Bachar his Stonemaster bouldering circuit on the granite eggs that lay scattered around the Hidden Valley Campground in Joshua Tree when he stopped below a three-inch-wide crack splitting the west face of a hundred-foot-tall rock called the Old Woman.

"Want to try something a bit bigger?" asked Long, pointing toward the route called Double Cross. Long was proposing "bouldering" a full-pitch rock climb or, in other words, free soloing it (a pitch is the distance one can climb in a single rope length; in the 1970s, most ropes were 150 feet long; today, 200 to 230 feet is standard).

"No way," said Bachar, who had never climbed more than a few body lengths above the ground without a rope. "That's crazy."

"If you climbed this route a hundred times, how many times would you fall?" countered Long.

Bachar thought about it for a bit and then replied, "None."

The climb, which turned out to be well within Bachar's comfort zone, was a revelation. Without the encumbrance of ropes and hardware, the feeling that Bachar got on Double Cross was better than doing drugs. He would later say that Long's question that day changed his life and that afterward, "there was just this weird twitch inside of me."

ONE OF THE FIRST THINGS a new climber learns is the numerical system used to grade the difficulty of routes. There are several different systems in use throughout the world. The American version is called the Yosemite Decimal System (YDS). It categorizes terrain into five classes. The encyclopedia of all things climbing, a book called *Mountaineering: The Freedom of the Hills,* breaks the classes down as follows:

> Class 1: A hiking scramble to a rocky gradient; generally hands are not needed.
> Class 2: Involves some scrambling and likely use of hands; all but the most inexperienced and clumsy will not want a rope.

Class 3: Moderate exposure may be present; simple climbing or scrambling with frequent use of hands. A rope should be available.

Class 4: Intermediate climbing is involved and most climbers want a rope because of exposure. A fall could be serious or fatal.

Class 5: Climbing involves use of a rope and natural or artificial protection (anchors in the rock) by the leader to protect against a serious fall.

The five before the decimal point of a rock-climbing technical difficulty grade simply denotes that it is fifth-class, that is, roped climbing. In the 1950s, when the Sierra Club first developed the system, fifth class was originally envisioned as including ten subgrades from 0 to 9, denoted as 5.0, 5.1, 5.2, and so on. The 5.0 grade was assigned to the easiest fifth-class climb, and 5.9 given to the hardest, which at the time was a route at Tahquitz in Southern California called Open Book. However, it quickly became apparent that a closed-ended system was not going to work because soon someone did a climb harder than Open Book, and then another climber bested that effort. So the system was revised and made open-ended. Then climbers began parsing the higher subgrades into easy, medium, and hard. So, for instance, 5.10 had three additional subdivisions: 5.10−, 5.10, and 5.10+. Eventually the pluses and minuses gave way to four increments of a, b, c, and d. Thus, 5.11a is only one tick harder than 5.10d and three ticks, or letter grades, less difficult than 5.11d. (In some cases, climbers have sliced it even thinner, e.g., 5.11b/c.)

Climbing grades are inherently subjective. A tall person might be able to reach past a featureless section to a beefy handhold, where a shorter climber might have to make creative use of faint ripples in the rock while stabbing desperately for the same hold.

But over time, a consensus develops around a particular climb's difficulty, and the system is remarkably consistent from one climbing area to the next.

Currently, the hardest sport climb in the world is a route called Silence in the Hanshelleren Cave in Flatanger, Norway. The climb was first envisioned and bolted by Adam Ondra in 2012, but it wasn't until 2016 that he began projecting the route in earnest. The bolts are spaced a body length or two apart, which means he'd fall anywhere from ten to thirty feet when the climb spat him off—something that happened hundreds of times. He finally found success, after some fifty days of working the route, in September of 2017. Ondra has tentatively rated the climb 9c, a French grade, which translates to 5.15d on the YDS.

So how difficult is a 5.15d? The YouTube video of the first ascent is worth watching. Ondra clings like an insect to an overhanging rock wall, angling out from the bottom of the cliff thirty or forty degrees beyond vertical. He climbs feet first, twisting his shoes into a flaring crack over his head. At the crux he winds himself into a Houdini-like contortion so extreme it's a marvel he doesn't tear his body apart. In the video's voice-over, you can hear Ondra joking that he actually used his own arm as a foothold. Higher up, he springs from one tiny hold to the next, going momentarily weightless, then catching himself, barely, with the tips of his fingers each time. After a sequence of several such moves in succession he reaches a larger edge, about the thickness of typical window-trim casing, where he "rests," steeling himself for the upper half of the climb, which features similar acrobatics.

IN THE SPRING OF 1975, Bachar dropped out of UCLA after his freshman year and headed to Yosemite. The electricity from that stormy night in Harrison's basement still crackled and, like an electromagnet, attracted a diverse group of individuals who shared the Stonemaster spirit. Now it was time for them to write the next chapter in the history of Yosemite climbing.

By the 1970s, the pioneers of Yosemite's golden age had come and gone. Royal Robbins and Warren Harding had left their marks with first ascents of the valley's largest, most spectacular cliffs, Half Dome and El Capitan, in 1954 and 1958, respectively. Yvon Chouinard, Tom Frost, Chuck Pratt, and many others had helped fill in the gaps. But while all of Yosemite's notable cliffs had already been scaled, these ascents were accomplished with the use of *aid*, meaning the climbers placed anchors—pitons, mostly— into cracks in the rock and hung from them in slings while hammering in the next steel wedge a few feet higher. For Bachar and the Stonemasters, the new game was to climb *free*, that is, without pulling on gear, resting on the rope, or standing in stirrups. Ropes and hardware were still used for protecting the climber against a fall, as a safety net, but never for upward progress. Every move had to be accomplished with the hands and feet alone.

Free climbing had played a role in the big first ascents by Robbins and his contemporaries—certain sections weren't difficult enough to require aid—but it had never been an end in itself when tackling the larger formations in Yosemite. The puzzle in unlocking the long snaking routes up 2,000 or 3,000 feet of rock wall was a tactical one: how much food, water, and gear to bring; devising systems for hauling it all up the cliff; where to camp on the wall; how many people should comprise the team. Warren Harding, who first climbed El Capitan over a span of two seasons, during which time he left his ropes "fixed" on the wall, had more in common with a skyscraper construction worker riveting I beams together than with this new breed of gymnast, who saw climbing as pure athleticism.

The fall-protection gear had evolved as well, from heavy steel pitons to lightweight aluminum chocks that could be placed and removed by hand. A climber could carry a few dozen of these "nuts" on a sling around his shoulder and hardly notice the weight, which enabled a quantum leap in difficulty. Whereas the hardest free climbs in the valley in the 1960s were rated 5.9+, give or take, by the mid-1970s the grades had been pushed well into the 5.12 realm.

And it was John Bachar, more than anyone else, who spearheaded the charge, not only by means of raw physical prowess but also by the panache with which he sought to imbue the whole free-climbing scene. He wore quirky hats, skinny shorts, and long tube socks with horizontal stripes that he pulled up to his knees. He also played the saxophone, having rescued the instrument from an ignominious death at the hands of Harrison, who was trying to convert it into a bong. At first, Bachar was all about Jimi Hendrix, but later, he found inspiration in jazz musicians like Miles Davis and Roland Kirk. He saw parallels between what these guys were doing with their instruments and what he was trying to do on the rock with his mind and body. He had surfed as a kid in LA, and the classic surf movies of his day depicting the Pipeline masters ripping down huge waves and always making it look easy—casual, even—left a lasting impression. Making a difficult climb look like no big deal, smooth and cool, just like jazz, became Bachar's trademark.

To Bachar and the other Stonemasters, smooth and cool meant moving fast, carrying a small rack of protection, and placing pieces far apart—"running it out," as climbers like to say. It was a form of self-expression demonstrating both the inner calm of a Zen master and the tenacity of a martial artist. And indeed, Bachar kept a picture of Bruce Lee, in mid-punch, taped to a page in his climbing journal. It was natural, then, that the seed John Long sowed in Bachar's psyche that day on the bouldering circuit in

Joshua Tree would eventually sprout and flourish. The ultimate expression of nerve and daring by Yosemite's self-styled highest-ranking black belt would be to leave the rope and gear behind altogether and venture up into the vertical abyss untethered.

But the Stonemasters weren't the first to climb rocks without a rope. Modern free-solo rock climbing can trace its roots back more than a century to an Austrian alpinist named Paul Preuss. In the early 1900s, Preuss authored more than three hundred first ascents—half of which he did solo. He disdained the use of equipment like pitons and even ropes because to his mind, they tainted the essence of alpinism, which was to climb mountains without the use of mechanical aids. But his boldness eventually proved his undoing. On October 3, 1913, while attempting a solo first ascent of the North Ridge of the Mandlkogel in the Austrian Alps, Preuss fell to his death. He was twenty-seven years old.

There is no record of anyone besting Preuss' free-solo feats until 1973, when a nineteen-year-old named Henry Barber, from Wellesley, Massachusetts—the same Boston suburb where I grew up—rolled into Yosemite after driving across the country in a Volkswagen bus. The jaunty newcomer, with his trademark white golfer's cap, which never left his head, kicked things off by "on-sighting" the first ascent of a route called Butterballs, a finger crack so perfectly sculpted that it had already been named, despite the fact that no one could climb it. The term "on-sight" had been adopted from the French climbing term *à vue,* which means a route is climbed with no prior knowledge other than its rating. In its most perfect sense, the climber doesn't even see the route until the moment he arrives to attempt it. Barber, wearing a few wraps of nylon webbing around his waist (proper sit harnesses with leg loops had not been invented yet) and a handful of nuts draped from a sling over his shoulder, waltzed up it on his first try. This was more than a first ascent; it was a statement: A kid from Boston had just put the West Coast climbers on notice.

That year, Barber, who kept meticulous records of his "tick list," logged 325 days of climbing. He became so comfortable on the rock that he began on-sight soloing valley test piece climbs, including Ahab, a notorious flaring squeeze chimney rated 5.10. No one had ever free soloed a 5.10 before, let alone on-sight. But these were mere warm-ups for what was to come. Before calling it a season, Barber walked up to what was at the time the longest free climb in the valley, a menacing gash splitting the 1,500-foot north face of Sentinel Rock. Two and a half hours later, he stood atop the tombstone-shaped wall, having ascended the Steck-Salathé route alone and without any equipment. It was the first time a major rock formation in Yosemite had been climbed without a rope. But what made this ascent truly mind-bending was that Barber had never done the route before. He found his way through acres of vertical terrain with no prior knowledge of what lay before him. Barber had invented a new sub-breed of climber, the on-sight free soloist, and he was now its sole practitioner.

Years later, over coffee at his house in North Conway, New Hampshire, Barber told me that after he soloed the Steck-Salathé, the Yosemite locals, who were ruthlessly competitive, started giving him the "stink eye." He'd show up at a campfire in Camp 4, and everyone would stop talking until he left.

"It could have been a jealousy thing, or I could have been an asshole," he said, alluding to the fact that he had a reputation for being abrasive back in those days. "I don't know, but it just got worse over the years."

So Henry Barber moved on. While the Stonemasters did their thing, largely within the confines of a single granite-walled valley in Northern California, he traveled the world, pushing standards everywhere he went. In Dresden, Germany, he climbed in the local style, chalkless, barefoot, and with jammed knots for protection. In Australia, they still talk about "Hot" Henry's visit in 1975, when, in a matter of days, he pushed free-climbing grades not one but two numbers higher.

IT WAS LEFT TO ANOTHER social maladroit, John Bachar, to drive ropeless climbing in Yosemite to the next level, which he promptly did the next year, in 1976, when he free soloed a multipitch 5.11 called New Dimensions. The route was only one grade below Fish Crack, which was considered the hardest climb in Yosemite at the time. A ropeless ascent of New Dimensions was as bold a statement as anything conceivable in the world of rock climbing, but not everyone was impressed or inspired. Some climbers saw Bachar as foolishly reckless. Shortly after the historic climb, a note appeared on the Camp 4 bulletin board: "Tell Webster's to change the meaning of *Insanity* to 'John Bachar free-soloed New Dimensions.'"

"He was socially awkward," says Long, "a borderline sociopath. He was his own guy and didn't get along with a lot of people."

Upon hearing of a contingent of climbers who doubted his claimed exploits, Bachar posted a now infamous note on the climbers' camp bulletin board that read, "$10,000 to anyone who can follow me for a day of free soloing. John Bachar." There were no takers. But according to Long, it wasn't all about bravado and showmanship. Long thinks Bachar's solos were more about self-affirmation than proving himself to everyone else. "He did a lot of it quietly and invisibly, with no fanfare. No one knows how much he really did."

When Bachar soloed the Nabisco Wall, a 250-foot 5.11c that includes Butterballs as its second pitch, in the spring of 1979, only a few of his closest friends were present to witness the feat. There was no film crew. No photos. Word had already spread, though, by the time Bachar got back to Camp 4, and he found himself accosted by climbers saying things like, "You're fucking nuts, man." Nabisco Wall was considered *the* valley test piece, and anyone who climbed it *with* a rope could consider himself a "hard-man" or "hard-woman" (there was a small but vital female Stonemaster contingent, led by the likes of Lynn Hill and Mari Gingery). Bachar had cemented his place in the pantheon of the world's all-time greatest rock climbers. But he wasn't finished.

He had upped the ante on the Nabisco Wall, but it wasn't until 1980 that he found his limit as a free soloist. The route was called Moratorium, and Bachar decided to climb it on-sight. To keep things adventurous, he didn't tell anyone what he had in mind, nor did he query other climbers who had done the route. If he had, they would have told him it was hard for the grade and that the crux was not the kind of climbing anyone would want to do without a rope. Three hundred feet above the ground, he found himself barely holding on in a slippery open book, the crease in the back too thin for his fingers to fit inside. Fully committed, unable to reverse the moves he had already made, Bachar punched through. Afterward, as he hiked down the back, he felt hollow. "I'd gotten away with something," he later told a friend. "I hadn't conquered anything. The mountain had just let me off."

THOUGH HE SURVIVED Moratorium that day and added another notch in his belt, the rigid strictures he had drawn up over the years began to isolate Bachar from other climbers. In the early 1980s, the ethic he championed was to climb routes from the ground up. If he fell, he immediately lowered off, pulled his rope down, and started again from the bottom. Adhering to this style, which came to be called traditional climbing, the Stonemasters (and others who followed their lead) had hit a ceiling that was preventing them from pushing grades beyond 5.13. Most of the obvious cracks in the valley had been climbed, and the only way to keep pushing higher and harder into uncharted territory was to quest out onto the blank faces between the crack systems. Face climbs generally offer only nubs and indentations and don't have fractures in which to place chocks or cams, or even pitons, so the only option if you want protection is to drill a hole in the rock and place a bolt.

Bachar was okay with bolts as long as they were placed by the leader, while climbing from the ground up. For a number of years, Yosemite climbers had maintained a consensus that allowed for the use of small metal hooks from which they would hang so as to free their hands for drilling. Several notoriously difficult and dangerous routes were thus established, including Bachar's own three-pitch tour de force in the Tuolumne high country, the Bachar-Yerian. The route is graded 5.11c X, with the "X" indicating that the bolts are so widely spaced it's likely a climber would die were he to fall at certain junctures along the route.

Bachar's ethic was noble—no one disputed that—but only a handful of people in the world were good enough, let alone bold enough, to climb according to his rules. Most people wanted to experience the joy of being high on a rock face, the world stretched below like a sublime painting—without having to lay their lives on the line.

In Europe, the birthplace of climbing, a new style was coming into vogue. Rather than go from the ground up, French, Spanish, and Italian climbers were rappelling from above and bolting routes with power drills. Where a hand-drilled bolt might take half an hour to place, a power drill could do the job in seconds. This new practice came to be known as "rap bolting." Once the bolts were in situ, the first ascensionist would "work" the route by climbing from bolt to bolt, resting on the rope along the way. When they had the climb fully memorized and rehearsed, an attempt would be made to climb the whole thing in one go without falling. If successful, the climber would say he had "redpointed" the route. The term comes from the German word *Rotpunkt,* which means "point of red." It was coined by Kurt Albert in the 1970s after he began painting a red dot at the base of routes in the Frankenjura that he had free climbed.

This new style was called sport climbing, and it was much safer than traditional climbing. Sport climbing soon became the world standard, and by utilizing these modern tactics, grades broke the 5.14 mark for the first time in the late 1980s. But Bachar would have none of it. He called its practitioners "hang dogs" and famously stated around this time that climbing without risk isn't really climbing.

At first the other Stonemasters backed him up, but it was hard to sit on the sidelines and watch as others, who were willing to embrace the new ethic, got all the glory. Yosemite was becoming a backwater. Cutting-edge climbing—and climbers—moved to Europe. In the mid-1980s, Ron Kauk, the only Stonemaster who could match Bachar's prowess on the rock, traveled to France to see what all the hubbub was about. Once he got his first taste of sport climbing, he immediately saw how it would open up huge potential in Yosemite. When he returned to the valley, he established some of the first sport routes. Higher grades soon followed. One of these routes, on Cottage Dome in Tuolumne, was a line that Bachar had been trying to climb ground up.

"All I wanted was a little rock saved for me," said Bachar, years later. "But they wouldn't even give me that." He retaliated by flattening the bolt hangers on one of Kauk's routes. An infamous altercation in the Camp 4 parking lot ensued.

"What gives you the right to take someone's route out?" asked Kauk. Bachar replied that it was no different than what they had done to his project on Cottage Dome. With the speed at which they could install new routes on rappel, he explained, there would soon be no terrain left for him. Bachar says that Kauk threw a punch but pulled back inches from his head. Kauk says he didn't and that he walked away disgusted with his old friend, who had once been like a brother. Mark Chapman, Kauk's climbing partner, stepped into the fray and told Bachar he would kick his ass if he ever chopped his bolts again. Bachar taunted him to just get it over with, and Chapman snapped. He punched Bachar hard enough in the neck that one of Bachar's arms went numb and he ended up in the hospital. Bachar pressed charges, and Chapman, an old friend and fellow Stonemaster, was arrested for assault.

Things quickly went downhill from there for Bachar. By 1990, he had few friends left in the climbing community. Many of the old Stonemasters felt that he had put climbing ethics before friendship. Bachar was bitter that the new generation of climbers seemed to have no interest in carrying forth the traditional hard-man style, which he had risked his life to enshrine. His shoulder was wrecked from years of high-level climbing, and his marriage was falling apart. While he was working through a divorce, his house in Yosemite burned down in a forest fire, and the park service tried to take his scorched land by eminent domain.

Bachar disappeared, and so did the Stonemasters' lightning.

CHAPTER FOUR

The Stone Monkey

Charlie Honnold had named Alex and his sister as beneficiaries of his life insurance policy. Alex's share of the interest on the bonds was about three hundred dollars a month, which was just enough to fund the itinerant climbing lifestyle that he envisioned as his escape from living with his mom. He borrowed her old Chevy minivan; loaded it with his climbing gear, a sleeping bag, and a few changes of clothes; and gave his mom a hug. In April of 2005 he headed off to find out what he was capable of.

In Joshua Tree National Park in Southern California, Alex wandered around the Mojave Desert among the bulbous, egg-shaped rocks, looking for things to climb. He wasn't necessarily seeking to be a soloist, but he was alone and far too shy to seek out partners in the campground. "Soloing goes with being a total loser," he later told his friend Chris Weidner. "You show up at a crag with no friends and you do your thing." He had a guidebook, but he often sized up routes and boulder problems by studying them from the base. How featured was the rock? How steep? How grainy? How tall? If his intuition told him he could do it, he climbed it.

Things sometimes got weird when he ran into other people. A part of him wanted to show off, but only if the climbing was well within his comfort zone. If the climbing was hard, near the limit of what he was capable of on-sight free soloing, which at the time was 5.10c or so, he couldn't have spectators. One day he was climbing such a route, which featured a short roof that was high enough off the deck for a fall to be fatal. His hands were jammed into a crack above the overhang, and as he was screwing up his nerve to commit to the move, he looked down and saw two tourists staring up at him. Alex froze, then retreated to a comfortable stance. He would wait until they left. But the tourists lingered, and Alex found himself wondering whether they were judging him, if they thought he was a coward for his obvious trepidation. Finally they left, and Alex pulled the roof. Later, reflecting on the incident in an essay published in *Rock and Ice* magazine, he wrote: "After that, soloing became even more solitary for me because I feared doing something stupid when people were watching. Yet it was still a difficult balance, since there are always people at climbing areas, and I often just wanted to climb. And honestly, sometimes it was nice to impress people. But pride is dangerous since it leads to recklessness or overconfidence, which have no place in soloing."

As winter approached, Alex bummed a ride north to Bishop, on the east side of the Sierra Nevada. The minivan had died and he was now getting around on an old, green mountain bike he had inherited from his dad. He stationed himself in a campground called the Pit. In the morning, he'd ride to the Happy Boulders or to a sport-climbing area called the Owens River Gorge. At the latter, Alex spent his days soloing, mostly out of necessity. He still didn't have any partners.

Alex's obsession at the time was to tick off as many routes as he could. His goal was twenty-five pitches a day, which he would compulsively record in his black book every night in his tent. He was on-sighting these routes, then downclimbing them, which, according to his rules, allowed him to count each route twice. He stuck with this program day in and day out in order to climb, as he later put it, "crappy little faces with no appeal besides the tick I could put in my guidebook." One day he headed up a 5.9 arête—an outside corner as opposed to an inside corner or open book. By now a route of this difficulty felt routine and somewhat casual. About twelve feet above the ground he slipped, landing in the dirt with a thud. After he realized he wasn't hurt, he looked around to see if anyone had seen him fall. There was no one in sight. He sat for a few moments contemplating what had just happened. It was his first unexpected fall while free soloing, and it could just as easily have happened higher up the route, high enough for him to be dead. He brushed himself off and climbed the route. A week later, it happened again from a similar height, this time while downclimbing a 5.10. Again, he walked away unhurt, and no one, besides himself, witnessed the fall.

By November, he was back at his mom's. He still didn't have a car, so he bummed rides from Sacramento-based climbers to Jailhouse Rock, a blocky, overhanging basalt cliff rising above the Stanislaus River, near Jamestown, California. Alex was still learning to apply his indoor skills to real rock, but he was tearing through the grades—with a rope. By spring he had ticked several 5.13s.

One day at Jailhouse, he met Mandi Finger. She was six years older and an experienced climber who was breaking into 5.13. When I spoke with Mandi twelve years later, in 2017, she told me Alex was too shy to talk to her, so she initiated a conversation. She discovered a young man who possessed a wealth of knowledge about almost any topic she might bring up. Within days of meeting, they decided to set off on a road trip in Mandi's Volvo station wagon.

For the next few months they traveled from one climbing area to the next across a vast swath of the western United States. In

August, they celebrated Alex's twenty-first birthday at a bar in Squamish, British Columbia. Some local guides bought Alex a drink called a muff diver—a shot of Kahlúa with a cherry floating in it, buried under whipped cream. Alex declined, telling the small crowd that had gathered around to watch that he didn't drink. The Canadian guides wouldn't hear of it. Of course he would dive the muff. How could you not? For Christ's sakes, it's your twenty-first birthday, they cajoled. They got borderline aggressive. It got awkward. But Alex stuck to his guns.

Alex and Mandi ended up dating, off and on, for nearly four years, though Alex claims that the length of the relationship "depends on how you define dating." Years later, Mandi kicks herself for staying with Alex as long as she did, claiming it was always "his way or the highway. He did not compromise."

What was Alex like back in those days, before he became famous? I asked her. "He was an asshole," she says. "All he cared about was climbing. He was obsessed. You don't do the stuff he does and come down and be normal. It's a package deal."

YOSEMITE NATIONAL PARK LIES about 150 miles due east of San Francisco in the Sierra Nevada. It encompasses 1,200 square miles, about the size of Rhode Island, most of which is roadless wilderness where intrepid hikers can explore granite domes, snow-clad peaks, and pristine alpine lakes. But the vast majority of the park's 4 million annual visitors skip the backcountry and beeline for Yosemite Valley, a seven-mile-long by one-mile-wide glacier-carved vale that lies on the park's southwestern corner at 4,000 feet above sea level. Here, the tourists clog the loop road and throng to overpriced hotels and crowded campgrounds, where the hum of RV generators and the squeals of children fill the air.

My first pilgrimage to the Ditch was in 1989. As I emerged

from the Wawona Tunnel on Highway 41 and saw the valley for the first time, I nearly crashed my Honda CB650 swerving into the parking lot of the famous overlook called Tunnel View. A few seconds later I was standing on a stone wall, gobsmacked by the panorama that lay before me. It was early May, and the alpine high country above Half Dome, still covered in snow, seemingly floated in the sky on the far end of the valley. Cascades poured down gullies on both sides of the valley, but these were mere trickles compared to the six-hundred-foot Bridalveil Fall, which plunged from a tiger-striped wall in the foreground. The floor of the valley was lush green and densely forested. Trees rose up the slope to the edge of the overlook, where two ponderosa pines, sticking up above the rest, framed the view.

I remember taking my time soaking it all in before turning my attention to the titanic cliff that loomed over the north side of the valley directly across from the falls. I had not anticipated how intimidating it would feel to stand face-to-face with El Capitan. If I hadn't spent years dreaming about climbing that wall, I could have simply trembled in awe of its immensity and pondered the retreating Ice Age glaciers that carved it from the earth's bedrock more than 10,000 years earlier. But I had long ago decided that scaling El Capitan would be my rite of passage as a climber, and for that reason, the cliff seemed to mock me, as if laughing at my audacity. Ansel Adams took a famous black-and-white photo from Tunnel View back in 1934, and he put it on the cover of his classic book *Yosemite and the Range of Light*. I had studied that photo until I felt as though I knew the place, as though I had taken its measure, but I now realized that nothing could have prepared me for how small I would feel in this valley of giants. It was shocking and a bit embarrassing how quickly I abandoned the idea of trying to climb El Capitan. Sure enough, that first season in the valley I never got higher than a pitch off the ground.

―――――――――

YEARS LATER, I took an interest in learning more about Yosemite's early history. The story the park service peddles at the visitor center hides some unpleasant facts. Before the tourist hotels and the guided nature walks led by the famous naturalist John Muir in the 1870s, Yosemite Valley was home to a polyglot tribe of Native Americans (mostly Miwoks, Paiutes, and Monos) who called the place Ahwahnee (which means "Gaping Mouth") and themselves Ahwahneechee ("those who live in the Gaping Mouth"). The troubles began when a carpenter named James W. Marshall found flakes of gold in the American River in 1848. This discovery set off the California gold rush, which drove tens of thousands of fortune hunters into the Sierra Nevada. Conflicts between the prospectors and the indigenous tribes who lived in these mountains soon followed.

By 1850, the natives living in the foothills of the Sierra Nevada were becoming increasingly concerned about how many white settlers were moving into the region. In hopes of driving the white men out of the area, they began raiding settlements. In December of that year, a war party attacked a trading post owned by a man named James Savage, killing three of his men. Local settlers had been looking for an excuse to go to war with the Indians, so they petitioned the governor, who approved the formation of a volunteer militia called the Mariposa Battalion. Savage was given the command. In March of 1851, the federal Indian commission signed treaties with six tribes. The treaties stipulated that the tribes would be relocated to a reservation in the San Joaquin Valley. The Ahwahneechee's chief, Tenaya, hadn't showed up for the meeting. A few days later, Savage and his army of 518 men found Tenaya at a village called Wawona. Tenaya tried to persuade Savage against continuing north, where it was rumored there were more villages.

In 1851, San Francisco was a quintessential boomtown, having been transformed, practically overnight, into one of the most important cities in the American West. In the three years since the gold rush began, the city's population had grown from 1,000 to nearly 30,000. Its harbor was bustling with ships that were arriving by the day from all over the world, including the Far East. The forty-niners and their wagon trains were streaming east into the Sierra Nevada, but there still wasn't a single non-native on the continent who knew about the existence of Yosemite Valley. And Tenaya was trying to keep it that way.

Savage and his men had been hired by the US government to root out every single Ahwahneechee, so they continued their march through the foothills, taking turns breaking trail in waist-deep snow. On March 21, they crested a ridge and descended into Yosemite Valley.

One of the soldiers in the battalion was a physician named Lafayette Bunnell. Four decades later, in 1892, he would publish a classic book about the campaign called *Discovery of the Yosemite and the Indian War of 1851.* In it, Bunnell writes about seeing the "frightful rock chief" from a spot that is probably not far from Tunnel View.

> None but those who have visited this most wonderful valley, can even imagine the feelings with which I looked upon the view that was there presented. The grandeur of the scene was but softened by the haze that hung over the valley,—light as gossamer—and by the clouds which partially dimmed the higher cliffs and mountains. This obscurity of vision but increased the awe with which I beheld it, and as I looked, a peculiar exalted sensation seemed to fill my whole being, and I found my eyes in tears with emotion.

Bunnell was so enthralled by the majestic view that he was still gazing into the distance, in a sort of reverie, while the rest of the battalion continued its descent into the valley. Savage called to him to get his head out of the clouds if he didn't want to be scalped by Indians who might be hiding in the woods hoping to pick off stragglers. In his book, Bunnell recounts his reply: "If my hair is now required, I can depart in peace, for I have here seen the power and glory of a Supreme being: the majesty of His handy-work is in that 'Testimony of the Rocks.' That mute appeal—pointing to El Capitan—illustrates it, with more convincing eloquence than can the most powerful arguments of surpliced priests."

His book recounts the effort he made to record the names the Ahwahneechee had ascribed to virtually every feature in the valley. Then, without apology, Bunnell renames everything. The valley's biggest cliff seems to have more than one native name. Tul-tuk-a-nú-la is a Miwok word meaning "Measuring Worm." The name comes from a creation story about El Capitan. Two bear cubs, their bellies full of berries, fall asleep on a rock, which grows up underneath them into a towering cliff. All the animals in the valley try to climb the wall to save them, but they find it impossible. Finally, an inchworm, the least likely of all the valley's creatures, offers to help. Inch by inch, it scales the wall and saves the bear cubs.

The other native name for El Capitan is To-to-kon-oo-lah, which means "Rock Chief." Bunnell writes that when he asked Tenaya about the origin of the name, the chief took him to an overlook with a view of the cliff and "triumphantly pointed to the perfect image of a man's head and face, with side whiskers, and with an expression of the sturdy English type." Translating Tenaya's "Tote-ack-ah-noo-la" into Spanish, Bunnell named the wall El Capitan. Most important, he also named the valley itself (with input from the other soldiers), "Yosemity." The name probably comes from the Miwok word *yohhe'meti,* which, according to Bunnell's book, means "grizzly bear." It was the name other tribes called the Ahwahneechee because of their renown as hunters of these bears. Bunnell writes that in the valley "their [grizzly] trails were as large and numerous, almost, as cow-paths in a western settlement."

The Mariposa Battalion would lead three sorties that spring, two of them into Yosemite Valley. What the soldiers did to the Ahwahneechee is the part that's been edited out of the story at the visitor center's replica Native American village. Apparently, the park service has decided that people would rather not know that the US government–sanctioned Mariposa Battalion torched the Ahwahneechee's villages, looted their food stores, and killed Tenaya's favorite son in cold blood—then brought the great chief to see the body. "In no fewer than seven separate incidents [in Yosemite Valley] they killed at least twenty-four to thirty Ahwahnees, and perhaps many more," says Benjamin Madley, a historian at UCLA and the author of *An American Genocide.* This number was a fraction of the total number of Native Americans killed during the six-month campaign. The battalion, which would be well paid for its service, disbanded on July 1, 1851. In the end, it succeeded in driving the Ahwahneechee out of their ancestral home to a reservation on the Fresno River, where they would face death and starvation.

Over the next few years, Ahwahneechee survivors trickled back into the valley, including Tenaya, who was allowed to leave the reservation. (The US Senate never ratified the treaty that Tenaya had signed.) By 1860, hotels had sprung up and tourists began to outnumber the natives. The hotel owners hired the Ahwahneechee to pose for photos with their guests. But they asked them to dress like Plains Indians, in tasseled buckskins and feathered headdresses, because this better fit the stereotype of what an American Indian should look like.

By the 1950s, the park service decided that the Ahwahneechee Village was an eyesore and a new rule was established, whereby only employees of the park service and its concessionaire would be allowed to live in the park. The last dwelling was destroyed in 1969. Today, in addition to the faux village at the visitor center, a project is under way to rebuild one of the original Ahwahneechee villages, called Wahhoga, on its former site. It currently has on display a few conical bark dwellings called *umachas*.

By THE DAWN of the new millennium, a modern version of the Stonemasters had taken over the Yosemite climbing scene, and with a tip of their hat to the previous generation, they called themselves the Stone Monkeys. The Monkeys, like their predecessors, broke new ground on the valley walls, establishing some of the world's most important long free climbs, such as Freerider, El Corazon, and the Quantum Mechanic. They also took seriously their responsibility to carry on the feral, rebellious antics their predecessors had enshrined into valley climbing lore. When the Monkeys weren't practicing their craft on the valley's towering cathedrals, they were generally making a nuisance of themselves, loitering around a slackline (a tightrope of nylon webbing strung between two trees), staging drunken bicycle demolition derbies in parking lots, making a ruckus in Camp 4 with all-night parties, and stalking tourist picnic tables in search of unfinished meals they could scavenge. At night, the Monkeys retreated to their various illegal bivouacs, where they hid from the park rangers like chimpanzees roosting in the jungle canopy, safe and secure from predators.

Most Monkeys had at least one nickname, many of which were created by Brian "Coiler" Kay, who lived in the same cave for so many years that it is still known to this day as the Coiler Cave. Coiler was the troop's bard, and he'd entertain the Monkeys around the campfire at night with his singing and strumming. If he wrote a song about you, there was no chance it would be complimentary.

"Clear out the parking lot, here comes Mr. Way. Do you have a tissue, because he's got an issue."

"Swills McGills got a plan now, he's gonna swill, swill, swill, swill, then he's gonna drill, drill, drill, drill."

Aaron Jones once climbed twenty-one Yosemite big walls in a single season. This meant climbing on El Capitan in August, when it can be one hundred degrees for days on end. Most of the Monkeys had moved up to Tuolumne Meadows or were spending their days hiding in the shade by the side of the river, drinking malt liquor. Jones kept at it until he literally roasted himself alive on a route called Tempest. The third-degree burns earned him the nickname "Burn-Face Boy."

Dean Fidelman, aka "Bullwinkle," bore the distinction of being both a Stonemaster and a Stone Monkey. Fidelman is an award-winning photographer who has been chronicling Yosemite climbing since the 1970s. He still shoots in black and white and processes his film in the dark room at the Ansel Adams Gallery in Yosemite Valley. One of his best pieces of work is an annual calendar called *Stone Nudes,* each month of which is a photo of a beautiful woman bouldering in the buff. (He tried a *Stone Dudes* version, which is filled with pictures of the Monkeys, but it wasn't a big seller.)

Ivo Ninov, a Bulgarian climber and BASE jumper, didn't have a nickname but was as core a Monkey as there ever was. Ivo couldn't leave, or get busted by the rangers, because he had overstayed a tourist visa and was in the country illegally. Ivo never referred to himself in the singular, even if he was alone. Instead of saying "I," he would always say "the Monkeys." His favorite saying was "The Monkeys are sending."

For some Monkeys, it seemed, the rock climbing served more

as a means to inebriate themselves in the most outlandish ways than an end in itself. Ammon McNeely, "the El Cap Pirate," held the record for the most different routes on El Capitan (sixty-one). He was so fond of malt liquor he attached beer koozies, like gun holsters, to the sides of his harness so he could fortify himself with liquid courage while leading hard aid routes. Once, while rope soloing a route called Eagles Way, he took a huge fall and ended up hanging unconscious, covered in blood, on the end of his rope. Yosemite Search and Rescue (YOSAR) soon arrived at the base of the cliff with a bullhorn.

"Do you need a rescue?" they yelled up the wall.

The loudspeaker woke McNeely from his drunken, concussed stupor. He sat up, looked around, and then yelled, *"Fuck you,"* so loudly that supposedly people in Camp 4, two miles upvalley, heard his answer. Then he climbed back up the rope and kept going.

The biggest character by far, though, was Charles Tucker III, known to all as "Chongo Chuck." Chongo was a holdover from the nineties, post Stonemasters and pre Stone Monkeys. Valley climbers in those days called themselves the Chongo Nation, in homage to their spiritual leader, who symbolized the never-ending battle with the park service, aka "the Tool." The maximum stay in the park was thirty days, so a climber had to get creative if he or she wanted to stay for the entire season, which lasts about six months. Most just flew under the radar, camping clandestinely or anonymously by various schemes, but Chongo was too big a freak to keep a low profile. He dressed like a gypsy in multiple blowsy layers of cotton shirts and loose-fitting hospital-style pants. His skin was leathery and wrinkled. His blond hair, flecked with gray, was long and stringy. He was handsome nonetheless, with sparkling blue eyes set in a face that told the tale of someone who had lived hard. He claimed to have spent ten years in Mexico City and had no recollection of what he did there.

Chongo played a constant cat-and-mouse game with the park rangers, and his preferred method of evasion was to spend as much time on El Cap as possible. He loved nothing more than to sit in his portaledge high off the deck, smoking reefer and contemplating life's great existential questions. The problem was that he didn't quite have the fitness to climb El Cap under his own steam, so he invented a new sport called big-wall hitchhiking. He'd choose a route, hang his portaledge on it five or six feet above the ground, and wait for a climbing party to come along.

"Hey, do you mind fixing a couple ropes for me?" he'd ask.

Then he'd draft for as long as he could, often bartering cheap Mexican brick weed for more rope fixing, until the team would realize that it literally had a monkey on its back.

"This is cool and all, but we're gonna have to cut you loose, sorry, man."

Chongo would set up his portaledge, smoke a fat bowl, and wait, like a trapdoor spider, for the next unsuspecting party. In this manner he usually set the record for the slowest ascent on every wall he climbed.

One time, when he was between walls and holding court in the cafeteria, he told a story about getting stranded for days on the side of El Cap. No one was coming up the wall and the route was too steep to rappel, so he settled in and embarked on a vision quest to unravel a vexing philosophical dilemma. It took him three days, but he eventually figured it out, and it was heavy.

"What was it?" I asked, leaning in, hungry for Chongo's hard-won wisdom.

"I forget," he replied.

To be a Stone Monkey was indeed to stay stoned much if not most of your waking moments. There was, after all, no other way to claim legitimate lineage to the original Stonemasters—the crew that famously set themselves up with a lifetime supply of pot in

1977. In January of that year, word trickled into Camp 4 that a plane filled with 6,000 pounds of red-haired sensimilla had crashed into a remote lake in the Yosemite backcountry. The DEA knew about the wreck but was able to remove only a small amount of the contraband before getting shut down by a blizzard. Luckily for the Stonemasters, the DEA decided to leave the plane and finish the job in the spring. Several of the Stonemasters, including Bachar, hoofed it more than ten miles through the snow to the crash site, where a hobo camp had formed in the woods on the edge of the lake. The scene was a veritable melee, with drug-crazed climbers hacking and sawing through the ice and sometimes fighting over the bales of weed that littered the lake. Bachar chopped a hole through the ice and snagged a forty-pound bale printed with a pot leaf, which he later sold in allotments as small as a quarter ounce. With the 8,000 dollars he netted, he bought a 1968 Volkswagen bus. Rumor has it that nearly a ton of weed was procured from "Dope Lake" before the rangers finally figured out that their little secret was known by virtually every climber in California. For the next year or so, the aviation-fuel-laced joints making the rounds in Camp 4 and El Cap Meadow burned extra-bright and crackly.

But amid the destruction of brain cells, the hard-core Monkeys got after the valley walls with a vengeance. And none more savagely than "the Dark Wizard," Dean Potter. More of an ape than a monkey, Potter stood six feet five inches tall and had the build of a boxer, with a barrel chest; wild, unruly brown hair; and a large aquiline nose. When he wasn't climbing or illegally BASE jumping off the valley's lofty walls, he could usually be found in El Cap Meadow, shirtless and barefoot, walking a Monkey slackline.

He was known as much for his moody temperament as he was for his prowess as an athlete. The Monkeys loved Potter like a brother, but that didn't stop them from at times calling him "Mean Dean." When he was up, Potter was an unstoppable force of nature, and his energy was the best drug of all for the other Stone Monkeys. When he was down, he would often channel whatever angst or emotional turmoil he was going through into free soloing. He distinguished himself in 2000 with the second free solo of Astroman. A few days later he reclimbed some of the key pitches for a camera crew. The full-page photos splashed across the climbing magazines made Potter a household name among climbers the world over. He went on to set numerous speed-climbing records, such as his solo linkup (accomplished partly with a rope) of Half Dome and El Cap in 1999 and his on-sight solo of the California route on Patagonia's Fitzroy in 2003. In 2006 he pulled off the hardest graded free solo ever done in Yosemite, a 5.12d crack called Heaven. What was perhaps most impressive about the climb—or disturbing, depending on whom you talk to—was that Potter's maximum grade at the time was about 5.13b, only two ticks higher on the scale. He wasn't preternaturally lithe, all tendons and sinewy muscle with a freakish strength-to-weight ratio, like Adam Ondra. Hauling his 180-pound frame up the wildly overhanging Heaven with no rope, treading so close to the line between life and death, displayed a disturbing compulsion to risk it all. It worried some of his closest friends.

And that was just the climbing. The Dark Wizard also took slacklining into the realm of extreme sport by stringing lines between cliffs, sometimes thousands of feet in the air. He called it highlining. Unlike tightrope walking, which is done on a taut steel cable with a balance pole, slacklining uses nylon webbing or rope, which still has some stretch no matter how taut it's pulled, so it sways and bounces under a person's weight. The slackliner undulates his body, snakelike, while waving his arms overhead from one side to the other in order to keep his center of mass above the line. When he was feeling inspired, Potter would highline without a tether.

As an accomplished BASE jumper, Potter took to sometimes free soloing with a parachute, a sport entirely of his own invention, which he called freeBASE. This allowed him to push his free soloing out to the edge of his climbing ability. His most notable freeBASE took place in 2008, when he climbed the 1,000-foot-long 5.12+ Deep Blue Sea on the north face of the Eiger (13,025 feet elevation) in Switzerland.

As a speed climber, free soloist, highliner, and wingsuit BASE jumper, Potter was without peer. He rampaged around the world practicing what he called his "arts," perhaps in acknowledgment of the Wizard moniker. By the mid-2000s, he was one of the most recognized and respected outdoor athletes in the world. He and his wife, Steph Davis, a top female climber, were *the* power couple of climbing. Thanks to lucrative contracts with companies like Patagonia and Black Diamond, they made a nice living and owned homes in Yosemite and Moab.

In the early morning light on May 7, 2006, Potter started up the slender east leg of a sandstone formation called Delicate Arch. The forty-six-foot-tall arch is the centerpiece of Arches National Park in Moab, Utah, and appears on the state's license plate. Potter had decided that he would free solo the formation as way to "commune with nature." It was also a chance to get some footage for a documentary film about his life called *Aerialist*. As he climbed upward past an overhanging bulge in the soft sandstone, two cameramen dangled from ropes above him. When he got to the top, he put on a harness he had previously stashed on the summit and rappelled back to the ground. He reportedly soloed the arch a total of six times that morning.

It was well-known that the arch was off-limits to climbing, but Potter, having carefully parsed the exact wording of the regulation, decided that it didn't strictly prohibit someone from *free soloing* the formation. That afternoon, Potter sent the footage to Patagonia, where a woman in the marketing department released it to various news outlets. When the story broke in *The Salt Lake Tribune* the next day, the condemnation was swift and furious.

Utahans were livid that some daredevil had violated a revered and fragile symbol of their state's natural wonders. The climbing community was even more disappointed; not because Potter had climbed the arch—climbers have never been known as rule followers—but because one of their heroes, a man who had always preached about the spirituality that drove his climbing, had the hubris to brag about something that he should have kept to himself.

The park service moved quickly to close the loophole that prevented it from charging Potter with breaking the law, and then it went a step further and drafted a new regulation prohibiting slacklining *and* the establishment of any new fixed anchors in the park. Thanks to Potter, the opportunity to establish new routes in Arches National Park was now severely limited. In one morning of climbing, he had done more damage to the climbing community's relationship with land managers than anyone in the history of the sport.

Outside magazine and the Access Fund, a nonprofit that protects access to climbing areas, sent people to the park to inspect Delicate Arch. Using spotting scopes and telephoto lenses, they documented the existence of deep grooves that had been worn into the rock on the summit of the formation—the kind of grooves that form when ropes saw back and forth on sandstone. Potter claimed that his crew had not created the grooves, but he refused to disclose how he got a rope on top of the formation to begin with. An old trick used by desert climbers was to shoot a string over the top using a bow and arrow. I later heard from a friend who was there that day that they used a tennis racket to hit a ball with a line attached to it over the top. Potter and his crew were not the first people to stand on top of Delicate Arch, and the grooves in the rock were likely from numerous previous ascents and rappels, but since the others were anonymous, he was the one left holding the bag.

Patagonia, which had built its brand on an ethos of conserving the environment, was horrified. The poster boy for their company had just desecrated one of the most sacred landmarks in the country. Initially, they stood behind Potter but told him he had to apologize, which he did, in an open letter to the outdoor-climbing community.

Around the same time that Patagonia released Potter's statement, I received an e-mail from him. The subject line read "I NEED HELP!" Though I never knew Potter well enough to consider him a buddy, I was in his larger circle of friends and associates. The e-mail ended with a plea to call or write Patagonia's CEO, Casey Sheahan. Potter even suggested the wording I could use in his defense:

> I object to the criticism of Dean's climb of Delicate Arch. It was not illegal. No harm was done to the rock. It is unfair and libelous to criticize Dean on the basis of inaccurate reports and unsubstantiated opinions. I respect Dean's no-impact climbing style, and I think it is completely in line with Patagonia's strong environmental ethics. Thank you for supporting Dean.

Hundreds of people did call and write Patagonia to defend Potter, but in the end it didn't matter. Within a few weeks of the incident, Patagonia terminated its contracts with Dean and Steph. Not long afterward, Potter free soloed Heaven.

CEDAR WRIGHT, AKA "MR. MAGOO," inhaled deeply, tilted back his head, and barked, "Oughh, Oughh." His guttural cry, meant to sound like a monkey's call but closer to that made by an old dog with worn-out vocal chords, floated up the orange shield of rock that loomed above him high on the west face of El Capitan. Someone was up there rappelling down the wall, and if it was a fellow Stone Monkey, he'd return the call. But whoever it was didn't reply.

"Holy shit, it's that Honnold kid," Cedar called to his partner, Nick Martino, when Alex came into view. Martino was fifty feet to the side of where Cedar was hanging at the belay for pitch 24 of Freerider. It was the pair's third day on the wall, and they were hoping to top out that evening. Neither of them knew Alex, but they certainly knew of him. For the past two weeks, the Monkeys had been all atwitter, as if a cobra had just slid into their nest, because some kid had come out of nowhere and free soloed two of the burliest routes in Yosemite—Astroman and the Rostrum— back-to-back in the same day. Only one other person had ever done this—Peter Croft, twenty years before, in 1987.

Croft's feat had stunned the climbing world and shifted the paradigm of what people thought possible, just as Bachar's boldest free solos had a decade earlier. By 2007, Croft was a revered fixture in Yosemite, universally held in high esteem. He was quiet—taciturn, even—but had an easy, winning smile and was always friendly when approached. He went about his business with little fanfare, a rarity for someone in his league. Unlike so many other sports, climbing has no arena; there are no grandstands at the base of the cliff. Nor is there a scoreboard or official results. If a climber wants his exploits known, he or his partner often just has to tell someone. Climbers call it "spraying," and for really good climbers, the ones with sponsorships and endorsement contracts, it's generally seen as a necessary evil. And yet there's no getting around the unseemly fact that it's bragging, and every climber knows it in his heart. Consequently, many climbers struggle to affect a low-key demeanor while letting it slip that they just did such and such hard route and the crux was wet and they were already tired from doing such and such other hard route.

But no one denied that Peter Croft was a genuinely humble hard-man. While other elite climbers of his era parlayed their exploits into a comfortable living, what little Croft had in the way of sponsorships or endorsements he supplemented by working unglamorously as a guide. And he did so to fund the simplest of lifestyles, living in a small house with his wife, driving a beater hatchback, and climbing every day.

Word might never have gotten out about Croft's Astroman-Rostrum linkup if it weren't for a chance encounter Croft had with Bachar that day. By Bachar's account, Croft's hands were covered in chalk and he had the unmistakable look in his eyes that said he'd just been to another planet and back. Bachar knew the feeling, knew Croft had just done something big. He asked Croft what he had been up to. Croft dodged the question by taking a big bite of his sandwich. But Bachar wasn't going to let him off the hook until he'd spilled it, which Croft eventually did, sheepishly.

Bachar was floored. The 1,000-foot Astroman represented the next level in free soloing, a climb that calls for every club in a Yosemite climber's bag, from thin, delicate face climbing to wide cracks, like the infamous Harding Slot. The moves entering the slot, where the crack flares from two inches to a foot wide, are horribly insecure. Bachar had made the route's first free ascent in 1975. Never in his wildest dreams did he imagine free soloing it. The Rostrum was a shorter, slightly easier climb downvalley, but it was still above Bachar's free-solo pay grade. He had considered soloing it when he was in his prime but never quite mustered up the gumption.

Now, the first person to repeat Croft's masterpiece, and only the third to free solo Astroman, was a dorky kid from Sacramento no one had heard of. The word circulating among the Monkeys was that he had been climbing outdoors for only three years. It wasn't unusual for a gym rat to transfer onto real rock and start pulling down big numbers at a crag like Jailhouse, where the movement is similar to indoor climbing. Gym climbing had been exploding in popularity. With tens of thousands of young kids getting into the sport, it was inevitable that the overall level of climbing would rise accordingly. In the 1990s, there were only a handful of people capable of climbing the rarefied grade of 5.14. Ten years later, you could go to the local gym in any big city and probably find young kids climbing that hard. But no one had just shown up in Yosemite Valley and almost immediately mastered the vast repertoire of crack-climbing techniques needed to do a route like Astroman, let alone free solo it.

The Monkeys had seen the kid around; a few had spoken to him and climbed with him. But he was standoffish, which rubbed some people the wrong way. Rumor also had it that he drove his white Ford E-150, which someone had nicknamed the "Pedophile Van," down Highway 140 every night to a pullout just outside the park boundary. The Monkeys took pride in their outlaw status, sleeping illegally under boulders, on ledges at the base of El Capitan, or in their vehicles in unoccupied campsites. But this Honnold kid actually followed the rules. *Who does that?* wondered Cedar.

It was a serendipitous place to meet for the first time, nearly half a mile off the deck on the side of El Capitan, because at that moment Martino was stuck. He'd been trying to lead a pitch known as the traverse to Round Table Ledge, which goes straight sideways for eighty feet. Martino fell near the end of the pitch and now hung fifteen feet below the horizontal crack system. He wanted to try again from the beginning, do it in proper traditional style, but since the pitch was a horizontal traverse, there was no way to rappel back to the anchor. But maybe now this Honnold dude could throw him the end of his rope. Alex obliged, and a few minutes later Martino was pendulum swinging across the cliff, jerking Alex around like a marionette controlled by a mad puppeteer.

JUST LIKE IN HIGH SCHOOL, Alex made no effort to try to fit in with the eclectic posse of misfits who called themselves the Stone Monkeys. Cedar, who soon became a close friend of Alex's, says that Alex thought the whole Stone Monkey scene—the pot smoking, the drinking, the ape calls, the ridiculous singing and strumming around the campfire at night—was "stupid."

James "Peaches" Lucas was one of the few Stone Monkeys who could call Alex a friend in 2007. They had met the year before in Squamish and had climbed together a bit. "He was kind of an outlier," says Lucas, "because he didn't smoke or drink. He didn't know a lot of people, so he didn't hang out that much."

Lucas was the one who reported Alex's Astroman-Rostrum free solo linkup on SuperTopo.com, an Internet forum that is like Facebook for Yosemite climbers. The post didn't appear until six days after the event. In the interim, Alex had kept it under his hat.

Last week, (Wednesday I think—which ever day NPS did the big controlled burn in the Valley) Alex Honold free soloed Astroman. Honold climbed the route doing the boulder problem pitch as well as the 11b variation higher. Later in the day he soloed the Regular North Face of the Rostrum using the unprotected 5.10 variation at the second pitch (there was a party on the 11a) Honold has also onsight free-soloed Pipeline (A Squamish Offwidth testpiece), the Lighning Bolt Cracks on the North Six Shooter, and soloed Chud a 13a at Rifle.

> Just wanted to send some props out to Alex. He's pretty modest so I figured I'd spray for him. Good job man.

"It was kind of a surprise to a lot of people that you could come to the valley and not hang out and be social and just rock climb and treat it as a serious sport," says Lucas. "When you do that, and you're not spending all this time spraying, you get a lot more done. He's a really good example of someone who followed the textbook of what to do if you want to get good at climbing."

The new kid had some similarities to Peter Croft. When Croft made his first road trip to the valley from his home in British Columbia in the late 1970s, "he was like Huckleberry Finn or the Jungle Boy," said Jo Whitford, Croft's first wife, in an article in *Climbing* magazine. "He wore these old corduroy shorts, all jagged, that he'd cut off with a Swiss Army knife. He'd go out soloing all day, come down and hang out by himself, and sleep in the dirt. He didn't even own a sleeping bag." Her husband, she said, had a hard time interacting with people he didn't know well. "He thinks about things. He likes to find out about the truth."

Young Alex was seeking his own truth.

AT FIRST, everyone thought it was an April Fools' Day joke. The rumor bouncing around the climbing community on April 1, 2008, was that Alex Honnold had free soloed the Moonlight Buttress. It was not the kind of route that anyone would ever solo. It's a 1,200-foot monolith in southwest Utah's Zion National Park capped with a vertical headwall whose only weakness is a finger-width crack that cleaves the orange sandstone like an expansion joint in the wall of a parking garage. In 2008, it was still impressive when someone climbed the route roped up without falling. The idea of anyone topping it without a rope was ludicrous.

At first, neither *Climbing,* nor *Rock and Ice,* nor *Alpinist* magazine reported the climb on their websites, verifying in most people's minds that it was a hoax. Then, on April 8, all three published stories confirming the free solo with firsthand accounts from Alex. Among other things, Alex said he didn't know that it was April Fools' the day he had done it. He was living in his van and climbing every day, so one day blurred into the next, and he almost never knew the day of the week, let alone the date.

Astroman and the Rostrum—impressive as they were—one could understand being climbed without a rope. It had been done before. Both are rated 5.11c, and Honnold's best climb to date had been 5.14b. But the Moonlight Buttress is rated 5.12d, which (in the strange risk calculus climbers employ) trims the cushion, the margin for error, down to a grade and a half. Yes, people had shaved it this close before. Potter shaved it much closer on Heaven, but that route is a short, forty-foot-long single-pitch climb. Potter spent less than two minutes in the death zone. Moonlight Buttress, on the other hand, has one pitch of 5.11c and six consecutive pitches—almost seven hundred feet—of 5.12. Honnold had just annihilated everyone's notion of what a ropeless rock climber could do.

Alex had spent two days practicing the route on a solo toprope, hiking to the top and fixing down the wall. There were a couple of sections that he wanted to make sure he had fully dialed in. One was a face-climbing move on pitch 5 where the climber surmounts a feature called the Rocker Blocker. It's a five-by-three-foot loose block that teeters a few inches when you climb over it. Above the block is a long reach past a blank section to a secure hold shaped like an elephant ear. When Alex did the move, he looked down to see if he might land on the Rocker Blocker if he slipped when he was free soloing. Nope. The key hold was just a smidge too far to the right. If he fell, he might bounce off the side of the Rocker Blocker, but there was no way it would stop him from going to the ground.

He had planned to rest for one day and then go for it, but it rained, and you can't climb on sandstone when it's wet because the holds absorb water and become extra friable. Climbers in sandstone areas like Zion and Red Rocks go ballistic if you break this taboo and climb when the rock is wet, because you could break a key hold and destroy a route. In Alex's case, the consequences were a bit more severe.

So he sat in his van in a movie theater parking lot by himself, running through the climb in his mind for hours on end. He thought about the individual moves, the sequences, how he would use his feet above the Rocker Blocker—and how heroic it was going to feel hanging up there on Moonlight Buttress with nothing but the tips of his fingers between him and eternity. But he also thought about how things could go wrong and what it would feel like if he slipped. Rather than hide from this reality, he explored it, right down to picturing how it would feel to hit the ground at terminal velocity. In his mind's eye, he hovered above his crumpled, bloody body. It was all part of his preparation. He wanted to think about it now, thoroughly, so he didn't have to when he was up on the wall. Get it out of his system, so to speak. This way there wouldn't be any surprises. People walked in and out of the movie theater, but no one noticed Alex sitting in his van. Later, he realized that he had been so lost in his head that he couldn't remember if he had gone to a movie or not.

The night of March 31, he cooked himself mac and cheese on his Coleman double burner and afterward he watched a police drama called *The Shield* on his laptop. At eight P.M. he went to sleep.

The next morning, he drove into the park early. Like Yosemite, the six-mile-long Zion Canyon is lined with some of the biggest cliffs in the country, including the Court of the Patriarchs— Abraham, Isaac, and Jacob—a cluster of three soaring towers of vermillion Navajo sandstone that Alex admired as he drove past. A mile from the end of the canyon, where it dead-ends at the famous slot called the Narrows, Alex pulled into a turnout below the north face of Angels Landing. On the other side of the Virgin River, Moonlight Buttress glowed in the morning sun. So far, Alex hadn't seen a soul, nor had he told a single person what he intended to do. He waded barefoot through the ice-cold emerald-colored river, holding his rock shoes in his hand, then scampered up the trail to the base of the buttress. The plan had been to wait until the route went into the shade at ten A.M., but he was so amped that he couldn't hold himself back. He stripped off all his layers down to a cotton T-shirt and hit play on his iPod, and as Bad Religion, a punk band, began to pump through his headphones, he grabbed the first hold and pulled down.

The average climbing party takes two days to climb Moonlight Buttress, sleeping in a portaledge on the side of the cliff halfway up, hauling bags full of provisions, and aid climbing most of the route. Alex topped out eighty-three minutes after he had set off from the base with a few songs left on his playlist.

On the descent down the back, Alex joined a popular trail leading to the summit of Angels Landing, where he passed dozens of tourists. His climbing shoes were too tight for hiking, so he carried them in his hand. A few people felt the need to let Alex know how foolish he was for hiking barefoot. Alex just smiled and chuckled to himself.

IN SEPTEMBER OF 2008, about five months after his free solo of Moonlight Buttress, Alex found himself alone and unroped near the top of the Northwest Face of Half Dome—and things were not going according to plan. One moment he was a hero, a demigod, and the next he was a scared twenty-three-year-old man-child, clinging to the side of a big, scary cliff that he had vastly underestimated. As his armor dissolved like an apparition, it felt like waking up from a pleasant dream into a nightmare. Alex had climbed himself into the ultimate dead end nearly 2,000 feet up the side of one of the most famous cliffs in the world, and no one but he himself could get him out of it.

He knew what he needed to do, because he had climbed the route a few days earlier with a rope. This move had felt hard, scary hard, and was the one crux on the whole route that he hadn't felt good about. But afterward, he told himself that he must have screwed up the sequence. When he got up there without a rope, he'd find a better, easier way to execute the move. The day before, he called his friend Chris Weidner, who had become his confidant, and told him what he was planning to do.

"What?" said Weidner. "Are you fucking crazy? You need to rehearse the hell out of it before you try to solo it."

"I've thought about that," said Alex. "And I've decided I want to keep it exciting." On Moonlight Buttress, Alex had done extensive rehearsal before the free solo. As a result, the climb had felt "gimmicky." He wasn't going back up to dial in the best sequence for this crux. He would figure it out when he got there.

But now that he was facing down the move, he realized he had sugarcoated it in his mind. This was simply and unavoidably a horribly insecure move, and without a rope to practice the different options for getting past it, he essentially had no choice but to do it the way he had a few days before, because at least he knew that sequence was doable. It meant pasting his right foot onto a tiny ripple and rocking his weight onto it while crimping two tiny creases with his fingers. If the foot didn't slip, he could then reach through to a good hold above. But if the foot did slip? Well, that outcome was unthinkable.

The spot he was stuck in was no picnic either. He wasn't on a ledge resting while he contemplated how to free himself from this mental prison. The creases he gripped with his fingers were too thin to hold himself up with just his hands. His feet were perched on two small edges in the rock. Most of his weight was on his toes, and his feet and calves were beginning to burn. Footholds like these have a tendency to degrade the longer you stand on them. The friction of the boot rubber against the rock creates heat, which causes the shoe to slowly ooze off the hold. It feels like falling off the mountain in slow motion.

He shifted his weight from one foot to the other, while doing the same with his hands. He kept reaching back to dip his fingers into his chalk bag like a frightened child grabbing for his security blanket. Alex needed to calm down. He took some deep breaths. *You've got this,* he told himself. But it didn't work. He knew he didn't have it, that he was teetering on the edge of control, that every second he didn't execute the move it was only getting harder. Half a dozen times, he threw his right foot onto the offending hold. *Do it, do it, do it,* he willed himself, but something wouldn't let him.

If he truly had no choice, he might already have dispensed with the move, whatever the outcome. But there *was* another option, just as a would-be suicide jumper can walk away from the edge: right in front of his face a shiny bolt protruded from the rock, and clipped to that bolt was a fat oval carabiner. It hung on the wall inches from his right hand. He could grab it, pull himself up, and reach past this horrible move. A body length above him the difficulty eased way off. If he used the carabiner, he could be on the summit in seconds.

He could hear the chatter of tourists up there. It was a warm late-summer afternoon. A few hundred feet away, dozens of people were taking photos, hugging, laughing, loving life. He looked up to see if any of them were watching him. It's a common thing for tourists to get on their stomachs and inch out onto a block called the Diving Board that overhangs the vertical northwest face. BASE jumpers use it as their launch pad. Thankfully, no one was watching him. Alex was in hell, but, as he would later recount in his autobiography, at least it was his own "private hell."

Just grab the carabiner, a voice inside his head whispered. *It's not worth it. Don't throw your life away for one dumb rock climb.* But another voice, equally powerful, said, *Wait, don't give up yet. You're one move away from the greatest free solo in history. Do you really want to throw away all the climbing you've done to get to this point?*

But some unconscious force in his mind simply would not open the gate and permit him to rock his weight onto his right foot. Each time he lifted it up and placed it on the subtle protrusion in the rock, he froze. He was about to give in and grab the carabiner, when he had an idea. By shifting the load bearing onto his middle and ring fingers, he was able to extend his index finger and lay the first pad on the bottom lip of the carabiner. He touched it ever so gently, making sure not to weight it even an ounce. This would be his compromise. He'd pull the move like this, and if the foot slipped, he'd hook his finger through the carabiner and hold on for dear life. It offered a slim possibility of survival should he blow it.

He threw his right foot onto the ripple and, with all his weight still on the toes of his left foot, inhaled deeply.

The gate opened.

He weighted his right toe and bore down as hard as he could on his fingertips, still making sure not to put weight on the carabiner. The foot held, and he snatched for an in-cut edge with his left hand. Done. He charged up the final crack leading to the summit and, as he topped out, passed about twenty people sitting on the edge of the cliff. He half expected—hoped—that someone would yell, "Holy shit, everybody, check it out, this madman just free soloed the Northwest Face of Half Dome." But no one said a word. A couple sat on a ledge a few feet away making out. The girl was cute. She paid Alex no mind. He might as well have been invisible.

Shirtless, panting, he looked at his chalk-covered hands and wrists and the veins bulging from his forearms. He looked around again. It was a beautiful sunny day; a hundred tourists were spread out across the summit of the dome, reveling in the views of the surrounding Sierra Nevada and congratulating themselves on the strenuous ten-mile hike to the summit of such a remarkable geologic formation. No one noticed him. Not one single person.

Alex took off his shoes, strung them through the belt of his chalk bag, and headed off for the cables leading down the slabs on the east side of the dome. And then, finally, someone addressed him.

"Oh my god," called out the tourist. Alex looked up hopefully. "You're hiking barefoot. You're so tough."

IN THE DAYS FOLLOWING the climb, Alex was bombarded with e-mails and calls from photographers and filmmakers who wanted to shoot him on the route. The same thing had happened after he free soloed the Moonlight Buttress. He told them all: "Thanks, but no thanks." All the mileage he had put in on the rock in recent months had caused the tendinitis in his elbow to flare up, and he just wanted to hang out at his mom's house, eat cookie dough, and keep binge-watching *The Shield*.

But in early 2009, Alex had a change of heart. Perhaps, he reasoned, it made sense to go back and re-create the climbs. People were calling them the boldest free solos in history, and it was a shame that he had no record of either of them, apart from a few notations in his Bible. His friend Celin Serbo, a photographer from Boulder, Colorado, had expressed interest in Moonlight

Buttress, and Alex had also been talking with another climber turned filmmaker named Peter Mortimer. Alex called them both and told them that he'd changed his mind.

The night before the re-creation, they went out for pizza in Springdale, the gateway to Zion National Park. As they sat around hashing out the logistics for the shoot, Mortimer shivered, like he had just seen a ghost. An image had flashed in his mind's eye—the wide-eyed kid sitting across from him free-falling down the side of Moonlight Buttress. In addition to being an award-winning filmmaker, one of the best in the climbing niche, Mortimer was also a skilled climber. He had climbed the route, so he knew exactly how hard and tenuous the climbing was. The plan had sounded great back in Boulder, but now that it was happening, he wasn't so sure.

After dinner, Alex headed for his van, and Mortimer; his assistant, Jim Aikman; and Serbo went to their hotel.

"Guys," said Mortimer a little later that evening, sitting on the edge of the bed. "I'm having second thoughts about what we're doing here."

"Me too," said Serbo.

They talked it over. Nothing had happened *yet*.

No one slept well that night. Mortimer tossed and turned as his mind worked through all the various layers of what it would mean if Alex fell. More than anything, more than the fact that it would destroy his career, that people would blame him for encouraging—if not subtly pressuring—Alex to do the climb again for the cameras, he couldn't bear the thought of Alex dying. "I didn't know him that well," says Mortimer, "but I liked him and felt close to him. He was one of the most refreshing people I'd ever met because he was so real and genuine. There was no pretense, no bullshit. You knew you were talking to the real Alex." The central question swirling in his mind was whether Alex might be doing this for the wrong reasons. They were in Zion to re-create one of the most badass climbs in history. How exactly could you see this as anything but self-aggrandizement? *What is my responsibility here?* wondered Mortimer.

"Hey, dudes, what's up," said Alex casually, in his deep baritone voice, when they met up for breakfast the next morning. The whole scene felt surreal to Mortimer, as if they were gathering to go look at the pretty rocks from one of the tourist overlooks. But he played along, projecting a confidence he didn't feel.

"Cool, man, yeah, let's do it."

Two hours later, Alex was standing on a ledge the width of a staircase tread, eight hundred feet off the deck. Serbo and Mortimer hung nearby, framing up their respective shots. They had all hiked up the back of Moonlight Buttress and rappelled off the top. Alex had never intended to repeat the entire free solo for the cameras; rather, he would do just the final four pitches of the route, which contained the most visually striking and dramatic moves. He slipped off his harness, clipped it to the end of the rope, and called up to Serbo that he could pull it up out of the shot. It was eight A.M., and the temperature was still only in the low fifties, but a light breeze made it feel colder. Alex wore long gray pants and a red T-shirt with a light blue polypropylene long-sleeve underneath. His only accouterment, apart from the rock shoes on his feet, was a purple chalk bag held to his waist with a piece of nylon webbing. A gray-handled toothbrush, for brushing excess chalk off hand-holds, was slotted in an elastic sleeve on the side of the bag.

Staring down the wall, they could see three aid-climbing parties below. Two were starting up from the base, and one had spent the night in a portaledge a few pitches above the ground. Mortimer recalls Alex looking down at the "gumbies" and saying something like, "This is bullshit, all this posing. I should just solo the whole route again. Freak all those people out. Show them what real climbing is all about."

But the show, such as they had construed it, was set to begin, so Alex jammed his fingers into the perfect crack splitting the headwall above him and stepped off the ledge. The walls on either side of the crack were sandy and smooth, almost without imperfection. The only possible purchase was in the crack itself. Alex buried his fingers in it and twisted his arm and wrist to lock them in place. He tucked the tips of his toes into the crack as well. As he reached for the next finger lock, his continued existence hung from the digits of one hand. On the tighter jams, the ones where the crack pinched down to half an inch, he could get only the tips of his index and middle fingers into the crack. But most of the time he was able to sink all four fingers to the hilt. When the jams were shaped like peapods, tapering down into tight constrictions, he would slide his fingers into the crack with his thumb on top. The meat of these jams rested on his pinky. He loved these "pinky locks," because they didn't require the same arm torque as thumb-down jams, and he could extend to his full wingspan between moves.

Staring through the viewfinder on his camera, Mortimer gasped at the footage he was capturing. This film was going to make them both famous. But what Alex was doing—it was inhuman. On a visceral level, it seemed to violate some unspecified law of nature. Mortimer felt sick.

As if in answer, Alex looked up the wall toward the two cameramen as he clung to the tiny fissure in the vertical wall of stone.

"Is this even cool?" he asked. "Do you want me to breathe hard and make it look like I'm scared or I'm trying?"

PART TWO

The Professional World

GREAT TRANGO, PAKISTAN

CHAPTER FIVE

Crashing the Gravy Train on the Vertical Mile

The rope yawned alongside the knife-edge ridge like a giant smiley face. Tied to its end, one hundred feet away to my right, another Alex (it was 1999, and I hadn't met Alex Honnold yet), the world's premier alpinist, Alex Lowe, was spread-eagled between slender pinnacles of granite. The opposing outward force of Alex's hands and feet pressing against the grainy rock created just enough friction to hold him in place. He had been moving fast, but he now appeared stuck, stymied by a crux move harder than anything yet encountered on the nearly 6,000-foot wall we had climbed to get to this point.

A few minutes earlier, Alex had passed up a spot where I thought he could have placed a piece of protection, an anchor in the rock that would have made the fall he was now staring down a lot less dangerous. *Why didn't he place that piece?* I wondered. *Did he not see it?* If it had been my other climbing partner, Jared Ogden, I would have yelled, "Hey, get something in," but I hadn't said anything because Alex and I weren't getting along, and I was afraid he'd think, once again, that I was bossing him around. There was also a distinct possibility that he was deliberately making the pitch more dangerous because it was faster not to stop and dink around with gear. I had figured that he'd find a way to anchor his rope when the climbing got hard, but that didn't happen; the drooping strand of orange cord between him and our belay was attached to nothing.

Jared, roosting beside me with a leg on each side of the narrow ridge, held Alex's rope in his belay plate. He looked at me, wide-eyed, and his expression said it all: *Alex is pushing it a touch too far.* The ridge was like the back of a Stegosaurus, with rocky pinnacles protruding like horns from its spine. On both sides, sheer rock walls dropped almost vertically. The wall to my left was the one we had spent most of the summer climbing. It fell away for more than a mile straight down to the glacier, which I couldn't see anymore because a churning cloud bank was flowing around the bottom half of the mountain, boiling up its flanks like steam rising from a volcano. One by one, the surrounding summits were disappearing into the murk. How long, I wondered, until the approaching storm would consume us, too?

The virgin west summit of Great Trango Tower, 20,260 feet above sea level, loomed only seventy-five feet above Alex's head. I was a stone's throw away from a place I had been dreaming about for half of my life, since that fateful day I first learned of this magnificent monolith in the Wellesley Free Library. But as the clouds closed in, I could think only of our packs—containing our sleeping bags, some food, and a stove—which we had stashed on a small ledge several hundred feet below our present position. We didn't even have a water bottle or a puffy down jacket with us, and if we didn't get back down to that ledge before nightfall and the arrival of the storm, we might well die of exposure.

I willed myself not to calculate how far Alex would fall if he slipped, whether his rope would cut on the sharp spine of the ridge if he fell off the other side, or how we could possibly get him down if he was critically injured this high up on the mountain. *It's Alex Lowe out there, Mark,* I said silently to myself. *He won't blow this.* But the cramp in the left side of my chest clamped even tighter. I knew that Alex had already taken three big falls on the route so far, that he had been knocked unconscious by rockfall on pitch 13, that only one day earlier he had been so ill we weren't sure if he would be joining us on this bid for the summit. Alex, despite the hype that surrounded him, was human, just like Jared and me. And if he inched too far out on that limb, and it broke off, there was a decent chance he was taking all of us with him.

WHILE WE GENERALLY TOOK TURNS pushing the route up the wall, we also each vied and connived a bit for the better pitches of the route. Jared and I sought the beautiful cracks and corners up the sheer sections of cliff that offered exposed and exhilarating climbing but also enough protection points to keep the climbing at least relatively sane. Alex, on the other hand, sought out the nasty, scary pitches, the ones with the highest stakes, exactly like what he was now battling.

Jared and I called him our "secret weapon," but in the climbing community he was known as "the Mutant." He picked up the nickname in 1995 on Denali, the highest peak in North America. Alex was hanging out at the 14,000-foot camp with two other elite climbers, Mark Twight and Scott Backes, when they got word that three Spaniards were freezing to death high on the West Rib. A few hours later, having been deputized by the park service, the trio was picked up by an army Chinook helicopter and skid landed at 19,500 feet, just below the summit. When they reached the Spaniards, one had already fallen, one was frozen and incoherent, and one was still able to move. Twight and Backes started working their way up with the guy who could function, leaving Alex behind to wait with the other. But Alex got impatient, as he was wont to do, so he tied the guy to his harness and started dragging him up the mountain back to the helicopter. When the snow got too deep, he threw the Spaniard on his back and kept climbing upward through steep terrain. The incapacitated climber, with all his frozen gear, weighed more than Alex.

ALEX LOWE WAS A MAN custom-built for such superhuman feats. His upper body was triangular, bulging arms hanging from broad shoulders tapering down to a narrow waist. His outsize, scar-covered hands often sported "gobies" and "flappers," climber-speak for the cuts and flaps of skin you get from stuffing your paws into rough-sided cracks. His barrel chest housed a set of lungs that could have sped him through the Tour de France had he chosen to ride bikes instead of climb mountains. In 1993, he was invited by the Russian Mountaineering Federation to take part in a kamikaze-style climbing competition on a 23,000-foot peak in Central Asia called Khan Tengri. The field included many of the best mountaineers in Russia. Alex didn't just win; he crushed the previous best time by more than four hours—a record that still stands today.

In March of 1999, a few months before we left for Trango, the cover of *Outside* magazine featured Alex, with his craggy jaw and blue steel eyes twinkling beneath bushy brown eyebrows, standing astride a virgin spike of rock in Antarctica. The caption read: "The World's Best Climber." It was a moniker he scoffed at, famously saying around the same time, "The best climber in the world is the one having the most fun." His enthusiasm and love for climbing could be contagious—if you could keep up with him. He more or less held his climbing partners to the same standards he set for himself, so if you weren't getting up at four A.M., downing a pot of jet-black coffee, and then cranking off pyramids of four hundred pull-ups before breakfast, you might find climbing with him a bit intimidating.

ALEX WASN'T GOING TO BACK DOWN, so he pushed off with his right arm and leg, unhitching himself from the crucifix-like stem and falling toward the pinnacle on his left. His body swung through the thin air, and just as gravity began to exert its inexorable pull, his right hand slapped onto a crystalline knob. At the same moment, he threw his right leg around the backside of the pinnacle. His body sagged, but Alex dug in with his right heel, straightened up, and stayed stuck on.

With no actual holds on which to stand or pull himself up this arête, he began a complex dance of intricate oppositional movement: one hand gripped the edge while the other slapped around the corner, fingertips groping blindly for the tiniest crease or edge. He smeared his toes against any slight depressions or nubs, countering the pulling forces of his arms. A well-placed heel hooked around the arête gained him enough purchase to reposition his hands a few feet higher. He scummed whatever square inch of his body he could—calf, hip, forearm—against the rock. Alex had simian intuition and this "body English," as climbers call it, allowed him to grip a smidge less forcefully, thus saving precious kilojoules of energy. In any setting this would have ranked among one of the more impressive pieces of climbing I had ever seen. Here, at 20,000 feet, in cold, wintry conditions, after weeks of strenuous climbing, I was witnessing a masterpiece. He was now less than a body length away from easy ground, and I allowed myself to exhale. But then, on what would have been his last flurry of sublimely played notes, a string broke.

A tiny trickle of water, dripping from a dollop of snow sitting atop the pinnacle, had soaked the last few feet of the arête. Alex kept reaching over his head, but his fingers couldn't find a grip on the wet rock. He shot a quick glance between his legs, and all he could see was a bulging rock twenty feet below. It stuck out enough that he'd hit it, but it wasn't big enough to stop him. He'd bounce and then fly off the back side of the ridge. "I'm downclimbing," he yelled, his body quivering as he slid down the arête. In place of the precision he normally employed while dancing up his pitches was a desperate, uncontrolled, all-out grovel to keep himself from falling. The world's best climber was coming unglued.

Jared braced a leg against the block in front of him to catch the fall that now appeared imminent, as Alex, clutching a golf ball–size crystal of quartz with his left hand, looked backward over his right shoulder, gauging the distance to the other pinnacle. "Watch me," he yelled, swinging his right leg backward like a martial artist winding up for a roundhouse kick. Gravity took over as his body hinged outward like a barn door. His leg found nothing but air. For a split second he was facing outward, away from the rock, looking right at us. Then he peeled off and went airborne.

SIX MONTHS EARLIER, I had been reminiscing with a buddy from college about our few triumphs and far more numerous mishaps as fledgling alpinists, in the front lobby of a warehouse turned corporate headquarters in San Francisco's Mission District. John Climaco and I had met at Middlebury College in Vermont after my brightly colored climbing rope—conspicuously displayed in the doorway of my dorm room—caught his eye. Climaco, a far more experienced climber, took me under his wing and introduced me to ice climbing and mountaineering.

Climaco had called me a few weeks earlier with the news that he had just scored his dream job producing websites for an Internet startup called Quokka that was hoping to be a Bloomberg-type terminal for sports. He was organizing his own Quokka-sponsored expedition to the unclimbed north face of Gasherbrum 1, an 8,000-meter peak in the Karakoram. Quokka, he said, had deep pockets and was seeking other trips to feature on its website. "Perhaps you have an expedition you'd like to pitch?" he had said.

At the time I was newly married and expecting my first child. My wife and I lived on a private dirt road in the woods of northern New Hampshire. Broadband wasn't yet available on my street, so I was still dialing up with a 56k modem to access the Internet. When I got off the phone with John I logged in with my AOL browser and a familiar male voice said: "You've got mail." I typed "quokka.com" into the header. Nothing happened. Then my computer crashed. It took twenty minutes before I finally pulled up Quokka's home page, which featured a full-screen pixelated image of a sailboat crashing through a stormy ocean. Graphics and various tabs covered the image. I clicked something and my computer crashed again. Quokka via dial-up was maddening, but I saw enough to understand that with a fast Internet connection this was a website in which one could get lost.

Climaco brought me to a glass-walled conference room with exposed pipes crisscrossing the ceiling and introduced me to his boss, Brian Terkelsen. In 1993 Terkelsen had co-founded the Eco-Challenge with *Survivor* mastermind Mark Burnett. The two had spent years developing reality-TV formulas that centered on relationship dynamics. I didn't realize it at the time, but Terkelsen was sizing me up as a potential character in what he deemed essentially another type of reality TV show. But that's not what he told me at the time. Quokka, as Terkelsen explained, was aiming to use the

Internet to cover sports in a whole new way. Instead of turning on the TV and digesting whatever the producers had decided to show you, Quokka would put viewers in the driver's seat, allowing them to feel as though they were inside that NASCAR or aboard the sailboat voyaging nonstop around the world. Gail Bronson, an analyst with IPO Monitor in nearby Palo Alto, called Quokka "sports on steroids."

Terkelsen said they would send us to San Francisco State to get our VO_2 max and body fat index measured. Up on Great Trango, we'd wear heart-rate and oxygen-saturation monitors. This data, along with anything else they could think of, would be a click away on the site. I nodded as he tossed out terms I'd never heard before, like "biometrics," "digital-media assets," and "real-time data." As we worked our way up the wall, he said, we'd document the action with pictures and videos and "dispatches" we'd write on tiny laptops in the portaledge at night. All this "content" would be beamed down to technicians in base camp who would collate it and upload it via satellite to the World Wide Web. We would show, in the most visceral way, in "near real time" what it *feels* like to climb one of the biggest cliffs on earth. Most important, Quokka would foot most of the bill for the expedition and pay the climbing team a talent fee.

SAN FRANCISCO IN THE LATE nineties was a heady place, the center of the dot-com bubble. Climaco, who had passed up law school to get in on the action, was offered a stake in the company in the form of shares he could cash in at Quokka's IPO. He was hoping to follow in the footsteps of a classmate from Middlebury who had gotten in on the ground floor at Yahoo. When Yahoo went public in April of 1996, James became a twenty-something-year-old instant multimillionaire. Many young bucks wanted to get the IPO done and cash out. There were plenty of dot-coms in that sense like Quokka, but Quokka was a signal of something else, too. This dot-com whirlwind would play a part in transforming the way climbers engaged, not only with one another but also with the pursuit itself.

It WASN'T ONLY THE TECH sector booming in the midnineties. By 1996 the North Face had grown into the world's largest outdoor clothing and equipment company. Doug and Susie Tompkins had launched the North Face brand thirty years before on October 26, 1966. (The Grateful Dead played at their grand opening, and the Hells Angels worked the door. Rumor has it that Electric Kool-Aid was served.)

Within two years of founding the North Face, the Tompkinses sold their interest in the company for 50,000 dollars. It was then bought and sold a dozen times before it was acquired by an investment group in 1994 for 62 million dollars. It fell to the new CEO, Bill Simon, to prep the North Face to go public, and he had a radical idea. Typically, when a clothing company needed photos for an ad campaign, it hired models, went somewhere scenic, and did a photo shoot. Instead Simon used a substantial portion of the company's marketing budget to fund a team of professional climbers and skiers. He recruited a dozen of the world's leading rock climbers, alpinists, and extreme skiers, including Alex Lowe. Greg Child, an Australian expat who climbed the North Ridge of K2 in 1990, was offered a contract worth 75,000 dollars a year, plus benefits and stock options. "For the first time in my life, I had a real salary, and my job description was to climb my ass off and travel the world putting up first ascents," says Greg.

The North Face had just made professional climbing a plausible career—one that allowed this handful of "athletes" (a then novel term for people living on the fringes of respectability) to earn a decent living. Almost immediately after its inception, Simon sent the Dream Team—Lowe, Child, Californians Conrad Anker and Lynn Hill, plus a handful of others—accompanied by outdoor photographer Chris Noble, on expedition to an alpine version of Yosemite Valley in Kyrgyzstan called the Aksu.

WHILE THE DREAM TEAM MADE headlines, I was living the more traditional climber's existence—squatting illegally in a cave in Yosemite National Park. I loosely associated with the ragtag community of Chongo Nation climbers who bridged the Stonemasters and Stone Monkeys eras. When we weren't out climbing, we'd congregate to drink malt liquor and swap spray at a worn-out fiberglass picnic table outside the deli in Yosemite Village. In the late fall of 1995, a few of us huddled around a dog-eared copy of *Climbing* magazine. We took out our frustration of being nobodies on the "sellouts" who graced the magazine's pages.

"How the heck do you get in on this gravy train?" one friend asked, after turning the page to a story about the North Face Dream Team and their recent expedition to the Aksu.

"No idea," I replied. I had no job, and the twenty-four-ounce container of Old English in my hand had been purchased with the proceeds from collecting nickel refund soda cans that morning. My day had started with a half-eaten "lodge breakfast"—some scrambled eggs and crusts of toast—that some tourists had forgotten to bus from their table in the cafeteria.

The North Face climbing team would probably have remained nothing more than a pipe dream for me were it not for the one guy sitting at the table that day who actually had the balls to step up and shout that he was worthy of being sponsored. Warren Hollinger was a disciple of the self-help guru Tony Robbins, and he was the most charismatic and unapologetic self-promoter I'd ever met. Standing six feet four inches tall, with a huge mop of curly brown hair and a ruddy, freckled face, Warren was a smooth talker and an inspired climber. He wasn't gifted with uncommon finger strength, but he was making a name for himself by climbing some of the most dangerous routes on El Capitan.

Warren's purpose in life was to train himself until he could look around and say, like José Canseco famously quipped in the late 1980s, "Right here, right now, I'm the best in the world." And as soon as he felt like he was the best, he planned to quit, sell his climbing gear, and set off on his next endeavor—to sail around the world. While I was sitting in my cave plotting where I could find my next twenty-four cans—a case was the maximum they'd take at the recycling center—Warren was on the phone selling Conrad Anker, one of the founders of the Dream Team, on the idea of the North Face supporting our upcoming expedition to Polar Sun Spire on Baffin Island.

Anker was one of the few people in the world who had been to the east coast of Baffin Island. He had kayaked into the remote Sam Ford Fjord in 1992 with Jon Turk, and the pair had paddled right beneath the 5,000-foot north face of Polar Sun Spire en route to climbing their own first ascent on a nearby tower. So Conrad threw us a bone. They couldn't give us any cash, but the North Face would supply us with state-of-the-art Gore-Tex jackets and bibs for our climb. Thanks to Warren, I now had my foot in the door with one of the biggest sponsors in the outdoor industry.

BAFFIN ISLAND IS LOCATED in northern Canada, north of Hudson Bay and west of Greenland. The island's 500,000 square kilometers is covered with lake-studded plains, glaciers, fjords, U-shaped valleys, and towering granitic walls. Though climbers have been visiting and exploring Baffin Island since the 1930s, and in earnest since the early 1970s, the world was not properly introduced to the vast untapped climbing potential on the island's fjord-riddled east coast until the explorer and adventure photographer Eugene Fisher reported in the 1995 *American Alpine Journal* that "on the east coast of the world's fifth-largest island are a series of 26 fjords, some 18 to 70 miles in length, that contain some of the tallest vertical rock walls on earth, walls that exceed even the fabled faces of Mount Thor and Asgard. . . . Yosemite Valley would count as a minor side fjord if it were located along this vertiginous coast."

I first read these words in the Yosemite Lodge cafeteria in the company of Warren and a few other climbers. The article boasted of five El Capitans and two Great Trangos in one fjord, and practically no one had climbed there. My grubby friends and I figured this had to be a wild exaggeration, but I called Fisher and he gave me a detailed explanation of the triangulation method he used to determine the heights of the walls.

Jeff Chapman, my buddy from the Crazy Kids days who accompanied me up Cathedral Ledge with our Chuck Taylors and clothesline, eventually caught the climbing bug and ended up being one of my main partners in college. So Warren and I added him to the team. I had gotten lucky a few months before the trip when someone collided with my Subaru in an icy parking lot. The car still drove, so instead of getting it fixed, I used the insurance money to pay my share of the expedition expenses. In early May 1996, our Inuit outfitter, dragging us behind his snow machine on a large wooden sled called a komatik, dropped us on the frozen sea below the north face of Polar Sun Spire.

We had planned for thirty days on the wall, but when two weeks had passed and we were still battling our way up a massive overhang on the bottom half of the wall, we knew we had to start rationing our food. Dinner, the highlight of each day, was a single Lipton noodle soup pack that we'd split three ways.

On June 16 my parents drove to the airport in Portland, Maine, to pick me up. This was before the days of satellite phones, so I had no way to communicate with the outside world to let them know I still had 2,000 feet of big wall hanging above me, we were running out of food, and the ice in the fjord was beginning to melt. If it broke up and turned into pack ice before we could top out, we'd be stuck back in the fjord for six more weeks waiting for ice out, when the Inuits could come in and get us with a boat. I had no way of telling my parents—or anyone else—that our survival might depend on our success hunting seals with ice axes.

We topped out two weeks later, on July 2. We were supposed to radio our Inuit friends when we got back to base camp, but when the ice breakup was imminent and they hadn't heard from us, they rode out to Sam Ford Fjord to check on us. As we were straggling into base camp, we heard the drone of their snow machines laboring over the slush-covered sea ice.

When I got home, I went golfing with my dad. After seventy days in the Arctic, the grass was greener, the buzz of the crickets more all encompassing, the sky a deeper shade of blue than I remembered it. When my dad swung his three wood I'd swear I saw tracers as his club whooshed through the air. I felt like I was high, but I wasn't on drugs. After some introspection, I realized the strange sensation I was experiencing was from being in the "now," something I had only previously experienced while climbing or skiing powder. After living in the moment for thirty-nine days on the side of an Arctic big wall, I found I could enter the now when I was strolling down a fairway or looking out the window at a birch tree swaying in the breeze. That's what cemented it, when I knew I had found my calling, the reason I was alive—to seek out and climb the great big walls of the world, wherever they might be.

WE NAMED OUR ROUTE the Great and Secret Show, after a Clive Barker horror novel we all read while on the wall. The tallest big wall in the world at the time was John Middendorf's and Xaver Bongard's Grand Voyage on the east face of Great Trango Tower, at 4,400 feet. When we topped out on Polar Sun Spire, our altimeter read 5,000 feet. The climb had started about 250 feet above sea level, which made the wall around 4,750 feet tall. But we didn't want to overstep, so we called our route 4,300 feet (two years later we flew past the summit in a Twin Otter, which again pegged the summit at 5,000 feet). We won a Golden Piton Award from *Climbing* magazine, which named the Great and Secret Show one of the best ascents of 1996. I put together a submission of my best photos from the climb and sent them all to the North Face, along with a ten-page "trial report" on the jacket and pants. My goal was a simple one: to give Conrad more than he was expecting. The expeditions I now wanted to go on weren't cheap, so somehow I would have to work my way up to the Dream Team.

I HAD BEEN READING ABOUT Jared Ogden's exploits for a few years. He had recently won the ice-climbing competition at the Winter X Games, beating out Alex Lowe, among others. Two years earlier he had climbed the north face of Nameless Tower (the smaller but more visually striking of the Trango siblings), vaulting him to legendary status in my book. In the magazines, his photo often ran alongside Alex Lowe's.

We met at a coffee shop in North Conway, New Hampshire. "Hey, dude," said Jared, "thanks for offering to show me around." He stood about five feet eleven inches tall and had a small silver hoop in his left ear. His shaggy blond hair and the way he spoke, dropping the word "dude" multiple times per sentence, reminded me of a California surfer. I had heard through the grapevine that he was brash and cocky, but I found him easygoing and self-deprecating. He played the drums on the dash of my still-dented Subaru on the way to the cliff as we talked about climbing. "Take me to your hardest route," he said matter-of-factly, when we pulled into the parking lot.

As far as I knew, the hardest route at Frankenstein Cliff was a two-hundred-foot-tall, six-foot-wide green-tinged pencil of vertical ice called Dropline. I had recently led it for the first time, a rite of passage for a wannabe hard-man ice climber.

"Here it is," I said proudly, after a short hike down a railroad track, pointing to where it hung from a dark brown cliff looming above a copse of birch trees.

Jared peered upward, then looked at me and said, with a tone that I found mildly condescending, "Is there anything harder?"

"Seriously?" I replied.

"I don't want to waste my time climbing that thing," said Jared. *Okay,* I thought, *maybe now I'm beginning to see why some people think he's cocky.*

We shuffled farther down the tracks to a spot called the Hanging Gardens, a forty-foot overhanging cliff festooned with glittering icicles.

"Fuck yeah, dude," said Jared. "This is what I'm talking about."

Several of the icicles touched the ground. These were established routes with names like Within Reason, Without Reason, and Clawcicle. Jared fired all of them as his warm-up and then walked up beneath an overhang in the center of the cliff that had three widely spaced daggers of ice, none of which came near to touching down. The descent for Frankenstein's Standard Route passes directly under this wall, and while I had climbed here many times and had previously done the routes Jared had just dispatched,

I had never once given more than a passing glance to the section of cliff he was now eyeing. No one had. In New Hampshire, climbers talked about whether a route was "in," meaning, was there enough ice to climb it safely. As I was about to find out, Jared's definition of "in" was a little different from ours. "Put me on belay," he declared. "I'm gonna lead this."

The hanging daggers were barely big enough to hold his weight, and he couldn't actually strike them to set the picks on his axes or they would have snapped off. So he gently tap-tap-tapped until the pick of his ice ax had poked a hole through the translucent curtains of ice. If he kicked even slightly, the icicles would break, so he twisted the front points on his crampons back and forth to make tiny divots, which he gingerly used as his footholds. In several sections there were no foot placements and he dangled solely from his axes, cranking one-arm pull-ups like a chimp swinging from one tree to the next. To protect himself from hitting the ground, he slotted camming devices into chinks in the rock and pounded some pitons into the ice-coated cracks. By the time he pulled over the lip, a small crowd had gathered, and a hearty cheer rang through the cold woods. With his very first climb in New Hampshire, Jared had just added a full grade to our rating system.

Word got around, as it always does with climbers, and that night we were invited to dinner at an Indian restaurant by Ruthann Brown, a local woman who worked in marketing for Polartec, the company that makes the fleece and filling for the North Face jackets and sleeping bags. Also in attendance was her partner Randy Rackliff, a friend who had been at the Hanging Gardens that day, plus two special guests, Alex Lowe and Greg Child, who were in town for the Ice Fest. It was my first time meeting these legends, and I tried to play it cool even though I was feeling high from sitting at the same table and sharing a beer with two of my climbing heroes. Greg immediately established himself as the group's entertainer. His wit and mental sharpness, and the inventiveness in the way he used language and the natural flow of the conversation to create humor, was unlike anything I had ever experienced. Ruthann, in particular, appeared to be in love with Greg, and at one point she said, "Greg Child, something about you makes me wild."

"Thank you, Ruthann," said Jared. "Now I know what I'm going to call my new route—Something about You Makes Me Wild."

Alex shared in the good humor, but I had the sense his mind was elsewhere. Before calling it a night, we made a plan to take Alex to the Hanging Gardens in the morning, where he had hoped to make the second ascent of Jared's route. And he did, but not before it spit him off a couple of times. Granted, the icicles had been hacked up and there wasn't much left to work with, but still, Alex Lowe, who was universally acknowledged as one of the best climbers in the world, had barely made it up Jared's route.

BY THE TIME JARED LEFT New Hampshire, I realized I had learned something from him that would forever change the way I climbed. Skillwise, I wasn't that far behind him, yet he was climbing at an elite level, and I wasn't. Why? I had just spent several days witnessing exactly what made him so great: the heart he put into his climbing. Climbing with Jared made it painfully obvious that I wasn't trying my absolute hardest—not even close. Spanish climbers have a saying for the way Jared climbed—*a muerte*—to the death. It doesn't mean you're trying to kill yourself, but rather that you're going at the climb with a grittiness and determination that leaves everything you've got on the cliff.

The caveat was that you could flick this switch only when you were ready, when you understood your limits instinctively and knew right where that imaginary line is that you can't cross. Flick the switch before you're ready, and you might well be going to your death. Jared showed me that it was time for me to flick it and that I was ready. And that all I had to do was decide I wanted it that badly.

It was time for something big.

FOUR MONTHS LATER, I was on my way to Pakistan with Jared to climb Shipton Spire, a rock tower that lies a few miles up the glacier from Trango Towers. Our team consisted of the two of us, plus our cook, Karim. We hired nine porters to help us carry our equipment on the fifty-mile trek to base camp. When we arrived in the lush meadow on the edge of a rubble-strewn glacier below the tower, and Karim realized we would be working on the climb for the next six weeks, he asked if he could go back to his village and return when we got down. We gave him some spending money and off he went.

Weeks later, at our high camp, we got pinned by a snowstorm that kept us tent-bound for several days. We had one Walkman between us, and we'd lie side by side on our sleeping pads, each with one headphone, listening to Jared's mix tape *Funk You to Death*. Whenever a decision needed to be made, I would throw out an opinion, expecting Jared, like Warren always had, to counter. But he never did. Not once. In Jared I had found a true kindred spirit and a partnership in which we made a team that was far stronger than the sum of its individual parts.

Shipton Spire's first ascent had been made only two years earlier by Greg Child and three other guys, but they hadn't actually stood on the 19,700-foot summit. They turned back somewhere around fifty feet from the top, afraid that the overhanging snow mushroom that capped the peak would fall off if they tried to climb it. Jared and I found better snow conditions, and in the middle of the night we took turns belaying each other up to the tippy-top of the mountain, a blade that culminated in a pyramidal spearpoint of snow so tiny I didn't dare try to stand on it.

DOORS WERE BEGINNING TO OPEN. Conrad brought us both onto what he called "the B Team." Then Greg Child and Alex Lowe invited us to team up with them for a *National Geographic*–sponsored expedition to Baffin Island in the summer of 1998. Our job was to find Baffin's biggest unclimbed wall, scale it, and come home with an article for the yellow mag that Greg would write and a film for National Geographic Television.

There was drama on that Baffin trip, mostly between Greg and Alex. As a junior member of the team, a "subbie," I managed to stay neutral and in a way felt honored that both Greg and Alex had confided in me. "The camera guys are like moths to a candle with Alex," said Greg during one of these confessionals.

High on Great Sail Peak, we sat through a six-day storm at a hanging portaledge camp tucked under a small roof. When the storm broke, Jared and I, stiff and cranky from a week of inactivity, set off up the fixed ropes to push the route higher. The sun broke through the clouds, illuminating a thick white blanket lying over the valley, above which we dangled on the white static lines like spiders on a thread. A ten-year-old with a point-and-shoot could have made award-winning photos on that day, so Jared called down to invite Gordon Wiltsie, the team's still photographer, to come up with us to shoot.

"Thanks for the offer," said Gordon, poking his head out from the portaledge in which he was lounging, "but I've already got a plan to do a photo shoot of Alex brushing his teeth." I can't remember Jared's exact choice of words, but it had a lot to do with where Gordon should put his camera.

THE EXPEDITION COOK, Gulam Rasoul, once told Greg Child that the name Trango probably comes from the Balti word *tengo*, which means "hair-oil bottle." There are two bottles that rise from a ridge between the Trango and Dunge Glaciers. The more northerly tower is called Nameless, a flawless obelisk of granite whose summit is guarded on every aspect by sheer 3,000-foot walls. Its neighbor, Great Trango, is one of the largest pieces of exposed granite in the world, a complex massif of gullies, hanging glaciers, and soaring rock faces. The 5,000-foot pillar on its east face was first climbed by Norwegians in 1984. High on the wall, the team of four realized they didn't have enough food, so two of them rappelled down. Five days later, they saw their companions top out the wall and reach the east summit. But on the descent, something went wrong and the pair disappeared. Their bodies were later spotted at the base of the wall, before being buried in an avalanche.

The Trango Towers, while impressive, are mere foothills when compared to the 8,000-meter giants that lie forty miles to the north along Pakistan's border with China. Everest may be the tallest mountain in the world, the crown jewel of the Himalaya, but any serious mountaineer will tell you that it's not the world's ultimate peak. That distinction has always belonged to the world's second highest, K2, aka the "Savage Mountain." The rather unimaginative name derives from the mid-nineteenth-century Survey of India, during which the six highest points visible from Mount Haramukh in Kashmir were named K1 through K6. The K, of course, stands for Karakoram, a Turkic name for the black gravel that covers many of the dry glaciers in this region. As of 2016, only three hundred or so people have stood on K2's summit, while around 5,000 have climbed Everest. Even the easiest route to

K2's summit, the Abruzzi Ridge, is far steeper and more technical than Everest's standard South Col route. The summit of K2 is the most elusive, dangerous, and hard-to-reach place on earth. For every four people who stand on top, one dies trying to get there.

When viewed on a map, the three-hundred-mile-long, east-west-oriented Karakoram appears to be the northwestern extension of the Himalaya, but it's technically its own distinct range, separated from the Himalaya by a fifty-mile-wide plain bisected by the Indus River. Both mountain ranges were formed by the collision of the Indian and Eurasian tectonic plates, but the Karakoram was formed more recently and has grown more quickly, and this has resulted in its mountains being more heavily glaciated and densely packed.

In the center of the range lies an area informally known as the "third pole," an ice cap that holds the planet's largest reserve of freshwater outside the polar regions. One of the glaciers that spokes off the third pole is the Siachen, which runs for more than forty miles down the center of a disputed area over which both Pakistan and India have claimed sovereignty since the mid-1980s. Hundreds of troops are stationed along the disputed border at heavily fortified high-altitude camps. Every year more of the troops die from exposure to the Karakoram's harsh weather than from combat.

The Karakoram is also far less populated than the Himalaya. Unlike Nepal's, its topography is ill suited to farming or raising livestock. Once you venture forth from the main towns, there are no Balti villages, no lodges or teahouses, no amenities of any sort—just raw mountains, glaciers, ice, and rock.

I APPLIED FOR A PERMIT to climb the northwest face of Great Trango in the fall of 1998, not long after we returned from Baffin. Jared and I had talked about inviting Greg and Alex but decided we'd have more fun if it was just the two of us. We had gelled as a two-man team the previous year on Shipton Spire, and all the negativity of the Baffin trip made us both wary of ruining that chemistry. I took point on the application, and in the blank where it asked for the expedition leader, I put my name.

In the past four years, Jared and I had both been successful on every big climb we had attempted. After we returned from the Great Sail Peak expedition, the North Face promoted us to the A Team. We were now pulling down a modest salary from "the firm," and between other small sponsorships, writing gigs for *Climbing* magazine, and slideshow tours, I was making a modest living as a "pro" climber. I had "sold out," but after years of dirtbagging and banging nails in Colorado, I was deeply in love with my new job. I had no boss, I made my own hours, and I climbed all the time.

So I was crushed when the North Face rejected my first official expedition proposal as a member of the A Team—to give Jared and me 12,000 dollars so we could attempt the unclimbed northwest face of Great Trango Tower. We had thought it was a sure thing.

"What do you think about inviting Alex?" I asked Jared one day. It went without saying that our sponsorship prospects would be significantly improved if we added the Mutant to our team. Jared agreed we might as well, since the trip evidently wasn't happening otherwise.

I called Alex, and he signed on without hesitation. "I've always wanted to go to Trango," he said. With Alex Lowe on the roster, we refloated our sponsorship proposal to the North Face. This time the answer was a resounding yes. Then Climaco called to tell me about Quokka.

WE ARRIVED IN BASE CAMP on June 22, 1999, following a train of 148 Balti porters who carried close to five tons of food and equipment. Our team included two climber-cinematographers, Mike Graber and his assistant, Jim Surette. These guys had been hired by NBC Sports to make an hour-long documentary about our climb for a new expedition television series sponsored by the North Face and hosted by Sting. The Quokka team included a field producer named Greg Thomas and a British satellite technician named Darren Brito. Our Pakistani contingent included a military liaison officer, a cook, and a high-altitude porter.

Our camp was situated on the back side of a lateral moraine bordering the eastern edge of the Trango Glacier. It's an idyllic spot lying alongside a small lake fringed with a grassy meadow, which in late June was peppered with tiny pink and yellow wildflowers. In every direction, our camp was surrounded with towering granite walls, which had the effect of making us feel like tiny specks of dust in a grand, unforgiving universe. Of all the walls that surrounded us, the northwest face of Great Trango, the one we had come to climb, was by far the most intimidating.

The entire bottom half of the wall, roughly the same height as El Capitan, was a crackless, homogenous, water-polished slab. We stared at it for hours with a pair of high-powered binoculars but saw no obvious line of weakness. The slab, we soon realized, was a bowling alley for loose rock, a kind of gutter that collected every errant stone that came loose from the acres of storm-lashed wall that hung above it.

Shortly after arriving in base camp, I awoke in the middle of the night to a roar that sounded like a 747 taking off nearby. Seconds later, a hurricane-strength blast of wind flattened my tent, pressing me facedown into my sleeping pad. I knew it was an avalanche, and that if I stayed where I was, I'd be buried alive. So I desperately fought my way out of the flapping nylon. Outside, I watched the brightly lit Quokka communications tent go fully airborne, with Brito riding it like a magic carpet. When it was five feet off the ground, the lights went out. Screams filled the air. Whoever it was, I couldn't tell, must have thought he was about to die. The rushing air was laden with slush, which shellacked me from head to toe. I couldn't see anything and there was nowhere to run, so I crawled back into my tent and huddled in the fetal position. A minute later, an eerie silence fell over camp. The debris—television, refrigerator, and car-size chunks of ice that had peeled off a hanging glacier—had stopped five hundred yards short of camp. Trango was saying hello.

OUR EXPEDITION HAD GOTTEN OFF to a wobbly start. Jared was the first to go down, falling prey to a nasty bug he picked up shortly after we arrived in Islamabad. Greg Thomas caught it from Jared on the approach; then Alex woke up with a sore throat just as we arrived in base camp. None of us, perhaps with the exception of Jared, who did multiple forays up 14,000-foot peaks in Colorado before the expedition, were fully acclimatized, which made the timing of the illness particularly bad for Alex. Jared had recovered by the time we got to base camp, but over the course of a few days the cold dropped into Alex's chest, where it blossomed into a nasty bronchial infection.

One morning I entered the cook tent and found Alex in his customary seat stirring a bowl of oatmeal. He had dark bags under his bloodshot eyes, and the skin on his face had a corpse-like gray pallor. "I feel like shit," he said in a nasal voice. A standard comment for any sick person, but not Alex Lowe. He was a stoic and not one to admit weakness. It was the first time I'd ever heard him confess he wasn't doing *great*.

I knew it hurt him when Jared and I headed off up the hill to lead the first pitches of the route, leaving him behind to convalesce. Our plan was to climb the wall in capsule style, meaning we would fix ropes and then use them to rappel back down at the end of the day. The next day we would climb back up the ropes to our high point with mechanical ascenders and foot loops—a process we call "jugging." At the high point we'd pull more ropes out of our packs and then lead higher, laying more lines behind us as we went. Eventually the commute would become so long that we'd set a camp, pull the ropes up from behind us, and use them to restart the same process.

On the fourth day of working our ropes up the slab, we came back to camp and Alex was gone. Thomas said he had decided to head down to a camp on the Baltoro Glacier called Paiju to try to recover at a lower elevation. That evening, Jared and I were sipping whiskey in the communications tent, which was set up like a CIA listening post with a horseshoe of tables covered in laptops, modems, batteries, and electrical cords spiderwebbed across the floor. Thomas opened his laptop and dialed into the satellite through the three-foot-wide dish sitting in the sand outside the tent. It took a while for the site to load, but slowly a line of text, overlaying a photo of the massive granite face that hung above us, came into focus.

"There's a bad vibe in camp." Alex Lowe.

Speechless, I looked over at Jared, who frowned and shrugged his shoulders. Thomas and Brito looked at us feigning bemusement, but it was obvious they knew this was coming. I was being informed for the first time—by a website—that my team was apparently infected with poor morale. And now thousands of the site's followers around the world knew all about it too.

Quokka had pulled and twisted the quote from a dispatch Alex had written that day, shortly before he departed.

> . . . current plans are to head off alone for a few
> days and convalesce away from mounting unsym-
> pathetic "get-off-your-ass-you-slacker" vibes (real
> or imagined). A group of dear friends and old

> climbing soul mates are camped at Paiju. . . . I'll
> spend a night or two in the company of good friends.

Alex, I was starting to think, had a tendency to project his feelings onto others. The slacker "vibe" he was feeling had to be coming from himself, I reasoned. Jared and I certainly understood he was in no shape to climb—and not for lack of grit or motivation. But, at the same time, he may have picked up on something more subtle. Jimmy Surette was spending a lot of time with us on the wall in Alex's absence. He was a legendary climber in his own right, a close friend and soul brother who lived minutes away from me in New Hampshire. Jared and I had been talking, quietly, about the possibility of Jimmy taking Alex's place if he didn't recover. We kept this talk strictly among ourselves when we were well away from camp, but now I wondered if Alex had somehow picked up on it.

He returned three days later, reenergized and psyched to get to work with us on the wall. No one mentioned the dispatch, and in the interim I had convinced myself it was nothing more than a manifestation of Alex's frustration at not being involved in the beginning of the climb. When he finally got on the rock, he climbed like a madman, charging up his pitches and, in the process, proving that even in his weakened state he was the strongest climber on our team.

On our way back down the lines at the end of one day, I was setting up my rappel and fumbling a bit. I wore long pants and a long-sleeve light blue turtleneck. Under my helmet I had tucked a bandana to cover my neck. My nose was white with zinc. Alex was standing next to me, and we made for an odd-looking couple because he was wearing nothing but a pair of polypropylene boxer shorts; no shirt, no helmet. I had been using a device called a shunt for a rappel backup. It attached to the rope above my belay device, so that if I got hit by a rock, or for any other reason lost control of the rope, it would lock and keep me from falling to my death. It took a little extra time to get it hooked up, and apparently it was more time than Alex had, because he grabbed the rope beneath my device, said, "See ya," and stepped off the ledge. Like I had done on Cathedral Ledge as a kid, Alex was now sliding Batman-style down the rope, attached with nothing but his hands.

"What the fuck is he doing?" said Jared, who had just touched down from the rope above.

Alex slid a few body lengths down the eighty-degree wall before he was struggling to hang on. He threw a foot onto a small hold and unweighted the rope enough to give it a few wraps around his arm. When I caught up with him back in camp, his arm looked shredded. Graber asked him what had happened, and Alex mumbled something incomprehensible.

A couple of days later, we were prepping some gear to take up to the wall when I made a mundane comment to Alex.

"I don't give a damn what you think, Mark," he said, locking me in an icy stare.

Whoa.

We stepped out of camp, away from the ever-present cameras. I sat down on a rock and looked up at Alex, who was standing over me. "You're being bossy and manipulative," he said. "And you're trying to hog all the attention for yourself. I didn't appreciate how seriously you would take being the expedition leader."

FOR THE NEXT THREE HOURS we explored the interpersonal dynamics of our team. Our lines of communication had become so jammed up that we were actually figuring out how each other felt by reading about it on the website. Alex and I had gotten along fine in Baffin, where I had taken a subservient role, but as expedition leader, I had set myself up for the mother of all head-butting sessions with climbing's alpha dog. "I'm seriously questioning whether I want to continue with this climb," he said.

When I looked up at the wall that towered above me, knowing I had lost the solidarity of my team, I realized that my dream climb suddenly had no meaning. I had been fantasizing about climbing Trango since I was a teenager, but now all I wanted to do was go home.

"You know, I read some of that stuff that you wrote to Lauren [my wife] about me," Alex said.

"You read my e-mail?" I shot back.

"It popped onto the screen while I was reading mine," he said.

"I'm sorry if any of that hurt your feelings, Alex, but you shouldn't be reading my e-mail," I told him. "I bet if I read your e-mails to Jenni [his wife] there would be stuff in there I might not be too psyched about."

"Yeah, you're probably right," he said.

"Even if we don't do the climb," I said, "I do want to leave here as friends."

"Me too," said Alex.

We decided the only way to save our expedition was to bail on Great Trango, at least temporarily, and head off up Nameless Tower. No film guys, no cameras, no dispatches, just the three of us, climbing a mountain, with no strings attached, no Quokka playing the puppeteer. Alex and I shook hands on the plan, and as I looked earnestly into his eyes, I thought I saw a glimmer of goodwill.

Back in camp we convened a meeting in our cook tent to share what was going on with the rest of the team. With the cameras rolling and the three of us sitting in plastic chairs at the end of the table, Alex kicked it off.

"Mark and I have issues," he said. "We find ourselves in a crucible that is new to us and is bringing out some of the best in us and, more importantly, some of the worst in our characters."

"The energy hasn't been good, and you can't do this wall without it," I added. "It's impossible."

Graber and Thomas went along when we told them that we were putting the Great Trango circus on hold to run off for a few days of soul-brother R & R. But they did remind us that we had already spent 50,000 dollars of someone else's money and that thousands of people were already following our progress via the website. Thomas had been bragging to me about how he was going to be set for life after the Quokka IPO, and I'm sure he saw his stock options flash before his eyes as he contemplated the possibility that this entire dog and pony show might implode.

After the team meeting, we headed up our fixed lines to get our equipment for Nameless. When I pulled onto the ledge at our high point, about 1,500 feet off the deck, Alex was waiting. He had unhooked from the rope and was standing about ten feet away. He strode toward me purposefully, and I felt my adrenaline spike. Then he opened his arms and gave me a heartfelt hug. We both choked up a bit and apologized for all the grief we had caused each other.

My dispatch later that night ended with these words:

> . . . It's weird, because I think we're now better friends than we've ever been. Sometimes, when you go through these traumatic moments, it makes the relationship stronger in the end. I don't think you'll be hearing any more about bad blood between Alex and I [sic].

To this day I still wonder what hand Brian Terkelsen might have had in the drama that was swirling around me. After all, we were only a week into our expedition, and it was already playing out like a crude version of *Survivor*. "On *Survivor*, people say one thing to your face, then do their 'confessional' to the camera," said Terkelsen, years later. "Trango was the exact same, but more raw and real."

The next morning it was dark and gloomy, and we decided to postpone our launch up Nameless for another day. Thomas, with some help from Graber, went to work on us, and by our third cup of coffee had talked us out of our plan.

WITH OUR ROPES FINALLY FIXED to the top of the slab, it was time to launch our bid for the summit. Everyone was looking forward to getting onto the headwall, where we'd no longer have to worry as much about dodging rockfall. In fact, the day before, Alex had been hit in the head and knocked unconscious by a falling rock while ascending one of our lines. Luckily, this time he had been wearing a helmet.

We had no way of knowing how long it would take us to climb the 3,000-foot headwall that loomed above our high point, so we took a guess and settled on packing up twenty days' worth of provisions. We laid it all out in the sand, and the food alone covered an entire six-by-six-foot blue tarp. Here's the list:

> 60 Snickers and Mars bars
> 120 Clif Bars
> 25 pounds homemade Montana beef jerky
> 50 pounds trail mix
> 30 pounds granola
> 4 gallons powdered milk
> 8 gallons Gatorade mix
> 60 freeze-dried dinners
> 2 huge bags of dried papaya and pineapple

dozens of soup packets
dozens of hot chocolate packets
10 pounds of Peet's coffee

On another, bigger tarp we laid out everything else: a dozen butane canisters, a hanging stove, mugs, eating utensils, extra clothing, sleeping bags, first aid, headlamps, plus all the communication gear for the website, including mini laptops, memory cards, batteries, cables, and a huge antenna. We packed everything into six urethane-coated haul bags, trying to stack things in the order in which we would later need them. After a soul-destroying, hernia-inducing day of hauling the six "pigs" up the El Cap–size slab, we collapsed on the ledge at the base of the headwall, knowing the most grueling part of this whole endeavor was now behind us.

We had been working on the upper headwall for a few days when Alex opened up the minicomputer one evening and it was dead. "Thank god," I said. "Now we don't have to type dispatches anymore." That little computer had come to embody everything I hated about Quokka, and I had dreamed about smashing it to smithereens with my wall hammer.

"It doesn't seem to be getting power," said Alex. "I know Darren could fix this thing. I think I'm going to rap off in the morning and bring it down to him."

"Really, Alex?" said Jared. "That seems like a waste of time. I'm with Mark—let's call ourselves lucky. We can still do voice dispatches with the radio."

"I wouldn't feel right not trying," replied Alex firmly, and I knew that was the end of the discussion. The next morning, ignoring our entreaties, he rapped down the fixed line, which we had left in place so Graber and Surette could continue filming us. Alex spent twenty-four hours in base camp and was back the next day with the computer, which Darren had been able to fix. Everyone at

Quokka thought Alex was a total hero, but Jared and I felt betrayed. It was the first time one of us had openly bucked the majority-rules mantra we had followed for settling disagreements.

Alex now treated the computer like it was his personal property. He kept it in his ditty bag with his first aid kit, and if I wanted to use it to write a dispatch or to check my e-mail, I had to ask him for permission. We were sitting outside one evening, watching the sunset while Alex pointed the radio modem toward base camp and began uploading our e-mail. "Hey, is there anything for me?" I asked. I had written my wife, Lauren, and Climaco before the machine had broken, and I was hoping they had e-mailed me back. Alex stared intently at the machine and made no reply. There was no acknowledgment I had spoken, not even a glance in my direction. I tried to look over his shoulder, but he kept turning farther away so I couldn't see the screen. I could see his face, though, and something was wrong. He was breathing deeply and clenching his jaw. I remember thinking, *Is he reading my e-mail again?* Alex continued to ignore me, so I went back to my bivouac. The weather was clear, so we had all found our own ledges to lie out on. I dozed off, and when I awoke Alex was standing over me, fists clenched, his body shaking.

"What did you write to Climaco?" he demanded.

"What? What are you talking about?" I replied.

"I said, what did you write to Climaco?"

"Did you read my e-mail?" I asked.

"Yes," he replied.

"What the fuck, dude?"

"I had a feeling you were talking about me behind my back, and I was right," he said. "What did you tell him about me?"

"I told him the truth, Alex," I replied, "that I'm trying to win back your friendship, but the harder I try, the more you push me away. That you're kind to Jared but disrespectful to me. I told him that the bad blood between us is getting worse, not better. That I'm having a miserable time and I don't want to be here."

Alex stormed off, and it wasn't until the next day that I read Climaco's e-mail. It was harsh. Among other things, it said that Alex was an egomaniac. Climaco, now the CEO of a pharmaceutical company, says he wrote that Alex "may be the greatest climber in the world, but he's also the greatest showman," and "Remember Mark, this climb was your dream, not his." He says he's lost his e-mail and mine, but he doesn't remember me bagging on Alex. The essence of it, he says, was that I was miserable and planning to quit the expedition. Climaco says he came down so hard on Alex because he was trying to bolster me in an effort to convince me not to quit. He felt certain that if I did drop out, it would ruin my budding career as a professional climber.

When I woke up the next morning, I expected the expedition to be over, but instead, Alex grabbed his pack and set off up the fixed lines. He didn't say a word to me, and I wondered if he knew that despite the rancor between us, I still admired him. He reminded me of my dad in that it was almost impossible to get his approval, but when I did, when he made "the face"—raising one eyebrow and then breaking into a huge shit-eating grin—it felt sublime.

Alex was pushing our high point up a hairline crack when huge fluffy snowflakes began to fall from the sky. I was two hundred feet below, unhooking haul bags for Jared, who was pulling them up while he belayed Alex. Soon Alex disappeared into the gloom and we were engulfed in a blizzard. Frothy waterfalls began coursing down the wall all around me. A trickle began seeping from the crack right above my head, and in the course of ten minutes it turned into an icy shower. I was clipped into two bolts and had nowhere to go, and before I could escape, water was pouring down my collar, soaking me to the skin, and filling my boots. By the time I released the last bag for Jared I was shivering and borderline hypothermic. "I have to get out of here," I yelled over the wind as I put myself on rappel. The route was overhanging and traversing, so instead of sliding right down to the next anchor, I ended up hanging in space at the bottom of a V of rope—the end, attached to the next anchor, was twenty feet up and to my right. To get to the anchor I would need to jug myself up, but the atmospheric conditions had caused a thick sheath of rime ice to form on the rope. The teeth on my ascenders wouldn't hold on the icy rope, and I was so cold I wasn't sure how much longer I could go before my hands stopped working. My only option was to delicately scrape the ice off the bow-taut line with the blade of my knife. By the time I crawled into my sleeping bag I was shivering uncontrollably, but I could still hear the *ting-ting-ting* of Alex's hammer ringing against the steel pitons he was driving into the wall high above. The Mutant . . .

Over the next several days, the storm settled over us like a sickness. But the dark clouds outside were benign compared to the one that churned over Alex and me inside the portaledge. I tried to win him back with kind gestures. I offered to tear my book in half because he had finished his. "I'm good," he said. I tried to talk to him about his family. "Whatever," was a typical response. Eventually I gave up. The three of us lived together in a space the size of a dining room table, but Alex and I didn't speak or make eye contact for days at a time.

When I came down from getting soaked in the waterfall, my boots had been so wet I had left them outside. Days later, they still sat in the gravel where I had dumped them, now frozen solid, glazed in a layer of ice and snow. It wasn't like me to give up on taking care of an essential piece of equipment. Until this point, I had slept with them in the bottom of my sleeping bag every night. I wondered if my partners were picking up on the message I was trying to convey: *I'm done.*

It took me hours to work up the courage to articulate the thought that had been running like a broken record inside my head for days. I hated Quokka and everything it represented—the voyeurism, the posing, the hype. Most of all, I hated them for driving a wedge between us. It had all sounded great back in San Francisco, but I had been naive about how it would feel to climb with this many strings attached. It was time to pull the plug on this puppet show.

"Hey, guys," I finally said. "I don't want to be here. I want to go home."

"Me too," said Alex, without hesitation.

We were about to call down to base camp to tell them we were bailing, when the rainfly stopped flapping for a few seconds. "Did you hear that?" I asked. Auditory hallucinations are common when you're stuck in a tent for days on end, so I figured it was just my imagination. Then a voice became distinct. Alex unzipped the door, and about a hundred feet away stood a man wearing a blue warm-up suit and an old-fashioned orange helmet. A Russian team had arrived to attempt the same face, but we had a two-week head start, so we never thought we'd see them up on the wall.

We waved, and soon the three of us were shaking hands with Alexander Odintsov, a legendary forty-one-year-old Russian alpinist. While we had been sitting on our butts in the "storm," feeling sorry for ourselves, the Russians had been firing off the lower wall in less than half the time it had taken us. It was a cold, blustery day, and I'll never forget Odintsov saying something about the weather being pretty good. "Ha ha, good joke," I replied, but he just stared at me with a confused look on his weathered face.

Instead of a harness, Odintsov wore a carpenter's tool belt, similar to the one I used to wear when I worked as a framer in Colorado. But the leather pouches were filled with homemade titanium pitons rather than sixteen-penny nails. When he noticed how intently I was observing his unusual approach to carrying essential equipment, Odintsov reached into his pouch and pulled out a few of the pins. He seemed to know each one personally and even had pet names for some of them. "This one I made myself," he said in Russian-accented English, holding up a scrappy chunk of metal, "and this one I call the Figure of One." Most shocking was the fact that he carried the pins loose in his tool bags. If he fell, and the carpenter's belt didn't rip right off his body, surely some or all the pitons would spill out and tumble down the mountain.

"What if you fall?" I asked.

"Don't fall," he replied, stone-faced.

Soon we were joined by the rest of the team: Yuri Koshelenko, Igor Potan'kin, and Ivan Samoilenko. "Hello, Mark," said Samoilenko, greeting me with a warm smile and a firm two-handed shake. "You were right, this is a good cliff!" A few months earlier I had bumped into Samoilenko at an outdoor industry trade show in Salt Lake City. We got to talking about upcoming projects. When he pulled out a picture of Great Trango's east face, I unveiled, unwisely, I now realized, a closely guarded photo of the face on which we were now getting reacquainted.

Odintsov told us about their "project"—to establish Russian routes on the ten biggest cliffs in the world. Great Trango was number five. Alex had met Odintsov in the Aksu in 1995, year one of the project, where they both established first ascents on Peak 4810. Odintsov followed up with another new route on the west face of Rocky Aksu in 1996, then scaled Norway's Trollveggen in 1997. In 1998, he and his team put up a futuristic new line on the north face of Bhagirathi III, in India.

That night, we all sat in a circle on a flat spot outside our portaledge, passing around a small tin cup, which the Russians kept filling with grain alcohol. The mood was warm and jovial, like a bunch of old friends telling stories at their local pub. I sat next to

Koshelenko, and when he passed me the cup, he put his hand on my shoulder and looked into my eyes. I can't remember what he said, but his warmth and goodwill felt like the first rays of sunshine after a long, nasty storm. I looked across the circle at Alex and Jared, both of whom were beaming—it didn't take much grain alcohol to get a buzz at this altitude.

The plan to bail was never mentioned again.

For the next several days we climbed alongside the Russians, who had found their own crack system running parallel to ours. We'd climb side by side during the day; then at night we'd meet in camp for more grain alcohol and stories. "What do you guys think about us all joining into one big team?" said Alex one evening, holding the tin cup in his battered hands.

"This is a fine idea," said Odintsov.

But Jared and I weren't so sure. The Russians climbed in a militaristic style they had been taught back in the Soviet days, when mountaineering was an official government-sanctioned sport like track and field or gymnastics. Accordingly, each team member had a specific job. Only Odintsov and Koshelenko led pitches; the others provided a supporting role. As part of a seven-man team, Jared and I figured that we'd be relegated to schlepping bags, cooking, and setting up camp. So we vetoed the proposal. Technically, it was a democratic vote, two against one, but all of the Russians and Alex were for it, so it could have been interpreted as five against two. It was the one awkward moment we shared with the Russians.

On July 24, we set off up the ropes we had fixed on the upper headwall. It felt good to be committing to the final leg of the climb after festering on the ledge for the past eleven days. If all went according to plan, we'd be on the summit in a week. As we hauled our six pigs behind us, the Russians cheered us along as they tinkered away on their route a few hundred feet to the right.

Later that evening, we set up our first hanging portaledge camp at 18,450 feet below a gray, left-facing open book that soared for hundreds of feet toward the route's most notable feature—a massive roof system that guarded access to the summit ridge. As the sun set, we stared out the door of the rainfly at the towers lining the west side of the Trango Glacier—Uli Biaho, the Cat's Ears, Shipton Spire, and the Mystery Phallus—while they slowly darkened into jagged silhouettes haloed by a rising moon. We sat quietly—Alex and I sharing the top bunk, Jared down below—letting the magic of life in the vertical realm wash over us.

"You know, I want to spend more time at home with the family," said Alex. His sons, Max, Sam, and Isaac, were ten, seven, and three. I knew how he was feeling because I now had a six-month-old son of my own. Alex loved his family, and he felt guilty about spending so much time away from them. And so did I. We wanted it all—to climb big first ascents and be stand-up family men in the gaps between expeditions.

"I've been thinking about a new career, one that doesn't require so much travel," he continued. "It's one of the reasons I'm so psyched about this project. I think this could really be a good opportunity for all of us. I love writing, and I see this website as a way to showcase what I'm capable of outside of climbing." The Trango website had given Alex a powerful new conduit through which to connect with his legions of fans. He knew the Internet offered a whole new platform from which to inspire his followers to pursue their own dreams, and he was working hard to make sure he was leveraging this opportunity for all it was worth. Alex would stay up late into the night meticulously crafting his dispatches. Quokka had asked us to write about hauling, knowing it was the element of this whole enterprise everyone hated the most. The difference between how Alex and I approached the assignment revealed our very different personalities and writing styles.

Here's what I wrote:

Luckily I found a way for you to simulate this experience if you're interested. First, you'll want to find the right location. I was thinking about a cement wall on the south side of a K-Mart in Arizona. In mid-July. Make sure it is at least 90 degrees. Place a chair about ten feet from the wall so that the sun is beating on your back and neck. Now put on a 75-pound weight belt, but make sure it is loose so it slides around a bunch on your hips—the chafing is very important. Take a bungee cord, tie one end to the weight belt, and find some way to attach the other end to the wall. Make sure it has just enough stretch so you can drop into a deep knee bend. . . . Standing in front of the chair, lift your left foot and place it on the seat. Rock your full weight onto the left foot, so that you're up on your tippy toes with the right. Now drop back onto the right foot, making sure the bungee is pulling hard on the weight belt—again, chafing is important. Repeat this process ALL DAY LONG. . . . Now imagine you're doing this for fun. Actually, this is what you've been dreaming about all year. And the good times aren't reserved just for today. You're going to be sitting behind K-Mart ALL SUMMER. . . . This is serious blue-collar work, for which there is little tangible reward. You could jug loads all day and there would still be plenty of stuff waiting to be brought up. Such is the nature of a heavy-handed big wall climb. You would have to be numb in the head to actually enjoy this stuff.

AND HERE'S ALEX'S take on the same subject.

> Hauling inevitably elicits predictable groans and grunts from most climbers, but I actually find solace in the rhythmic cadence of throwing my weight against the resisting bag, over and over again until it gradually flops up onto the ledge like some great inanimate leviathan. I play mind games, of course. I chant the complete names of my wife and sons in sync with each haul, resting only once the entire family has been named. Kind of nice really—meditation on a subject very dear. While hauling the seventh bag to the top of the lines today, my reverie was interrupted by a passing shadow. A huge raptor with a wingspan easily reaching six feet was effortlessly gliding past on the updrafts. I'm not sure what the Balti name is, but no matter—such majestic creatures transcend encumbering monikers. Goraks, raven-ish birds that are ubiquitous throughout the Himalaya, are with us constantly. They dive and soar with such seemingly joyful purposelessness, I can't help but conclude that sheer mischievous fun is the motive.

Now that we were getting closer to the summit, Quokka was pumping up its PR efforts, and most days we had to give interviews to American radio stations. Our handheld Yaesu radio had been configured to patch through the satellite dish in base camp, allowing us to use it like a telephone. One night at high camp we called a station in San Diego to do a morning show with two Beavis and

Butthead–type comedians whose shtick was to entertain their listeners, as they sat in rush-hour traffic, by riffing off each other and making their guests look like idiots.

"So who exactly works at the 7-Elevens in Pakistan, anyway?" asked one of the guys.

"You've been watching too much *Simpsons,* dude," replied Jared.

"How do you guys go to the bathroom up there?" asked the other.

"You ever heard of a mud falcon?" I replied.

The next day, we were interviewed by Bob Edwards of National Public Radio (NPR). The conversation was refreshing compared to the gutter talk we'd spewed across San Diego, and the piece, which aired on *Morning Edition,* played on hundreds of radio stations across the United States, reaching millions of listeners. Afterward, the website went viral—although that term hadn't been invented yet. Quokka was inundated with e-mails, which Brito would sometimes beam up to us. Most of the e-mails were complimentary, people wishing us good luck and asking questions like "Is there less gravity at altitude?" But there were some haters. These folks all said the same thing: "What kind of an egotist goes out and risks his life for something so pointless?" "Who is going to rescue you (and pay for it) when it all goes wrong?"

One thing was certain: Expedition reporting had come a long way since George Mallory and Sandy Irvine were dispatching letters with carriers on the 1924 British Mount Everest expedition. In 1953, news of Sir Edmund Hillary and Tenzing Norgay's first ascent of Everest was sent via a runner from base camp, who took four days to reach the nearest telephone. Thirty years later, high-altitude filmmaker David Breashears broadcast the first live TV images from Everest's summit. Now, at the dawn of Y2K, there we were documenting an entire two-month-long expedition in close-to-real time.

ALEX GOT SICK to his stomach and couldn't climb one morning. Jared and I left him to sweat it out for the day and headed up the fixed ropes hanging above camp. When I was fifty feet up, I looked down between my boots, which were still wet, and saw Alex hanging a brown-spackled pair of long johns out the door of the ledge. That afternoon, 1,000 overhanging feet above camp, Jared tackled the most spectacular pitch of the entire route—a twenty-five-foot horizontal ceiling, split down the middle with a razor-thin crack. Jared nailed his way out the roof, slamming knifeblade pitons, like a blacksmith, one after another into the upside-down crack. Free climbing was out of the question, so Jared aid climbed using the same techniques developed by Royal Robbins and Warren Harding forty years earlier during Yosemite's golden age. What I remember most from that lead was the sound of the pitons being driven into the rock. With each hit, the tone would rise as the iron bit deeper and deeper into the rock. The ringing peal of metal against metal echoed within the cathedral-like amphitheater below the roof, and from years of pounding iron into rock, I could tell how solid each piton was from the tone it gave off as it inched into the mountain. Hours later, when Jared turned the lip of the roof, he let loose with a cry like a wolf howling at the moon that I'm sure they must have heard in base camp a mile below: "Aaay-ooooo."

Alex was sleeping when we got back to the ledge that evening, and we did our best not to disturb him as we slid inside and boiled water on the hanging stove for our nightly freeze-dried meals. In the morning, I awoke to Alex's alarm at four A.M. I looked out from the mummy hood of my sleeping bag and there he was, firing up the stove for our morning brew as per his usual. He made eye contact, and I was surprised to see he was making the face, one bushy eyebrow up in the air, a childish grin stretching from ear to ear. "So, should we go for it?" he said matter-of-factly, as if he hadn't been ill for the past twenty-four hours.

When I poked my head out the door of the ledge I saw long wispy mares' tails blowing in from the south. We all knew, from hard experience, that these clouds were the leading edge of a storm front that was blowing in from the Indian Ocean. So while Alex made coffee, Jared and I loaded our packs with the essentials for a fast and light push for the summit—stove, sleeping bags, bivy sacks, pads, and a light rack of climbing gear. It was time to leave the portaledge, the pigs, and all the other detritus behind, and go full out for the summit.

NINE HOURS LATER, on a knife-edge ridge seventy-five feet below the summit, Alex missed the karate kick and barn-doored off the side of the mountain. He bounced once and then disappeared over the far side of the ridge.

The force of the fall jerked Jared violently, but he held on, and a few seconds later all was still and we couldn't hear anything but wind and our own ragged breathing. Terrified, fearing the worst, Jared and I yelled Alex's name into the void. There was no response. "What are we gonna do?" asked Jared, reaching down and plucking the rope, which was jammed between two rocks and as taut as a bowstring. As I contemplated how I could traverse across the tensioned rope, I felt it come slack in my hand. "He's alive!" yelled Jared, as he quickly reeled in rope. A few minutes later, Alex popped back up onto the ridge, threw both arms over his head, gave us a double thumbs-up, and yelled, *"Yeah, boyzz!!"* at the top of his lungs.

"Are you okay?" I yelled.

"I'm great," he called back. To our amazement, Alex then proceeded to put himself back into the same exact position from which he had just fallen. Jared shot me a worried look but didn't say anything. Seconds later, Alex was back on the arête. He slapped his way up to the wet hold, snagged it with his right hand, and pulled down on it with everything he had. This time, shakily, he pulled through.

"That was fucking insane," I said to Jared, who just shook his head in disbelief. It was the boldest bit of climbing I'd ever seen.

These thoughts were quickly forgotten thirty minutes later, when the three of us were hugging and high-fiving on the summit in the twilight. "Uh, guys," I said, interrupting the reverie, "isn't that the *actual* summit up there?" The fifteen-foot-tall block was coated in a thin layer of ice, which meant it wasn't possible for us to scale those last couple of body lengths.

"I think we're close enough," said Alex. "Let's get out of here." It was midnight by the time we reversed the tricky horizontal pitches on the ridge and arrived at the sloping six-foot-wide snow ledge where we had stashed our packs. I stomped out a coffin-shaped hole in the snow for my bivouac, and as I slid into my sleeping bag, the last thing I saw was Alex sitting down with his back against the wall. It was a long, cold night, and when I awoke, it was snowing lightly and the mountain was enveloped in cloud. My Gore-Tex bivouac sack was covered in a shiny glaze of ice. I was surprised to see that Alex was still sitting where I had last seen him the night before. Something didn't seem right, so I bundled up and shuffled over to see how he was doing.

"I can't get this stupid thing off," he said, wrestling with his jacket.

When I leaned in to help, I saw that his left arm was so swollen that the sleeve of his coat might as well have been painted onto his body. "You're hurt," I said.

"I guess so," he replied. In our hectic, half-crazed effort to get to the summit and back down, Jared and I had never assessed Alex after his fall. He had told us he was "great," but I now realized that must have been the adrenaline talking. After he had gone back up and dispatched the arête, we both assumed he had somehow come through the fall unscathed. I carefully looked him over and found that his elbow was severely contused and his hip had a puncture wound that appeared to go right down to the bone. Worse yet, he was mumbling and seemed confused. In the few minutes I'd been working on him it had begun to snow more heavily and the wind was building. Snow was piling up on his shoulders and pooling around his legs, and the visibility had dropped to a few body lengths. It was time to get the hell off this mountain.

By one P.M. we were back at our portaledge. We climbed inside and made some hot chocolate, unsure of whether we should spend the night and risk getting pinned by the storm, or break down camp and continue rappelling. We were all antsy to get off the wall, and when I looked out the door of the rainfly, I spied a patch of blue sky—a classic sucker hole. By the time everything was packed into the six pigs, it was snowing again.

The snow turned wet and gloppy. Waterfalls began flowing down the wall, soaking me to the skin as I searched for the bolted anchors we had placed on our way up. Through the mist, I spotted the Russian portaledge, with its Day-Glo pink rainfly, far across the wall. They must have seen me, too, because I heard one of them yell, "Did you make the summit?"

"Yes," I shouted back.

"Congratulations," yelled the Russian team, in unison.

We had planned to reverse our route, but the line of our ascent was steep and traversing. After only a few rappels I realized there was no way it was going to happen. As darkness fell, I committed to forging a virgin descent down a blank headwall whose contours were a complete mystery. The face was gently overhanging, so I had to kick off the wall to keep my body swinging back and forth on the rope; otherwise, I'd end up dangling in space with no way to reach the cliff. Each time I swung in, I would quickly pan the wall with my headlamp, looking for cracks in which I might build my next anchor. If I didn't see anything, I'd push off hard with my feet, letting the wet ropes zip through my rappel device, praying I would find something before I reached the ends.

After I'd found and built each anchor, Jared and Alex would lower the pigs to me, and I'd dock the hanging circus to the constellation of pieces I had haphazardly shoved into the cracks. In the middle of the night I touched down on a table-size ledge flowing with an ankle-deep river. I tried to remove a piece of gear from the sling over my neck, but my fingers were wooden and no longer following my commands. Water was pouring all around me and all over my body, streaming out of my jacket cuffs and my pants legs. I remember being surprised that I suddenly had an urge to pee—it felt odd to deal with a bodily function when I was in full survival mode and unsure if I would live through the night. When the steaming stream gushed forth into the beam of my headlamp, I reacted instinctively, shoving my numb, pruned fingers directly into the flow of warm urine, like I was washing them under a faucet. As sensation slowly returned, and my fingers curled with the exquisite pain known as the "screaming barfies," I vowed to myself that this would be my last big climb.

By the time we finally stumbled into base camp twenty-four hours later, I was already reconsidering the vow.

By a strange coincidence, or perhaps not, Quokka had its IPO the day we summited. This was the day when the three hundred employees, most of whom had been lured into taking the job with the offer of stock options, were supposed to hit the jackpot. A couple of weeks earlier, when we were halfway up the wall, Quokka had offered to let us in on the action: Rather than the 4,000 dollars we were supposed to be paid as talent, they would give each of us the equivalent amount in stock options. We couldn't believe our good fortune. When Quokka had its Netscape moment, we figured we would double, triple, or maybe even quadruple our investment.

Of course, that's not how it went down. The hard truth was that Quokka was ahead of its time: There just weren't enough people with access to broadband to make the website commercially viable. Worse, Quokka hadn't been able to figure out how to monetize its business. The few banner ads and sponsorships they were able to sell dried up after the IPO flopped. Layoffs followed, and Climaco moved on. A year later, the dot-com bubble burst.

I'D BEEN HOME FROM PAKISTAN for about a week when I called Chris Eng at the North Face. He had been hired as the athlete team manager less than a year earlier. We exchanged a few pleasantries, but I couldn't get him to open up and bro down like we always did. "So what trips are you working on?" I asked. Another long, awkward silence. "Well," he said, "looks like our next big one is an expedition to the north face of Jannu."

"Uh . . . yeah," I replied. "I know all about it, obviously, because it's my trip. Jared and I have been planning it for years."

"Well, actually, it's going to be Jared and Alex," he said.

I called Jared, who sheepishly admitted that he and Alex had been talking. They had decided to team up, and I was out. "No hard feelings, right?" he said. I couldn't help but wonder if maybe this was more serious than just being uninvited on a trip. I called Greg Child for advice, and he said, "Watch your back, Mark." I couldn't call Alex because he had already left for his next expedition to the

South Face of Shishapangma, an 8,000-meter peak in Tibet. When we had parted ways at the airport, he had given me a hug. "We're good, right?" I had said. "Totally," he replied.

THE NEWS BROKE about a month later on a website called MountainZone, a competitor of Quokka's that was covering the Shishapangma expedition. Alex and a cameraman named Dave Bridges were missing.

It was October 5, 1999—a month and a half since we had returned from Great Trango. They had been acclimatizing on the lower apron of the South Face with Conrad Anker when they spotted a small avalanche break loose about 6,000 feet above them. It appeared benign at first, but the face was loaded with snow from a recent storm, and the avalanche quickly propagated. As it barreled toward them, Conrad ran sideways. Alex ran down. Bridges followed Alex. Right before the avalanche struck, Conrad dove onto his chest, burying the pick of his ice ax as deeply as he could into the snow. When the blast hit, the lights went out. Conrad doesn't know what happened next, but when he came to, he was only lightly buried about a hundred feet from where he had self-arrested. Blood dripped from a wound on his head. The snow, warmed from the kinetic energy of its particles colliding on its slide down the mountain, instantly set up like quick-set cement. Conrad walked across its surface looking for his friends—but there was no trace of them.

I WAS WITH MY WIFE and nine-month-old son when we got the call. I said to Lauren, "Okay, he's missing. But it's Alex Lowe. He's probably stuck in a crevasse or wandering around dazed and confused on some glacier. He'll be back." But as the days stretched into weeks and then into months, and the call that he'd been found never came, it slowly sank in that Alex was gone.

As I processed the shock and grief of Alex's death, criticism of our Great Trango ascent began to mount among the so-called purists of the sport. Steve House, one of the guys Alex had visited when he was convalescing in Paiju, was leading the charge. House was a staunch proponent of what people were beginning to call "modern lightweight tactics." That year he wrote a piece for the *American Alpine Journal* in which he meticulously detailed all the many reasons he was unimpressed with our climb. In the author's note at the beginning, House wrote:

> In the year 2000, the cutting edge of alpinism is not fixing ropes, placing bolts, using oxygen or high-altitude porters . . . re-leading pitches for the camera, making e-mail dispatches from the bivouac or climbing with partners whose only purpose is documentation. These are ideas that according to some will define cutting-edge climbing in the future. I think that these ideas will simply define a new specialty within climbing that I'll call "business climbing." Business climbing will divide our talents and degrade the amount of cutting-edge climbing that will be accomplished. . . . Was the 1999 American Great Trango Tower expedition a milestone in the history of climbing? No. Were their accomplishments equitable with the amount of publicity it garnered? Absolutely not.

House's article was espousing a modern evolution of the alpine-style climbing that the legendary Tyrolean mountaineer Reinhold Messner first brought to the Himalaya in the 1970s. The ethic of alpine style is that you start at the base of the mountain with your pack, climb as high as you can each day, find a bivouac, and then continue on in like fashion until you reach the top. Messner and his partner Peter Habeler were the first to climb Everest without supplemental oxygen, in 1978. Beforehand, Messner had famously said that he would climb Everest by "fair means" or not at all. In his landmark 1971 essay, "The Murder of the Impossible," Messner decried the growing trend of climbers using oxygen and excessive amounts of equipment to bring down a mountain's difficulty, rather than rising to meet the peak on its own terms. He wrote, "Today's climber doesn't want to cut himself off from the possibility of retreat: he carries his courage in his rucksack."

Before Messner arrived on the scene, Himalayan peaks were usually climbed in "expedition style." The idea is simple: You lay the entire mountain, from top to bottom, with ropes. It's a laborious way to climb a mountain, but it's relatively safe and the nylon umbilical cord offers a fast and efficient way to get off the mountain if someone gets hurt or sick or bad weather comes in. The problem comes once the climbers have made the summit. At this point, all they want to do is get down safely, and as a result, it's common for the fixed lines to be left behind. By the time the next season rolls around, the ropes are often unusable, shredded from the wind or frozen into the slope, which means a new set must be laid. On popular 8,000-meter-peak trade routes like the Abruzzi Ridge on K2, there are so many old ropes in place that it's virtually impossible to climb the mountain without stumbling over them. If you're like Messner or House, and you want to climb these routes in their natural state, you're out of luck.

Expedition style is how most of the 8,000-meter peaks were first climbed, and for the most part, it's how they are still climbed today. If you sign on with a commercial expedition, even to smaller mountains like Nepal's Ama Dablam, you pay for the privilege of using the umbilical cord, which is typically set by local high-altitude Sherpas or porters. You show up, attach your ascenders to the rope, and up you go. This extreme *via ferrata* is a big part of why so much controversy swirls around Mount Everest every spring. The job of establishing the fixed ropes on Everest is especially dangerous because the umbilical cord has to be run through the Khumbu Icefall, an unstable section of glacier riddled with ever-shifting crevasses and ice towers called seracs. The job is outsourced to Sherpas, who put their lives on the line each season to establish the ladders and ropes their clients need to climb the mountain. When a massive avalanche broke loose from the Western Cwm and swept across the Khumbu Icefall in April of 2014, sixteen Sherpas lost their lives—while their clients sat safely in base camp.

Climbers have been arguing about style since Edward Whymper first climbed the Matterhorn in 1865. While there have never been official rules that dictate how a mountain should be climbed, there have always been various unwritten ethical codes. On Great Trango, we knew we were violating some of those codes—using too many fixed ropes and bolts, "spraying" about ourselves on the Internet, and posing for the cameras—but the compromises seemed unavoidable if we were going to document the climb in the way we had promised our sponsors. We found ourselves in the same position Ron Kauk did when John Bachar flattened his bolts ten years earlier. Only now it was our reputations being flattened.

HOUSE HAD BEEN INFLUENCED by a prominent American alpinist named Mark Twight, who was pushing to protect the sacredness of the climbing experience by taking Messner's idea of fair means even further. A year after our Trango ascent, Twight, House, and Scott Backes completed a route on Denali called the Czech Direct in "single-push style," meaning they started at the base and climbed more or less nonstop for sixty hours until they reached the top. They carried a stove for melting snow, but no tent or sleeping bags.

Afterward, Twight wrote an article for *Climbing* magazine, entitled "Justification for an Elitist Attitude." In it he wrote:

> I'm an elitist prick, and I think posers have polluted mountaineering. They replace skills and courage with cash and equipment. They make the summit, not the style, the yardstick of success. Only marginal minds or true individuals used to discover mountaineering. Lack of social support forced them to be autonomous, to turn climbing into a lifestyle isolated from society. We had community back then. Now I'm embarrassed to call myself a climber, because close on the heels of the admission some dilettante will ask whether I've read *Into Thin Air* or done Everest.

The night before the trio set off on their climb, House read to them from Yukio Mishima's *Sun and Steel*.

> Pain, I came to feel, might well prove to be the sole proof of the persistence of consciousness within the flesh, the sole physical expression of consciousness. As my body acquired muscle, and in turn strength, there was gradually born within me the tendency towards positive acceptance of pain, and my interest in physical suffering deepened.

According to Twight, this passage spoke to what his team was seeking. "We were on Denali to prove the existence of consciousness," he wrote. "I've tried to explain the crack we peeped through, but even close friends can't understand. What truth we learned is locked in our three hearts alone."

This ultraminimalist style became known as "light and fast"

alpinism. Now even carrying bivouac gear was seen as a devolution of the sport. Some called it "disaster-style," on account of how little room for error you had when climbing the world's biggest alpine faces with little more than the clothes on your back. Either way, most climbers thought it was an unrealistic ideal: There were only a handful of alpinists in the world who had the skill and desire to climb abiding by this new ethos. And as Twight had just unapologetically made clear, everyone else had no business on the mountain.

A FEW YEARS LATER, it was Odintsov and the Russian Big Wall Project who came under fire from House. They had just completed a famous "last great problem" of the Himalaya—the North Face of Jannu. That 11,000-foot wall tops out at 25,295 feet and had been attempted more than a dozen times by some of the world's best alpinists. After Alex passed away, Jared put me back on his team, and along with Kevin Thaw, we made our own attempt in the fall of 2000. After Great Trango I needed to rediscover the soul of climbing, to find the joy that I had experienced on climbs like Polar Sun Spire and Shipton Spire. While I found House's sanctimonious attitude and arrogance insufferable, I agreed with his assessment of our Great Trango climb to some extent (not least because the heavy logistical burden Quokka placed on us ruined much of the fun), and it was a good life lesson to take his criticism to heart.

We turned back 3,500 feet up Jannu, at the base of the upper headwall, after almost being caught in an avalanche. But we had fun.

Odintsov and his team succeeded where all other teams had failed, and their Jannu ascent was nominated for the prestigious Piolet d'Or—an award given out by the French Guides de Haute

Montagne each year for the world's best mountaineering ascent. (In 1999, our two routes on Great Trango were nominated—the Russian Way and Parallel Worlds—but neither team went home with the prize, a golden ice ax.)

At the award ceremony in Grenoble, France, in 2005, nominees were asked to give short presentations about their climbs. House, who was nominated for a brilliant solo ascent of K7 in Pakistan, used his presentation to criticize the Russians for the heavy-handed expedition style they had employed on Jannu. Nonetheless, the Russians won, and afterward, a tense conversation took place between House and Odintsov. Later, in an article in the French magazine *Vertical*, House wrote, "The Russians did climb the north face of Jannu . . . but they also mutilated it with their heavy style. The Piolet d'Or pretends to award ascents that represent the 'evolution' of alpinism. I maintain that the Russians' ascent of the North Face of Jannu is irrelevant to modern alpinism."

In a letter to *Alpinist* magazine, House editorialized, "Ever since the great alpinists of the previous generation brought alpine style to the Himalaya, any other style of ascent is a gross and unacceptable step backward into the past, and a great strike against all that is beautiful about the pursuit."

Like us, Odintsov never responded to House's criticism, at least not publicly. I had always wondered what he said to House when they spoke at the Piolet d'Or ceremony in Grenoble. I wanted to ask Odintsov, "Am I the only one who finds all this drama among the climbing elite unseemly?" In 2006 I e-mailed him and asked him about the exchange between him and House in Grenoble. He wrote back immediately.

Such disagreements legitimately exist between people of different age and mentality, born on different continents. It would be strange if those disagreements didn't exist at all. Yet there exists a category of people with a firm knowledge of how one is supposed to live. For them, personal happiness isn't enough; they need to make others happy. To them, it's absolutely necessary that everyone around them live life by their patterns. If such a zealot is given no power, he is merely amusing and is quite harmless. But God forbid that he is given the means to try out his recipe on others. The Russians are personally familiar with such experiments. The one bad thing is that such discussions lead to disunion among people practicing this wonderful sport. Climbers, including their elite, have little association with each other as it is. To the Atlantic Ocean that separates us, do we have to add a swamp of discussion on who's better?

LOOKING BACK ALMOST TWO DECADES, it's hard for me to separate the drama with Alex from the experience as a whole of working for Quokka. The intent was to let people experience, in a whole new way, what it's like to pioneer a first ascent in the Karakoram. It was a worthy goal, I suppose, one we all believed in at the beginning. But in the end, the expedition turned into something more like an episode of *Survivor*. We banded together when necessary, but we weren't a team. And for this reason, among many others, the Quokka experiment was a failure—and a mistake.

In the years since, I've come around to admitting that I wasn't blameless in the falling out with Alex. At the time, I denied vehemently that I was being bossy and overbearing, but it can't be a coincidence that my ex-wife and at least one close friend have told me that I sometimes act exactly as Alex described me.

I can't speak for the others, but I know that my own awareness of being on a stage—a stage on which I was competing for the limelight with "the world's best climber" (whether I wanted to or not)—precluded the Zen I had always found in climbing. The act of trying to share what makes climbing such a singular experience had robbed it of its essence and sucked all the joy out of a climb I had dreamed about since I was a Crazy Kid.

CHAPTER SIX

The Secret Weapon, Mr. Safety, and Xiao Pung

W here's your helmet?" I asked.

"Uhhh, I don't have one," replied Alex Honnold sheepishly.

"What do you mean? You forgot it back in camp?" Before I finished my question, I knew the answer.

"Uhhh, no. I mean I didn't bring one on the trip."

"*Intentionally?*"

"Sort of. I don't actually own a helmet."

The conversation could have been comical if we had been anyplace other than where we were. Imposing walls of crumbly granite hung above us in every direction. The gully was about thirty feet across, its walls polished and striated by the debris-ridden flash floods that coursed through it like a flushing toilet every time it rained. It was not the kind of place you ventured without a helmet.

Below us, the gully dropped out of sight into a mist-filled cauldron. If we were canyoneers, we could have kept rappelling into the abyss. Six miles farther down the canyon and 10,000 feet below, the gully would eventually spill us into the South China Sea. At the time, only three parties had ever successfully negotiated the canyon, one of which barely survived.

A few months after the Trango expedition, I found myself in a dusty base camp below a volcanic spire in northern Cameroon. Around the campfire one night, my two South African climbing partners regaled me with tales of a mysterious jungle canyon lined with titanic cliffs. With each round of the whiskey bottle, the walls grew, until a giant beetle landed in the dirt in front of one of the South Africans. He promptly snatched it up and popped it into his mouth. When he was done chewing, he declared that the walls might be 10,000 feet high, nearly twice the height of Great Trango Tower.

"Pleeeease, just tell me where it is," I begged.

"Yeah, well, the thing is, we can't tell you, because we're thinking about climbing it ourselves," said the one who had eaten the bug.

"You're the last guy we'd tell," said the other.

I HAD MOSTLY FORGOTTEN ABOUT that whiskey-addled conversation when, many years later, I came across a book entitled *Descent into Chaos*. It told the story of a doomed British Army expedition that attempted the first descent of Low's Gully, the world's deepest slot canyon, located on the north side of Mount Kinabalu in Borneo. One look at the cover, which showed a jungle gully flanked with towering cliffs, and I knew I had found the secret climbing paradise the South Africans had teased me with back in 1999.

The British Army envisioned the expedition as a training exercise, but the leader, Lieutenant Colonel Robert Neill, vastly underestimated what he was getting into. Of the dozen men comprising his team, only one had significant climbing and canyoneering experience. Three of the men, who were Chinese, were out of shape and had never rappelled before. On February 21, 1994, they dropped into the gully with six days of provisions.

Early on, the team split into two groups. The stronger members forged ahead, while the stragglers struggled to keep up. The original plan was to leave their ropes fixed in place as they descended, so that they would have a means of getting back out if the gully proved impassable, as sometimes happens in canyons. But they quickly realized they had not brought nearly enough rope. A decision was made to "pull through," meaning the ropes were pulled down and reused. Now the only way out was down.

The details of what then transpired have been the subject of two books and a movie, but the short version is that the stronger half of the team eventually emerged from the gully, barely alive, eighteen days later. And they had no idea what had happened to their weaker teammates.

The largest rescue mission in the history of Malaysia ensued, involving more than a thousand men, most of whom tried, unsuccessfully, to work their way up the gully from below. The Malaysian and British air forces flew countless helicopter sorties, but the gully was always maddeningly enshrouded in fog and mist.

On day thirty-one, just before the Malaysian government was about to call off the search, a helicopter pilot spotted the six men huddled on a ledge on the side of the gully at 7,200 feet elevation. All twelve members of the expedition survived the ordeal, but Low's Gully was forever tainted.

By the time I contacted the Sabah Parks administration in 2008 with a plan to rappel into the depths of Low's Gully and then climb the giant cliff hemming its west wall, several more expeditions had ventured into the canyon, including a second British Army expedition, which again had to be rescued by helicopter. So the park's superintendent had declared Low's Gully off-limits. I never found out why, but the officials with whom I was communicating decided not to share this crucial piece of information.

THE CLERK AT THE FRONT desk of the hotel in Kota Kinabalu told me that only one other member of my team had arrived—a

Mr. Honnold. It was the middle of the night, but after two days of shuffling across twelve time zones, I was too frazzled to sleep, so I plopped into a chair and opened a bottle of duty-free vodka. Taking my first sip, I heard a knock on the door. Through the peephole I saw Alex Honnold standing in the hallway wearing nothing but a pair of boxer shorts. I invited him in, and he took a seat on the bed. It was the first time I'd sat face-to-face and talked with the guy, and I was immediately captivated by his eyes, which were deer-in-the-headlights huge.

"Vodka?" I offered, holding up the bottle.

"I don't drink," he said. "Never have. I don't smoke or use caffeine either." So that's why the Brits had nicknamed him "the Monk," I thought to myself. But then he qualified his teetotaling with an awkward admission: "Actually, I do have one vice—fornication."

"What did you bring to read?" I asked, having long since learned you could never have too much reading material on a climbing trip.

"I brought five books," he replied. "And I'm glad I did because I've already read two." Alex rattled off some titles that included *The Brothers Karamazov* by Fyodor Dostoyevsky and several philosophical treatises on atheism.

We talked a bit about Half Dome. It had only been about six months since the free solo. People were calling it the boldest rock climb in the history of the sport. Alex told me the story, explaining how he "lost [his] armor" on that slabby face move on pitch 21. "I should have spent more time preparing the route," he said.

"So what about El Cap?" I asked. In the two years since he had turned the world climbing scene on its head, he had already established himself as the best free soloist in history. And everyone knew that a free solo of El Capitan was the holy grail of rock climbing. Whoever did it would go down in history as the greatest climber ever. Dean Potter had been eyeing it. No disrespect to the Dark Wizard, but everyone knew it was beyond him. This kid sitting across from me, however, was operating in a whole new realm. It still seemed far-fetched, and I doubted it would actually happen, but every new generation of climbers pushes the boundaries beyond what the previous one thought possible. It was an obvious question to ask, though somewhat impertinent. Climbers tend to be coy about their grandest ambitions and likewise respect one another's reticence. But Alex had an air of frank openness, which suggested to me that he wouldn't mind my asking. And I was damn curious whether he would seriously consider it.

"I do think about it," said Alex, "but right now it's way too scary. Maybe someday, though. We'll see." With that, he stood up, arched his back, and started toward the door.

"Well, it was good to finally meet you," he said as he was stepping out.

"Actually, we've already met," I replied. Alex looked at me inquisitively, tilting his head to the side, then shrugged and headed out the door.

That meeting had been only a few weeks earlier, at a rock-climbing festival in the desert outside of Las Vegas. It was dark and noisy, and the only thing I remember from the encounter, apart from its brevity, was the handshake. As Alex's mitt closed around mine, I felt like a little kid shaking hands with a giant. It was a peculiar sensation, because I'm taller and heftier than he is, and he didn't have a commanding presence otherwise. He stood hunched forward, shoulders drooped, dark eyes hidden under his hoodie like some shadowy character from a *Star Wars* movie. Afterward, I wasn't even sure if we had made eye contact.

I didn't want to invite Alex on the Borneo expedition. It had been Conrad Anker's idea. He'd been the captain of the North Face Global Athlete Team and a leading figure in the climbing community ever since my misadventure on the Great Trango

Tower with Alex Lowe and Jared Ogden nearly ten years earlier. It was Conrad's job to scout for the next batch of talent. Shortly after the Half Dome free solo, he signed Alex to the team. I'd seen Conrad over the years being careful not to bring on people whose personalities don't mesh with those of the rest of the North Face athletes. The crew usually hovers around forty to fifty people, with an equal number of men and women spanning various disciplines from big mountain skiing to ultrarunning and specialists in every type of climbing. A guy might be the best climber in the world, but if he's insufferable to hang out with, he's never getting a contract from Conrad.

From the way Conrad was selling me on Alex, it was clear he had fallen under this kid's spell. "He could be our secret weapon," Anker suggested, a young, fearless gun to send out on the sharp end when the silverbacks are tapped out and a tough pitch needs to be fired. I had used similar phrases about Alex Lowe once upon a time, and the resonance was not a happy one.

There were, of course, commercial considerations. The North Face planned to use Jimmy Chin's photography from the expedition for a national advertising campaign. Alex Honnold, who had never been on an expedition before, was to be the new poster boy, it seemed. The firm needed photos of him in action, and the Borneo expedition was the best fit of the trips heading out that year. There was also the fact that Jimmy and another North Face climber, a filmmaker and artist named Renan Ozturk, were planning to make a film about the expedition, the theme of which they were thinking could be "Young and Old." Just like that, not quite forty, I was the old guy.

I was diplomatic when Conrad made the ask, careful not to say what I was thinking at the time, which was, *Hell no! I don't want to climb with that maniac. He'll kill me.* Conrad knew as well as I did that the choice of climbing partners is critical. In this case, all signs certainly pointed to the fact that Alex Honnold and I were not operating on the same wavelength.

I had always put climbers in one of two categories: those who'd had the wake-up call, and those who hadn't. Until a climber has experienced a serious accident, it's easy to feel invincible, to fall into the trap of thinking *Bad things happen, just not to me.* Conrad, having lost several of his best friends to climbing accidents, and having nearly died himself on Shishapangma with Alex Lowe and Dave Bridges, certainly had his eyes wide-open. But what about Honnold? His eyes appeared to be wide-open, but were they really? Did he recognize how close he was to the edge?

BEFORE I LANDED IN KOTA KINABALU, or KK as the locals call it, my idea of Borneo was pretty much the common caricature: a primitive jungle island crawling with hungry cannibals with bones stuck through their noses. KK, I discovered, is a thriving first-world metropolis that serves as a popular vacation destination for Asians, especially Japanese. Ringed with tropical beaches, KK, which is home to about 450,000 people, reminded me of Honolulu. What I didn't know is that Borneo, the world's third-largest island, is divided among three different countries. Three-quarters of the island is Indonesian territory, while the northern portion is mostly part of Malaysia, except for a 2,200-square-mile enclave on the north coast owned by the tiny nation of Brunei.

We spent several days sweltering in the equatorial heat of KK as we dealt with logistics like sorting and organizing our gear, buying food, and picking up last-minute supplies. What the rest of the team didn't know was that I was making regular trips to the Sabah Parks administration office to work on our permit, which I still didn't have. Every day, I was shuffled from one office to the next. The various officials were mostly pleasant, but no one was willing to tell me whether I would be given a permit or not.

By the time we finally pulled out of KK in two vans, one carrying us and the other all our equipment, I still didn't have permission for us to rappel into Low's Gully. I felt like I was gambling with someone else's money, and I had gone all in. When we got to the park headquarters at the trailhead for Mount Kinabalu, I would find out if the superintendent was going to fold or call my bluff.

On our way out of town we pulled into an electrical supply store. We had stopped at this shop on an industrial backstreet the day before to get an adapter for the generator that Jimmy and Renan would use to charge their camera batteries. Our outfitter, a middle-aged Malaysian man I'll call Paul, walked into the store and came out a few minutes later followed by the beautiful young woman who had sold us the adapter. She was petite but had a voluptuous body, with long black hair and sleepy eyes. She slid into the front seat between Paul and our driver, placing a small Hello Kitty bag down by her feet. She looked back at us and smiled but said nothing. I assumed Paul knew her and she was bumming a ride, perhaps to see family who lived out near the park.

But when we got to our hotel outside the park entrance that evening, she was still with us. We all piled out of the van and walked out into the road for our first good look at Mount Kinabalu, which had appeared out of the clouds. The mountain was more of a massif than a single peak, comprised of two rocky plateaus connected by a ridge of toothlike summits. Jungle-covered foothills rose to a point where the vegetation abruptly stopped. The upper reaches of the mountain, nearly 10,000 feet above us, appeared bare and weathered. In the middle of the crenelated summit ridge was a distinct U-shaped notch that I recognized as Commando Cauldron, the entrance of Low's Gully.

Paul came out of the front office and threw a pile of keys onto a picnic table. The six of us, plus the woman, whom we had nicknamed Hello Kitty, stood there looking at the keys. Conrad grabbed one, gripped the shoulder of Kevin Thaw, an old friend and frequent partner we had invited to round out the team, and disappeared into one of the rooms. Jimmy and Renan did the same. There were two keys left. I grabbed one and headed up a staircase leading to the second floor, looking back to see if Alex was following me. He wasn't. By a simple process of elimination, he had been left to share the last room with our new friend. When I emerged twenty minutes later, after taking a shower, the rest of the guys were sitting at some tables under an awning out front. Alex and Hello Kitty were nowhere to be seen. The door to their room was closed, curtains drawn.

The next morning we met early for breakfast at a restaurant across the street from the hotel. "Where's Kitty?" I asked Alex, who was staring back at me from across the table, his face expressionless.

"Still in bed, I guess," he replied.

She walked in a few minutes later with her long black hair tousled. Barefoot, she wore nothing but a pair of panties and a loose-fitting T-shirt. She was a well-built woman, and it was obvious she was not wearing anything under her shirt. As she reached over the breakfast buffet to fill her plate, everyone could see. Alex just sat there eating a bowl of cereal and made no comment.

AT THE PARK ENTRANCE, several rangers eyed us suspiciously as we unloaded dozens of duffel bags from our bus. We had about 1,200 pounds of food and equipment. We each planned to carry a fifty-pound load, which meant we'd need to hire about twenty porters to carry the rest.

"Who's the leader of this group?" said an officious-looking man wearing an army-green uniform with a red-and-blue patch on the breast.

"Uhhh, that would be me," I replied.

"Come with me," he said grimly, as if he had just discovered that one of the duffels was full of drugs.

He brought me to an office on the second floor of the park headquarters, where a short man with close-cropped salt-and-pepper hair sat behind a big desk. He didn't stand as I approached, and when I reached across the desk to shake his hand, he crossed his arms and scowled. Since the park service had known for months what I wanted to do, I gave it to him straight. We were a six-man team sponsored by the North Face, on assignment for *Men's Journal* magazine. We had come to Borneo to climb a first ascent on one of the big walls rising from the depths of Low's Gully. The man, whom I assumed to be the superintendent, stared back at me saying nothing, so I kept blabbing.

"It is forbidden to enter Low's Gully," he finally said.

"But?"

"It's strictly out of the question."

"But?"

"I said no," he barked, with a finality that caused my chest to tighten with fear.

I slumped into my seat, feeling sick. I would have to go outside and break the news to Conrad. The guy who had given me my big break as a climber was happily sorting loads in a parking lot a few yards away—for an expedition on which I had already spent more than 10,000 dollars of someone else's money. An expedition that wasn't happening. *That's it,* I thought. *My career is over.*

The superintendent was glaring at me, as if contemplating whether he could have me arrested. I felt a tap on my shoulder. My heart jumped as I spun in my seat, expecting to see a park official with a billy club and a set of handcuffs. But it was Jimmy, who had slipped in quietly.

"Hey," he whispered, leaning in close, "let me take over here." I motioned to the other chair, but Jimmy shook his head. "No, you should go. I've got this."

As I was exiting the room, I looked back over my shoulder and saw Jimmy stepping around behind the superintendent's desk. He had his iPhone out and was holding it horizontally in front of the superintendent. Jimmy put his arm on the guy's shoulder, then said, "Did I ever tell you about the time I skied Mount Everest?"

Twenty minutes later, Jimmy walked out with our permit in his hand.

JIMMY CHIN AND I FIRST crossed paths in Yosemite in the late nineties. Like a lot of us, he was living out of a beater Subaru, hiding from the Tool, and cutting his teeth up on El Capitan. He had no sponsors and almost no money. Not long after, I remember running into him at the North Face booth at the Outdoor Retailer trade show, where he was trying to score, unsuccessfully as I recall, a free jacket.

A few months earlier, Jimmy had picked up a camera for the first time. While sitting in a portaledge on the side of El Capitan, Jimmy's friend Brady Robinson taught him how to operate his Nikon FM camera. While bivouacked on the summit after completing the climb, Jimmy awoke to a dazzling sunrise. To the east, the craggy, snow-covered peaks of the High Sierra framed the silhouette of Half Dome. In the foreground, a few feet away, Robinson, bathed in orange rays of alpenglow, lay in his sleeping bag, still sound asleep. Jimmy grabbed Robinson's camera and snapped off a few frames, thinking nothing of it. It was beautiful but the kind of scene a climber sees all the time.

The photo turned out to be a gem: perfectly composed, the exposure and depth of field spot on, the scene as classic as they get. Robinson sent the slide to the clothing and equipment company Mountain Hardwear, which paid him five hundred dollars for it. He gave the money to Jimmy.

"It was like, wow, I only have to take one photo a month, and I can be a climbing bum for the rest of my life," says Jimmy. He had told his parents he was going to spend one season in Yosemite and then apply to business or law school—a plan that had been laid out for him since he had learned to walk. But at the end of that season he called home from a pay phone in the parking lot of Camp 4 and told his parents he was going to Pakistan to climb big-wall first ascents. He wouldn't speak to them again for more than a year.

But Jimmy didn't know the first thing about launching an international expedition, so he showed up one Monday morning at Mountain Light, the office and gallery of the award-winning adventure photographer Galen Rowell. Jimmy didn't have an appointment and Rowell was a busy man, so he was offered a seat in the waiting room. Apparently, Rowell was very busy, because Jimmy spent the entire week hanging out in the waiting room until finally, on Friday afternoon, Rowell walked up and introduced himself. "I gotta give you credit for your perseverance," he said. Rowell took Jimmy into his office and gave him a personal slideshow about his recent expedition to a fairy-tale land of unclimbed rock towers in Pakistan called the Charakusa Valley. As Jimmy was leaving, Rowell reached into the carousel and handed him a transparency of the valley's most striking unclimbed spire. "Make sure you take a camera," he said.

WHEN I WALKED INTO OUTDOOR RETAILER in the summer of 2000, Jimmy's photos from that expedition to the Karakoram were everywhere. And it seemed as though everyone was talking about this kid from Minnesota who could climb hard and shoot magazine-quality photos on the fly. The images he created, more than just being beautiful, had a gritty authenticity that set Jimmy apart from other photographers.

IN THE LATE 1940s, Jimmy's parents were teenagers caught up in China's Communist Revolution. When Mao Zedong declared victory and established the People's Republic of China in 1949, their families joined millions of Nationalist Party sympathizers who fled to Taiwan. In 1962, they immigrated to the United States, where they met in the library studies program at Vanderbilt University. The Chins eventually settled in Mankato, Minnesota, as librarians at Minnesota State University. Jimmy's sister, Grace, was born in 1967, and then "Xiao Pung" (Chinese for "Chubbs") arrived in 1973.

Xiao Pung was a precocious child. By age three he was playing classical violin, practicing martial arts, and speaking English and Mandarin. By five he was competing in swimming and tae kwon do, winning nearly every race or match he entered.

One day when he was six, Jimmy came home from tae kwon do practice after a snowstorm. His father, Frank, was waiting for him at the end of their long driveway, which was covered in a foot of snow. "He didn't say anything and just handed me the shovel," says Jimmy. "He trained me by crushing me."

Each summer, the Chins would travel to Taiwan, where Jimmy and his sister spent long days hunched over their paintbrushes, working diligently to master the art of calligraphy and the thousands of characters that make up the oldest written language in the world. For ten of the most formative years of his life, Jimmy spent his summers immersed in an ancient culture deeply infused with Confucian and Taoist philosophy.

According to Grace, the mantra in the Chin household was

"Push harder; accomplish more," to become better than everyone else so you could be a doctor, a lawyer, or a CEO. "Dad's philosophy was that whatever you did, it wasn't good enough," says Grace. "Because obviously you could try harder and do even better."

But as can happen when a child is put under too much pressure, Jimmy rebelled. In middle school he started sneaking out in the middle of the night and stealing his parents' car. Showdowns with his father—and sometimes the local police—escalated until his mother shipped Jimmy off to Shattuck–St. Mary's, an elite Episcopal boarding school in Faribault, Minnesota.

For 130 years, Shattuck had been famous for its Crack Squad— one of the oldest, most decorated military drill teams in the country. The Squad was essentially a secret society run entirely by students. Tryouts took place in the Armory each fall. Like Fight Club, the first rule of the Squad was that you didn't talk about the Squad, and the second rule was that you didn't talk about the Squad. "The first time I saw their forty-five-minute drill executed without a single command, I was mesmerized," says Jimmy. "As a kid brought up to be a multidisciplinary perfectionist, the Squad was totally irresistible." By junior year Jimmy was captain of the Squad, only the second time in the group's history the honor had been given to a non-senior. "He had this way of gaining your confidence and trust by taking the time to understand you and making you feel a part of what was going on," says Dan Fleak, a fellow Squaddie, who was a year ahead of Jimmy. "He never demanded respect—rather showed that he deserved it through his actions."

Away from the overbearing influence of his father, Jimmy had grown into a leader. He got straight As, dominated on the athletic fields, and was a black belt martial artist. At the beginning of his senior year, he was on track to apply to Harvard, Princeton, and Stanford, but he still had an anti-authority streak that frequently put him at odds with the school's administration. "Teachers either loved me or they hated me," says Jimmy. Then he got caught with a girl in his room. It was the kind of offense that normally warranted a brief suspension, but the headmaster, who was not one of his fans, decided to expel him.

His parents enrolled him in a more liberal prep school, where he started climbing and smoking pot. On weekends, he went on epic road trips to Joshua Tree National Park in Southern California. He'd drive through the night, climb as many pitches as possible, then hightail it back to Minnesota for class on Monday morning. His father eventually found out what Jimmy was up to when he checked the odometer on his Subaru. In one month, Jimmy had driven 10,000 miles.

At Carleton College, Jimmy majored in international relations. In a comparative religions seminar, he was introduced to the *Tao Te Ching* and the *I Ching,* the ancient Chinese divination texts that form the religious and philosophical basis for Taoism. "These books spoke to me," says Jimmy, "probably because of the Confucianism I learned as a youth in Taiwan. Taoism taught me to focus on the process, and not to be attached to preconceived ideas of what I thought the outcome should be."

AT THAT SAME TRADE SHOW, Jimmy came by the North Face booth, where a friend introduced him to Conrad Anker. Anker had recently returned from his traumatic avalanche experience on Shishapangma. His broken ribs had healed, but he still wore scars on his face. He took an instant liking to Jimmy. "My first impression was of a guy with charisma and intelligence, but a complete lack of ego," says Anker. "He was pretty refreshing compared to some of the people you meet in the climbing world." Soon the two were teaming up regularly, and under Anker's tutelage, Jimmy quickly developed into an uncommonly strong climber and, more important, proved himself to be one of those rare individuals who also had the talent and work ethic to document the climbing experience with his camera.

Two years later, Anker and Jimmy were pulling carts across the Chang Tang Plateau in search of the birthing ground of the Tibetan antelope for *National Geographic*. The team included the late Galen Rowell (he would die in a plane crash in 2002), who was now Jimmy's hero and mentor, and alpinist Rick Ridgeway, a member of the team that made the first American ascent of K2. David Breashears, famous for his *Everest* IMAX movie, had dropped out at the last minute, and Anker had suggested that Jimmy take over as the expedition cinematographer—despite the fact that he had never shot film or video. Jimmy, whose last name means "gold" in Chinese, nailed the assignment, and when Breashears saw the footage, he hired him as a high-angle cameraman for an expedition to Everest in 2004. On that trip, Jimmy filmed and summited alongside Ed Viesturs, America's preeminent high-altitude mountaineer.

A year later, Jimmy photographed and filmed five different expeditions, including one to Mali on which he had his own Quokka moment while shooting for a cable channel called Rush HD, which had partnered with the North Face on an adventure-based television series. "The cameramen were awesome guys, but the directors and producers didn't get it," recalls Jimmy. "They kept trying to dictate where and how the team would climb. It became the tail wagging the dog."

This was also the year that Jimmy and I teamed up for our first expedition together, to Pitcairn Island, the famous hideout of the mutineers of the HMS *Bounty*. While leafing through the photographic insert in a book titled *The Bounty*, I found myself spellbound by a picture of a small boat attempting to land in Pitcairn's Bounty Bay.

Majestic rock spires rising directly from the South Pacific dominated the background of the circa 1825 painting. I discovered that forty-seven people, most of them seventh- and eighth-generation descendants of the mutineers, still made a living on Pitcairn Island. The one-and-a-half-square-mile island, which has no airstrip or ferries, is located halfway between Panama and New Zealand and is known as the world's most remote inhabited place; the nearest landmass, Australia, is 3,000 miles away. The shoreline is completely encircled with cliffs, and along its seven-mile circumference there is not one cove or harbor where a boat can safely anchor. To get there, I convinced the North Face and *National Geographic* to split the cost of chartering a sixty-six-foot sloop that we would sail from French Polynesia to Pitcairn.

Unfortunately, the majestic rock spires in the romanticized nineteenth-century painting turned out to be far less impressive in real life. In fact, the rock on Pitcairn Island wasn't technically rock; it was compressed volcanic ash that crumbled in our hands like sunbaked mud when we tried to climb it. Jimmy ragged me mercilessly about the fact that I had dragged him across the world to climb rock "that wasn't even rock." But he always did it with a gleam in his eye. After all, I had put him in a position to capture some of the most unusual images ever shot by a climbing photographer. One photo, in particular, of me walking across a tide pool with crumbling rock spires in the background, a North Face pack held proudly over my head, would later grace billboards and magazine spreads all over the world.

But "boondoggle" was the word going around the North Face headquarters when they got Jimmy's photos, some of which showed Greg Child and me playing badminton on uninhabited coral atolls—with cocktails in our hands. It would be years before they let anyone on the team go on an expedition that involved a boat.

THE TRAIL TO THE SUMMIT of Mount Kinabalu, muddy and narrow, twisted and wound its way below waterfalls and along spiny ridges bordered with wind-stunted trees. Pitcher plants of every possible size and color littered the ground. Birds darted from tree to tree. Colorful butterflies floated in the air all around us. The slopes of Mount Kinabalu host ecosystems of dazzling diversity. Botanists are still finding new species every year within the six unique ecological zones that lie along the mountain's 10,000 feet of vertical relief, which stretches from jungle plains to the 13,455-foot summit. The latest tally puts the total number of plant species on Kinabalu at approximately 6,000, more than in Europe and North America combined. This number includes eight hundred species of orchids, six hundred species of ferns, and twenty-seven different types of rhododendrons.

As we climbed higher, the wind picked up and we entered a cloud forest, where everything was coated in electric-green moss that grew up the trunks of the trees and hung beard-like from the branches. Orchids grew from niches in dead logs and in the crotches of the trees. I kept sniffing for the park's most famous plant—*Rafflesia arnoldii,* aka the "stinking corpse lily." It's the word's largest flower, and its petals can grow to more than a meter in diameter. Its smell, as one might guess, is said to be nauseating. But I never smelled anything except myself and the pungent, peaty forest that enclosed us.

In late afternoon, a monstrous, crescent-shaped building materialized out of the gloom—the Laban Rata rest house. We stopped in for a quick cup of soup in the cafeteria, which was packed with tourists, most of whom were Japanese. The standard itinerary for a Mount Kinabalu ascent is two days, with an overnight in this famously overpriced hut on the way up. Most of these people would leave at two A.M., hoping to summit in time to catch the view of the sun rising over the Celebes Sea.

Not far above the hut, at around 11,000 feet above sea level, we finally broke above the tree line. The porters left the main trail and began angling up a dike in a steep slab of rock. The mist had now coalesced into a light drizzle. Bubbling rivulets coursed down the rock in little grooves, pouring over our hands and feet as we scrambled toward a col between bulbous summits. Soaked to the skin, with the temperature in the low forties, I longed for the sweltering heat we had left behind in KK. It was almost dark when I looked up and saw two porters on their way down, without their loads. Over the next ten minutes all twenty of our porters blew by us. "I bet they just dropped their loads on the col and called it good," said Jimmy.

When Jimmy and I finally crested the col at sunset, we found Conrad and Alex sitting on the apex of the ridge next to a giant pile of duffel bags. It was raining, the wind was gusting, and it would be dark in a few minutes. There was nothing even vaguely resembling flat ground anywhere.

"Mind if I bivi with you?" asked Alex, looking mildly concerned.

"Of course, check and see if you can find any good spots for the tent down the ridge. I'm going to check over here." Half an hour later, neither of us had found anything, so we just pitched the tent next to the pile of bags. It was an awful spot, a jumbled pile of boulders, but it was no worse than anywhere else. After guying out the tent, we unzipped it and looked inside. I burst out laughing. Alex didn't laugh, but he did smile when he saw the jagged spine of rock running down the middle of the tent floor. "We'll find a better spot in the morning," I said, crawling in. I went to work leveling my side by filling the nooks and crannies with rolled-up duffel bags, books, and anything else I could find. With the foundation laid, I inflated my Therm-a-Rest pad and laid it over the mess. Pumped nice and stiff, it covered the chaos underneath well enough. Next, I reached into the bottom of my duffel and pulled out the pillow from my bed at home, which was warm and dry inside a black Hefty trash bag. I propped the pillow against the back wall and reclined while emitting an exaggeratedly loud sigh of contentment. Alex, who was still sitting in the door of the tent, gave me a bemused look. "You brought your pillow," he said.

"Of course," I replied, relishing the moment. "I always do. Didn't you?" Alex didn't answer. He crawled in and threw his pad down on his side without making any effort to improve it.

"This is so cool," he said sarcastically, looking up at me from the coffin-like trench, his pad folded around his shoulders like a taco shell. "I can't believe how much cool stuff I'm learning from you guys."

In the morning, Conrad and I took on the mission of finding a way down into the gully, while the rest of the team stayed behind to work on our base camp. The biggest drawback to the camp wasn't its precariousness; it was the lack of water. The only source I could find was a soupy puddle skimmed with a layer of black gumbo in which floated a giant white dead bug. Another unwelcome discovery was a robust population of giant jungle rats mounting a campaign to capture our food stash.

According to my research there were two routes down into the gully: the path taken by the British Army back in 1994 via a place called Lone Tree and an alternate route established by a Spanish team back in 2000. As absurd as our plan was starting to seem, we weren't the only ones to have the idea of rappelling into Low's Gully only to climb back out. The Spaniards did it in 2000, followed by a British team in 2004. It was disappointing we wouldn't be the first, but it was also encouraging (considering I was known for leading wild-goose chases like the Pitcairn expedition) to know that reputable climbers had deemed the canyon a worthy objective.

After we'd crested a ridge directly above camp, the ground dropped away before us into what appeared to be a bottomless trench. From the stygian depths rose a towering spire, like something out of a Tolkien novel. The bottom section of the wall was invisible, hidden within the dark confines of Low's Gully, but from where it emerged from the blackness it arced upward in a clean, unbroken shield, streaked with tiger stripes of white, green, and black. The first 2,000 feet of the wall appeared to be overhanging, and then the angle eased for the final five hundred feet, which culminated in a shark-toothed pinnacle piercing a cerulean sky. I felt a tingling of excitement: Now that I was seeing the wall firsthand, it appeared every bit the kind of challenge and adventure I had structured my life around. But before we could think much about the climbing, we needed to negotiate a long and treacherous rappel into the forbidding chasm.

THE NEXT DAY, after rappelling about 2,000 feet, I stood in an algae-covered riverbed, feeding rope through my belay device. Above me, Alex aid climbed a bolt ladder, which had been drilled nine years earlier by the Spaniards. We had intended to pioneer our own route up this cliff, but eons of flash floods had polished the bottom few hundred feet of the wall porcelain smooth and it made no sense to drill bolts alongside the ones that were already in place. We decided to follow the Spanish past this toilet-bowl blankness until we found a good spot to branch off into uncharted territory.

But Alex was doing it all wrong. Instead of walking up his *étriers* and hanging in his harness between moves, he was pulling himself upward using only his arms. By this point I had climbed at least fifty big walls, and I had never seen anyone do it this way.

"Hey, there's an easier way to do that," I yelled up.

"I know," he called back. "I want to do it this way, so I can get more of a workout." I laughed, my cackle echoing in the cavelike chamber. It was ridiculous what he was doing, but wasn't that the whole point of climbing: to bend over backward and make life as difficult as possible?

On the second pitch, I was thirty feet above Alex's hanging belay when I came upon a detached flake blocking the path forward. I lightly tapped my knuckles on the block, like I was knocking on someone's front door. It reverberated like a drum. All four sides were cracked, and I wondered what was holding it to the wall. "Just free climb around it," called Alex, when he saw that I had stalled out. But the rock was covered in lichen and there were no good holds to pull on—other than the block itself. What I did next is the climbing equivalent of grabbing the handle on a skillet to see if it's hot. I slid a small camming device into the crack on the bottom of the flake and gave it a tug. As the cam lobes flexed outward, whatever flimsy bond that was adhering the block to the wall came unglued. A horrible grinding noise filled the air. A chunk the size and shape of a cinderblock slammed into my chest, tearing through three layers of clothing and taking a bite out of my chest muscle before continuing its flight downward.

"Rock!" I screamed, as I watched it spin through the air making a sound like a swooshing samurai sword. Alex leaned to the side nonchalantly as the rock sailed past about a body length away. A few seconds later, it cratered into the gully below, sending a shock wave up the wall and echoing across the valley. My body shook with adrenaline. Blood oozed from the gash in my chest. I leaned the rim of my helmet against the wall and gazed between my legs at my helmetless partner. We shared a look, but nothing was said.

Two DAYS LATER, Alex and I rappelled back into the gully. This time, we weren't going back to base camp at the end of the day. Our task was to push the route forward while Conrad, Kevin, and Jimmy followed behind, hauling up the gear we'd need to spend the next week living on the cliff. It was exciting to think that somewhere up on the wall, I didn't know where, we would bivouac in portaledges that night. We had reached the point where it was time to branch off the Spanish route, and my mind was filled with that feeling of giddy anticipation that comes with going off the map, outside the known world.

Alex had shown up that day wearing a light blue helmet. He had quietly borrowed it from Renan, who was staying behind to shoot long shots of us working our way up the wall. This cliff was a filmmaker's dream because it started in a pit, which meant Renan could shoot down and across at us from various vantages in Easy Valley.

By late morning, I found myself in a precarious position, hanging from a camming device wedged between two plates of rock that moved when I shifted my weight. Sand and pebbles were sifting out from beneath the plates, which is never a good sign. My excitement at pioneering a route through terra incognita was replaced by dread as it sank in that the path I'd chosen was a minefield. I tapped the rocks to the side and above me with my hammer, like playing a xylophone. Each piece had its own unique tone, but nowhere could I find the sharp metallic ring given off by solid rock. I felt like I was playing a real-life game of Jenga. Were I to choose poorly, like I'd done on the second pitch, and accidentally dislodge the wrong piece of stone, it was possible I could unload a dump truck's worth of loose rock onto myself, Alex, and everyone else down below.

"Go for it," yelled Alex impatiently, from his perch twenty feet below me. "It's not dangerous if you tread lightly." He was right. This type of climbing, what we call *choss,* had once been my specialty. In my day I had free climbed some notoriously sketchy routes, including Stratosfear in Colorado's Black Canyon, the East Face of Mount Babel in the Canadian Rockies, and most of a new route on Mount Dickey in Alaska. But you need confidence, and a lot of it, to free climb on loose rock. And right then, perhaps because I was still spooked from pulling the rock off on the second pitch, or because I now had three children, or simply because I wasn't as strong as I'd once been, I had none.

When I called for the bolt kit, Alex didn't hide his disgust. "Seriously?" he said. "You're going to drill?" When I affirmed that indeed was my plan, he said I was being "super old-school," a thinly veiled way of telling me he thought I was a wimp. Drilling a bolt is the one way in which climbers permanently alter the landscape. Once that four-inch-deep hole has been bored into the rock, it will be there forever. For this reason, many climbers, myself included, try to avoid using bolts, if at all possible. I had to weigh the question of whether I was "murdering the impossible" against the chance that I would fall, pull out all my protection, and break my legs when I hit the ledge where Alex was holding my rope. Picturing myself crumpled and broken was all the convincing I needed.

An hour later, I pulled onto a sloping ledge three feet deep and fifteen feet long. I had climbed only about a third the length of a normal pitch, but this shelf offered a perfect location for our bivouac—and I was happy for an excuse to stop and build an anchor. The cracks I'd been following had petered out, and the next weakness was hundreds of feet away, across a long section of overhanging gray rock that appeared entirely devoid of weaknesses in which to place protection. If I were to continue, it would mean drilling a ladder of bolts up the wall. No one wanted to see that

happen, least of all an impatient and pacing Alex Honnold, waiting to be let out of his cage.

Time for the secret weapon, I said to myself as I reeled in the rope
for Alex, who was in a sour mood when he joined me on the ledge.
"What the hell have you done to my cams?" he demanded. I had
undone some rubber bands on the slings of his camming devices
because I needed the carabiners to build my anchor. My pitch had
been short, but I'd been so scared that I managed to stick most of
our rack into the mountain. I explained why I thought it didn't
make sense to have the biners banded onto each camming device
for multiday big-wall climbs. "I think I know how to take care of
my cams and biners," he said.

"Why don't you clip in?" I asked. Alex was standing next to me
on the ledge, and he wasn't connected to anything. I thought this
was a stupid and unnecessary risk, and I told him so. But I had lost
all credibility in his eyes, and he was done being mentored by "Mr.
Safety"—the nickname he had given me somewhere along the
way. He stayed untethered.

I assumed Alex had always been a nitpicker, but his friend Chris
Weidner later told me that Alex's attitude began to change in
2009. Weidner first met Alex in 2006, before he was famous, and
he says that in those early days, Alex was soft-spoken, thoughtful,
and generous to a fault. When they climbed a route called Golden
Gate on El Capitan in 2007, Alex practically dragged Weidner up
the wall. "He was a really, really supportive partner, even though,
compared to him, I sucked." But over the next few years, as Alex's
fame grew and he became a public figure, Weidner says he also
became more self-centered. "I don't know whether he was getting
a little older and more comfortable in his skin, or what," recounts
Weidner, "but he definitely changed a bit, and I wasn't too psyched
about it." According to Weidner, Alex couldn't understand why
his friend wasn't as motivated or as strong as he was, or why he

didn't see things the same way he did. He was showing zero empathy and being selfish "in the way that a psychopath is selfish," says Weidner.

"It was insane how obsessive and nitpicky he was: 'Why do you need to drink that cup of coffee, why are you drinking that wine, why do you put so much salt on your dinner?'" It got so bad that Weidner stopped using salt because it was easier than battling Alex about it.

As ALEX GRUMPILY put the rubber bands back onto his cams, Jimmy joined us on the ledge. He grabbed the carabiner of hooks and went through them with Alex like they were keys on a key ring. There was the talon, the sky hook, the fish hook, the pointed Leeper, and the flat Leeper. We even had a custom hook I had shaped on my grinding wheel at home. I called it the Hawk, for its beak-like point and because I came up with the idea for it while listening to a classic rock station of the same name on El Capitan. Jimmy placed the hooks on variously shaped edges on the wall in front of us, explaining why he chose one over the other, and showing Alex how to test if a placement was solid. He put the sky hook, which is shaped like a shepherd's crook, onto a chip the size of a silver dollar. When he weighted it, the metal dug behind the tiny flake and popped it off like a dead toenail. "Choose wisely," said Jimmy, chuckling as he gave me a knowing look.

Just a few months before, Jimmy had led a pitch like this at 20,000 feet in the Indian Himalaya on Mount Meru. More than twenty different expeditions, which included some of the best alpinists in the world, had attempted the route previously, but no one had come close to success. Jimmy's masterful lead, which Conrad later named the House of Cards due to the rock's instability, proved the key to the route. But the team ran out of food and fuel and ended up turning back just one hundred meters shy of the summit.

Alex set off, moving slowly upward, making long reaches between small holds I couldn't see. He kicked some of the footholds to test their integrity before stepping on them. *Good,* I thought. *He's showing some caution.* His route meandered right, then back left, then straight over a bulge to a small stance twenty-five feet above, where he was splayed out on the wall like a gecko. His rope whipsawed in the air, and I tried to calculate if the wall was steep enough that he would miss the ledge if he fell.

"That's far enough," called Jimmy. "Try to find a good hook placement and get a bolt in." Crimping an edge with his left hand, Alex reached down and pulled the hooks off the gear loop on the right side of his harness. He chose one and placed it on edge in front of his chest. He gave it a little downward tug, and, satisfied it was good, he clipped his harness to it with a short sling called a quick draw and slowly eased his weight onto it while still holding on with his fingers in case it popped off.

"Is it normal for the hook to flex?" he called down nervously, as his life hung from a quarter inch of chrome-moly steel balanced on a chip of rock the width of a matchbox.

"Perfectly normal," I yelled back. Then Alex drilled his first bolt. Moving up toward what looked like a ledge, he stretched the rope to its end, placing four more bolts along the way. When he called down off belay about two hours after he had set off, Jimmy and I looked at each other.

The guy had just on-sighted loose, overhanging 5.12 on a jungle wall in Borneo. And he made it look easy. I wasn't confident I could follow his lead, even with the rope overhead, so I seconded the pitch by clamping mechanical ascenders to the rope and ratcheting my way upward. When I got to the anchor, I looked up at Alex. His brown eyes were wide-open, and the way he looked at me was entirely different than he ever had before. The grumpiness was gone, and in its place was a glow that came not just from his eyes and the huge shit-eating grin that covered his face—it seemingly radiated from his entire being. I felt as though I had just come in from the cold and was now standing next to a blazing fire. And I realized why Conrad had fallen under Alex's spell when they climbed El Niño together on El Capitan. Being near Alex when he was luminescent felt really good. "That was sick," said Alex. "I'm so stoked." We went for a high five, but I turned my hand sideways and clasped his giant fingers. He looked at me and smiled, and I now knew that we could give each other as much shit as we wanted, and it would never damage our budding friendship.

Jimmy led another pitch, and then the three of us rappelled down the ropes we had fixed to our camp. Two portaledges, cocooned inside white rainflys, hung one above the other, with four haul bags neatly hanging outside the doors. Conrad and Kevin were ensconced in the upper ledge, so the three of us moved into the lower one. The ledge was designed for two on the top bunk and one in a hammock strung underneath.

Jimmy explained to Alex that, as was customary, the three of us would Rochambeau to see who got stuck with the hammock the first night. After that we'd rotate a different guy down below each night. "It's okay," said Alex. "I'm fine with the hammock." He slipped over the aluminum bar and left us to lounge in the comparative luxury of the double-wide platform above. He seemed happy to trade a less comfortable bunk for some private space.

We had decided not to bring a stove, to save weight, so we dined on salami, cheese, and crackers, which we passed between the two ledges in a gallon-size Ziploc bag. For dessert we shared a block of caramel-filled milk chocolate. Off in the distance, past a row of pink and purple clouds that appeared to be marching across the South China Sea, I could see the hazy outline of a distant island. I wondered if I was looking at the Philippines.

"Hey, Alex, what are you going to call your pitch?" asked Conrad, who was drawing a map of our route, what climbers call a topo, in a small yellow notebook. On a big-wall first ascent, it's a custom to give names to significant pitches or features.

"I hadn't even thought about it," replied Alex, "but how about 'the Emily pitch—beautiful and intimidating.'" "Emily" was Emily Harrington, a twenty-two-year-old whom Conrad had recently signed to the North Face team. She was around Alex's age and one of the best female climbers in the world. She was also spunky and quite attractive. Alex had a huge crush on her. He knew that in the small world of the climbing community, word gets around, and she'd eventually hear about the "Emily pitch" (she did). I never would have had the gumption to do something like that when I was Alex's age.

I looked over at Jimmy, who had turned away from watching the sunset and was staring at the inside of the rainfly. I followed his gaze and for the first time noticed how beat-up the fly was. Little nicks and cuts riddled the fabric, and I recalled Conrad back in KK saying that we needed to seam seal it and repair the holes. But we had never gotten around to it.

"This is the same ledge we used on Meru," said Jimmy wistfully. "It was so cold up there that all three of us slept up on the top bunk."

"Are you ever going back to try and finish it?" I asked.

"No fuckin' way," he said. "I'm done with that thing."

(Two years later, Jimmy would return to Meru and finish the route with Conrad and Renan.)

Later, as the three of us settled in for the night, Alex grew quiet and I figured he had fallen asleep. I'd noticed in base camp that he usually went to bed right when it got dark. He was one of those guys who just had to close his eyes and he fell asleep and snoozed right through until morning.

"You know, I'm kind of feeling like a pansy," announced Alex, out of the blue.

"How so?" I responded. "You just did the sickest lead I've ever seen."

"I know," he replied, "but it scared me. I shouldn't have gotten so scared."

CONRAD, KEVIN, AND JIMMY headed up the ropes the next morning, while Alex and I dropped down to see if he could free climb some of the bolt ladders we had aid climbed on our way up. I was hanging off some bolts, feeding the rope in and out for Alex, who was working a difficult section, when the sun disappeared behind a cloud. Every morning so far, we had awoken to clear skies that slowly filled with clouds over the course of the day as the sun burned off the moisture that had settled overnight onto the jungle surrounding Mount Kinabalu. By midafternoon these clouds would build into towering cumulonimbus that would eventually envelop the mountain in torrential thunderstorms complete with booming thunder and lightning. At first I thought these clouds were the standard fare, but then it got dark, so dark it felt like nightfall. A stiff wind began to blow, and giant raindrops splattered off our helmets.

"Let's get the fuck out of here," I called down to Alex, as we raced back up our ropes to the portaledge.

By the time we got back to our camp, horizontal sheets of rain were blowing in from the north, dousing us as if someone was splashing buckets of water against the wall. We crawled into the ledge, but it wasn't much different from being outside. Waterfalls were now pouring down all around us, and I could hear a mighty roar emanating from the gully below, which had transformed into a raging torrent. Water poured through the holes in the fly, and the wind shook the ledge violently. We heard yelling and then the horrifying sound of giant things falling through the air. I peered through the opening at the top of the door and saw rocks the size of television sets whizzing through the gloom on all sides of the ledge. Somewhere up above, Conrad, Kevin, and Jimmy were still battling their way up the choss.

Alex had slipped down into the hammock, and against my advice had gotten into his sleeping bag. I had put mine in a dry bag that morning and clipped it up in the apex of the rainfly, where it still hung dry. Water was pouring in through the holes in the fly, and my nylon bed was filling up like a bathtub. There were two brass grommets on either end of the bed designed to serve as drains. I looked down over the edge and saw Alex's pale face in the opening of his bag. Water was pouring out of the grommets in a steady stream directly onto his sleeping bag. I knew the hammock didn't have a similar drain system, and since it was coated nylon, it had to be filling up with water. Alex was obstinately lying in a pool of water, in his bag, *because* I told him not to. He hadn't said it, but when I suggested he keep his bag dry until we got the water situation sorted, I imagined he thought, *Fuck you, Mr. Safety.* It was the perfect time to give the cocky little bastard some grief, but when I looked at his face enclosed in the sopping-wet fabric of his sleeping bag, his expression said, *Yeah, I'm an idiot. But I'm a stubborn idiot and I'm not giving an inch!* So I just smiled. Slowly, a mischievous smirk spread across Alex's face. And then we both burst out laughing.

I heard a noise outside and looked out the door to see Jimmy, soaked to the bone, dangling on a rope outside the portaledge.

"Conrad is going for it," he said.

"Still?"

"Yeah. He said he wanted to finish his pitch. Move over, I'm coming in."

Jimmy and I sat on our helmets and used our cups to bail water out of the nylon bed like sailors trying to keep their boat afloat.

Jimmy pulled out the camera and pointed it in my direction. Mostly, I was thinking about my warm bed at home.

"How's it going down there?" I yelled, leaning over the side of the ledge and locking eyes with Alex. I was only three feet away from him, but the roar of the gully below was so loud we could barely hear each other.

"Not good," he replied. "I just tried to kill some time fantasizing about women, but I just didn't have the heart."

"Wow, you must really be suffering," said Jimmy, who had popped his shaggy head over the ledge's aluminum frame, his head pressed against the soggy rainfly next to mine.

"How is it up there?" asked Alex.

"Wet," I replied, "and I'm bored. I wish I had brought a book." Climbers, always concerned about weight, don't usually bring books up on the mountain. Back in 2002, on a ski mountaineering expedition with Warren Miller Entertainment, I had gotten trapped for three days in a blizzard high on Mount Waddington in the Coast Range of British Columbia. To keep ourselves from losing our minds, my partner "Sick Rick" Armstrong and I had devised a game: We took turns making up stories about the cute little bear with the red Santa's cap on our Sleepytime tea bags. We played for hours at a time, each picking up where the other had left off and working hard to outdo the other guy by having the bear do completely outrageous, illegal, and immoral acts, which will remain between Rick and me. Stuck in storms at various bivouacs over the years I've told endless stories—some of them completely made up. I've read the directions on hot chocolate packs like they were *New Yorker* articles. Once, in Pakistan, I built a maze on the floor of my tent for an old tired fly I coaxed along by prodding him with a piton.

A few minutes later, Alex's giant hand came over the bar of the ledge holding a torn-in-half book. "Here, take this," he said. It was the first half of *The Brothers Karamazov*.

"Thanks."

"No biggie," he said.

In the morning, the rain had stopped, but we were still socked in dense fog and everything was drenched. I rolled onto my side and put my hand down into the bottom of my bag. It was sopping wet. Jimmy and I had slept in a pool of water. At that moment, I just wanted the trip to be over. I said as much to Jimmy, who was sitting up next to me, his face wearing a grim expression. Sipping on cold instant coffee, I laid out the reasons why we should bail. Jimmy didn't say much, but I knew he was on the same page. Alex, meanwhile, had extricated himself from his torture chamber and was standing outside the ledge urinating into the fog. He was silent, which I took as his tacit agreement that the climb was over.

Conrad and Kevin were also quiet, but I could hear them rustling around in their ledge. Jimmy had just begun expressing his own doubts when Conrad finally chimed in. "Enough with the whining," he said sternly. "It's time to get back to work." Jimmy and I looked at each other sheepishly, like two children who had just been chastised by their father. It was just another storm.

THE SUMMIT, which we reached three days later, was beautiful but anticlimactic, as they always seem to be. We work so hard and take so many risks on these climbs that I suppose it's inevitable that mountaintops hardly ever live up to the monumental billing we attach to them. The letdown is so common that some climbers have said that summits don't matter. It's a gallant idea, but if the summit doesn't matter, where exactly are we heading when we set off from the base?

Conrad had been right when he told me that I would learn a lot from climbing with "the kid." Alex Honnold had reminded me of the old climbing proverb: "There are old climbers and there are bold climbers, but there are no old bold climbers." He had helped me to see, perhaps for the first time, exactly how much I had reeled things in over the past few years. What I hadn't realized until Borneo was that if I kept reeling things in at the rate I was going, it was only a matter of time before I wouldn't have any desire to climb a first ascent like the one we had just done.

My parents, people who had never climbed a pitch in their lives, had always seen this eventuality. "How long do you think you can climb for?" my dad had asked me one day. Later, when I started having children, he had asked, "So what are you going to do when you're done climbing?"

"There is no next thing," I had replied. My dad understood something that I had failed to see or had been unwilling to admit—the sport to which I had dedicated my life was a young man's game. Sure, there were a few outliers like Conrad Anker, "old, bold climbers" who were still pushing the cutting edge into their fifties, but climbing with him had only reinforced the idea that I'm not one of those guys.

After my dad had told me that I was "worm food" when I died, I had been desperate to find something that could give meaning to my existence. But the harder I quested, the more elusive the answers became, and over time, I slowly became nihilistic. If life had an intrinsic meaning, I couldn't figure out what it was. Then I found climbing and, perhaps more important, the climbing tribe. Climbing became my passion, and the strength of that passion gave my life the orientation and purpose it had previously lacked. Climbing taught me what the fox meant when he told the Little Prince, "One sees clearly only with the heart. Anything essential is invisible to the eyes."

Somehow, I had failed to notice that I had crested my personal climbing arc and I was now sliding down the back. A decade earlier, I had been the young buck, and now there I was, at only thirty-nine years old, and the new guy was calling me a silverback and Mr. Safety.

And so I asked myself a question that had never occurred to me before: What would life be like without climbing? It was a question I wasn't prepared to answer, but now that I was no longer gazing upward, wondering, like Alex, where climbing might lead me, I saw, for the first time, the cracks that had formed in the foundation upon which I had built my life.

THERE WAS ONE LAST LOOSE end to take care of before we packed up camp and headed home—exit interviews. Jimmy and Renan had shot hours of video, and Conrad, Kevin, and I had given them plenty of material with which to develop the theme of young and old. We all said basically the same thing: It had been motivating to climb with a young gun like Alex Honnold. Every jaw-dropping lunge, every inhuman pull—even every rookie mistake—had served as a potent reminder that the fire that we saw inside Alex still burned inside us, too.

But for this theme to work, Alex had to acknowledge that he had actually learned something from the silverbacks.

"So?" asked Jimmy, as the cameras rolled.

Alex, sitting atop a boulder on the outskirts of camp, stared back at him blankly.

"Alex, come on. Conrad is one of the most accomplished all-around climbers in the world. He's been on more than forty expeditions. Can you honestly say you haven't learned anything from him?"

"But he's not really a climber," replied Alex. In his narrow view of the sport, which he was now revealing for the first time, if you couldn't climb 5.14, what you did in the mountains was some weird type of adventure hiking. And he wouldn't pretend to be impressed by it. He would later say that he'd felt like Jimmy had teed him up and then said, "Okay, now dance, monkey."

"Who the fuck does this guy think he is?" said Jimmy after Alex had left camp. "I was so incredibly respectful of my elders when I first came on the scene."

"Yeah, me too," I replied. "I still am."

"Well, I can tell you one thing," said Jimmy as he packed away his camera. "I'm never working with him again."

Alex ended up hiking down alone. Jimmy and I hiked down together, talking about Alex most of the way down. The guy was a cocky, elitist son of a bitch, and his failure to acknowledge that he might have learned something from the silverbacks was downright offensive. But then why did we still like the guy? Alex's smugness, his condescension, the way he would look at you while you were cutting him down to size and just smile—it was lovable. You knew he was thinking, *Dude, don't you realize what a fucking badass I am? Do you realize how foolish you sound, trying to tell* me *what's what?* In most people, this attitude would be insufferable, but in Alex it was somehow endearing, probably because he could actually back it up. Compared to the false modesty so common in climbing, his brashness was refreshing. He wore his ego right on his shirtsleeve like the logo of one of his sponsors.

A few minutes from the trailhead we came upon Alex sitting by the side of the trail. He had left camp an hour before us and he's a fast hiker, so he must have been waiting for a long time. "I've been thinking," he said. "You guys want to do another quick interview?" I left Jimmy to do his thing, knowing that Alex wouldn't want an audience while he was saying nice things about us.

CHAPTER SEVEN

Nonprofit

It was the name that initially drew him in. Dean imagined the sky was a deep blue sea that he would fall into if he slipped. When he saw the climb for the first time, a 1,000-foot gently overhanging pillar of gray and orange limestone on the northwest arête of the Eiger, he knew that it was the one. Even the grade, 5.12d, was just right—not too hard, definitely not too easy.

It was June 2008, and Dean Potter had been "living like plankton," in his words, at the base of the Eiger for more than a month. It had been raining most of that time. Afternoons especially were almost always foggy and wet. To pass the time, he and his cameraman, Jim Hurst, would take turns hiking down to the train station to buy beers from the vending machine. If they ever got a weather window, the plan was for Dean to freeBASE the looming pillar of rock that hung over their camp like a tombstone. Dean would free solo the climb wearing a BASE rig, Hurst would film it, and if everything went according to plan, they'd end up with a nice segment in Sender Films' next Reel Rock Tour—a major annual showcase for adventure sports.

Dean always maintained he didn't climb for accolades or fame, but ever since the Delicate Arch fiasco his reputation was badly in need of redemption. People still ranted about it two years later on SuperTopo, where they referred to it simply as "DA." Sometimes, when he was feeling low, he wondered if he'd ever live it down. It had even contributed to the end of his marriage with Steph. They weren't officially divorced yet, but they would be soon. And now this Alex Honnold kid had stolen the show. He was the new face of extreme sport, the guy all the sponsors wanted to associate with. Dean's career was in jeopardy of fading into obscurity. He needed some good publicity.

Whenever the weather was decent, he would solo up the Eiger's West Ridge, rappel down from the top, and rehearse different sections of the route. If conditions were favorable, he would BASE jump afterward from a spot called the Eiger Mushroom. He'd land down in the valley, grab some beers and maybe a baguette, then hike back up to their camp.

Deep Blue Sea would be Dean's first go at this brave new kind of extreme sport. FreeBASE wasn't quite free soloing, because he would be wearing a BASE-jumping rig, which meant that a slip didn't necessarily mean certain death. But it wasn't BASE jumping either, because the exit—if it occurred—was not a controlled event. If he slipped or popped off unexpectedly, there would be no horizontal vector to his launch; plummeting only inches from a cold wall of rock, he'd somehow need to find a way to orient himself in the air in order to track away from the cliff.

Would he be able to right himself and get enough separation from the wall to deploy his chute with any significant chance of a successful opening? He'd seen other jumpers' chutes hit the cliff, not open properly, or snag. A lot of those people were now dead. The best he could do to increase his odds was to make practice jumps with awkward, uncontrolled exits like falling sideways, falling on his back, tumbling. One day, while rehearsing the first crux of the route on the fourth pitch, he dropped a stone that he had carried down from the ridge in his pocket. *One one thousand, two one thousand, three one thousand, four one thousand,* he counted. Then he heard the crack as it impacted the low-angle slope at the base of the wall. The more he visualized falling off at the various cruxes on the route, the more he realized the parachute offered little more than a vague possibility of survival. If freeBASE wasn't exactly free soloing, it was far less similar to climbing with a rope. To attempt it on a route that he considered beyond his free-solo realm was pushing up the risk to an almost absurd level, even for the Dark Wizard.

THE LONGER THE TRIP DRAGGED on, the more pressure and stress Dean began to feel. He knew he was taking it out on Jim. They talked about it. Dean told Jim he felt bad about how he was treating him—but he couldn't help himself. He said he had to be hypercontrolling because if he couldn't control every little detail in his life, how could he maintain control when he was flying, free soloing, or highlining without a tether?

It was a flaw—an ill-fitted joint in the conglomeration of brooding personality and exuberant life-force that was Dean Potter. He knew he had been this way with Steph, too, and that it was part of what had driven her away. Now he was doing it to Jim. And Jim was one of Dean's oldest friends. Jim was thick-skinned, but a person could take only so much abuse. Dean had just ripped into him for not making the coffee according to his exact specifications. If he didn't ease off, Jim was going to snap. Who then would film Dean's art?

After several weeks camped at the base of the Eiger, they woke up one day and the sky was clear. Jim headed up the ridge to the top of the route. Dean traversed in to the wall on a ledge, bypassing the lower-angled pitches at the bottom of the route. As Jim rappelled down from above and Dean started up the climb, wispy clouds began to coalesce around the summit. By the time Dean set off on the crux fourth pitch, clouds were boiling up from below and sifting down the wall from above. Jim hung on his rope about twenty-five feet above him, framing the shot: Dean, wearing a green short-sleeve shirt, black parachute pants, and a small purple-and-black pack (containing his BASE rig), floating above a white cottony ether. Dean crimped a thin side-pull edge, reeled it in, and reached high and right for a brown spot where the rock was spiny, like the back of a puffer fish. At his full extension, the hold was still six inches out of reach. He tried again: same thing. "Fuck," he said quietly, to himself. Something wasn't right. Was it the BASE rig? Was it too heavy? He tried one more time, but the hold was just beyond his grasp. Then he realized his feet were too low, on the wrong holds. He resituated them and pulled again, but his forearms were now flushed with lactic acid and his fingers were uncurling from the holds. He was pumping out. The BASE rig felt like a lead weight on his back. He realized this was it: He would have to jump off. He looked over his shoulder into the opaque stew of cloud that had now completely socked in the north face of the Eiger. He was looking at a blind jump into a cloud with no visual cues to orient himself in the air—almost certain disaster. He had only one hope for survival. "Dude," he yelled. "I can't do it. You have to rescue me!"

Jim had been so absorbed in the filming that he hadn't realized the gravity of the situation. One moment he was staring through the viewfinder, watching Dean grope for the out-of-reach hold, the next he was frantically trying to save his friend's life. Jim quickly stowed the camera and reached down to drop the rope that he had coiled and clipped to his harness so it wouldn't be visible in the frame. Pulling back the handle on his Grigri, he slid down the rope, faster than was safe, until he was even with Dean. He kicked off the wall and got himself swinging like a pendulum. Dean was clinging to two tiny 5.12 crimps, and his grip was slipping. Any second, he would have to let go and take his chances diving into the white void. Jim swung in close. Dean looked over his left shoulder, and they locked eyes. Dean lunged. For a split second he was airborne; then he wrapped his flagging arms around Jim's waist in a bear hug and the pair flew back across the foggy north face of the Eiger in a giant messy heap.

When they stopped swinging, they looked at each other, shocked and disbelieving at what had just happened. Dean's custom-built BASE rig had a harness with a big D ring on it. Jim let go of Dean with one hand, found an ascender on his harness, and clipped it to the ring. He then fastened the ascender to the rope. Taking turns, they slowly and carefully worked their way up the fixed lines Jim had rigged earlier in the day.

When they were safe on the ridge at the top of the wall, Dean turned to Jim and said something to the effect that the rescue fiasco was all Jim's fault because he had pressured him to do the climb that day.

Jim was fed up. He started making fun of Dean, mimicking him, trying to get Dean to realize how silly he was being. "If you're doing it for the camera and you're not doing it for yourself," said Jim, "I think you're a fucking idiot." Dean shot back that Jim was fired. If that's the case, replied Jim, then I guess I'll just go ahead and delete this footage.

That's when Dean snapped. "You're not going to destroy my art," he roared, charging at his old friend.

Jim, an accomplished ultrarunner, took off up the hill, still holding the camera. It was raining now, and the entire mountain was enshrouded in thick fog. Visibility was only a few feet. Dean kept after him, and Jim kept running uphill toward the summit. When Dean eventually realized he would never catch him, he picked up a rock and whizzed it at his friend, just missing. Jim then grabbed his own stone and hurled it back at Dean. Stones flew back and forth for a few minutes before both men plopped onto the ground, frazzled from the adrenaline and dismayed at the absurdity of the fact that they were acting like toddlers—on the Eiger. It was drizzling, and they were both soaked. They had run so far up the side of the mountain in the whiteout that they no longer knew where they were. "I'm so fuckin' angry, I don't think I can find my way down," said Dean. Jim, still holding the camera, came down to where Dean was sitting.

"Hey, man, you seem to be in a crazy head space right now. How about if we do an interview?"

Two weeks later, Dean tried again, and this time he succeeded in making the world's first ever freeBase climb. And Jim filmed it. The footage ended up in the Sender Films Reel Rock Tour. At the end of the segment Dean says, "The thing I'm getting out of pushing my limits is that I turn impossible to possible. . . . The possibilities of what we're capable of doing if we believe in it is the most compelling thing I can think of." The botched attempt? The rescue? The rock fight? None of that made it into the film.

"El Cap is only a matter of time, but that time is looking shorter all the time," wrote Karl Bralich on SuperTopo in 2008. "I remember when the idea of even a free El Cap route was almost inconceivable but somebody soloing it? We have to be very careful about what we believe to be impossible."

In the four years since Moonlight Buttress and Deep Blue Sea, Alex and Dean had similar orbits, at the center of which was El Capitan. Everyone loves a good rivalry, and the Internet peanut gallery, which seemed to have chosen SuperTopo as its rostrum, loved to speculate about who would claim the holy grail of rock climbing. It was no longer a question of if but when—and whether it would be Honnold or Potter who would claim climbing's greatest prize.

"I obviously think about it, as does everybody else," Dean told *Outside* magazine. "And if I start obsessing on something, I'm kind of helpless but to go for it." But Dean was facing a real dilemma, because the most obvious route for a possible free solo began with a slab called the Freeblast. And it wasn't steep enough to be feasible for a freeBASE ascent, which was how he envisioned himself pulling off the feat. "Right now it's this puzzle that I can't quite figure out, so I don't have a definite plan."

But then Dean found a way to access the top six pitches of Freerider via a "magical passage" at the top of the west face. He got to it by downclimbing the top of a route called Lurking Fear and then traversing a massive horizontal break in El Cap's west face called Thanksgiving Ledge. Dean free soloed the U-shaped linkup in 2011, calling it Easy Rider and rating it 5.11d. Afterward, he told *Outside* that it could be "the first step towards a ground up freesolo [of El Cap]."

On the far left side of El Cap, where the base of the cliff turns sharply uphill, there's a route called the West Face, which is not to be confused with the west face, which is the entire half of the cliff that lies to the left of the Nose. The West Face is 1,800 feet high and rated 5.11c. Most people call it a grade V. (Grade is a separate rating system for the length of a route. Grade V and VI are considered big walls.) Around the corner on the cliff's east end there's another flank route, called the East Buttress, which is 1,200 feet high and given a grade IV. Every other route on El Cap is grade VI. No one has ever argued that the East Buttress is an "El Cap route"—it's only nine pitches—but climbers have long debated the status of the West Face. If you climb it, can you legitimately claim membership in the El Cap club? Most of the folks on SuperTopo don't think so—and, yes, they've argued the point ad nauseam. A guy who identifies himself only as bvb wrote: "the intimidation factor on WF is not the same as the frontside routes . . . right around the time that the exposure kicks in, the 11b/c fingercrack pitch, the wall suddenly shelters you and it's not like you're a fly on a windshield anymore."

In May of 2012, Dean climbed the West Face into Easy Rider with his friend Sean Leary. Dean told Sean that he was going to solo it soon and claim the first free solo of El Cap. Word spread through the Yosemite grapevine, but Alex had long known about Dean's scheme.

Two days earlier, Alex had scaled the three biggest walls in Yosemite with Tommy Caldwell—El Capitan, Half Dome, and Mount Watkins, all free, in twenty-one hours. This monster linkup entailed 7,000 vertical feet of difficult rock climbing—seventy-seven pitches up to 5.13a. Dean and Timmy O'Neill had pioneered the linkup back in 2001 but had aid climbed the most difficult sections. It was Dean's idea to train like a fiend and then one-up himself by free climbing the linkup. Back then, there really was no one he had to worry about beating him to it. But things had changed since Alex and Tommy had come on the scene.

Dean had been training for the free linkup with Leary. They were planning to BASE jump off the top of each of the formations to save time hiking down. Tommy and Alex, out of respect for the fact that the "Triple Crown," as they called it, was Dean's baby, had held off on trying it for a couple of seasons to give Dean the room he needed to get it done. But when the spring of 2012 rolled around and Dean still wasn't ready for it, they decided they had waited long enough.

Alex didn't want to scoop Dean yet again on the West Face, but he also didn't want to spend the rest of his life explaining to people why the West Face doesn't count as a real El Cap route. It's hard to explain an asterisk to a non-climber. Alex later told me that Dean climbing the West Face and claiming it as the first free solo of El Cap "would be the douchiest thing in the world. I couldn't tolerate that." After one rest day and one day of rehearsal on the route, Alex free soloed the West Face. He then told a couple of people and word got out. This was important so Dean would know it was a fait accompli and not try to claim it as a first of anything for himself. Of course a thread started up immediately on SuperTopo. Alex made a point not to claim it as the first free solo of El Cap. He later admitted that he did it "specifically to hose Dean," and that it was probably the most openly competitive thing he had ever done.

The next day Dean hiked up and retrieved his gear from his stash at the base of the West Face. He would never climb the route again. He also gave up on free climbing the Triple Crown. What was the point if it had already been done?

A few days later, Alex joined a crew that was heading out bouldering. When he got to the boulder field, Dean was there. "I was so scared he was going to beat me to death," Alex told me. But Dean was friendly and respectful. He never mentioned the West Face or the Triple Crown, but he certainly understood, probably better than any other person could, what Alex had accomplished over the past week. And he was man enough to tip his hat to his rival, who had just erased any last twinges of doubt about who the king of Yosemite was. It was time for Dean to find a new peg on which to hang his hat.

"IT'S GOOD TO BE THE KING," said Mel Brooks in the film classic *History of the World: Part I*. And indeed, being the king of rock did come with its share of perks. Thanks in part to a *60 Minutes* profile that aired in 2011, Alex was now as close to being a household name in America as any climber had ever been. He starred in a Citibank commercial, which he claimed paid more for two days' work than his sister, Stasia, who works in the nonprofit world, had made in the past five years. He had recently signed a multiyear, six-figure deal with the North Face. His agent was even working on a deal for Alex to free solo the world's tallest building—the 1,671-foot Taipei 101 in Taiwan—live, on TV. He was offered six figures for a climb that would take, at most, a few hours. It never happened.

But Alex was still living in his van, and his annual expenses were running about 15,000 dollars a year. He was now making more than ten times what he had a few years earlier, yet he wasn't spending any more than he had back before his career took off. His financial adviser wanted to talk about index funds, real estate, and IRAs. Alex had something different in mind.

Two years earlier, in the fall of 2010, Alex and I, along with a few others, including Jimmy Chin, had teamed up for an expedition to Chad, where we were the first climbers to explore a 23,000-square-mile area on the southern fringe of the Sahara called the Ennedi Plateau. We made first ascents of about twenty freestanding sandstone towers, but it wasn't the climbing that left an impression on Alex. The trip was Alex's first to the developing world and the first time he had witnessed true poverty. In 2010, the life expectancy for a Chadian was forty-nine years.

To get to the Ennedi we had to drive off road across the Sahara for three long days. About halfway across, in the middle of an endless plain reminiscent of the Bonneville Salt Flats, we rolled up on a pair of men astride two heavily laden camels. They wore scarves wrapped around their heads, and they just sat there, staring at us, their eyes wide. Then one of the men jumped down, fished a battered tin bowl from his sun-bleached saddlebag, and started milking his camel. When the bowl was half full, he jogged up to our vehicle and offered us the frothy brew. Alex tilted back the bowl and took a glug. We gave them bread and water. When they sauntered off, Alex asked our outfitter, "Who were those guys?"

"They're Toubous," he replied. "They're coming back from Libya. Those bags on the back of the camels are filled with salt and other staples they're taking back to their village."

"Wow," said Alex, slumping back into his seat in the Land Rover. The commitment it took for those guys to set off across the desert with no backup struck all of us. It was sort of like Alex on one of his free solos. Only these guys were just trying to live. Unlike us, they didn't have to create artificial challenges to make their lives hard.

There were six of us split between two jeeps, but Alex and I always seemed to end up in the same vehicle, probably because we were the only ones who wanted to talk. I could throw out any subject and be confident that Alex would have an opinion, or at least be willing to play the devil's advocate. Mostly we talked about climbing, but we also shared our thoughts on spirituality, atheism, the cosmos, the singularity, and a personal favorite of mine—mental telepathy. We didn't talk much about people, with one exception—John Bachar. Bachar had died in July the previous year. After free soloing what he personally reckoned to be more than 1.5 million feet of rock, he finally fell at age fifty-two. No one knows exactly what happened. He was soloing a 5.10a at an eighty-foot cliff called the Dike Wall near his home in Mammoth Lakes, California. Some climbers who were around the corner heard a loud *whoomph* that sounded like someone had dropped a backpack off the top of the cliff. When they ran over to see what had happened, they found him.

His death sent shock waves across the climbing world. How could something like this happen to a guy like John Bachar? Alex, as he explained that day in the jeep, refused to believe that Bachar simply slipped. It must have been a heart attack or a seizure, he reasoned. Perhaps a chipmunk scurrying across the top of the cliff had dislodged a stone that whapped him in the head as he was making a long reach. "Something must have happened," said Alex. "John Bachar would not fall."

At the time, I felt as though Alex was projecting. Bachar could have just slipped. Shit happens. But later, when I dug into the circumstances surrounding Bachar's death, I realized that Alex's intuition might have been on to something.

By 2006, Bachar was three years into a partnership with a new rock shoe company called Acopa. He was designing shoes and traveling regularly to Mexico, where the company sourced a special sticky rubber. Since his falling-out in Yosemite, he had found his way back to climbing and he was free soloing regularly again, up to 5.11. But what really gave his life meaning now was his son, Tyrus, who was nine years old. Bachar still played his old sax, and he loved nothing more than sharing his passion for music with Tyrus. That summer, he was on his way home to California from the Outdoor Retailer trade show in Salt Lake City when he fell asleep at the wheel. When he woke up, his car was upside down on the side of the road and he had a broken neck. His girlfriend, who was sitting next to him with her seat belt on, was okay, but his business partner, Steve Karafa, sleeping in the back seat, had been thrown from the vehicle. Karafa died at the scene.

It would be a year before Bachar was back on the rock, but he eventually started climbing again, and slowly, he eased back into free soloing. But he wasn't the same climber he used to be. The accident aged him. Not just because he broke five vertebrae in his neck but because he never forgave himself for causing the death of a close friend. His friends worried about him. Someone saw him soloing one day at the Owens River Gorge in Bishop. He didn't look solid. Dean Fidelman, who was working with

Bachar on a book about the Stonemasters, confronted his old friend about a month before he fell. "Are you okay?" he asked. "Are you solid?"

Fidelman says the question irritated Bachar, who spat back, "Yeah, I'm fuckin' solid, okay."

Two weeks before he fell, Bachar posted the following on SuperTopo:

> bachar
> Gym climber
> Mammoth Lakes, CA
>
> Anybody have any experience with cervical stenosis?
>   Cervical foraminal stenosis in particular?
>   What symptoms did you have? How did it start? What treatment(s) did you receive?
>   Did treatment work?
>   Just want to hear some climber's perspectives.
>
>   Thanks, jb

Dozens of people responded. A few days later, Bachar posted again.

> Thanks for the responses. Right now I am receiving deep tissue massage and accupuncture treatments which seem to be helping a little but I've only been doing them once a week for about 6 weeks now.
>   I still have weakness in my left arm and shoulder. It's almost like someone has a dimmer

switch and turns it down when I try to crank hard. I'm going to see what my surgeon has to say soon. I am going to continue therapy and see if that resolves the problems.

In the meantime I thought I'd see what, if any, experiences other climbers have had in order to start thinking about what I can do about this.

Thanks again people for speaking to this— it helps.

In the fall of 2012, Alex was climbing in Eldorado Canyon, a climbing area just outside Boulder, Colorado, with a friend named Maury Birdwell. They were driving back to town in the evening when Alex casually mentioned that he was thinking about starting a nonprofit. He said he wanted to use his fame and some of his disposable income to try to make the world a better place. He told Birdwell about the poverty he had seen in Chad and how it had changed his view of the world.

Birdwell is an Oklahoma native who cut his teeth as a climber in the Wichita Mountains. He'd established himself as a lawyer based in Boulder specializing in business, entrepreneurship, and nonprofit development. Birdwell had exactly the expertise Alex was looking for.

A few weeks later, Alex and I left for a sailing and climbing expedition to the Musandam Peninsula in Oman, where a magical fjord land on the southern shore of the Strait of Hormuz dazzled us. For three weeks, we explored the area's vast climbing potential— we found hundreds of miles of untouched cliffs lining the shore. We also learned about the Kumzari people, who live in remote fishing villages that can be accessed only by boat. The Kumzaris are a network of families with their own pidgin dialect, a legacy of the cultural collision that has been going on there since ancient times. Linguists don't know how their language developed, but it mingles Farsi, Arabic, Hindi, Portuguese, French, Italian, Spanish, even English. One theory is that the Kumzaris were originally nomads from the mainland who were pushed out onto the tip of the peninsula by Arab, Yemeni, and Portuguese invaders. Another, more intriguing theory (which I made up) is that their ancestors include shipwrecked sailors who washed ashore, perhaps as long ago as the Middle Ages.

Alex mostly did his own thing. I'd often run him into shore in the dinghy in the morning, and I'd watch as he'd wander off to explore a village and then, later, the unexplored cliffs behind them. No one except Alex knows where he went, whom he met, or how many first ascents he did. But one day he came back to the boat in the evening all excited about a mysterious fortress he had found on a high and lonely ridge that he had discovered after a long free solo.

"I can't imagine how they could have built it or what it was for," he mused, with a sparkle in his eye that I had only ever previously seen after he had done a difficult climb.

WHEN HE GOT HOME from the Middle East, Alex immediately called Birdwell. In the months since that climbing day in Eldorado Canyon, he had analyzed his options and realized that he couldn't find a more perfect partner for the Honnold Foundation. "Would you be willing to help me get this off the ground?" he asked.

"I was hoping you would ask that question," replied Birdwell.

A few days later they filed articles of incorporation and applied for 501(c)(3) nonprofit status. They built a website and a Facebook page and posted their mission statement. It reads: "The

Honnold Foundation reduces environmental impact and addresses inequality by supporting solar energy initiatives world-wide."

What they didn't publicize was the fact that Alex personally seeded the foundation with 50,000 dollars (about a third of his income that year)—the money his financial adviser had recommended he invest in a mutual fund. "Alex is not the most emotionally expressive person," says Birdwell. "But he still feels the connection just as strongly as everyone else. He's the kind of person who expresses himself through his actions."

Not long after they launched the foundation, Alex met a guy named Ted Hesser at one of his talks. At the time, Hesser, who is also a climber, was working for a clean energy market research firm in New York City called Bloomberg New Energy Finance. His job was to write research reports that focused on all the changes occurring in the industry. President Obama had made clean energy a key initiative of his administration and, as a result, the industry was at an inflection point. Technologies were changing faster than policies could be drafted to deal with them. A massive amount of investment was pouring into the clean energy space from both government and private sources. Hesser's job was to figure out who the winners and losers would be.

He started sending Alex his reports. These were twenty-to-thirty-page research papers so dense that Hesser says most of his clients didn't even read them, let alone understand them. But Alex read them. Carefully. And then he hit Hesser with astute questions that, without fail, cut to the heart of what mattered. It didn't take long for Alex to realize that the place where the Honnold Foundation could have its biggest impact was in rural Africa, where many people still didn't have access to electricity. More specifically, Alex was interested in pay-as-you-go solar systems. Hesser, who had been working in the industry for ten years, had already concluded that this very specific slice of the clean energy market was exactly the place where there was the most potential for creating transformative change. He hadn't held Alex's hand; he just sent him the reports, and Alex had figured it out all on his own. "Intellectually, logically, he pieced it together really quickly," says Hesser. "It was really impressive."

The Honnold Foundation's first project took place in the Kayenta region of the Navajo lands in Arizona, where Alex, Maury, and Cedar Wright worked with a partner called Elephant Energy to install solar panels on homes that had been waiting for years to be connected to the electrical grid. More projects followed, including an expedition to Angola that combined a solar project with the chance to climb first ascents in a largely unexplored mountain range.

But Alex wasn't using his star power to pump up the volume on the Honnold Foundation. He was giving away a substantial portion of his personal wealth, and doing so in a meticulously premeditated way, but without any fanfare or hoopla. Birdwell says that the reason Alex has been low-key about his foundation is that he doesn't want to brag about what he's done so far, because the scale, at least to date, has been too small. "He's trying to hit a really long ball," is how Hesser puts it.

"Alex has a really interesting relationship with money," says Hesser. "Giving away 30 to 40 percent of his income [each year] doesn't mean the same thing to him as it might to someone else. Alex doesn't worry about money the way most people do. It's part of his character, and it's part of what makes him so unique and special."

Hesser left me with a story about the time Alex gave a talk in San Francisco to a bunch of well-to-do professionals. Afterward, Alex was musing about how differently he views risk than the people in the audience. "Sure, they could lose all the money in their hedge fund one day," said Alex, "but they still go home and sleep in a nice bed at night. It's not like they die."

CHAPTER EIGHT

Secret Dawn Walls

The van careered around a bend on Highway 120, its tires squealing. Alex wasn't giving the road his full attention. He rarely did. Alex hates driving. "It's a waste of life," he once told me. Driving had always been a time to get things done, to catch up on his correspondence. Sometimes, on roads straighter than this one, he'd read long-form *New Yorker* articles. But on this dark night on January 14, 2015, Alex was pissed off. He was talking to Becca Caldwell on the phone, and she was sharing some unwelcome news. The plan—for Alex to carry Fitz, Tommy and Becca's twenty-month-old son, to the top of El Cap to meet his father when he summited the Dawn Wall—was off.

Tommy and his partner Kevin Jorgeson had been on the wall for the past eighteen days. Now, only a handful of pitches, all well within their ability, stood between the two climbers and the summit. Tommy had first dreamed up this climb back in 2007. At the time, no one had ever considered that it might be possible to free climb the tallest, most sheer section of El Capitan. It was an idea so far beyond the pale that Tommy, at least initially, was loath to admit he was even thinking about it. When he rappelled the wall for the first time, to feel it out, he discovered long sections that appeared to be impossible. But instead of turning him off, the impossibility of the project drew him in, deep. The Dawn Wall soon became his obsession. Kevin came on as a partner in the fall of 2009. Over the next few years, the two men spent months of their lives on the side of El Capitan, slowly piecing together a route. Now, seven long years since Tommy had first envisioned it, that climb was finally within reach.

Becca wasn't the one shooting Alex down. Like Tommy, she thought the plan was reasonably safe, even if Alex was planning to bring Fitz up the East Ledges, the climber's shortcut to the summit of El Cap that includes a five-hundred-foot cliff. Alex had planned to ascend fixed ropes with Fitz securely strapped to his back in a child carrier. *What could possibly go wrong?* The problem was that Patagonia, Tommy's main sponsor, had caught wind of the plan, and the corporate honchos weren't into it. What irritated Alex was the fact that people were being irrational and illogical, worrying about what-ifs that were statistically negligible. Sitting in the passenger seat was Joe Hooper, a journalist from *Men's Journal* magazine. Hooper was planning to accompany Alex to the summit. When Alex hung up the call, he turned to Hooper and said, "That's like typical PR shit, and it's so annoying. That's why she [the woman in Patagonia's marketing department] works in an office. The rest of us don't work in an office because we actually do things." He paused for a few moments, then added, "I fucking hate PR people."

WHEN ALEX AND HOOPER ARRIVED on the summit of El Capitan the next morning, Kevin and Tommy were a few hundred feet from topping out. About forty people had gathered to celebrate the momentous occasion. The crowd included journalists like John Branch from *The New York Times* and a feisty camerawoman from

ABC News wearing shiny fashionista combat boots. Becca was there, as were Kevin's girlfriend and his father. There were friends and sponsors and even some hangers-on—local dirtbags who didn't want to miss such a historic occasion. The eclectic ensemble reminded Hooper of groupies gathering backstage after a concert. Marijuana smoke wafted through the air.

The occasional patch of ice hid in the shadows, but the air was mild, the sky clear. Climbers were calling it "Juneuary." A couple of cameramen, dangling on ropes at the lip of the cliff, announced that Tommy had just reached the final anchor. But it was located just below the lip in a spot that no one could see. As everyone waited for Tommy and Kevin to scramble up into view, Alex scampered down the steep slab and disappeared over the edge. When Tommy topped out, Alex was right there. They hugged, and Alex hung out while Tommy belayed up Kevin. After congratulating his friends on the climb of their lives, Alex got out of the way. As the cameras whirred, the grizzled, bearded climbers stumbled up the final slab on wobbly legs that hadn't felt terra firma in nearly three weeks. In view of the crowd, Tommy and Kevin stopped and gave each other a hug.

Tommy, who had come down with a cold and lost his voice, appeared bewildered. He embraced his wife awkwardly. It was clear he wasn't comfortable sharing this intimate moment with all these people. He had climbed El Capitan about sixty times, but until now, there had never been more than a friend or two to greet him on top. Kevin, on the other hand, embraced the role of the conquering hero. He shared a warm, passionate embrace with his sexy girlfriend as the paparazzi's flashbulbs popped all around him. Someone handed them bottles of champagne. Tommy popped the cork on his and started drinking it. Kevin shook his up and sprayed it all around him like he had just won the World Series. The crowd cheered.

When the hubbub had settled slightly, Hooper approached Tommy to offer his congratulations. He was shaking his hand when a guy from Patagonia, who was acting as the master of ceremonies, and doing so somewhat heavy-handedly, shooed him away, telling him that Tommy was "off-limits."

A little while later, the Patagonia guy called out, "If we get a call, we've all got to go silent. It might be the president." A murmur rippled through the crowd.

"That would be sick if President Obama called," said someone. Obama did eventually call to offer his congratulations, but not until later.

Alex stood in the background quietly observing. Up until this moment, he had been the most famous climber in the world. But not anymore. That title now belonged to Tommy Caldwell. News of the intrepid climbers battling their way up the world's most difficult rock climb had gone viral shortly after they set off in late December. With access to a strong LTE signal, Tommy and Kevin had been using their smartphones to post daily updates to their Instagram and Facebook accounts from the portaledge at night. It was like reality TV, but you could comment and interact with the stars of the show. If you were lucky, they might even respond.

It wasn't always like this. Millennials don't know anything different, but those of us who climbed before the invention of the Internet can remember a day when expedition climbers unplugged from the outside world when they went off on expeditions. When I didn't arrive on that flight from Baffin Island back in 1996, my parents had no way of knowing if I was dead or just running late. At the time of the Quokka experiment on Great Trango, we had no idea how profoundly the rise of the Internet and social media would change the culture of climbing. By 2015, it wasn't just possible for professional climbers to keep their fans apprised of their exploits in real time; it was expected. Endorsement contracts often included stipulations about social media: how often to post, which hashtags to use, and even creative guidelines. For better or worse, social media was now the primary way climbers interacted with one another and it was how we broadcasted our accomplishments. And it was a rare soul who avoided getting sucked into the vortex.

THE MAJORITY OF THEIR NINETEEN days on the wall were spent at what they called their base camp, a portaledge situated about 1,200 feet above the ground. Fixed ropes connected to the ground and every few days some of their friends would climb the ropes, hauling up bags of supplies. On one of those supply missions, Alex came up with a load. When he got to the ledge, he looked at Tommy and said, "Dude, I was expecting this climb to look like this totally badass futuristic thing. What's up with that overhanging choss?" It was a typical Alexism, Tommy would later say, to look at something that most people would view as totally outrageous and "make it seem lame."

The crux of the climb was a section just above the camp called the Dike Traverse. About two hundred feet long, it followed a horizontal band of calcite on a smooth swath that was essentially a vertical friction climb. Tommy had been trying to find a path across the dike for years, and it's a testament to his doggedness that he never gave up, even after it had spit him off hundreds of times. And then, a week after leaving the ground, he finally unlocked an enigmatic sequence of moves that allowed him to squeak through. Afterward, he wasn't sure exactly how he had done it. There is no stronger motivator than competition, and seeing his friend succeed gave Kevin his own burst of inspiration, and he, too, succeeded on his next attempt. The pitch, which was probably the hardest ever done on a big wall, is rated 5.14d. But so is the next, pitch 15. Tommy redpointed it the next day, but

Kevin came up short. Then he fell again and again and again. With each subsequent attempt to climb the minuscule, razor-sharp holds, the skin on his fingertips grew thinner until the pad on his middle finger split. "The moves are hard but the issue is, you have to want to grab," said Kevin in an interview he gave journalist Andrew Bisharat, from the portaledge one night. "And you have to not give a fuck about how much it hurts. Which is kinda hard to do."

He superglued the cut closed, but he now had no choice but to tape the tip of his finger, which badly limited his ability to grip the rock. If the split kept getting bigger, it would start oozing blood right through the tape, which would act like lubricant and make it impossible to continue.

All this drama was being shared on Instagram and caught on film by a camera team that was living alongside Tommy and Kevin, documenting the climb for a feature-length film being produced by Sender Films. People began to wonder: What if Kevin is stymied by pitch 15? Will Tommy leave him behind? Would Kevin want to support Tommy and belay him to the top, if he wasn't able to share in the success? Would the climb still count if only one of them succeeded? While the Internet peanut gallery argued about arbitrary, hair-splitting semantics (including whether Tommy could legitimately claim a free ascent since he had seconded, not led, some of the easier lower pitches), Kevin continued to belay Tommy as he redpointed more pitches each day. Then at night, Tommy would belay Kevin as he attempted, day after day, to master pitch 15.

Just as it was looking all but certain that Kevin was out, he made one last-ditch effort to keep his bid for the Dawn Wall alive. With the tape slipping off his superglued fingertip, Kevin roared as he lunged for the final jug, the only good hold on the pitch. And this time, he latched it.

———————

THIS WASN'T THE FIRST TIME the world had waited on the edge of its seat to see if climbers would succeed on the Dawn Wall. A similar scene had played out forty-five years earlier. Back then they called it the Wall of Early Morning Light, and its first ascent in 1970 (accomplished with the conventional aid-climbing techniques of the time), by Warren Harding and Dean Caldwell (no relation to Tommy), marked the culmination of the greatest rivalry in the history of the sport.

The 1950s, a period known as Yosemite's golden age, saw the first ascents of the valley's grandest formations. Rock climbs of this magnitude, what came to be called big walls, were so tall that a climber would have to sleep on the side of the cliff on the way up. And since no one had ever attempted to climb cliffs of this magnitude, those who would pit themselves against these monoliths had to invent the sport along the way. Of the handful of climbers who were most active during this period, there were two men—Royal Robbins and Warren Harding—who, by the nature of their diametrically opposed personalities, would come to represent the yin and yang of the golden age.

Robbins was a serious man, a Berkeley intellectual who carried around leather-bound notebooks to record ideas stirred by the heady books he always seemed to be reading. He kept his hair in a military-style crew cut, was usually clean-shaven, and wore tortoiseshell eyeglasses. He was tall and powerful, with an athletic build and a commanding, almost imperious presence. A gifted free climber, he established the country's first 5.9-rated route in 1952—Open Book—at a crag called Tahquitz in Southern California, when he was only seventeen.

Robbins was a purist. For him it was not about getting to the top of the mountain; it was about the style in which he got there.

He espoused a minimalist ethic: a climber should leave as small a footprint as possible. It was a standard to which he held not only himself and his partners but all climbers. At the time he came of age, cracks were being permanently scarred through the use of pitons, which chewed away holes in the rock as they were repeatedly hammered in and out. Climbing needed rules if the cliffs were to be preserved for future generations, and as the sport's leading light, Robbins felt it was his obligation to make sure people knew what those rules were.

Harding was, in every respect, the polar opposite, a wild man who oozed charisma and had a ribald sense of humor. He drove fast cars, boozed with abandon, and was often in the company of beautiful women. His eyes seemed to be eternally twinkling with the knowledge of some diabolical plan in the offing. Short and wiry, with a high-pitched voice, he wore his hair long and often slicked with Brylcreem. He rarely shaved. His friends called him Batso, a nickname he garnered because he seemed to spend most of his time hanging upside down.

For Harding, climbing was anarchy. Anyone who didn't like the way he did things could go to hell. He called Robbins and his followers the "Valley Christians." And to counterbalance their virtuousity, he founded the Lower Sierra Eating, Drinking, and Farcing Society (LSED&FS), which was dedicated to gluttony and sloth. Their motto was "Semper Farcisimus." I once attended one of their parties—a celebration of Batso's seventieth birthday—which took place at a remote, obscure climbing area on the east side of the Sierra. I remember Warren, with stains of red wine all down his white T-shirt, staggering toward his tent shortly after dark. Later that night, after his cronies warned us several times to quiet down so they could sleep, they attacked us. One of my friends got beaten up by an old guy with a shovel.

There was one thing Robbins and Harding held in common,

and that was a deeply rooted competitiveness, especially with each other. In the battle for the first ascent of the valley's walls, Royal Robbins initially took the upper hand when he scaled Half Dome over seven days in 1954. Harding had been preparing for the same climb when he heard that Robbins and his team had already pulled it off. They met on top, where Harding offered congratulations. But inside he was seething. "In a fit of egotistical pique, we grumbled around the Valley for a couple of days, trying to figure out what to do," Harding later recounted. "Any climb less than Half Dome was beneath us; only a great climb would do."

So he decided it was time to attempt the valley's crown jewel, El Capitan, the highest, sheerest cliff in all of North America save Baffin Island (which at the time was undiscovered by rock climbers). His assault on the leviathan wall began in July 1957. Harding and his two partners—Mark Powell and William "Dolt" Feuerer—soon found themselves stymied by soaring hand and fist cracks that were too wide for the pitons they carried. Back on the ground, they explained the problem to their friend Frank Tarver, who solved it by cutting the legs off some old wood stoves and sawing them into makeshift pitons that fit the wide cracks. Today, this section of the wall is known as the Stove Legs.

It took Harding and a rotating team of climbers two seasons to complete their masterpiece up the center of El Capitan—a route that came to be called the Nose since it follows the cliff's central buttress. In contrast to the alpine style that Robbins and his team employed on Half Dome, Harding and his crew fixed hundreds of feet of rope, similar to the way Mount Everest was climbed in 1953. With this nylon umbilical cord, the climbers were able to commute up and down the wall and haul food and equipment to their various camps, including vast quantities of cheap red wine and, once, a whole Thanksgiving turkey, baked lovingly by Harding's mom.

Harding, Wayne Merry, and George Whitmore (Powell and Feuerer had dropped out) summited on November 12, 1958, having spent a total of forty-five days working the route. "As I hammered in the last bolt and staggered over the rim, it was not at all clear to me who was conqueror and who was conquered," wrote Harding of the experience in his book *Downward Bound*. "I do recall that El Cap seemed to be in much better condition than I was."

Robbins, for one, was unimpressed. The expedition style, the bolting, the fanfare that followed—it was almost too much to bear. His answer was to climb Harding's route in alpine style two years later. He managed El Capitan's second ascent, without the use of fixed ropes, in seven days. And thus began a game of one-upmanship that would consume Robbins and Harding for the next decade.

By 1970, there was still one wall that no one had attempted to the right of the Nose on El Capitan's southeast face, the tallest and most forbidding piece of rock in all of Yosemite, if not the world. It rose from a cavernous recess at the base of the cliff called the Alcove and soared skyward in a single uninterrupted 3,000-foot swath of continuously overhanging stone. Robbins had studied it with binoculars. While there were some cracks, too much of it was blank, at least to his mind. Whoever climbed it, if it was ever climbed, would have to drill ladders of bolts to connect the disparate crack systems. In Robbins' estimation, an ascent of the Wall of Early Morning Light, as it had come to be called, would require too many bolts. So he declared it off-limits.

Perhaps if Robbins had just kept his mouth shut, Harding would have turned his attention elsewhere, but when his nemesis declared the Wall of Early Morning Light out of bounds, the temptation proved irresistible.

Harding, then forty-seven years old, set off in October 1970, with his friend Dean Caldwell, who was twenty years his junior. This time, he would not leave an umbilical cord to the ground but would instead climb the wall in a single push. As Robbins had predicted, Harding was forced to place many bolts, especially in the first few hundred feet. The *tink-tink-tink* of his drill biting into the rock was clearly audible at the base of the mountain, where Robbins observed, fuming at the audacity of his rival.

At the beginning of their third week on the wall, a storm rolled into the valley. Harding and Caldwell were pinned in their "Bat tents," special hammocks with built-in rainflys designed by Harding's company, B.A.T. The initials—a clever play on his nickname—stood for Basically Absurd Technology. A crowd gathered in the meadow as the park service prepared to rescue the climbers, who they assumed were stranded. In fact, Harding and Caldwell were having a grand time camped on a ledge they named Wino Tower, where they sipped judiciously on a bottle of Christian Brothers brandy and rationed out sardines, bits of cheese, and canned fruit cocktail. Knowing that something was afoot below, Harding wrote a note, sealed it an empty tin can, and dropped it down the wall. A passerby picked it up and brought it to the rangers who were massing in the meadow. "A rescue is unwanted, unwarranted, and will not be accepted! We must be the most miserable, wet, cold stinking wretches imaginable. But we're alive, really alive, like people seldom are."

But no one had ever spent this much time living on the side of El Capitan in one continuous push, and the rangers were convinced that they knew better. The next day, ropes were lowered from the rim. After much heated yelling back and forth, Harding and Caldwell made it clear that they were fine and adamantly refused the offer of rescue. Harding would later say that if it had come down to it, they were ready to fight off their rescuers with piton hammers. When the media heard the story of the tin can and the climbers' refusal to be rescued, the story became front-page news, where it remained for the duration of the climb.

When Harding and Caldwell summited at noon on November 19, 1970, twenty-seven days after leaving the ground, they stumbled into a media frenzy not seen since Edmund Hillary returned from the first ascent of Everest. After living in a Bat tent on the side of a cliff for nearly a month, Harding was so overwhelmed by the crowd waiting on the summit, which included journalists, friends, and his girlfriend, that he scuttled off behind a rock, where he hid crying for several minutes. But when he emerged, still wiping the tears from his eyes, he was ready to take on the role of America's first climbing superstar.

From Yosemite he went straight to New York City and then to LA, where he and Caldwell appeared on talk shows and were interviewed by *Life* magazine for a feature article about their climb, and then later by Howard Cosell for ABC's *Wide World of Sports*. A lecture circuit followed, each show involving wild parties that usually lasted until the sun came up. Batso, of course, was always the last man standing. He was generous and as loose with his money as he was with women, and when the frenzy eventually died down, Harding discovered to his dismay that he had spent every cent he had made, and then some. A few weeks later, he was back working construction on a California road crew, just like he had been before the climb.

Robbins was deeply offended by the Wall of Early Morning Light, almost as if the 330 bolts had been drilled into his own hide. The order of things had been upset, and in a fit of self-righteousness, he declared that he would make the second ascent, and in the process he would erase the route by chopping off all the bolts. But at their first bivouac four pitches up, as he and his partner Don Lauria rested in their hammocks, Robbins began to have second thoughts. Neither felt sure they were doing the right thing, especially in light of the fact that the climbing was some of the most inspired they had ever done. In the morning, Robbins turned to Lauria and said that he had decided to quit chopping the route. He would later write, "[It's] good to have a man around who doesn't give a damn what the establishment thinks. . . . Harding stands out as a magnificent maverick."

His rival may have been playing the game by different rules, but he was playing the game and playing it well. Robbins realized that underneath all their differences, he and Harding had a lot more in common than either of them had ever wanted to admit. And with that realization, climbing's greatest rivalry—and Yosemite's golden age—came to a graceful end.

JOHN BRANCH of the *New York Times* got the first interview with Tommy and Kevin when they topped out. Jorgeson gave him the best quote when he said, "I think everyone has their own secret Dawn Wall to complete one day, and maybe they can put this project in their own context." He was echoing the same sentiment expressed by Maurice Herzog in the mountaineering classic *Annapurna:* "There are other Annapurnas in the lives of men." Honnold stood nearby.

The best climbers, the ones who truly stand out from the rest, the characters who have gone down in history, they've all had at least one superlative climb that defined them, a route that redrew the boundaries of human potential, setting a benchmark for the next generation. Even if Tommy and Kevin never climbed another significant route, they could coast on this one for the rest of their lives. Edmund Hillary and Tenzing Norgay had the first ascent of Everest. Reinhold Messner was the first to climb to the top of the world without supplemental oxygen. Harding claimed both the Nose and the Wall of Early Morning Light. Lynn Hill free climbed the Nose in one day. But Alex didn't yet have the one singular accomplishment that defined him, at least not to his own mind. Free soloing Robbins' route on the Northwest Face of Half Dome couldn't be the end, because there was one more obvious step to take. And Alex knew there was only one person who had any business even contemplating that next step.

What no one knew, not even his closest friends, was that Alex was already well into the process of free soloing El Capitan. Years ago, around the same time that Tommy quietly rappelled off the summit to see if there were enough holds to free climb the Dawn Wall, Alex was making a list of routes he might solo as stepping-stones on his way to the Captain. Each of the routes, in their own way, simulated sections he would face on Freerider, the route up El Cap he felt offered the best chance of success. El Sendero Luminoso, a 5.12+ in Mexico, which he climbed in January 2014, featured steep, technical face climbing like he'd encounter on Freerider's Boulder Problem. The University Wall, a 5.12– in Squamish, British Columbia, which he free soloed in August of the same year, had lots of burly wide cracks, like the one he'd face on the Monster Offwidth.

Alex had worked on the University Wall for several days prepping it for the solo, but he couldn't get it dialed to the point where he felt good about it. He would later tell me that he got it to about 95 percent. He had always felt that on a solo he should feel at least 99 percent certain of the outcome, and hopefully with a few .9s tacked on. So he set it aside and moved on to other things. Two and a half weeks later, still in Squamish, Alex was having one of those climbing days when everything feels easy. Small holds felt big. His feet felt as though they were glued to the rock. He had power to waste. So he walked up to University Wall and he started climbing. He had rehearsed an intricate sequence at the crux, which required pinching the bottom of a flake as he carefully ticktacked his feet along a series of barely perceptible nubs in the rock. These were the moves he was never able to feel quite right about. But when he got to the undercling, he locked off with his right hand and brought his feet up high. As he did, he realized he was feeling so strong that he didn't have to follow the tricky moves he had practiced. Instead, he simply reached high to a good hold above. He would later describe it to me as a moment of "transcendence."

From Squamish, Alex headed to the Needles, a climbing area in the foothills of the Sierras a few hours south of Yosemite. It was here that Alex had set his sights on another route on his list called the Romantic Warrior, a 5.12b. He had climbed it eight years earlier and had never forgotten a section called the Book of Deception, a tricky stemming corner at the top of the nine-hundred-foot route. It seemed like a good primer for Freerider's Teflon Corner.

A flamboyant and controversial climber from Southern California named Michael Reardon had already claimed a free solo of Romantic Warrior in 2005. Reardon was a former glam rocker turned actor turned movie director who was known for climbing naked and for leaving personal calling cards—panties and tubes of Vagisil—inside summit registers. What made Reardon's climb downright mind-boggling was that he claimed to have done it on-sight. Climbing records and the sport's accepted history have always relied on an honor system. When climbers claim to have done routes, they are taken at their word. But there have been a few notorious characters who famously dishonored the tradition. First there was Frederick Cook, who claimed the first ascent of Denali in 1906. The photo he supplied of his teammate planting a flag on the summit turned out to have been taken on an insignificant subpeak located many miles from the mountain. And there was Cesare Maestri, the Italian who still claims to have made the first ascent of Patagonia's Cerro Torre in 1959, a climb so far ahead of its time that it wasn't repeated until 2012. According to Maestri's account, his partner Toni Egger died on the descent when he was swept off the mountain by icefall, taking the camera and photographic proof of the ascent with him. Maestri claimed that anyone who repeated the route would find his bolts high on the wall, but when the north face of Cerro Torre was finally scaled by an elite team of modern climbers, they found no bolts and the route didn't match Maestri's description.

When Reardon claimed his free solo of Romantic Warrior—by far the boldest ropeless climb to date—doubts began to surface almost immediately. The gist of the controversy is captured in a post on SuperTopo that was written by someone with the handle Levy. He starts out by asking if anyone has actually seen Reardon solo anything. He wonders why, if Reardon is soloing so many hard routes, no one ever seems to witness the climbs. "He's a nice guy & friendly," writes Levy, "but in climbing perhaps more than any other 'sport,' personal credibility is everything. We have no judges or committees to say whether or not an ascent is legit or not so one must be taken at their word for their climbing feats. If somebody I know told me 'Yeah I saw him solo it' that would be enough for me. So far however, I have heard no credible reports of seeing the ascents M.R. claims."

One of Reardon's most noteworthy doubters was Peter Croft, who knew him personally. Croft told me that he liked Reardon, but that he had heard too many stories from "high-profile climbers" about Reardon lying about things he had done. "It's not like I'm 99 percent sure he didn't do it," says Croft. "I know that what Michael said did not occur." Croft mentioned a number of different stories, including other debunked solos claimed by Reardon in Britain and in Joshua Tree, but he said that if I was interested in learning the truth about Michael Reardon, I should check with Peter Mortimer.

In the summer of 2005, shortly after Reardon returned from a trip to the Needles, Mortimer visited him at his home in Southern California. Reardon told Mortimer, who was a close friend, that he had gone to the Needles by himself to check out some stuff and that it had been "a mellow trip." He said nothing about having done what at the time would have been the greatest free solo in the history of the sport.

A few months later, Mortimer heard that Reardon was claiming he had on-sight soloed the route. At first he was excited for his friend, but then he realized that Reardon was saying it had happened on the trip that he had told Mortimer was mellow and uneventful. So Mortimer confronted him. "Why didn't you tell me about Romantic Warrior?"

"It was so special, I needed to keep it to myself," replied Reardon. This, according to Mortimer, was completely out of character for a guy who loved the spotlight and was unabashed about wanting his expressions as an artist of free-solo rock climbing to be appreciated by others. When Mortimer expressed incredulity, Reardon shot back that he had photographic proof of the ascent. "That's bizarre," replied Mortimer, "because you told me you were there by yourself." The pictures do exist and are easily searchable on Google. They're reminiscent of the iconic image of John Bachar on New Dimensions. Reardon, wearing a red shirt and blue shorts, his mane of blond hair flowing in the breeze, clings to a crack in a right-leaning open book, hundreds of feet above the ground. Like Bachar, he's looking directly into the camera lens. But unlike Bachar, he's giving us the finger.

Mortimer contacted the photographer, Mark Niles, who admitted the pictures were from a re-creation. They had rappelled in from above and Reardon had posed, much like Honnold would later do for Mortimer on the Moonlight Buttress. "At that point I stopped believing him," says Mortimer. Reardon would later change his tune about the photos, telling *Rock and Ice* magazine that they were indeed taken during a re-creation a few weeks after the climb.

In 2007, Mortimer's partner at Sender Films, Nick Rosen, was in the midst of writing an article about the controversy when Reardon was swept into the ocean by a rogue wave at the base of a sea cliff in Ireland. The water temperature was in the low fifties, and the current quickly pulled him away from shore. By the time the Irish Coast Guard arrived on the scene, Reardon, who was forty-two years old, was gone. His body was never recovered. Rosen and Mortimer decided to drop it.

But there are still many credible people who believe that Reardon did everything he said he did. Duane Raleigh, editor of *Rock and Ice,* investigated Reardon's claims. He checked the time stamps on his photos, cross-referenced weather forecasts, and interviewed eyewitnesses. "It all checks out," says Raleigh. But that was before I shared Mortimer's account with him. Raleigh wants to know why Mortimer's information hadn't come out back when *Rock and Ice* was reporting on the controversy. "There's always been a little bit of doubt there," he says. "And now, maybe a little bit more."

One person who believed Reardon unequivocally was John Bachar. They were friends, and the two used to solo together regularly. Bachar told Raleigh that Reardon would climb circles around him. When the rumors began circulating that the Romantic Warrior climb was a hoax, Bachar, with a tip of his hat to the 10,000-dollar bounty he offered up back in the early eighties, offered free Acopa rock shoes for life to anyone who could keep up with Reardon for a day. There were no takers.

Alex, for his part, didn't care one way or another. As far as he was concerned, if Reardon said he did it, he did it. We're left with the question of whether any of this matters. Peter Croft, for one, thinks it does. "If history matters at all, we should give credit where credit is due," says Croft. "And history does matter, so it [the truth about Reardon] should come out at some point."

In September Alex drove into the Needles and spent the night in his van in a dirt pullout. The next day he ran laps on the route's crux pitches by rappelling in from above and self-belaying with a small aluminum pulley called a Micro Traxion. The device was designed for hauling bags through caves or up cliffs. It incorporates a ratchet that holds the load in place while you reset between pulls. In climber parlance this is known as "progress capture." Climbers figured out that Micro Traxions also work well for self-belaying on a fixed strand of rope. We call it "mini-tracking," in reference to the Micro's predecessor, the Mini Traxion, which was bigger and heavier but works in the same way. Alex put a locking carabiner through the small donut hole on the device and clipped it to his harness. As he climbed up the wall, the Micro rolled along the rope at his waist. If he fell, the ratchet, which is lined with tiny angled teeth, would cam against the rope, holding him in place. The beauty of mini-tracking is that it allows a climber to rehearse a route without needing another person to serve as belayer. This way you're not "wasting someone's else life," as Alex once put it to me.

When Alex got back to his van that evening, he realized he was out of propane. Which meant he had no way to cook the only thing he had for dinner—mac and cheese. He debated driving out to get fuel, but it was such a long way to where he could resupply that he might as well bail and head back to Yosemite. Should he just go for the Romantic Warrior route in the morning? It seemed like a bad idea. He had been planning another day or two of rehearsal, because the climbing had felt hard and insecure. He stayed the night, and in the morning, while eating an energy bar, he said to himself, *Fuck it, I'm going for it.*

At the base of the route, he tried to empty his bowels, but nothing happened. This was a bad omen, but he headed up anyway. The first four hundred feet of the route are relatively easy, and Alex made quick time. But as he approached the first crux pitch, he felt his insides begin to grumble. He was in the middle of a steep pitch, and there were no ledges anywhere. And it would be extremely poor style to shit right down the climb itself. Alex looked out left, where a flake of rock offered a horizontal handrail. He grabbed it and traversed sideways until he was twenty feet off the side of the route, hanging from 5.10 handholds on an overhanging wall. He slipped his small pack off one arm at a time and shoved it into the crack; then, hanging by his one hand, he pulled down his pants. He brought his legs up into a crouch and "space dumped" into the void. After taking what might have been the most daring poop in history, he wiped, pulled up his pants, and finished the route in good style. Afterward, he told a couple of friends what he had done, but he didn't report the climb to the magazines or post about it on his social media. And he never went back to pose for photos. Alex was keeping this one for himself.

By 2015, Dean Potter wasn't climbing much any more. Instead, he spent his time making illegal wingsuit jumps from various formations in Yosemite Valley. He had jumped from every major cliff in the park. Many of his launch points were firsts, and he was constantly on the lookout for new ones. Half Dome was a perennial favorite. He would hike up to the slabby west side of the dome via a secret trail with his dog, Whisper. At the base of the wall, he would put the dog, a blue heeler, into a pack and then free solo a

Jeff Chapman ascending a fixed line on the north face of Polar Sun Spire, Baffin Island, Canada.

© Mark Synnott

Crazy Kids of America, circa 1982. Top row, left to right: Paul Getchell, Muffy Arndt, Jeff Chapman, Scott Fitzgerald, the author, Bruce Barry, Ben Barr, unknown. Bottom row, left to right: Jesse McAleer, Amy Synnott, Robert Frost, Tyler Hamilton, Tyler Vadenboncoeur.

© courtesy of the Frost family collection

The mirror image of the shot above, taken by Jeff Chapman. The team spent thirty-six nights living in this portaledge while establishing their route called the Great and Secret Show.

© Mark Synnott collection

Warren Harding on the Nose in 1957, during the first ascent of El Capitan. It was Thanksgiving, and the team hauled up a whole turkey and a bottle of Chablis to celebrate the holiday. It would take forty-five days, split over two seasons, before the route was completed in November 1958.

© *Allen Steck*

A young Royal Robbins at Stoney Point, a bouldering area outside Los Angeles, where many iconic climbers of Yosemite's golden age cut their teeth in the 1950s and '60s.

© *Frank Hoover, courtesy of Dean Fidelman collection*

Lynn Hill. In 1993, she free climbed the Nose of El Capitan, a feat that many had deemed impossible. Afterward, she famously quipped, "It goes, boys."

© Dean Fidelman

John Bachar free soloing New Dimensions in 1982. His ropeless ascent of this 300-foot, 5.11-rated route in 1976 redefined the limits of what was thought possible. At the time, the hardest roped climbing in Yosemite was only one grade harder.

© Phil Bard

Top: The Stone Monkeys were known for their antics both on and off the rock. Here, Alex Huber, who made the first free ascent of Freerider in 1998, executes a difficult boulder jump outside Yosemite's Camp 4. Note the crash pads below in case he missed.

© *Dean Fidelman*

Left: Ivo Ninov (front), Dean Potter, and Charles "Chongo" Tucker (standing) relaxing in "Chongo's office" in Yosemite Valley. Sticks are used to protect the tree's bark from the slackline that is tied around it.

© *Dean Fidelman*

Dean Potter slacklining at Taft Point, with El Capitan visible in the background. It was near here that Potter and his friend Graham Hunt would later die wingsuit BASE jumping. The notch they tried to fly through is visible in the middle right of the photo.

© *Dean Fidelman*

Alex Lowe following the author's lead high on Great Trango Tower in the Karakoram in 1999. The cable in his left hand is a funkness device, used for yanking out recalcitrant pitons.

© *Mark Synnott*

Alex Lowe on the summit ridge of Great Trango Tower. A few minutes after this photo was taken, while leading the next pitch, he slipped and fell about 50 feet down the backside of this ridge.

© *Jared Ogden*

The final bivouac high on Great Trango Tower. The author discovered, shortly after taking this photo, that Lowe was badly injured from his fall and had spent the night sitting on the ledge without getting into his sleeping bag.

© *Mark Synnott*

From left to right: Jared Ogden, the author, and Lowe camped at the base of the headwall after a harrowing descent in a storm.

© *Jared Ogden*

From left to right: Conrad Anker, Jimmy Chin, and Alex Honnold on the approach to Low's Gully on Mount Kinabalu in Borneo.

© *Mark Synnott*

A young Alex Honnold on the flanks of Mount Kinabalu. This was Honnold's first international climbing expedition.

© *Mark Synnott*

Jimmy Chin on the wall in Borneo. Low's Gully, which drops 10,000 vertical feet over six miles, is visible below him.

© *Mark Synnott*

Sandstone towers on the Ennedi Plateau in Chad. The author led the first climbing expedition to this area in 2010. The team, which included Alex Honnold and James Pearson, climbed the first ascents of twenty towers, leaving thousands more for future generations of climbers.

© *Mark Synnott*

While exploring a canyon toward the end of the expedition, the team was accosted by knife-wielding bandits. This image is a screen grab from Renan Ozturk's video of the encounter.

© *Renan Ozturk, Camp 4 Collective*

Alex Honnold, the author, and Hazel Findlay in Devil's Bay on the south coast of Newfoundland, Canada, in 2011. Despite terrible weather they managed to climb the wall in the background, called Blow Me Down.

© Tim Kemple

Findlay and Honnold scope climbing objectives on Oman's Musandam Peninsula in 2012. The team spent three weeks exploring the area, sometimes called the "Norway of the Persian Gulf," aboard a catamaran skippered by the author. That afternoon, Honnold would free solo the wall at the head of the fjord, prompting the local inhabitants to tell the author they thought Honnold was a witch.

© Mark Synnott

Honnold gauging his pump after his free solo of an overhanging 1,800-foot cliff in Taghia, Morocco, called Rivières Pourpres. Honnold trained in Taghia with Tommy Caldwell before making his first attempt to free solo El Capitan in the fall of 2016.

© *Mark Synnott*

One of the many Berber bridges in the Taghia Gorge.

© *Mark Synnott*

Alex Honnold and Tommy Synnott.
© *Hampton Synnott*

The author (left) trick-or-treating in
Yosemite Village with Tommy Caldwell.
© *Hampton Synnott*

Dierdre Wolownick, Alex Honnold's mom, on Sunnyside Bench, about a week before Alex's first attempt to free solo El Capitan. Wolownick was not aware of her son's plan.

© *Mark Synnott*

Left to right: Peter Croft, Honnold, and Sanni McCandless, Alex's girlfriend, in "the box," as Alex sometimes called his Dodge ProMaster van. Alex elevates his ankle, which he damaged in a fall on Freerider earlier in the season.

© *Mark Synnott*

The author, pictured here, watched the climb from El Cap Meadow with a high-powered spotting scope. He described watching his friend that morning as "almost unbearable."

© *Mark Synnott*

Honnold scales the Enduro Corner, 2,500 feet above the valley floor, on the first free solo of El Capitan, June 3, 2017. Tommy Caldwell called the feat "the first moon landing of free soloing."

© *Austin Siadak*

An image taken through the viewfinder of the author's spotting scope during one of Alex's many training sessions on the route. A camera team, including Jimmy Chin, dangles nearby.
© *Mark Synnott*

The author attempted to free climb Freerider in 2002 but was unsuccessful. Here he is nearing the top of the Enduro Corner. This is roughly the same place Alex is climbing in the adjacent photo.
© *Cameron Lawson*

After completion of the climb, Alex told the author that on the way up the wall he was already thinking about his next goal. An hour later the author took this photo of Honnold on his hangboard.

© *Mark Synnott*

Alex received dozens of texts from his friends after the ascent. He joked that he needed an auto reply to respond to them all. The only equipment used for the climb, his shoes and a chalk bag, lies on the floor of the van below his legs.

© *Mark Synnott*

2,000-foot 5.7 called Snake Dike with the dog—and his BASE rig—on his back. At the top, he'd strap motorcycle goggles over Whisper's eyes and make sure she was securely fastened to his back, and then the two of them would jump off the Diving Board. On a good day, they would fly for more than a minute, swooping in near the cliff like a raven before banking out over the valley, pulling the chute, and floating to a soft landing in a small meadow alongside Mirror Lake.

Since Deep Blue Sea on the Eiger, Dean had only freeBASEd one other route, the Alien on the Rostrum in Yosemite. FreeBASE had been a visionary idea, but the fact that he was the only person in the professional climbing world interested in pursuing it said a lot about how dangerous it was. The main problem was that there weren't that many cliffs that were steep enough for it to be feasible.

But in a roundabout way, freeBASE had led to his next obsession, which he was calling human flight. The idea was to jump from the top of a cliff, high on the side of a mountain, fly down its side, and then land on a snow slope—without deploying his chute. And he had found the perfect place to do it in the Coast Range of British Columbia.

Dean had pitched the idea to *National Geographic*, and he brought me on as a writer, alongside Jimmy Chin, who would photograph the event. After signing a nondisclosure agreement, I was given the details. Dean, I learned, had been working with an aerospace engineer named Maxim de Jong to develop a custom wingsuit that featured body armor, similar to that worn by motocross riders and extreme skiers. The suit also included an "otter body" on its chest that would allow him to sled across the snow when he landed.

The story never came through, so I wasn't with Dean when he went to British Columbia and holed himself up in a small cabin with Jim Hurst, who was supposed to film the stunt for *The Aerialist*, the documentary about Dean's life that was now nearly a decade in the making. The jump didn't happen for reasons that remain obscure. I've always assumed it must have had something to do with the death of Dean's friend Sean Leary, who died in a BASE-jumping accident in April of 2014 in Zion National Park. It was Dean who found Leary's body on a ledge below the ridge he hit.

But Dean was still working with de Jong on a custom wingsuit that incorporated a vertical stabilizer. The deeper he probed into the aeronautics, the clearer it became that wingsuit design was inherently flawed. With the flying-squirrel wings on the sides of the suit, BASE jumpers could achieve glide ratios up to 2.5:1. But glide wasn't the problem. The issue was tracking. On most aircraft, directional stability and steering rely on the tail fin. Wingsuits don't have a fin, and this makes them more akin to a falling leaf than a torpedo. If a wingsuit BASE jumper makes even a tiny miscalculation in body position, he can lose control and find himself tumbling through the air like a piece of plywood dropped from a skyscraper. Dean believed that this design flaw was probably responsible for Leary's death, which gnawed on Dean's conscience since he had personally introduced his friend to the sport.

Another of Dean's favorite jumps in Yosemite was Taft Point, just up the road from where he lived on thirty acres in Yosemite West, a small town within the park. And it was here that he found himself on the evening of May 16, 2015, almost exactly four months since Tommy and Kevin had climbed the Dawn Wall. Dean, who was now forty-three, stood alongside his friend and frequent BASE-jumping partner, Graham Hunt, a twenty-nine-year-old who was one of the best wingsuit jumpers in the world. It was a beautiful evening. Ravens, creatures that Dean had long ago identified as his animal totem, were soaring on warm air currents high overhead. The rising warm air was a good sign, as it would help them track away from the cliff when they stepped off the edge.

But Dean wasn't feeling well. He had left Hunt a message earlier in the day saying that he wasn't up for flying. Later, he changed his mind. On a few occasions, they had flown through a notch in a ridge about 1,000 feet below the exit point. Since the conditions appeared to be perfect, they decided they would try for the notch. Jen Rapp, Dean's girlfriend, situated herself nearby to take photos of the jump.

"Are we ready?" asked Dean.

"Yes," replied Hunt, as he stowed his phone after a call with his girlfriend, who was on the valley floor trying to find the landing zone.

Dean exited first, followed a second later by Hunt. The images captured by Rapp show Dean beelining for the notch, with Hunt much higher and slightly behind. They disappeared from view; then Rapp heard two very loud sounds in quick succession. Was that *crack* the sound of their parachutes snapping open? She hoped so, but it didn't feel right. She texted both of them but got no response. Then she tried the radio. Hunt's girlfriend, Rebecca Haynie, waited down by the river. But Dean and Graham never landed. By the time YOSAR arrived, it was dark and too late to do a thorough search of the scene.

At first light, a California Highway Patrol helicopter located the bodies of the two men on a talus slope just below the notch.

Jim Hurst was on his way to the Grand Canyon when he heard that his friend had just died. He immediately changed course and headed to Yosemite. The search and rescue team hadn't been able to analyze the accident, and there were a lot of unanswered questions that were making it hard for their friends and families to understand how two of the world's best BASE jumpers could perish on what should have been a routine jump. There was speculation that they might have collided in the air; or perhaps they flew too close to each other and the resulting turbulence caused them to lose control.

Hurst and a BASE jumper named Corbin Usinger rappelled off Taft Point and explored the notch. They found a pine tree that was missing its top. By combining what they found on the scene with Rapp's photos, and calculating the angles and trajectories, they were able to speculate what might have happened.

The photos show that Dean was flying a lot lower than Hunt. This could have been due to the fact that his wingsuit was partially unzipped, something they discovered when his body was recovered. It looked like Hunt was making a turn to the left, which would have been consistent with him deciding not to fly the notch. But then he made a sharp turn back to the right. Why he did we'll never know, but that turn cost him his life. Hurst determined that from the angle at which Hunt was approaching the ridge, the tree he hit would have been indistinguishable from the green forest backdrop. The top of the tree, which was broken into four pieces and lying in the talus below the notch, was approximately eight inches in diameter. Dean made it through the notch, but he didn't have enough height to clear the lower-angled terrain in a gully on the backside. He ran headfirst into a rock wall going a hundred miles an hour.

In the final analysis, Hurst thinks Dean was too low and needed to deploy his chute and take his chances with a rough, unplanned landing high in the terrain, which probably would have resulted in traumatic injury. Thermals were rising on Taft Point, but the far side of the notch was a cold north-facing wall. A local pilot later told Hurst that it was a place notorious for rotors and downdrafts, exactly the type of air currents that pilots try to avoid at all costs. The thermal updrafts Dean and Hunt had deemed auspicious may have actually strengthened any downdrafts on the north side of the notch as cold air was sucked down to replace the rising warm air.

Hurst and Usinger climbed up to the notch and found the spot on the other side, about a hundred feet away, where Dean had hit. "If he'd had another four feet of elevation he would have made it," says Hurst. "The realization that he was going to die would have been like a quarter second." As they scrambled around the area, they found parts of their friend spread over a seventy-five-foot radius, like a Tibetan sky burial. According to Hurst, there were lizards sitting next to pieces of Dean's brain, waiting for flies to land. "That's something Dean would have loved," he says. Dean Fidelman, a close friend of Dean's, agrees. The scene was macabre, but it was a fitting end for a man "who had always wanted to become one with Yosemite."

ALEX AND DEAN had a complicated relationship, but Dean's death hit Alex hard. Years ago, when Alex was plotting his escape from his childhood bedroom, it was Dean he had watched in those *Masters of Stone* videos. They might have been rivals, like Harding and Robbins, with vastly different styles, but deep down they were uncompromising soul brothers who pushed themselves for the same simple reason: It gave them joy and offered an escape from the mundane drudgery of everyday life. In the years since Alex had scooped Dean on the West Face of El Cap, friends noticed that they were becoming closer, drawn by a mutual respect that seemed to grow stronger each year as they both became more comfortable in their own skins. A few days before Dean's final flight, the two had dinner together in Yosemite.

Six days after the accident, Alex wrote an essay about Dean for *Time* magazine. "He was a hero of mine growing up, representing everything badass about the climbing world," wrote Alex. "As a young gym climber, I thought what he was doing was impossible—and amazing." The public response to Dean's death, according to Alex, ranged from "deep respect for a man who greatly influenced his sport to unchecked contempt for someone who threw his life away, squandering what's most precious in search of the next cheap thrill." The contempt rankled Alex, perhaps because it hit close to home. And so he may have been projecting a bit when he wrote, "No one spends 20 years at the cutting edge of their sport by being an adrenaline junkie all the time. Most people had only seen his climbing and flying through short YouTube videos and never got a glimpse of the years of training behind them. Dean actually had a thoughtful and conservative approach, building up to things slowly over time as he became physically and psychologically prepared."

There were some who argued that Dean's risk-taking was immoral, but the way Alex saw it, these people were hypocrites because many of them risked their own lives on a daily basis by sitting on the couch eating potato chips. "I was 19 when my father died from a heart attack," wrote Alex. "He was a 55-year-old college professor and had led what was by all appearances a risk-free life. But he was overweight, and heart disease runs in our family. No matter the risks we take, we always consider the end to be too soon, even though in life more than anything else quality should be more important than quantity."

Following Dean's death, Alex called Weidner and confided to his old friend that he was feeling rudderless and unmotivated. He had been working hard on his autobiography with the writer David Roberts, but rather than finding motivation in telling his story, it was causing him to feel depressed. "Man, this is so lame," he said. "Here I am turning thirty, and all I'm doing is writing about how rad I used to be."

Alex had developed a cycle in which he went big every other year. It wasn't something premeditated, more just that his motivation seemed to ebb and flow on a biannual basis. The year before, 2014, had been an on year, but 2015 was turning out to be a year of low motivation. "I used to do cool shit," he told Weidner. "Now I'm just hanging out in my van feeling tired and unmotivated." It was possible that wearing the mantle of being the world's greatest free soloist was beginning to weigh on him. In that same conversation, he told Weidner, "This may be the first time I feel real pressure to perform."

The past year had been an emotional roller coaster. One of his friends had achieved his lifetime dream. Another had died in the process of seeking his. *What is the arc of my career?* wondered Alex. *Am I actively pursuing the things I care the most about?* One thing he knew for sure: He was burned-out. He needed to get a better perspective on things, to make sure he was heading in the right direction and living his life with intention. He needed to take a break from climbing for a while—something he had never really done.

He didn't quit cold turkey, but over the next two months he put climbing on the back burner. He spent his time reading, trail running, and going on long hikes. He dated a bit but didn't have a steady girlfriend. He spent hours alone in his van.

I spoke with Alex in early December. He was back at his mom's in Carmichael, California, hanging out in his old bedroom. He said he had been going through some of his old training journals and reading through his notes and to-do lists. One of them was titled "How to Be a Better Person." "I've definitely always thought about all that stuff," he said. I asked about his fall season and how it felt when he went back to climbing. He said he was surprised at how good he felt when he got back on the rock. One of the first things he did was head up onto El Cap, where he free climbed a difficult new route recently established by his friend Mason Earle. He expected to feel rusty and out of shape, but instead he was firing on all cylinders, climbing just about as well as he ever had. His motivation was flooding back in like a spring tide, and all signs were pointing to 2016 being an on year for him.

Could it be *the* year, the one he had been dreaming about since he free soloed Half Dome in 2008?

"Honestly, this was the first year I was like, 'Hmm, maybe,'" he replied when I asked him if he was still thinking about soloing El Cap. "It doesn't fill me with terror the same way it has in the past. So maybe it's getting closer or it means I'm becoming . . ." Alex trailed off and didn't finish the thought. He paused for a moment and then said, "We'll see, we'll see."

PART THREE

Topping Out

CHAPTER NINE

Amygdala

Alex, his arms by his sides, lay on a padded, gurney-shaped table in the radiology department at the Medical University of South Carolina. Sitting in a control room on the opposite side of a thick leaded-glass window, Dr. Jane Joseph watched as Alex slid head-first into the body-size donut hole in the Siemens Magnetom Trio fMRI (functional magnetic resonance imaging) machine. As his head entered the narrow tube and his shoulders brushed against the sides, a sudden and overwhelming wave of claustrophobia washed over Alex. His heart rate spiked. His breaths came fast and shallow. "Are you comfortable?" asked Joseph, her voice coming through a speaker inside the plastic tube. Alex nodded, but he wasn't okay—he was panicking. He had never had an MRI before, and he hadn't expected it to trigger a primordial fear. Phlegm from a lingering cold dripped down the back of his throat. Sniffling and swallowing repeatedly, he thought, *What if I choke?* Then came the loud noises. Buzzing, popping, and clicking surrounded him as the machine came alive and vibrated with energy. He felt it resonate inside his body. He wanted out.

But Alex had flown across the country to have this scan, so he took a few deep breaths and reminded himself that his fear was irrational. Nothing could hurt him in the tube. At any moment he could signal the technician, who could have him out of the machine in seconds. He flexed his will to regain control of his physiology. He felt his heart rate slow, and he calmed his breathing. The range of emotions from feeling relaxed to feeling panicked and back again had lasted three or four minutes. During this time, Joseph was doing an anatomical scan of Alex's brain but not yet looking for electrical activity. By the time she was ready to activate the fMRI, Alex had centered himself. Though no one knew it at the time, the test was essentially over.

IN DECEMBER OF 2014, Alex, Jimmy, and I gave a lecture in Grosvenor Auditorium at National Geographic's headquarters in Washington, DC. Afterward, we set up in the reception area to do poster signings. Alex's line stretched out the door; Jimmy's was nearly as long. Mine was embarrassingly short, but in it stood a man who stepped up to the table and identified himself as a neuroscientist. Glancing over at Alex, who was signing posters for his adoring fans, the man leaned in and whispered, "You know Alex's amygdala isn't firing, right?"

The amygdala is an almond-shaped nodule located deep in our brains. It acts sort of like the hub of a bicycle wheel, with the spokes representing its connection through the limbic system to a vast array of brain structures. The amygdala helps us to attach emotional value to stimuli that constantly swirl around us, and it is strongly associated with our most primal emotions, including sexual arousal and fear. If you've ever felt your pulse shoot up as a result of, say, being badly startled or seeing an erotic image, then you know your amygdala is firing.

That night, back at the hotel, I was reading about the amygdala online when I came across a reference to Urbach-Wiethe disease. It's a rare genetic condition that destroys the amygdala. This in turn led me to an article in *Discover* magazine about a person with the disease whom brain researchers had anonymously labeled SM-0426. The article was entitled "Meet the Woman Without Fear." Scientists have been studying her since the mid-1990s in hopes of better understanding fear and anxiety. They've dangled snakes and spiders in her face and had her watch scary movies like *The Blair Witch Project* and *The Shining*. Nothing fazes her.

When I later mentioned the neuroscientist's comment to Alex, he scoffed. "That's total BS," he said. "I experience fear just like everyone else." Alex had been asked many times whether he's a sociopath or if he has Asperger's, and he has conceded that he's probably "somewhere on the autism spectrum." But this was the first time someone had speculated that a basic structure in his brain was broken. And so I wondered if he was asking himself the same question I was: Is Alex Honnold's brain wired differently than the rest of ours, *or* has he found a way to master life's most primal emotion?

I COULD NOT HAVE IMAGINED the far-ranging implications of that seemingly innocuous encounter at National Geographic. A few months later, I shared the story with David Roberts, who was co-writing Alex's autobiography, *Alone on the Wall,* and he included it in the book. After that, the defective amygdala story became, in the popular imagination, Alex's superpower. It was as if Alex were a real-life version of Dr. Seuss' Mr. Sneelock, a savant whose magical skill, rather than being able to quickly tally huge sums, was to turn off fear. And this annoyed Alex, because he knew he experienced fear just like every other normal person.

What fascinated me was not the question of whether Alex had a working amygdala but instead why everyone, myself included, felt so compelled to probe for an explanation of how Alex can do what he does. Anyone who climbs and knows of Alex Honnold's exploits has had the "how does he do it" conversation with their partners between burns at the climbing gym or sitting around the bar with a round of beers. The question was the impetus behind countless magazine articles, films, blogs, podcasts, and, yes, this book. I wondered whether this fascination with Alex's brain reveals more about us, the people asking questions, than about him. Because for every individual who tips his or her hat to Alex's talent and nerve, there is another, like the Grosvenor Auditorium neuroscientist, who feels compelled to label him as abnormal—and perhaps pathologically so.

"People want to explain him away, they want it to be something that doesn't place a demand on them," says J. B. MacKinnon, a writer from Canada who arranged the brain scan and later wrote a widely read article about the results for *Nautilus* magazine. "Because if Alex is just an ordinary guy who managed to transform himself into this superhuman figure of fearlessness and cool under pressure, then they should be able to do that too. And nobody wants to believe that's the reality. We all feel this need to make him into something different and unique so the rest of us don't have to take any lessons from what he's done."

"I didn't think there was going to be a ghost in the machine," adds MacKinnon. "But if we looked at his brain and there wasn't anything [wrong], it really would raise the question: How the hell does he do it?"

"THIS IS SOMETHING I'M STARTING to wonder about myself," said Alex when MacKinnon called him and explained he had a neuroscientist lined up to scan his brain. "I don't think I'm abnormal, but I guess we can take a look." Alex knew that he couldn't have Urbach-Wiethe disease, because he did experience fear and always had. Fear made him need to poop before a big solo. Fear gave him high blood pressure before his first public speaking engagements. Fear caused the butterflies that fluttered in his chest when he was screwing up the nerve to talk to a pretty girl. And fear made his palms sweat when he watched videos of himself free soloing. Still, a seed of doubt had been sown. It would take three days out of his life to travel to South Carolina for the scan, but it was a unique opportunity that might lay certain questions to rest and silence those who dismissed him as a freak.

THE DAY BEFORE THE TEST, in early March 2016, Alex and Mac-Kinnon were walking the streets of Charleston, which is anything but a climbing town. At a café, they ran into a woman in her fifties who recognized Alex from seeing him on TV. She had never climbed before. A few minutes later they had a similar encounter with a younger woman who also said she had never climbed. Everywhere they turned, they kept bumping into fans. The next one was a man in his late twenties who was in awe that he had randomly stumbled upon his climbing hero. He followed the standard script: "Man, I can't believe you don't experience fear." According to MacKinnon, Alex struggled to hide his annoyance.

Years ago, John Bachar had a similar encounter at a gas station in Yosemite. A climber approached Bachar as he was filling his four-by-four. "How can you solo all that crazy stuff?" he said.

"You're soloing right now," replied Bachar.

MacKinnon now stood next to Joseph as the first images of Alex's brain appeared on the monitor. "That's a good-looking brain," she said. Joseph was referring not to the fact that it was extraordinary in any way but that it appeared at first glance to be normal and healthy, without the shrinkage or other degeneration she often sees in her lab. The amygdala was located near the bottom of Alex's brain, not far from the roof of his mouth, and it had not yet come into focus. Like most brain structures, there are two amygdalae, a right and a left. The ancient Greeks were the first to discover the amygdala when dissecting brains, and the name comes from the Greek word for "almond." Joseph told the technician to find Alex's.

A second later it came into focus, right where it should be.

"He has one!" exclaimed Joseph. She couldn't help but be pleased, since she knew too well how serious it would be if his was nonexistent or showed signs of disease. Now it was time to see if she could fire it up.

The test she administered has been used for decades. Subjects are shown a series of pictures that are meant to disturb or excite, and while they are viewing these images, the fMRI uses a strong magnetic field and radio waves to detect blood flow in different brain regions. The more blood flow, the more synapses that are firing. Images flashed on the screen in front of Alex's face: cockroaches, a close-up of a hissing snake, children burned by napalm, a woman shaving her pubic hair, a tarantula on a man's shoulder, a toilet filled with feces, a decaying corpse, a snarling dog, a riot scene with people throwing rocks, a gory close-up of a head that had been bashed so hard the eyes were sliding out of the skull.

Joseph told me she is loath to view these images even though she has seen them countless times. She admitted that while researching Alex before his arrival, she had found herself unable to watch YouTube videos of him free soloing. So at least for a low-sensation seeker, as she describes herself, the images spark strong responses.

The slideshow lasted about fifteen minutes; then Joseph started the second part of the test, which she calls the Reward Task. It was a game in which Alex could earn small amounts of money depending on how quickly he pressed the button on a clicker he held in his hand. While Alex clicked away, Joseph monitored a part of the brain called the nucleus accumbens. It's a structure near the top of the brain stem that processes dopamine, a neurotransmitter that carries electrical impulses between neurons. Most people think of dopamine as the chemical associated with lust, motivation, and addiction, but its function is complex and still not fully understood. What brain researchers do know is that the test Alex was undergoing is known to flood the nucleus accumbens with dopamine in reward-driven people.

When Alex emerged after half an hour in the tube, he looked at Joseph. "I can't say for sure [if my amygdala was lighting up or not] but I was like, 'Whatever.'" It felt, he said, "like looking through a curio museum."

AFTER THE BRAIN SCAN, Joseph gave Alex a personality test. Not surprisingly, he scored as twice as likely to seek high sensations compared to the average person. Yet the test also showed him to be well adjusted emotionally. He scored extremely high in the categories of conscientiousness and premeditation, low in neuroticism.

But there was one outlier. Joseph had assumed Alex would score low on disinhibition, a term used in psychology to describe the tendency to be impulsive and unaware or uncaring of social customs. A disinhibited person is also likely to be bad at assessing risk. Joseph had assumed that Alex was not overly disinhibited, because if he were, he would have already killed himself free soloing. But Alex had scored high in this category. I wasn't surprised, however, knowing what I do about climbing. I see it the opposite way: An inhibited person would never get into free soloing in the first place. But what I find interesting is that while Alex scored high in disinhibition, the test also indicated that he's highly analytical and punctilious—an unusual combination, according to Joseph. This juxtaposition may point to the tension that I have long sensed in Alex, something MacKinnon also noticed. He described Alex to me as someone who is "constantly suppressing some kind of internal intensity."

It took Joseph a month to study and prepare the results of Alex's scan. By this point Alex was in China, on his way to climb Getu Arch, one of the world's most difficult multipitch sport climbs. He was curious about the results, but he had already decided that whatever the brain scan revealed, he was not going to modify his behavior on its account. Joseph had e-mailed Alex four images, two of his brain and two of a control subject's brain. The pictures showed all activity that had occurred across the entirety of the two tests. The control subject was a rock climber and deemed a high-sensation seeker by the researchers. Alex had met him while he was at the university, and Joseph had scanned the man shortly after Alex. Joseph had made clear from the start that the test results of Alex's scan were not scientifically valid because there had been only one control. This was not a study that would be published in any medical journals.

"Is my brain intact?" asked Alex via Skype.

"It's perfectly healthy," said Joseph.

The images produced by fMRI brain scans use various colors to illustrate the strength of synaptic activity, similarly to how meteorologists portray the intensity of thunderstorms on radar maps. The image of Alex's brain showed two gridlines that formed a plus sign directly over his amygdala. The nodule was dull gray. The fMRI had not detected *any* electrical activity. Neuroscientists call this "zero activation." The only part of his brain that showed any color was the visual cortex—proof that he was actually looking at the images.

Now Joseph referred Alex to the image of the nucleus accumbens taken during the reward task. The results were the same. The neurons weren't firing. Zero activation during both tests was "highly unusual," according to Joseph. The control subject was given the exact same tests. Like Alex, he reported feeling no emotional stimulation. It was obvious to this subject what the game was, and he felt confident that his brain, which had seen him up countless difficult rock climbs, had not taken the bait. He was wrong. His amygdala and nucleus accumbens were both lit up like a Christmas tree.

THOSE OF US WHO KNOW and follow Alex weren't surprised when we heard the results of the scan. Over the past twenty years, he has focused intently on learning to control fear. It's been a gradual process, something he once described to me as "slowly expanding the bubble around my comfort zone." It's a progression every climber must follow, from first overcoming the irrational fear that ropes and anchors won't hold, on up to learning how to stay calm and loose when executing difficult moves, even if the fall would be dangerous.

Since he first envisioned free soloing El Capitan, Alex has known that he would need to take this process to a rarified extreme, training himself to control his innate fear response when climbing near the limit of his ability thousands of feet above the ground without a rope. So one possible interpretation of Joseph's findings is that he has succeeded brilliantly—assuming, of course, that his amygdala is actually capable of firing, ever. And this, Joseph emphasizes, the test could not determine. It only indicated that his amygdala doesn't respond in the same way to the same stimuli as do those of the vast majority of test subjects.

When Alex's book came out in the fall of 2015, I interviewed him for *National Geographic*. He told me that one of his prime motivators for writing it was to help people understand why he can do what he does: "I've done so much soloing, and worked on my climbing skills so much that my comfort zone is quite large. So these things that I'm doing that look pretty outrageous, to me they seem normal." He said that it makes "total sense" to him and that it's "easily understandable," but still, people don't seem to get it. "Maybe I should have explained it better," he said.

He used the analogy of driving on the freeway. It can be terrifying the first time a new driver pulls into speeding traffic from the on-ramp. But as you do it more and more, you become accustomed to the high consequences of a mistake, and after enough repetitions, it's a routine experience, like brushing your teeth.

I pointed out that it's a lot easier to keep your car in the proper lane than it is to hang from a pinky lock on a 5.12 finger crack. But Alex disagreed. He said it's only easy because I've done it a lot. "If you were some aboriginal dude who had never even seen a car before, you'd be like, 'Holy shit I'm about to die,'" he said. "Climbing to me is the very same thing. I've actually spent more time climbing than driving. Imagine New York City cabbies and all the outrageous things they do. That's kind of like me with my climbing. I've spent a ton of time hanging on pinky locks, so it's not a big deal."

The rationalization that his free soloing is no more dangerous than being a cabbie in a busy city is one that Alex has carefully constructed, probably because it's the keystone in the philosophical edifice he has built to justify the risks he takes. Try to tell him that free soloing is dangerous, and he will argue the point, every time. The closest I've come so far is to get Alex to admit that the "consequences" of a fall while free soloing would be "disastrous." But then he'll quickly point out that just because a consequence may be severe, its probability of occurring does not increase. The consequences, he'll say, are equally dire if your hand slips off the steering wheel and you swerve into the oncoming lane and collide head-on with a Mack truck. "Every time you go out on a highway you're running an astronomically small chance of being hit by a big rig. That's just the cost of doing business." According to the Insurance Information Institute, the lifetime odds of dying in a car accident for a person born in 2013 are roughly one in six hundred. Change the metric to dying in any kind of accident and the odds are one in twenty-four.

Engage Alex in this conversation, as I have on numerous occasions, and invariably he will quote his own homegrown statistic that no free soloist has ever fallen while pushing his limits. "It doesn't seem to be the way that people die," he has said. As far as I know, he is correct. Bachar died soloing 5.10, which could be considered moderate terrain, at least for him. Derek Hersey, the famed British free soloist who fell off Yosemite's Sentinel Rock in 1993, was on a route rated 5.9. To date, his is the only death ever attributed to free soloing in Yosemite National Park. (Afterward, someone taped a laminated photo of Hersey onto the rock at the start of the route. "We miss you Derek," it read.) Dan Osman, another free soloist, and a founding member of the North Face Team, was killed when his rope broke while he was practicing a sport he invented called "rope jumping." John "Yabo" Yablonski, the Stonemaster, and Earl Wiggins, an unsung Colorado climber, both noted free soloists, committed suicide. Charlie Fowler, the Coloradoan who on-sight free soloed the Direct North Buttress of Yosemite's Middle Cathedral in 1977, was killed in an avalanche in western China. Michael Reardon drowned in the Irish Sea. Dean Potter perished while BASE jumping. Henry Barber, who soloed the Steck-Salathé route on Sentinel Rock in 1973 (the same route on which Hersey would later fall) is still alive and well, as is Peter Croft, who, with little fanfare, continues to solo 5.12 at the Owens River Gorge.

"I think that the odds of me actually falling are very low," says

Alex. While I might disagree, I see how Alex needs to believe this, in order to do what he does. Otherwise, he'd be afraid to do it. And that fear, if it turned to panic at the wrong time, could kill him. Most of us look at our one-in-twenty-four chance of dying in some kind of accident the same way Alex looks at free soloing. We choose to go through life believing that we won't be unlucky because otherwise, we'd be too afraid to get in our cars or even leave the house. If hanging from a fingertip jammed in a crack 1,000 feet off the ground is just as ordinary an experience for Alex as negotiating rush-hour traffic is for the rest of us, then one might have to admit that his rationalization makes sense.

OUR NATURAL FEAR RESPONSE to danger is an evolutionary trait. We call it colloquially the fight-or-flight instinct. Essentially, our muscles become supercharged with adrenaline, which gives us extraordinary strength and energy to fend off an aggressor or run away. This was the greatest acute danger faced by our prehistoric ancestors, so presumably it's an appropriate and potentially life-saving physiological response to attack. But rock climbing is different. Yes, it demands strength and energy—in abundance for long, difficult climbs—but it also requires calm, finesse, and poise. You're not going to get up a 5.13 with an uncontrolled explosion of fury. An adrenaline bath might help you run faster than you ever have, but if you're trying to find the precise body position to unlock an enigmatic sequence of climbing moves, it would be like using a chainsaw to perform surgery. Succumbing to fear will all but guarantee the bad outcome that is causing you to be fearful in the first place. So Alex tries to deal with fear in the same way he would other basic emotions, like hunger. "When you're hungry, you set the feeling aside and eat when it's convenient," says Alex. "With fear, your pulse quickens, your vision narrows, and you're like, 'Oh my god, I'm feeling fear, oh my god, oh my god,' and then it cascades out of control and you lose your ability to perform. With free soloing, obviously I know that I'm in danger, and feeling fearful while I'm up there is not helping me in any way. It's only hindering my performance, so I just set it aside and leave it be."

Alex reported feeling panicked when he was first jammed into the tube. He said that no part of the test was as uncomfortable as the "oh no, I'm trapped in a box" moment he had in the beginning. Was his amygdala firing when he felt claustrophobic? Joseph hadn't yet activated the fMRI, so we don't know. But Alex says he recognized the irrationality of his fear, chose to set it aside—breathe it out, as he describes—and then felt fine. So perhaps his amygdala, if it had been firing, calmed down and essentially turned off. Nothing in the test was tuned nearly high enough to elicit emotional discomfort similar to the claustrophobia, so Alex's amygdala may have simply remained in the off position.

IN THE MONTHS FOLLOWING the brain scan, while Alex trained relentlessly for Freerider, I decided to dig deeper into the amygdala question. I contacted Joseph LeDoux, a neuroscientist at New York University who has been studying the amygdala for thirty-five years. He kicked off the conversation by telling me that writers have a tendency to oversimplify when trying to explain something as complicated as the brain. He said that contrary to popular belief, the amygdala is not the fear center of the brain. "The amygdala has a lot of consequences in the brain that affect our feeling of fear, but the feeling of fear is not generated by the amygdala. . . . The field [neuroscience] has always failed to make the distinction between fear as an experience and fear as a sort of implicit processing system, and it's caused a lot of confusion." According to

LeDoux, damage to the amygdala does not eliminate the conscious experience of fear; rather, it prevents the behavioral and physiological responses to threats—sweaty palms, spiking pulse rate, and tunnel vision.

When I asked LeDoux about the zero activation, he said it was a meaningless result because fMRI machines are tuned to detect a certain threshold of electrical activity. "The fact that the experiment failed to find it doesn't mean it wasn't there," he said. He told me that electrodes placed directly onto Alex's amygdala, that is, on the inside of his brain, not the outside, would indeed detect synaptic activity.

And LeDoux dismisses the possibility that Alex's amygdala is dormant. Instead he posits that Alex may have been born with a muted amygdala response relative to the general population, making him a genetic outlier, so to speak. He also says it's likely that Alex has desensitized his amygdala to be less responsive to threats, particularly those associated with heights, by routinely exposing himself to high places. "By self-exposing, training himself in those situations, he's going to reduce the amygdala activity, because that's what exposure does. And perhaps he has trained himself to be able to turn on that inhibition when he goes into those kinds of situations."

So how does it feel to stare death in the face and not be afraid? What does the world look like through those eyes? I was contemplating these questions at my mom's house in Florida when I happened to catch a segment on the *Today* show about Nik Wallenda and the Big Apple Circus. Nik is a member of the famed multigenerational family of aerialists known as the Flying Wallendas. The segment was about a horrific accident that had taken place the month before. The troop was attempting a world record eight-person pyramid on a wire twenty-eight feet above the ground, with no net, when someone on the bottom faltered. Five of eight people fell to the ground; three, including Nik, managed to catch the wire. No one died, but Nik's sister broke every bone in her face. The story reminded me that the last time I had seen Nik on television he had been walking across the Grand Canyon on a tightrope. The death-defying walk, which he did without a tether, was broadcast live on the Discovery Channel. I remembered it as one of the most mesmerizing performances I had ever witnessed.

I sent Nik a message on Facebook, and he called me the next day from his home in Sarasota, just up the road from where I sat in my mom's home on the Gulf Coast. It turns out Nik is a big fan of the world's greatest free soloist.

"I say it all the time. Fear is a choice," said Nik. "You can decide whether you want to be scared or not." As an example, he referenced a haunted house. "I can go in there with the expectation of being scared to death, or I can go in there, and go, 'These people are paid to scare me. Why would I be scared of this? It's not real.'"

Whether you are fearful of heights, financial problems, or your spouse being unfaithful, Nik said it's our choice whether we want to "allow it to take root." He compared fear to a weed in your garden. If you don't pull out the weed, it spreads and takes over. "As soon as I experience any thought of fear, I kick it out immediately. I counter it with, 'No. I know what I'm doing. I've done this my whole life. I've trained for the worst cases.' I always counter negative with positive in every aspect of my life. I truly have no question in my mind that fear is a choice."

IN THE FINAL ANALYSIS, what may be most remarkable about Alex is that he is both a "super sensation seeker" and, at the same time, an individual with an unusually high degree of emotional regulation. These two traits are often antithetical, but the fact that they coexist within Alex may have a lot to do with his ability to tread so close to the edge.

What concerns Joseph is that a high-sensation seeker like Alex may find that he constantly needs to up the ante, to bring himself ever closer to the edge of his limits in order to get that hit of dopamine his brain is accustomed to getting. Evidently, her test wasn't tuned high enough for Alex's nucleus accumbens to fire—perhaps not even close—but it's fair to assume that Alex is a reward-driven individual. As MacKinnon points out, everybody climbs for the reward. Why else would we do it if not for some psychological payback? The problem with getting caught up in an endless game of one-upmanship, even if it's just with oneself, is that it can lead to addiction and other pathological, self-destructive behaviors. In her lab, Joseph sees this most often with drug users and gamblers, but it's easy to imagine how it could happen to a free soloist.

Alex had survived because he tempered his drive to explore his limits with sober premeditation, diligence, and patience. If he didn't have control of his impulses, he might have gone for El Capitan without a rope years ago. Joseph didn't know about Alex's secret plan (neither did MacKinnon, although he had his suspicions), but she did have a parting word of advice for Alex: "Don't let the impulsivity win out over the conscientiousness."

CHAPTER TEN

The Source

"A lex falling through the [camera] frame to his death," said Jimmy, "that's what I think about. And if I'm already seeing it, I can only imagine what it would be like if it happened." Jimmy and I were sitting in white plastic deck chairs on the roof of Gîte Tawj-dat, a climbers' guesthouse in a remote village called Taghia in Morocco's High Atlas Mountains. The *gîte* (French for "vacation house") sat in the back of a cirque ringed with red-hued limestone towers that poked into a hazy sky. They call this place the Yosem-ite of Africa, and for the past two weeks, Jimmy and his crew had been racing around filming Alex and Tommy Caldwell as they raged up the spires that towered above us. A few days earlier, the pair had succeeded on a monster linkup of three of the longest and most difficult routes in the canyon. They were calling it the Taghia Triple Crown. I had arrived a couple of days later, in time to spend one day with Tommy before he flew back to the States. Alex was staying on for another week. He had told me over the summer that he might "scramble"—a euphemism he often uses for free soloing—one of Taghia's big walls to finish off the trip.

Jimmy had declared a rest day, the first since they had arrived. The crew, totaling half a dozen, included a director of photography, a sound guy, a high-angle cameramen, a producer, a "data wrangler," and a professional rigger, most of whom were close friends of Alex's. They were scattered around the guesthouse tinkering with their gear. Alex was in his room, probably binge-watching *Spartacus.* He'd told me the day before that he had downloaded all four seasons off Netflix before the trip, and he was already on season three.

I hadn't seen Jimmy since that day on the tram in Jackson Hole. He looked drained as he slouched in his chair and sipped mint tea from a chipped ceramic mug. There were bits of something, probably twigs or leaves, tangled in his shaggy black hair. He said he was having trouble sleeping because he worried that the film he was making about Alex "might put undue pressure on him to do something he might not do if there wasn't a film being made of it." Like Alex soloing Les Rivières Pourpres, a sixteen-pitch 5.12c on the 1,800-foot tooth of rock that rose in the back of the gorge above Jimmy's left shoulder. "And that's really, really heavy," said Jimmy.

Jimmy was articulating the same thing he had told me when we spoke by phone in August. Being Alex's documentarians meant that we might one day watch him fall off the mountain. And worse, at some level, we'd be complicit in his death. Looking into Jimmy's eyes, I could see that it scared him, not just because he would lose a friend but because he knew it would be a dark cloud hanging over him for the rest of his life. It was one thing to contemplate it in the abstract at his home in the Tetons, another to live it, as he was now.

And it wasn't just Alex whom Jimmy worried about. For the past two weeks he and the crew had been moving nonstop through high-angle technical terrain. They had been doing plenty of their own climbing and occasional free soloing to get into position to film Alex and Tommy. It was at a far lower grade, say, 5.6 instead of 5.12, but they were wearing huge packs filled with ropes and camera gear, and the chance of someone dislodging a loose rock onto another, or Alex himself, was ever present.

TWO DAYS EARLIER, I had traded a Toyota Land Cruiser for a donkey where the road ended at a bustling village called Aguddim. The drive from Marrakech had taken five hours, leading south and east across the flat desert of lowland Morocco up into the High Atlas Mountains. The tarmac followed the ancient path of a historic trans-Saharan caravan route connecting Marrakech with Timbuktu. Beyond Aguddim, no roads penetrate the most remote parts of the High Atlas, and I proceeded on foot, following the donkey as it clopped along a dusty trail with my green duffel bag strapped to its back.

Taghia lies at the same latitude as El Paso, Texas—thirty-one degrees north. Its 6,600-foot elevation keeps it much cooler than Marrakech. Prime climbing conditions tend to run about a month earlier than they do in Yosemite, making it an ideal choice for someone looking to get tuned up for a season of free climbing big walls. Alex first visited Taghia in 2012 with Hazel Findlay, who joined our Oman sailing and climbing expedition later that same year. He told me they had a "thing" on that trip and that something about the place, which he couldn't quite put his finger on, set him up for what turned out to be the best Yosemite season of his life. That was the year he and Tommy climbed the Triple Crown and then he broke the speed record on the Nose of El Capitan with Hans Florine.

"Yeah, I could go anywhere in the world," he said, gesturing toward the High Atlas Mountains, "but where's better than this?"

The muleteer led me to a sprawling two-story house surrounded by a tall stone wall. I ducked through a doorway into a courtyard lined with trees and tossed my duffel bag on a wooden bench. A slim, narrow-faced man with light skin emerged from a doorway, gently took my right hand in his, and said, *"As salaam alaikum"* (Peace be unto you).

"Wa alaikum as-salaam" (And unto you peace), I returned, having learned the proper reply from my past travels in the Muslim world.

Said Massaoudi, the owner of this *gîte,* looked to be in his mid-fifties. He built his guesthouse in 1994, shortly after French and Spanish climbers discovered the gorge's untapped climbing potential. During prime climbing season, March through April and September through October, his guesthouse bustles with foreign climbers, mostly Europeans, who pay 150 dirhams (about fifteen US dollars) a day for room and board.

Said lives in a portion of the downstairs with his wife, Fatima; their three daughters; and a married son who has a baby. The home, which appeared to have had rooms haphazardly added on as needed, was set up like a hostel, with a large common room on each floor, bathrooms with pit toilets, a hot shower, and at least a dozen double-occupancy guest rooms.

Said, like all of the three hundred or so inhabitants of Taghia, is a Berber. The name Berber is a derivation of "barbarian," from the Greek word *barbaros.* Berbers have lived in northern Africa for thousands of years, and they are well-known as traders who braved the Sahara to establish caravan routes connecting sub-Saharan Africa to the Iberian Peninsula and beyond. One of those routes, reported to have been in continuous use for at least seven hundred years, passes directly through Taghia Gorge via the same path I'd followed from Aguddim to Said's *gîte.*

I FOUND THE TEAM'S EQUIPMENT and other stuff upstairs. One whole wall of a large living room was stacked waist-high in black plastic Pelican cases. Apparently, the crew was out, because the place was quiet. I poured myself a cup of tea and stepped onto a porch that offered an unobstructed view down the valley through which I had just hiked. A stream ribboned the valley bottom, sparkling in the midday sun. Terraced fields rose from its banks, quilting the surrounding hillsides in varying shades of green—sage, lime, olive, emerald. Scattered among the lush fields I could see dozens of snug little hobbit homes, built with mud and dry-stacked limestone blocks that looked as though they had grown from the earth like the fig and almond trees that surrounded them. Closer by, a man was spread-eagled in a tree twenty feet in the air whacking walnuts to the ground with a long stick. Sounds of a bustling village filled the air: children playing, babies crying, the bray of donkeys, dogs barking, the constant buzzing of insects. I knew, from having studied the High Atlas Mountains on Google Earth before the trip, that the vast wasteland of the Sahara lay just on the other side of the mountains that rose behind the *gîte*. More desert lay to the north, east, and west, but Taghia, fed by a fabled spring called the Source, is an oasis.

I was trying to figure out the line for a famous route called Babel that climbs the left side of Taghia's version of El Capitan, a 2,800-foot cliff called Tagoujimt n'Tsouiant, when I noticed two young women marching purposefully down a switchback cut into the slope below the mountain. They looked to be in their twenties and, as they clearly weren't Moroccans, I guessed it was Alex's girlfriend, Sanni, and her sister, Jaime. A few minutes later, they bounded up the stairs. Sanni was effervescent and appeared genuinely pleased to meet me. She shook my hand warmly and said Alex had told her I was coming. Petite, with blond hair down to her shoulders, twenty-four years old, she had a smile that would make most men melt. Jaime is older, more reserved, and I wondered if she might be wary of her little sister dating a guy like Alex Honnold (I would later learn this to be the case). We sat down at a table in the living area, and they told me that they'd just done a big hike. The rest of the team had spent the night on top of one of the mountains.

I had never met Sanni (short for Cassandra), and the only thing I had heard about her was that she had "dropped" Alex while climbing at a cliff called Index in Washington State. I learned the details, like most of the climbing community, in a publication called *Accidents in North American Mountaineering*. As the title suggests, it makes for grim reading.

It was March of 2016, early in the season for rock climbing in Washington State. But it was warm and sunny, and Alex was leaving in a few days to climb Getu Arch in China. He was about to run up a moderate 5.9 crack called Godzilla when Sanni's parents, who were climbing with them that day, asked if he would use their rope and set the climb up as a toprope (toproping is when the rope is run through an anchor at the top of a route and the belayer is situated at the base of the climb; it's the way most ropes are set at indoor climbing gyms). This way they wouldn't have to lead it and they could run laps on the climb while Alex and Sanni went to climb something harder. What no one realized was that the rope they handed Alex was too short for Godzilla. After Alex finished the climb, Sanni began lowering him. Everyone was chatting and having fun, when she felt the end of the rope slip through her fingers. A split second later it popped through her belay device. Sanni screamed. Alex, now without a belay, dropped ten feet into a pile of rocks, landing hard on his butt and side.

Sanni rushed to his side. "Are you okay?" she asked with a gasp.

"Hold on," said Alex, while he assessed his injuries. His elbow was bleeding, and his body was hurting all over. Jaime and her boyfriend, who were also climbing that day, took charge of the scene and ran through the ABCs—airway, breathing, circulation—then they did a "chunk check." It appeared nothing was broken, so Alex got up and, with a hand from Sanni and her dad, hobbled down to the van. They drove straight to the hospital. Sanni was in back with Alex, bawling most of the way. An X-ray didn't show any breaks, but considering the mechanism of injury, the doctor suggested a CT scan. It revealed compression fractures in two of his vertebrae.

The next night, back in the van, Alex tried to break up with Sanni. "I want to be a good climber," he said, "and I have to make sure that my life is supporting me becoming a better climber."

"Listen," replied Sanni, "we're not going to do this thing where you break up with me, go off and do some angst soloing, and then we get back together. . . . You don't have to be angsty to be a good climber. This was a terrible accident, but I don't think it's something that's going to happen again."

Alex wasn't taking any responsibility for the accident. As the vastly more experienced climber, it was his job to "close the system" before leaving the ground. The standard way to do this is to tie a barrel knot in the end of the rope. If he had done that, the knot would have jammed against Sanni's belay plate when he ran out of rope, preventing it from popping through. Sanni had been climbing for only about six months and had barely climbed outdoors, so it was unfair to put the blame on her for a housekeeping safety detail. Alex, the same guy who showed up to climb a choss big wall in Borneo without a helmet, has always been resistant to the sport's long-established safety protocols. Perhaps when you free solo big walls, tying knots in the end of the rope seems a bit silly.

"We hadn't fallen in love yet," Sanni told me. "In his mind, it was like, 'I wanna do what's best for climbing, and if you're not best for climbing, and being around you sets me back, then I don't want to date you.' And I think it was also part of this weird secret desire to have some angst, so that he goes and climbs better."

And so Alex went to China, where the running joke of the trip was "My girlfriend broke my back, and then I tried to break up with her, and she didn't let me, so I guess we're still dating."

"BEFORE WE START, I'm just going to get through the annoying questions, the things I don't like very much, and cover some of the basics about fear and death. Because that's what everyone always asks me about, and I just want to get that over with." Alex, wearing a plain red T-shirt and asphalt-colored chinos, was standing behind a podium on the stage of Town Hall Seattle. He mentioned the "annoying questions" a second time, then cued up a five-minute film about his 2014 free solo of El Sendero Luminoso in Mexico.

With its vaulted ceilings, large stained-glass windows, and wooden pews, the Great Hall felt like a place of worship, which it was up until the 1990s, when the Fourth Church of Christ, Scientist sold its church to a group of civic-minded Seattleites. The Great Hall can seat more than eight hundred people, and it was packed. Sanni sat in the middle of a row toward the back. Her friend, an avid climber, had asked her if she wanted to go to see Alex Honnold.

"Who?"

Sanni had just started climbing in September in a local gym called Vertical World and had never heard of Alex Honnold or any other professional climbers.

TOWARD THE END OF THE PROGRAM, a man stood up and said, "Several years ago you mentioned that one of your primary motivators for soloing Half Dome was to get more attention from women. Would you say that has happened, and do you have any crazy stories you'd be willing to share?" Someone catcalled from the back of the hall.

"Yeahhhhh . . . well, I'm single, so obviously I still need to solo harder walls," Alex deadpanned. The crowd cheered. "When I first was living in the van and road-tripping, my first interview in *Rock and Ice* I was like, 'Oh, I'm in the magazines, and now I'm gonna get laid.' But it did not work at all. It's surprising how, even after being in a bunch of films and being on the cover of things, it turns out that personality is more important. So, it's still not really working, but thanks for rubbing it in."

This guy is sassy, thought Sanni. Sure, he was a bit awkward, a bit goofy, but he was still "super cute." And there was something else. "I don't want to say it's fearlessness," she was telling me now, as we sat across from each other in the *gîte*, "because I know it's a word he stays away from, but he had this readiness to go, this total competence." Sanni had been single for almost two years since graduating from UNC Chapel Hill. She was working at an entry-level marketing job and living in a house with four girlfriends. They all wanted to meet guys, but money was tight and the bar scene was grim. She tried dating apps and went on occasional dates, but no one captured her imagination.

At the end of the presentation, a long line formed to purchase *Alone on the Wall* and have it signed by Alex. Sanni and her friend decided to buy one copy and share it. Alex worked his way through the queue, just like he had at every other event he'd done in the years since he had become famous. As each person stepped to the front, he locked them with his doe eyes, flashed a toothy smile, and said a few kind words. Many of the younger people wanted selfies with Alex. He tried to make each one quick. The line stretched across the Great Hall, and he had to be efficient if he was to get back to his hotel at a decent hour, where he hoped to watch some *Harry Potter* before bed.

In each book, he wrote the same thing, "Alex Honnold," followed by two words that sum up his philosophy on life: "Go Big." Alex told me that at one such event, a buxom woman arrived at the front of the line and asked Alex if he would sign her breasts. "Uh, are you serious?" Alex stammered. In answer, she pulled up her shirt, under which she wasn't wearing a bra. As the rest of the people in line gazed in awe, Alex grabbed his Sharpie, wrote his name on her left breast, and then, almost as an afterthought, wrote "Go Big" on her right one. Sanni was a bit more discreet. She said hey and gave Alex her most charming, dimpled smile, and when he handed back the signed book, she passed him a note.

Later that night, back at the hotel, Alex pulled it out of his pocket.

"Because you made me laugh and why not. Sanni." And her number. He racked his brain to try to remember the woman who gave him the note, but he had given hundreds of autographs that night, and all the faces blurred together. But he grabbed his phone and sent a quick text to say thanks and that he was leaving the next morning at five A.M.

Two weeks later, Alex was on his way back to Seattle for a talk at REI. He had forgotten about the woman at the Seattle Town Hall.

Sanni, though, had been thinking about Alex, and when she saw an announcement that he was coming back to Seattle, she texted him. A few days later she picked up Alex and Cedar Wright at the climbing gym and took them to dinner. After their talk at REI, she brought Alex back to her house for a bonfire party in his honor.

"Right away, there was a really strong connection," she tells me. Alex left again, but a few days later he invited Sanni to fly to Vegas to climb for a weekend in Red Rocks. Sanni said yes.

I'm going to Sin City to hang out with a guy I barely know, who lives in a van. What's the worst that could happen?

As I SIPPED a cup of tea in the *gîte*'s common room, Alex appeared in the hallway. I had been wondering where he was hiding and had not seen him come in. Perhaps he'd been in his room all afternoon. He looked around with one eye scrunched shut, said, "Hey," and something like "I feel like death" and then shuffled into the bathroom. I'd seen him like this before, suffering from an acute migraine. They don't strike him often, but when they do, it's like Superman and kryptonite.

I didn't see him again until nine A.M. the next day. "Morning, kiddies," he said. He looked tired, but his face wore a knowing smile, as if he was laughing inwardly at the notion that we were all children and he the only adult among us. The migraine had passed, and his superpowers were building back up. He carried a book in his hand, which he placed on a shelf behind the dining table, next to the *gîte*'s guest book. I saw on the binding it was *Open*, Andre Agassi's autobiography. I hadn't read it but had seen some reviews, and I knew it focused on Agassi's struggles with fame and how he came to hate tennis, the sport around which he had built his life.

Alex stepped up to the sink attached to the wall outside the bathroom and examined his face in the mirror. Bare-chested and barefoot, he wore only his well-loved black climbing pants. As he stood there brushing his teeth and examining himself in the mirror, I looked around and noticed that every eye in the room was on him. Alex weighs around 160 pounds, which isn't light for a five-eleven rock climber. Every muscle from his waist up is chiseled into his frame. I imagined that punching him in the gut would feel like hitting a wall. His shoulders are broad for the size of his frame, and his arms are long and borderline freakish on account of the ape-like hands that hang from their ends. His fingers are so thick they actually look buff, like they have miniature muscles in them. And instead of hanging straightish, they appear naturally curled like a gorilla's. They're so thick I wonder if he can even straighten them. His fingernails, on the other hand, are surprisingly normal. Most climbers' nails get banged up so badly that at least one or two end up looking like Ruffles potato chips. Mine are sometimes so bad I find myself trying to hide them from certain people. Alex's are scratched, but they're not deformed.

"It's a little embarrassing," said Cheyne Lempe, one of the high-angle cameramen, "but every time I see him I get a little starstruck."

WE SCOOTED DOWN A NARROW path that ran along the bank built to divert water from the river into a canal running straight to Said's *gîte*. The trail, red and muddy, stood out starkly against the vibrant green grass growing along its edges. Where the canal connected with the main river that fed it, we hopscotched across to the other side on flat limestone rocks that rose a few inches above the rippled water. A wider trail led us past a small square of hard-packed red dirt where a few young men sat on a stone wall holding phones in their hands. A 2,500-foot-high limestone tower called Oujda loomed overhead. At the bottom of the cliff, some fifty to one hundred feet above the ground, dozens of rivulets poured out of cracks in the face—the magical spring they call the Source, the place that gives Taghia its *baraka* (spirit). Green beards of moss hung beneath the gushing founts, reminding me of a romanticized painting I'd once seen of the mythical Hanging Gardens of Babylon. Before crossing the boggy slope below the Source, I looked downstream. The Ahansal River flowed northward from its headwaters, sparkling in the sun, its banks green and radiant against the brown foothills of the High

Atlas Mountains. In the other direction, upstream of the Source, the riverbed was dry. The boundary of the oasis formed by the Source was as stark and abrupt as the vertical walls that rose from the sandy corridor into which we were filing.

WE SHUFFLED ONE BY ONE into the slot canyon, which narrowed until I could touch the walls on either side at the same time. The way ahead was blocked by an overhang capped with a water-polished boulder. Here the Berbers had jammed a juniper tree trunk between the walls of the canyon. Such makeshift ladders can be found all over these mountains, similar to the *via ferrata* that crisscross the Dolomites in Italy, only made of wood and stone instead of iron. I was told that many "Berber bridges" are the handiwork of the Ait 'Atta, a nomadic tribe of goat and sheep herders who winter in the Sahara and in summer lead their flocks up into the High Atlas. For a thousand years, the Ait 'Atta have been allowed access to the high pastures of these mountains in exchange for providing security to the inhabitants of Taghia and Aguddim against enemy tribes from the Sahara.

The Berbers cross this makeshift bridge multiple times a day, and I think they even lead goats across it, but apparently I wasn't the only one who thought it was sketchy. Some climbers, it wasn't clear who, had created a bypass by drilling a bolt into the canyon wall about fifty yards upstream. By utilizing an *étrier* clipped to the bolt, our crew, which included some of the best climbers in the world, was able to bypass the Berber bridge.

Once we were past this crux, the canyon opened up to the width of a dirt road. As I stared up between the overhanging walls at a tiny arc of sky high above, I marveled at the geologic forces that sculpted these natural cathedrals from rock that was once the bed of an ocean. With a little bit of imagination, I could picture the three mountains that towered above me back when they must have been one giant plug of rock.

ON A SMALL LEDGE at the base of Taoujdad, Alex attached a Micro Traxion to a black rope hanging on the wall. The cliff rose like the prow of a spaceship, seeming to overhang every inch of its 1,800 feet. I followed the rope upward with my eyes, knowing it traced the route Alex planned to free solo. A thousand feet overhead I lost the line where it disappeared above a blocky overhang. On the hike into this valley, the wall had looked reddish in the midday sun, but now that I was standing at its base I saw that its color was closer to orange, with blotchy patches of pink, white, and gray. The route was marked by tiny white splotches—handholds covered in chalk, like a 3-D game of connect the dots.

Alex set off with a water bottle and a spare Micro Traxion swinging from a gear loop on the back of his harness. I asked him why he didn't attach the second device as a backup, and he said he thought one was better because it was simpler and cleaner. He had heard stories of people falling and having the two devices jam against each other such that neither clamped down on the rope. His point was that sometimes less is more.

That morning, back at the *gîte,* Dave Allfrey, the team's rigger and a close friend of Alex's, was in the hallway sorting through his gear. He said he was going to mini-track Rivières Pourpres, and with a serious look, he told me about a superstition he has about Alex and his big free solos. For a number of years, he has been climbing routes with a rope before Alex goes and solos them. He's not sure how it started, but the superstition is that Dave needs to feel good on the route and complete it without falling for it to be okay for Alex to climb it without a rope. "I need to report back [to Alex] that it felt easy." As he's climbing, he keeps an eye out for anything that might be amiss—loose holds, edges that have too much chalk. If there's a key hold that he thinks Alex might not notice, he marks it with a small dab of chalk called a tick mark. "When I do try to drop myself into his shoes," said Dave, "sometimes it's distracting, and I find myself not climbing as well because it throws me into an uncomfortable mental space." Alex, who is not superstitious in the least, finds the whole thing a bit silly.

"Get some, Mark," Alex called from above, when he looked down and saw me setting off on my own mini-track adventure. There was a problem, though: I hadn't anticipated mini-tracking in Morocco, and so I had not brought my rig. When Alex invited me that morning to go up with him, I scrounged up some gear, but the devices I was using weren't Micro Traxions. My setup wasn't sliding smoothly up the rope. I had to keep reaching down with one hand to manually pull the rope through the system, which was difficult because the route was steep and unrelenting. The manufacturer's website specifies that the Micro Traxion can be used for self-belay, but it should always be backed up in some fashion. Most climbers, myself included, use two. I clip both to my belay loop, but I extend the top one and hold it up by clipping it to a bungee cord (actually an old headlamp strap) around my neck.

The diciest part of mini-tracking is the transition at anchors. This entails clipping a lanyard to the anchor to secure myself, removing the Micro Traxion from the lower rope, and putting it back on the rope above. There is no room for error, and mistakes made at these changeovers have resulted in a number of fatal accidents.

A prominent New England climber fell to his death in 2014 at my home cliff, Cathedral Ledge, while mini-tracking. No one knows exactly what went wrong, but he was found at the base, unclipped from the rope. Another New England climber, while climbing Moonlight Buttress (the route Alex free soloed in 2008) in Zion in March of 2016, heard a whooshing sound coming from above and assumed it was rockfall. He looked up and saw to his horror that it was a man, still alive, free-falling to his death. An investigation revealed that he was mini-tracking high on the route when he somehow came unhooked from the rope.

I HADN'T WARMED UP, and there were no rests. And even if I had, the route was above my current pay grade. By the time I was 120 feet up, my forearms were burning. I pumped out on the second pitch, meaning my arms got so tired that my fingers opened and let go of the holds against my will. I fell back on the rope. As I hung there and shook out my arms, all I could think about was the horror of how it would feel to pump out while free soloing. I knew the climbing was easy for Alex and that this would never happen, but still, the thought of it made me slightly nauseous. I was also dubious of the integrity of some of the holds I was pulling on. A few were nothing more than congealed blobs of calcite that had leached out of the limestone. I yanked on one of them while I was hanging there, and it felt solid, but I knew that some holds, especially on limestone, feel secure right up until they break off. We call them "time bombs."

I hung on the rope or fell at least once on most of the pitches, but I eventually worked out the kinks with my rig and there were sections I climbed well. It was thrilling to be high off the deck in Morocco, pulling hard on small holds. At the anchor of the sixth pitch, about halfway up, I met Alex, who was on his way down. He had climbed the entire route in about ninety minutes.

"What are you doing?" he said.

"I'm working my way up," I replied. "What does it look like I'm doing?"

For a brief moment, I thought Alex was about to give me some kudos for making it as far as I did.

"This is like when they let a normal guy into the pool in the Olympics," said Alex.

All I could do was laugh. "You really can be a dick sometimes," I replied. "I thought I was doing well."

"Well, for a middle-aged father of four, you're doing great."

MIKEY SCHAEFER, Jimmy's director of high-angle photography and all-around right-hand man, walked up behind Alex and began kneading his shoulders. Alex bent his arm like a chicken wing and rotated it around as if rowing a boat. "I've got something going on with my right shoulder," he said. Mikey dug in with his short but powerful fingers. Alex sighed. His head dropped, and his chin settled onto his chest.

"Is that gray hair?" asked Mikey, whose own bushy mop and rug-thick beard were flecked with silver strands. Though he stands only five foot four, Mikey is a giant in the climbing community. He's not a household name like Honnold or Caldwell, but among climbing's cognoscenti, he is revered as a quiet badass who operates under the radar, despite being one of the best all-around climbers in the country.

"Yeah," said Alex. "Think about all the stress I experience." Everyone laughed, but I couldn't tell if Alex was being sarcastic or not. In all the years I have known him, I have never actually seen him appear stressed-out.

Said appeared carrying a sombrero-shaped, brightly painted ceramic dish called a tagine. Steam poured from a volcano-like spout and filled the room with the mouthwatering aroma of a stew Fatima had been slow cooking all afternoon. Berbers have been cooking with tagines for hundreds of years. It's an ingenious design; the spout traps the escaping steam, which condenses and drips back into the stew, slow cooking and tenderizing inexpensive cuts of meat with a limited amount of water. The dinner menu at Said's is tagine, tagine, and tagine. The only mystery is what kind of meat you'll find inside. It could be goat, lamb, or chicken. That night it was chicken. The other ingredients were carrots, potatoes, squash, onions, and other bits and bobs I couldn't identify. It was seasoned with spices typical of a Moroccan kitchen, including turmeric, ginger, and coriander. Said appeared with a second tagine, this one meat-free for Alex, who has been a vegetarian since 2012. I dug in heartily with a large spoon. The chicken melted off the bone, and the flavor was bold and spicy and unlike anything I'd ever tasted. Said returned throughout the meal with endless loaves of bread baked in his homemade clay oven. We drank tea flavored with mint that Said's daughters had picked from the side of a stream a few yards from the house. Everything had come from within one hundred yards of where we sat. The only exception was the flour in the bread, brought in by donkey from the market in Aguddim. Once a month, the king subsidizes the delivery of a discounted fifty-kilo bag of flour for every family in Morocco.

The kitten must have smelled the tagine. It darted in the door, wove its way between our legs, and jumped up onto the couch with Alex. Someone mentioned how the creature looked well. It had been so scrawny and emaciated when the crew first arrived that people weren't sure it was going to make it. Said had been putting out bowls of milk, and the crew had been slipping it plenty of snacks.

Alex then casually said he wouldn't care if someone killed it. All eyes in the room turned on him: eyebrows raised, looks of bemusement, and grumbles of disapproval. Having known Alex for eight years, I've heard this sort of comment before. You might even call it a signature Alexism: first, that it occurred to him to contemplate whether he cared at all about the cat, second, that he decided he didn't, and third, that instead of keeping his mouth shut, he decided to share this gem of a revelation with the rest of us. I wondered if he would have still made the comment if Sanni and her sister were there—they had left the day before. Sanni didn't say why she was leaving early, but she did tell me that she had never watched Alex free solo. Perhaps she wanted to keep it that way.

"I didn't say I would kill the cat," he added. "Just that it wouldn't bother me if someone else did." I looked back at Alex stroking the kitten with his huge hand. A smug smile had replaced the poker face, and I knew that it was all a game, a game in which the object is to make your companions uncomfortable, to force them to stop talking about climbing, for once, and to think.

Seconds later, we were back to talking about climbing.

THE NEXT MORNING, Alex sat at the table chewing on a stale piece of bread, tapping a meaty forefinger against the screen of his phone. The shaky Wi-Fi signal we'd been pulling in with a Moroccan cell booster wasn't working. "It seems slightly warmer today," he said. Just a casual observation about the weather? Maybe, except the temperature had a lot to do with how well his fingers would adhere to the rock. And in an hour, he would be hanging from his fingertips with 1,000 feet of air sucking at his heels.

Someone bumped into a red plastic bucket in the hallway, and it clattered loudly. "Hey, you just kicked the bucket," said Alex, trying to lighten the mood.

A banana-shaped canvas pouch filled with Scrabble tiles sat on the table in front of us. "Want to play?" I asked Alex.

"Sure," he said, "but you have to let me win so you don't shatter my confidence."

As I divvied out the pieces, the kitten jumped up onto the couch and Alex picked it up, cradling the little creature in one of his giant hands and scratching the top of its head with his other. Alex told me that he had just been e-mailing with some folks from his high school in Sacramento. They were inducting him into their Hall of Fame at a ceremony in October, and they had a few questions, like how did his education at Mira Loma High prepare him for the things he's doing now.

"So?" I asked.

"I just told them that I never really gave a shit about my education, but that school did help shape my overall worldview."

Alex looked down at the pieces on the table in front of him and began moving them around like he was playing a shell game. In seconds, he had eight words interconnected in a crossword puzzle: *Jab-jetty-lieu-taze-bane-cane-came-been.* I had two: *nun-cunt.* I suck at Bananagrams.

"I'm pretty sure 'cunt' is slang," said Alex. "Is 'glinty' a word?"

I said I didn't think it was, but it turned out I was wrong. Alex added it on.

Clair Popkin, the director of photography, signaled me. It was time to go. He and I and a local Moroccan named Hassan El Mouden who had been working for the crew as a porter had a plan to climb up the back side of Taoujdad and wait for Alex on top of Rivières Pourpres. "Good luck, my man," I said to Alex, clasping his hand in a kung fu grip.

Alex stared at me with his big brown eyes and smiled.

LIKE THOUSANDS OF TIMES BEFORE, Jimmy hooked his daisy chain to the two-bolt anchor, unhooked his rappel device from the black static line he had just slid down, and shifted his weight onto the tether. "*Off,*" he yelled, the signal that the rope was free and Mikey could come down. Jimmy secured himself to the next rope, transitioned off the anchor, disconnected his daisy chain, and started rappelling down the next rope. The rock was gray and weathered, slightly less than vertical. Jimmy walked down the wall, carefully placing his feet so as to avoid any loose rocks.

When French sport climbers first established Rivières Pourpres and other routes snaking up this vast acreage of limestone cliff, they climbed the route from the ground up, taking five days to inspect, clean, and protect it. In addition to placing a dotted line of expansion bolts for anchoring ropes, they pried off any loose blocks and flakes of rock that might pose a danger while climbing. It's standard practice when establishing bolted routes and creates a relatively safe climbing experience for both the first ascensionist and all other subsequent climbers. Jimmy's crew had reconnoitered camera positions off to the side of the route so they could film Alex as he climbed past. These sections of rock, well beyond arm's reach of the route, had never been touched, let alone scoured for loose rock. Dislodging a deadly missile onto a fellow cameraman—or even Alex himself—was always a real and nerve-fraying possibility and one Jimmy was assiduous to avoid at all times.

So Jimmy couldn't believe it when he looked down and saw a backpack-size block sliding out from under his right foot. The terrifying sound of rock grating against rock filled the air, and there was nothing he could do to stop what was about to happen. Two of his close friends, Dave Allfrey and the sound guy, Jim Hurst, Dean Potter's old friend, were somewhere down below.

"Rock, rock, rock," he bellowed. The boulder bounced several times, leaving puffs of dust each time it hit the wall and filling the air with a loud cracking that reverberated through the canyon. Spinning violently, it hit a grassy terrace sixty feet below, where it exploded and dislodged several more rocks. Jimmy looked down and watched two dozen softball- to football-size stones raining down toward Dave and Jim.

FOUR HUNDRED FEET BELOW, Dave heard the cracking and the call of *"Rock"* that is every climber's nightmare. *I'm a fuckin' magnet for this stuff,* he thought as he looked up and saw the sky above him filled with black projectiles that whistled like incoming artillery. In the spring of 2015, he had been pummeled by a filing cabinet–size fin of rock that Cheyne had inadvertently dislodged onto him on a first ascent in Baffin Island. Dave had shown me the scar, which looked like a shark had taken a bite out of his back. Now he sucked himself in close to the wall, tried to make himself as small as he could under his helmet, and waited to find out if it was his time to die.

THE NEXT THIRTY SECONDS PASSED in slow motion for Jimmy. He heard the rocks hit the canyon floor, then an eerie silence. The radio crackled to life. "I'm okay," said Dave, "but holy fuck was that close." Jim Hurst came on the line and said he was also okay.

Jimmy hung on the rope, his hands over his face.

"DO YOU HEAR THAT?" I said to Clair and Hassan. We were sitting on the summit of Taoujdad. The "trail" up the back had included a section of 5.5 free soloing near the top. It was easy, but some of the rock was vegetated and loose, and the exposure was real. A fall from anywhere on this section would have been fatal. Just below the top, Clair's radio had crackled with the news that Alex was starting up.

"Yeah, what is that?" said Clair. Wind blasted the summit, sieving through the scraggly bushes that clung to jumbled piles of rocks. A gust blew up the wall from the direction of the sound, and we both heard it more clearly. It sounded like, *"Alex, Alex, Alex."*

A jolt of adrenaline hit my chest, and I felt like I was in a car skidding off an icy road at high speed. "What the hell is going on?" I said to Clair, as we both started scrambling down a steep ridge to see if we could figure out what was happening. Fifty feet down, the wall dropped away below me into a dark abyss. I looked over the edge and saw something that my brain had difficulty processing. A dark-haired man in a short-sleeve blue shirt was walking a tightrope stretched between Taoujdad and a similar tower on the other side of the gorge. The line, I could see, was made of nylon webbing—a slackline. It must have been 1,000 feet across and a similar distance above the ground. It was windy, and the line vibrated like a guitar string. The man swung his arms back and forth over his head as his body whipsawed from side to side like a skier on a slalom course. Another gust carried his calls in our direction.

"Allez, allez, allez." The yelling that had almost given me a heart attack was this guy cheering himself on in French.

After the panic had washed through me, I felt an intense anger toward this overly exuberant acrobat. His obnoxious hooting and hollering must have been a serious distraction to Alex. That the guy probably didn't even know Alex was soloing the wall to which his line was attached didn't matter to me.

"That guy needs to shut the fuck up," I said to Clair, looking up at him and realizing that he was filming.

OVER THE COURSE OF TWO weeks in Taghia, Alex had climbed nearly two hundred pitches. Of those, 140 or so were 5.12 and above. The amount of difficult rock climbing he had done in Morocco was unprecedented, and it had taken a toll on his body. The big toe on his right foot felt tender as he stepped onto a tiny foot nub on the first hard move of the route. Miles of climbing on razor-sharp limestone had also calloused and dried out his fingertips. His index and middle fingers, in particular, felt too dry where they gripped the rock. Alex worried that the thickened skin made his fingertips less sensitive to the nuances in the holds he was gripping. Calloused skin can sometimes cause a fingertip to "skate" off a hold, like a foot slipping on a banana peel. His fingers needed moisturizing. So he popped the last phalanx on his right index finger into his mouth and gave it a quick suck. The middle finger was next. He looked up and saw Cheyne off to his right dangling on the black rope he had used for mini-tracking two days ago. Cheyne was leaning over, camera up to his eye, so focused on composing the shot that he didn't notice Alex's consternation.

A few hundred feet higher, Alex screwed up a sequence and found himself in the middle of a small roof facing a move he hadn't rehearsed. This pitch is rated 5.11d, a grade at which Alex has a large margin for error, but the rock was steep, there were no rests, and he was feeling more pumped than he had on any of the previous three times he had done this section. He was tense, overgripping a bit because he wasn't trusting his sore foot. He hadn't yet found the flow.

What the fuck is that? Someone was yelling. Alex looked over his left shoulder and spotted the French slackliner.

"Allez, allez, allez," the man cheered himself, over and over. *Who does that? Who cheers for himself?* The Frenchie fell. Caught by his long tether, he dangled like a spider on a thread eight feet below the line. At least he had stopped yelling.

Most of Alex's weight was hanging from a deep pocket he underclung with his left hand. He had buried his fingers so deep he wasn't sure if they would come back out of the mountain; it's something he tends to do when free soloing. His right hand was on a smaller edge, and the next move was a big one. His feet were splayed out below. He looked around—Frenchie bobbing on his tether, two guys dangling on ropes up and to his right, one jugging up from below. He may have been soloing, but he certainly wasn't alone.

MIKEY SETTLED HIS FEET AGAINST a reddish streak in the limestone, rotated his torso to the left, and stared down the wall through the camera's viewfinder. Alex seemed to be moving smoothly now. *His foot is barely on the pedal. He's giving what? Like, 50 percent, maybe 60?* Mikey knew the climbing wasn't as easy as Alex made it look because he had done the route himself when he first got to Taghia. He had struggled on one of the moves Alex was about to pull—1,200 feet up an overhanging wall.

Afterward, when I talked with Mikey about the experience of filming Alex free soloing, he described some of the thoughts running through his mind. "He's running at low rpms, barely revving his engine, but still, I feel like I'm watching someone on top of a building who's about to jump. And it's sucking the energy right out of me. This must be like war photography. The chance of someone dying—it's not a point-zero-zero sort of thing; it's a percentage point, like multiple points. It could happen. I wouldn't want to do this job every single day for a year. Oh man, that would be really bad odds."

Mikey had been trying not to dwell on the fact that shortly before leaving for Morocco, the climbing tribe had sustained another loss. Kyle Dempster, thirty-three, and Scott Adamson, thirty-four, two of America's best alpinists, had disappeared in late August while attempting the unclimbed north face of the Ogre, a 23,000-foot mountain in the Karakoram. A storm blew in on the second day of what was supposed to be a five-day mission. The pair was last seen by their cook halfway up the face. Most of the crew knew them personally.

ALEX PULLED HIMSELF onto the route's only decent ledge 1,400 feet above the ground, as Mikey continued filming.

"Hey, how did you get up here?" said Mikey. "Where's your rope?"

Alex laughed. Jimmy was nearby on a separate rope a bit above Mikey, jugging up to get in position to film the next pitch, which was by far the most dramatic on the entire route—gently over-hanging, smooth gray rock with streaks of orange and red. Big moves between positive holds. The rating: 5.12c. Alex slipped off the heels of his shoes and shuffled a few feet across the ledge. He turned his back to Mikey, who was still rolling, and let out a sigh. A stream of urine arced through the air.

THE JANGLE OF CLINKING CARABINERS drew my attention to a notch between two fins of scaly gray limestone one hundred feet below. Jimmy, panting and dripping with sweat, was hustling to top out before Alex, so he and Clair could shoot Alex summiting from two different angles. He pulled the huge black camera case from around his neck and threw it down in the rocks by his feet.

"Did you hear what happened?" he asked me as sweat dripped off the tip of his nose. "I almost killed Dave and Jim."

A few minutes later, we heard whistling. Alex, wearing a bright red shirt, black pants, and a yellow chalk bag, scrambled up onto the summit, all nonchalant, as if he were strolling down the side-walk to get a pack of gum from the corner shop. Jimmy and Clair had their cameras trained on him, while Alex stood there, staring at his forearms.

"That felt like work," he said, to no one in particular.

"How did it go?" I asked him.

"I was overgripping and a little tight on the whole bottom part. I didn't really loosen up until I got to the crux. That actually felt pretty good—smooth, easy. I don't think I've actually ever soloed anything like that before. It was wild. Overall, I would give myself a B-minus. But I've had solos where I was more on edge, like Romantic Warrior." He then reminded us of the story that had become legend among those of us who follow his exploits. "I was so gripped on that one I took a dump on pitch 3."

With that he grabbed the pack we had brought up for him with his shoes and a water bottle, threw it onto his back, and walked off.

Hassan had been sitting a few feet away, absorbing everything. He's twenty-five years old, six feet tall, and movie-star handsome. The entire time I had been in Taghia, Hassan had been wearing a tight, light blue cotton V-neck sweater with no shirt underneath. He lives in Aguddim, speaks fluent English, and works as a translator and guide. He's also a budding climber, a member of the first generation of Moroccans to venture up these cliffs with ropes and quickdraws. Hassan had told me earlier that all the Moroccan climbers know about Alex and Tommy. They had watched the coverage of Tommy's Dawn Wall ascent on CNN. "Everybody wants to meet them," said Hassan. Alex and Tommy are famous in Morocco, even among non-climbers. Which explained the Moroccan woman who saw us walking back from the cliff and called out, "Alex, I want to marry you."

"He [Alex] is an inspiration for young people here. It's making me motivated to get more into climbing," says Hassan. "But it worries me, because it's dangerous."

When Alex left, I turned to Hassan. "What do you think?"

Hassan looked me in the eyes and shook his head. "He's crazy."

Mikey showed up a few minutes later and plopped down on the summit next to Jimmy. They both looked dog tired, as anyone would after a long, sweaty day humping heavy loads through the mountains. But more than just physically exhausted, they appeared mentally frazzled, shell-shocked almost. Jimmy stared across the canyon with an expression that looked pained and aggrieved. I had been through a lot of emotional, pressure-packed moments with Jimmy over the years, but I had never seen him like this before. No one spoke for a while.

Then Jimmy said, "Today was awful for me. . . . The thing is, I was hyperfocused. I knew the most dangerous thing that could happen would be to kick off a rock. It was all I was thinking about. The place I put my foot, fifteen people had already gone over that ground. It kind of made me lose my stomach. I was like, 'Fuck this shit.' I told Mikey, 'The last thing I want to do right now is shoot somebody soloing.'"

"And I had to be like, 'Hey, he will be up here in thirty minutes. You got a job to do. Put it in your pocket and think about it later,'" said Mikey.

"This shit is fucking gnarly," said Jimmy. "And I knew it would be like this, I mean, I knew it would be dangerous like everything else we do. But with this shit—with this many cameramen—the chances of hurting someone else . . ." His voice trailed off, and he looked down at the ground, which was covered in loose rocks.

Any climber who ventures out of the gym or beyond manicured sport-climbing crags has had close encounters with rockfall. It's part of the game and a risk you learn to mitigate rather than eliminate. When I'd heard Jimmy say that he'd knocked off a rock above Jim and Dave, I wasn't surprised. It is a common occurrence. I've had my bell rung at least a dozen times by golf ball–size rocks that have taken chunks out of various helmets I've owned over the years. But I've always been roped in when this has happened.

The real reason this incident was so chilling was because we all knew that it could have happened when Alex was on the wall. Without the security of a rope, he can't squeeze in tight, dive for cover, or shield his head with his arms. And he doesn't wear a helmet since it would be useless if he fell from any appreciable height—not to mention it's just not his style. My stomach churned as I imagined a shower of rock shrapnel peppering him amid a hard sequence. I know what it feels like to get whapped with a small piece of stone. Even a peanut-size rock hitting Alex in the head might cause him to falter if it happened at the wrong moment.

Dave said afterward that he could feel the rush of wind on his ears as watermelon-size chunks of rock shrieked within inches of his skull. Yes, he was wearing a helmet, but it wasn't going to offer much in the way of protection against rocks that big, which would have ripped his head off his body. Jimmy was now bearing the full weight of his decision to take this job on. Jon Krakauer's perfectly rational advice that *someone* would film Alex, and that Jimmy should be "the guy" because he was the most qualified to do it, seemed utterly worthless in this moment, like, "Somebody's going to ski off the summit of K2, so it might as well be you."

In Jimmy's film *Meru*, he has a line about how the best alpinists are the ones with the worst memories. Only those who can selectively forget the misery and near misses are willing to return again and again to attempt big, dangerous climbs. While this project didn't involve the physical discomfort of a Himalayan expedition like Meru, it certainly offered its own set of horrors.

We all just sat there, listening to the wind whistle through the notches in the rock, staring off at the parched hills surrounding the tiny oasis of Taghia. "I don't want to do this job for the rest of my life," said Mikey. "All the stress is just going to ruin me. I've seen other shooters that work in the mountains, and they've seen it go bad, and now they're paranoid, because they hit their threshold.

We could be doing car commercials or shooting models in Mexico." Mikey paused and appeared to be deep in thought, like he was imagining those bikini-clad models on the beach. I looked at Jimmy, and he was finally smiling. He does photo shoots with supermodels on occasion. "But none of that work is really meaningful," Mikey added. "You're just selling shit. Here we're actually trying to show somebody special."

LATER, BACK AT THE *GÎTE*, everyone hung out on the roof watching the sunset. All that was left of the trip was to pack up and head home. It would have been the perfect time to break out some beers to celebrate, but Alex and Jimmy don't drink and consuming alcohol is against the law in the Kingdom of Morocco. After Rivières Pourpres, Alex had gone and soloed a classic multipitch 5.11. In total, he had soloed an El Cap's worth of hard rock. It had been one of the most impressive days of free soloing in the history of the sport. Alex wasn't glowing and animated like I'd seen him after other big successful days—too much hadn't gone well for everyone. But he was more chatty than usual, and a question I'd been pondering came to mind.

He had read three books in Taghia. *Open, The Push* (Tommy's autobiography that he shared with Alex in real time via thumb drive as he was writing it at the *gîte*), and *The Signal and the Noise* by Nate Silver. Somehow, he had also found time to watch at least three seasons of *Spartacus*. *The Signal and the Noise* is all about statistical probability and why most predictions fail. In the book, Silver explains what he calls the prediction paradox: "The more humility we have about our ability to make predictions, the more successful we can be in planning for the future." I found it interesting that the world's greatest free soloist was reading a book about probability in the weeks leading up to what could be called the ultimate gamble. I wondered where Alex put his odds of success if he decided to go for it. It's a pretty loaded question to ask someone, but given his mood and the tie-in to the book, I decided to toss it out.

First, he talked about other people's odds of pulling it off. His friend Brad Gobright, an up-and-coming free soloist? "If he woke up one day and decided that he didn't care if he lived or died, he'd run a 35 percent chance of dying. There are a ton of dudes who, if you put a gun to their head, they'd have a 70 percent chance of living" to claim the first free solo of El Capitan. "Obviously these are unsatisfactory odds for most people," he added.

Alex said that while training in Switzerland that past summer, he had visited his friend Ueli Steck, a brilliant forty-year-old climber nicknamed "the Swiss Machine." Steck is a household name in Europe, known for constantly breaking his own speed records on classic routes in the Alps, like the North Face of the Eiger. Steck is to alpine climbing and mountaineering what Alex is to rock climbing.

They had gone on a hike in the hills above Steck's home and talked about "when you just take the chance." Steck told Alex that on some of his big climbs, he "seizes his moment and just goes for it," acknowledging that when the stakes are high enough, he's willing to roll the dice. Steck was undoubtedly referring to his 2013 solo ascent of the 8,000-foot South Face of Annapurna, a 26,545-foot mountain in Nepal. This climb is high on the short list of the boldest Himalayan coups in the history of the sport. Annapurna, the tenth-highest mountain in the world, is often called the "deadly mountain." As of 2012, 191 people had stood on Annapurna's summit, and 61 had died trying to get there or on their way back down—a fatality rate of roughly 32 percent, the highest of any 8,000-meter peak.

Steck had attempted the face twice before. On one of his failed bids, in 2007, he was hit by rockfall while climbing unroped low on the face, causing him to fall 1,000 feet. In 2013, when he finally succeeded, Steck was climbing with a Canadian named Don Bowie, who bowed out the day before the pair planned to set off. Rather than be denied a third time, Steck set off alone carrying a small backpack and two hundred feet of six-millimeter rope. According to his own account, he climbed nearly nonstop for twenty hours, free soloing every inch of the face, including mixed climbing on the crux rock band that required him to use his ice axes as hooks on vertical rock at 23,000 feet. On the summit, he briefly took in the view, then turned around and climbed and rappelled back down the way he had come up. He was back in camp twenty-eight hours after he set off. "If I climb anything harder than that, I think I will kill myself," said Steck afterward.

"I'm looking for something repeatable," said Alex, as he lounged in a plastic chair on the roof of the *gîte*. "[Mark] Twight's whole summit or death—either way I win—that's not really my scene. But I do think a bit about it. Maybe for El Cap I just need to embrace that mentality. Some things are worth it."

As an example, Alex mentioned his University Wall free solo. After rehearsing the route, he could only get his odds up to about 95 percent. So he set the project aside.

"Then one day [six weeks later] I was like, 'Today is my day,' and I just went up and did it. Sometimes you have to choose your moment, which is the opposite of today—a Tuesday morning at the office—time to clock in. Soloing is so much about confidence. Today I should have been ultrastrong, but I actually felt slightly weak."

When Jimmy and I had first started talking about this project, he had suggested I join his crew as a rigger and work alongside Dave helping fix anchors and ropes for the cameramen. At first, I loved the idea, because it would intimately embed me with the crew. But I've done a lot of rigging over the years, and I fully understand the dangers involved. When I stepped back and thought about it carefully, contemplating all the loose rock, the sharp edges, and how much danger I'd already been exposed to in my life, I decided it wasn't worth the risk.

In 2008, not long after an expedition to Kashmir with Kevin Thaw and Peter Croft, I retired from high-risk Himalayan expeditions. My marriage was falling apart, and my sense of responsibility of being a father was growing on me as I approached my forties. A sober assessment of the odds of survival if I kept pushing the limits indefinitely—which were all too stark given the deaths of too many close friends and associates—left me with no delusions of immortality. And so I let go of the ambition, which had burned since I first found climbing as a youth, to compete with the best alpinists and adventurers of my generation. I still climbed and skied and traveled the world. I just did so with a greater margin of safety than before. I said no to many opportunities. I chose to focus more on my guiding business, my writing career, and other interests like sailing that have expanded my horizons in new ways. And I spent more time with my kids and got them involved in some of my adventures.

There had been several times over the years, since I had first gotten to know Alex, that I wanted to grab him, shake him by the shoulders, and say, "Dude, if you don't step back from the edge, you're gonna miss out on a lot of good living." I felt that same impulse on the rooftop in Taghia.

Instead, I said, "There's a lot of things that you still need to experience, Alex."

"Yeah," he replied, looking mischievous and not missing a beat, "like threesomes."

CHAPTER ELEVEN

"Her Attitude Is Awesome"

When was the last time you talked to Alex?" asked Chris Sylvia, my boss at the North Face. It was my twentieth year on the Global Athlete Team—as they now called it—and Chris was the latest in a series of a dozen or so managers with whom I had worked over the years.

"A couple days ago, why?"

"He took a bad fall and destroyed his ankle. He doesn't know if it's broken yet, but he showed it to me on FaceTime and it looked really bad. Black and blue and swollen all the way up to the knee. I've never seen him so down."

When I got off the phone I texted Alex. "Hey just heard about your fall really sorry to hear that you got hurt but glad you are ok just wanted you to know I'm sending good vibes your way." Instantly, the three little iMessage bubbles lit up. Alex, who is usually climbing and slow to respond, was tapping the tiny keypad on his phone with his sausage-like fingers.

> "Thanks dude, appreciate it. I got it looked at today
> and it's good so I think things won't be too bad.

Pretty optimistic. Just almost climbed 12c in the
gym one footed. Which is something at least. It
might be ok in a week or two according to the doc."

I called Jimmy. The phone rang once, then switched to a foreign dial tone—a common scenario for Jimmy, who is constantly
traveling around the world working on photo shoots and film pro-
ductions. He didn't pick up, but a couple of minutes later he called
me back. "You heard about Alex, huh?" he said. "I guess we're
going to postpone a week, but Alex has done major damage to the
ligaments in his ankle and you know how long it can take for that
kind of thing to heal."

"What happened?" I asked.

"I'm not sure," he replied. "I haven't heard the details yet. I just
know that his ankle is destroyed, and that I've now got a serious
problem on my hands. My team has been booked for months, and
I can't just cancel or postpone on them—they are all counting on
the work and have turned down other jobs. And now there's nothing to film. He was climbing so well in Morocco and our whole
team was really starting to gel. We had all this momentum, and
now . . ."

Afterward, I sat at my desk, thinking back to the spring of
1997, when I took a similar fall on El Capitan. My partners
thought I was overestimating the extent of my injury, so they taped
up my ankle and we kept climbing, setting a speed record in the
process on a route called Lost in America. Two days later I got it
X-rayed and found out I had broken my ankle. I was in a cast for
six weeks, and the day after it was removed I flew to Pakistan to
climb Shipton Spire. I thought back to how shaky I had been on
that climb, how worried I was that I'd fall again and reinjure it. I
remembered how it had taken a year to regain my confidence as a
climber. How would Alex handle it?

TWO AND A HALF WEEKS later, Jimmy and I sat in his van outside the Majestic Yosemite Hotel (formerly the Ahwahnee), waiting for a text from Alex. We'd just linked together two classic routes—Super Slide and Serenity Sons—on a cliff called the Royal Arches. Neither of us had been climbing much, and the linkup, which Alex free solos in a couple of hours, had taken us all day. Now the plan was to go find Alex. Neither of us had seen him since Morocco.

We found him half an hour later, sitting at a high-top table in the corner of the Mountain Room Bar with Mikey Schaefer and two other guys I didn't know, a guide for the Yosemite Mountaineering School and another climber. There were glasses of water on the table. These guys had been here for a while, but no one had ordered anything. Alex looked like he'd just gotten out of bed. His black hair was tousled and unruly, as usual. He wore his standard getup, a pair of black softshell pants and an orange puffy jacket that had brown stains down the front. I gave him the kung fu grip handshake with a half hug / back slap—standard climber greeting.

"So let's see the ankle," said Jimmy. Alex slipped off his right shoe and peeled down his sock. His ankle was huge. Deep purple, pink, yellow, and orange bruises, like the colors of a sunset, ran from the tips of his toes to just below his knee.

"Whoa," said Jimmy.

"This is nothing," said Alex. "You should have seen it two weeks ago." Alex told us that he had been climbing and hiking every day. His orthopedist told him that since it wasn't broken it was okay to get out and push his ankle as much as he felt comfortable. For Alex, this meant soloing 5.9 instead of 5.11 and 5.12. He told us about some multipitch climb that he soloed up and down that day, in his approach shoes.

As we got caught up, a climber from another table came over to say hey to Alex. I had never met him, but I knew who he was— Kevin Jorgeson, Tommy Caldwell's partner on the Dawn Wall. He was dressed from head to toe in Adidas and sporting almost as many corporate logos as a NASCAR driver, including a Day-Glo green ADIDAS across the front of his hat. He's a distinctive-looking character, with a Cheshire-cat grin and a close-cropped beard. His smile is so wide that it has permanently etched deep creases into his cheeks.

I was sitting right next to Kevin, so I couldn't help but eavesdrop. He and Alex were talking about Adam Ondra, the twenty-three-year-old Czech wunderkind, currently the world's best sport climber, who had just arrived in the valley to attempt the second free ascent of the Dawn Wall. Apparently, he had never trad climbed before, which meant he would need to learn how to jam his fingers and hands into cracks and place protection, on the fly. For the past several months Jorgeson had been sharing "beta" via e-mail with Ondra—giving him precise details of the route's trickiest passages and strategy suggestions like where to place portaledge camps. Jorgeson had come to the valley to do some of his own climbing and to support Ondra in person, even though Ondra had stated publicly on social media that he planned to one-up Tommy and Kevin, to improve on their style, by climbing the route from the ground up, and in a more speedy fashion. Ondra had said he hoped to do it in a week. It struck me that Ondra's plan was a good thing, because it was likely to draw media attention away from Alex and his top secret mission to free solo Freerider. Alex didn't mention it to Jorgeson there in the bar, but I suspected he already knew.

A FEW DAYS LATER, I was strolling through Yosemite Village with my wife, Hampton, and our seven-month-old son, Tommy. I had vowed to avoid one of the biggest problems of my first marriage—being away from home too much—by bringing Hampton and Tommy with me on my travels whenever possible. *National Geographic* had rented me a cabin in the town of Foresta, a small inholding within the park that was a twenty-minute drive from the valley floor, so that I could report closely on the unfolding story of what would certainly be the most sensational rock climb in history. I'd been ribbing Hampton about how unfair it was that she got to stay in a house on her first visit to Yosemite, whereas I had only graduated to having a roof over my head after years of hiding out in the talus field above Camp 4. I promised that one day soon I would give her and Tommy a tour of my favorite caves.

The village is home to most of the park's rangers, and some of the more senior ones live in a row of houses that fringe a meadow below the imposing Northwest Face of Half Dome, a cliff that illustrates the power of glaciation perhaps better than any other geologic feature on earth. "That's the wall that Alex free soloed in 2008," I told Hampton, gesturing toward the dome that looks like it has been sliced in half with a guillotine. Hampton looked up and just shook her head.

I texted Alex to see if he was around. "Yeah, come say hi. I'm hangboarding at Mikes," he replied.

We found Alex a few minutes later sitting in his van, which was parked in the driveway of Mike Gauthier, Yosemite National Park's chief of staff. The house is a one-story ranch with a large attached garage. A fire pit and a weathered picnic table sit in the middle of a yard that has been left to grow wild. Through the massive oak trees growing all around the house I could see sections of upper Yosemite Falls. California was in the midst of a record-breaking drought, and the waterfall was barely a trickle. Normally, the falls' roar fills the valley, but on this day it was silent.

"Hey, Hampton," said Alex, giving her a hug. They had met once previously in Moab, the day before I asked her to marry me halfway up a four-hundred-foot sandstone rock spire (the plan had been to propose on the summit, but Hampton doesn't climb much and I had underestimated the route). Alex took Tommy's tiny hand—about the size of one segment on Alex's index finger—and gave it a shake. "Nice to meet you, Thomas," he said, looking our little man in the eyes with a bemused smile. "Welcome to my home," he said proudly, gesturing toward the interior of his Dodge Ram ProMaster 2500. He had traded in his old van, a smaller Ford Econoline, after nine years and 190,000 miles. A futon set on a wooden frame about three feet above the carpeted floor took up the rear. Underneath was a storage area where he kept his climbing gear in crates. Above the bed sat a bookshelf, about two-thirds full. It was dark back there and I couldn't quite make out the titles, but I recognized several guidebooks to Yosemite and the Sierras, and I supposed the rest were probably environmental nonfiction, the subject he was currently most passionate about. Across from the door, a countertop ran from the edge of the bed to the back of the driver's seat. It housed a propane range with a double-burner stove top and a small oven below. "My friends convinced me I should have an oven," he explained, "but I don't know. I'm not much of a baker." A small sink without a faucet was adjacent to the stove, beneath which sat a minifridge. Cabinets made of some kind of blond hardwood, perhaps maple, hung above and below the countertop. The handles were different-colored lobes from Black Diamond Camalots—a type of camming device. It was an eye-catching detail added by his friend and climbing partner Mason Earle, whom Alex had hired to customize the interior.

"My ankle is doing a lot better," he said, pulling up his pant leg. And indeed, it did look a lot less swollen and bruised than it had two days before. "Sanni's mom turned me on to this castor oil compress I've been wrapping it in at night and it seems to be working."

Perhaps the van's most distinctive feature was the hangboard bolted above the door. Two feet wide and eight inches in height, it was routed from a single piece of yellow poplar featuring variously sized grips intended for finger strengthening. BEASTMAKER 2000 was branded into the wood in the upper right corner. "Check out these forty-five-degree slopers," he said, fingering two ramp-like grips on the top of the board. I reached up to feel them. They were baby-bottom smooth, with nowhere to grab. "Supposedly there are humans that can hang these," he said, "but I'm skeptical." All the holds on the Beastmaker are designed to mimic the features a climber might find on real rock. On the outside of the bottom row are the "monos"—two divots just big enough for the tip of one finger. Rumor has it that Ondra can do a one-arm pull-up on this tiny pocket.

Alex had spent the morning mini-tracking a route called the Excellent Adventure. It's a difficult crack climb, rated 5.13, that breaches an eight-foot horizontal roof at the top of the flawless pillar of gray and orange granite known as the Rostrum. Excellent Adventure is a variation to the last pitch of the North Face (5.11c), a route that many believe to be the best free climb in Yosemite. Peter Croft was the first to free solo the North Face of the Rostrum in 1985; then, two years later, he combined it with Astroman—the free solo linkup that established him as the boldest valley climber of his generation. All told, Croft soloed the North Face of the Rostrum a total of fifty or sixty times, sometimes downclimbing it. And it was during one of his many forays up this wall that he spotted the line that would become the Excellent Adventure. I can still remember the photo that ran in *Climbing* magazine back in 1989 when Croft and Dave Shultz did the first ascent. At the time it was one of the hardest pitches in Yosemite, and to this day it is rarely climbed.

"I climbed it with one rock shoe and one approach shoe, and it felt pretty good," said Alex. "I might try to scramble it when my leg feels better," he added nonchalantly.

I nodded and said nothing. In my previous incarnation as Mr. Safety, I might have called him out. *Free solo the Excellent Adventure? Are you out of your mind?* But things were different now. I didn't want to say anything, or do anything, that might mess with his mojo. So instead I nodded and very quietly said, "Hmmm," as if he had just told me he was going to the store to buy some chips. Still, my mind struggled to process what I had just heard. In my years of climbing and hanging out with Alex Honnold, I've learned that when he mentions he *might* do something, he's already made up his mind he *is* doing it. And, of course, then he does do it. At times like this, I could still get caught off guard and find myself sitting there, my jaw on the proverbial floor, stupefied at the audacity this guy could wear so comfortably, like one of his well-loved red T-shirts. Evidently the injury had done nothing to disturb his confidence.

Alex looked down at his phone. Beastmaker has an app, which offers a multitude of different workouts with names like Beasty, Crimpcentric, and Pocketcentric. To complete a full workout requires hanging from the board, off and on, for an hour or so. As we chatted, the app was counting down a two-minute interval between sets. When the timer hit zero the background on the app turned from green to red.

"Time for my next burn," he said, stepping up to the board and gripping a half-inch-wide edge on the bottom row of holds with the fingertips on his right hand. He settled onto his fingers, lifted his feet in the air, and reeled himself upward with one arm. At the top, with his chin even with the bottom of the board, his head nearly touching the ceiling of the van, he locked off for a couple of seconds, then slowly lowered himself back down. Climbers call this a "one-armed negative," and before that moment I had never actually seen someone do one.

"I'm glad you guys came by," he said. "These workouts are pretty boring, so it's nice to have people to chat with between burns."

He reached for a journal with a black cover sitting on the counter and jotted down some symbols to denote the set he had just cranked off. He explained that he has different symbols for the various holds on the board. I looked over his shoulder as he flipped through a few pages. The book was filled with what looked like hieroglyphics. For years, Alex has been recording everything he does related to climbing, every route, how long it took, little notes on how it felt, plus the details of every training session, including every hangboard set. "I've got stacks of these notebooks at home," he told us, "going back to around 2004."

"Is it actually useful to record all that info?" I asked.

"Believe it or not, I do look back on it occasionally, and I can see how much I'm improving—or not." He put down the book, opened the minifridge, and pulled out some hummus and a loaf of bread. "And I've been making progress. Earlier in the summer I couldn't even hang the half-pad edge, but now I can."

There are two things Alex trains to improve his prowess on the rock—power and endurance. The latter is something that he has in almost unlimited supply, and he maintains it by running, going on long hikes, and soloing and simul-climbing a mind-numbing number of pitches every week. He once free soloed one hundred pitches in a morning—that's more than the average weekend warrior climbs in a year. His legendary endurance is a big part of what sets him apart from other climbers. And it's what has allowed him to climb things like the Yosemite and Taghia Triple Crowns. Tommy Caldwell is the only climber I know who can keep up with him in the endurance arena.

What Alex lacks, at least to his own mind, is power, or what climbers call "contact strength." The ability to hang on tiny holds hinges on two things: the thickness of finger and forearm tendons and the ratio of this tendon strength to body weight. This type of strength can be trained and increased, as Alex's black books bear out, but, just like the ability to run fast or jump high, if you're not born with unusually strong tendons, you will never rock climb at an elite level. As a climber, Alex is naturally gifted, probably more so than 99 percent of the population, but his maximum grade of 5.14c is still a full tier below the highest echelon of climbing, where the grades top out at 5.15d. The difference between sport climbing and the big-wall linkups that Alex specializes in is like the difference between sprinting and distance running. One relies primarily on power, the other on endurance. Alex is a long-distance thoroughbred, not a sprinter, and no matter how hard he trains, he will never be able to pull as hard as the world's best sport climbers, guys like Chris Sharma, Adam Ondra, and Alex Megos; just like how Haile Gebrselassie will never beat Usain Bolt in the hundred-meter dash—and Bolt will never beat Gebrselassie in the 10,000 meters. The point is that while sport climbing and big walls are part of the same sport, they're entirely different disciplines. One of the things that makes climbing unique, though, is that the different disciplines can be combined. The Dawn Wall, which combined powerful cutting-edge sport climbing with the drawn-out effort of a medieval siege, is a perfect example. Tommy Caldwell told me in Morocco that in 2014 he invited Alex to join him on the Dawn Wall when Kevin got hurt. But Alex declined because he didn't think he was strong enough. "I've only climbed 5.14c," he told Tommy, "so how do you expect me to climb 5.14d up on El Cap?"

"I think Alex was selling himself short," Tommy told me. "He could do it; I'm just not sure if he has the attention span for something like the Dawn Wall."

Since I first met Alex, he has always been quick to point out climbers who can crank harder than him: "You know Alex Megos did Realization in one afternoon, right? That's just sick." (Realization is widely regarded as the world's first 5.15a, established by Chris Sharma in 2001.) It bothers Alex that he's lauded as one of the world's best rock climbers, when there are teenagers popping up in climbing gyms all over the country who can pull harder than he can. Earlier in the year he recounted a story of getting burned off by a fourteen-year-old girl at an indoor climbing center in Denver: "I was like, wow, I can't climb that route. I wish I could climb as hard as that little girl." He routinely gets questions about whether he will compete in the first Olympic climbing competition, which will take place in Tokyo in 2020. "People don't get it," he said. "I just can't perform at that level."

AFTER A FEW MORE SETS, the app said it was time for a longer break, so Alex sat down on the floor with his back against the cabinet and ate his sandwich. I passed him little Tommy, and Alex plopped him into his lap. After a few minutes, Tommy, who had recently learned to sit up, began leaning forward, which turned into a slow-motion fall. There was plenty of time for Alex to grab him, and Hampton and I both assumed that's what would happen. But for some reason, Alex just sat there. Tommy toppled out of his lap and bonked his head on the corner of the doorframe. It was one of those wipeouts where the baby doesn't cry at first, making you think, *Maybe it wasn't as bad as it looked*—then he explodes like a volcano. Tommy's ear-splitting wails soon filled the van. Hampton scooped him up and gave me an annoyed look that said, *What the fuck is up with your friend?*

"Wow, I just crippled little Tommy," said Alex with a sheepish look on his face. "Sorry about that. I guess I'm not cut out to be a father."

A few minutes later, Sanni pulled up in a green Subaru. "Hey, everyone," she said, hopping up into the van and cooing over Tommy for a minute before wrapping her arms around Alex. She had spent the past two weeks hiking the John Muir Trail, a 215-mile trek through the Sierra wilderness. She had started in Yosemite Valley the week before and ended on the summit of Mount Whitney, the highest point in the continental United States, 14,505 feet above sea level. The back of her truck was filled with groceries she had bought outside the park, and she set to work stocking everything into the van.

JIMMY PICKED me up the next morning at eight A.M. An electrical storm had blown through overnight. A massive lightning strike had awoken Hampton and me in the middle of the night. It shook the foundation of our little cabin. The lightning had struck a tree outside Jimmy's house, just up the hill from ours. The tree came down, taking out power to all of Foresta and landing on the roof of Jimmy's brand-new van. "Can you believe this shit?" he said, pointing at the crunched-in roof.

We drove down into the valley, past El Cap Meadow and Yosemite Falls, to the Upper Pines Campground, where we found the Caldwells in Site 68. The Pines is located near the head of the valley, and the towering walls to the east—namely, Washington Column, Half Dome, and Tenaya Peak—block the sun until mid-morning. The temperature gauge on Jimmy's dash read thirty-eight degrees. The Caldwells' van was parked next to a picnic table. The door was open, but the windshield was frosted. Tommy emerged carrying his seven-month-old daughter, Ingrid, who was chewing happily on a toothbrush. I had never met Becca, Tommy's wife, but when she came out with Fitz, their three-year-old son, I realized that I had run into her at the post office the day before. Strangely, I had briefly mistaken her for Beth Rodden, Tommy's first wife, a top female climber who lives in Yosemite. They are both good-looking, athletically built women with long brownish blond hair and blue eyes.

CHEYNE, MIKEY, JIM, AND CLAIR—all of whom had been on the crew in Morocco, plus a new camera assistant named Jacob Bain, fanned out around Alex. I hung back, hiding behind the van so I wouldn't be in the shot. When they were fully out of view, I trailed along, keeping several hundred feet behind.

I caught up as Alex and Tommy were gearing up at the base of a climb called the Great Escape. The valley runs from east to west and dead-ends below Half Dome, above which looms the Sierra high country, an alpine zone of rocky peaks that form the crest of the Sierra Nevada. East-west is an ideal orientation for a rock-climbing venue, because it means that the cliffs lining the valley, for the most part, face north or south. Having both sunny and shady offerings makes it possible to rock climb year-round in Yosemite—yet another reason it's the world's climbing mecca. Climbers always prefer to be a little cool rather than a little warm, because chilled rock offers excellent friction, whereas hot rock does not. And even though it was only in the upper thirties, Tommy and Alex still preferred to climb in the shade rather than in the blazing sun, which was now baking the cliffs on the other side of the valley. Typically, on a day like today, the temperature differential between the north- and south-facing sides, a distance of less than a mile, was probably thirty to forty degrees.

Unlike most of the routes in Yosemite, the Great Escape is a bolted face climb, similar to the type of routes these guys had climbed together in Morocco. It's rated 5.11+, and it fit the goals for the day because Tommy had a family outing planned and could spare only two hours to climb with Alex. "Check it out," said Alex, holding up his rock shoe. "You can actually see the scuff mark on the rubber where my ankle impacted with the rock."

Tommy grabbed the shoe and inspected it. "How did it turn?"

"Like this," said Alex, using his hand to simulate the way his ankle rolled outward when it hit.

"Is that your worst climbing injury?" said Tommy.

"Yeah, maybe the most acute because I'm crippled and I can't climb hard. I honestly thought it would be doing a lot better by now. It's been twenty-four days."

The conversation turned to Adam Ondra. The day before, as a warm-up for the Dawn Wall, he had attempted to free climb the Nose, the same route Warren Harding pioneered up El Cap back in 1957. It remains the cliff's most popular route, and for most climbers it's the most accessible way to scale El Cap using a combination of aid- and free-climbing tactics. Five years after El Cap was first free climbed via the Salathé Wall by Todd Skinner and Paul Piana in 1988, the Nose still eluded climbers seeking an all-free ascent.

"IT GOES, BOYS."

In climbing lore, these now-famous words rival even George Mallory's "because it's there" quip about why he wanted to climb Mount Everest. It was 1993, and a new giant, standing all of five feet two inches tall, had emerged. Lynn Hill, like many other notable rock climbers of her generation, grew up in Southern California. As a youth she competed in gymnastics, then started climbing in 1975 at the age of fourteen. By the late 1970s she had fallen in with the Stonemasters, whom she routinely amazed by matching and even one-upping the best male climbers of her generation. By the mid-1980s she was competing on the World Cup and trading titles with Catherine Destivelle, a Frenchwoman who until Hill's ascendancy was widely regarded as the best female rock climber in the world. In 1986, Hill finished second to Destivelle in the famed Arco Rock Master competition. In an interview with *Rock and Ice* magazine in 1992, Hill tells of the time she asked one of the Rock Master officials why there was such a disparity in prize money between the men and women. His response: "If the women climb without their tops, then we'll pay them the same."

Hill's first attempt to free climb the Nose was in 1989, but neither she nor her partner Simon Nadin were able to master the tiny crack splitting the Great Roof on pitch 22. She returned to competitions and the next year won a World Cup in which she bested not only all the women but all the men as well. That same year she became the first woman to climb the grade of 5.14. She chose a route called Masse Critique because the first ascensionist, a Frenchman named J. B. Tribout, in a fit of a chauvinist hubris, had declared the route so hard that a woman would never climb it. Hill once again proved she was as good as, if not better than, the best male climbers. In 1993, in the best shape of her life, she returned to Yosemite with the goal of free climbing the Nose. She worked the route for several months, and then over five days in May she climbed it from bottom to top, leading every pitch. She gave the route a 5.13b rating (it has since been upgraded to 5.14a). At the time it was the most difficult big-wall free climb in the world. But she wasn't done. She trained fervently for another six months, then returned and climbed the route free in a day. More than twenty years later, it was still ranked by many as the greatest rock-climbing feat in history.

Ondra, keeping to the tradition of one-upmanship, had announced that he would try to on-sight the route—in a day. Ondra's stated objective would be like a figure skater nailing a new Olympic-caliber routine on her first try or a pianist sight-reading

Rachmaninoff's third piano concerto and playing it flawlessly. He made it to pitch 22 without falling, but after the Great Roof spat him off several times in a row, he abandoned the free-climb attempt and just motored as fast as he could for the top, climbing mostly free but pulling on the occasional piece of gear when he needed to.

"I texted him one word: 'Respect,'" said Alex.

THE NEXT MORNING we were back at the Great Escape, though I wasn't quite sure why because Alex didn't have a partner to climb with. *Would he actually try to solo it with a bum ankle?* This was hard to imagine, considering he hadn't managed to get a rock shoe on his right foot yet, and the Great Escape is known as a sandbag; even to Alex, who is infamous for downgrading. (He once declared a route I was struggling on in Maine a 5.6—we later found out it's six grades harder.)

Alex spilled a pile of rock shoes out of his pack at the base. "I'm gonna mini-track it one more time and if it feels good I will probably scramble it," he said. After some experimentation with the variously sized shoes, Alex slipped a size 41 onto his good foot and an approach shoe on his hurt foot. "I'm going to switch to the rock shoe higher up where it gets harder," he said, clipping a right-footed size 42 to the back of his harness. His final piece of preparation before he set off up the wall was to girth hitch a sling to the belay loop on his harness to use as a tether for the transitions at the anchors. But instead of attaching it to a locking carabiner, which is standard practice, he used a non-locker. Locking carabiners have a mechanism that prevents the gate from opening accidentally. It's a cardinal rule that if a climber is clipped to a single carabiner, it should be a locker. In all my years of climbing, Alex is the only one I've ever seen who routinely breaks this rule. I call lockers "daddy biners," and in recent years I have been using them for clipping protection midpitch. *Well, at least he's using a tether,* I thought. In Borneo he sometimes didn't even attach himself to the anchors.

When he touched back down thirty minutes later, he announced that he was heading off to "take a poo."

"It's funny," he said, "because I already went, but once I got up there and started visualizing all the moves and imagining climbing them without a rope, I suddenly had to go again. I guess it's kind of true what they say about pooping yourself when you're afraid."

When he returned a few minutes later, he sat down in the dirt and slipped back into his two different-size shoes. "My ankle hurts," he said to no one in particular as he stretched the 42 onto his still-swollen right foot. Before he left the ground, he took his phone out of the pocket of his puffy coat, gazed at the screen briefly, and stuffed it back in. I assumed he was checking the time. As Alex entered the first crux, a sideways move that forced him into an iron cross, his arms spread to their full index, I realized that it had been a long time since I had watched him free solo, probably not since Oman. In Morocco I waited for him on top of Rivières Pourpres, so I didn't actually witness the act. Suddenly, I felt a little sick, like I was standing on the deck of a boat hobbyhorsing in a churning sea. Some primal instinct compelled me to look away. I knew he could slip. And if he did, I didn't want to see it.

The holds are tiny. Long reaches to crimps the width of matchboxes. Footholds the size of peas. I know because I had mini-tracked the route the previous day—and I had fallen all over it. The rock is not impeccable. *Could he break off a hold?* I wondered. As if in answer, pebbles ripped down through the canopy of yellow oak leaves overhead, making a noise like a BB gun. I wasn't wearing a helmet, so I moved farther out from the base, just in case someone broke off a bigger piece, like had happened in Morocco.

I looked around for Mikey, but he had disappeared. I hiked down the hill and found him down by the trail, with his back to the wall, tinkering with his phone. He apparently had no interest in watching Alex climb.

"Why do you think he's doing this?" I asked. "Why risk his life for a nothing of a route?"

"I think he's just trying to keep himself in the free-solo mind-set," he replied. "In the long run, it's going to make the main event safer."

Right then, I heard a sharp noise. My heart skipped a beat. Mikey kept his head down, but I looked up as a sudden pang of fear constricted my throat. I saw Alex splayed out across the rock, his left arm fully outstretched, his right close in by his chest pulling sideways on a tiny black crystal, probably a basaltic intrusion, which I remembered as one of the shittiest holds on the route. Cheyne was jugging up his rope to get back above Alex. The noise was the rope slapping against the rock.

I watched for a bit. Alex flagged his right foot and hopped up on his left—one, two, three moves in a row. His movement, which I had only ever witnessed as a fluid, choreographed dance up the rock, looked all herky-jerky. There was no question—he was babying his ankle on a 5.12 free solo.

"Thirty-seven minutes round trip," he declared a few seconds after reaching the ground. "That's probably the speed record on the Great Escape. Now it's time to go spray all over the Internet."

"Why this route, Alex?" I asked.

"I heard that Dean and Stanley [Sean Leary] used to simul-climb it with five draws when they were training for the Nose record. It's something to work on while I recover. Need to keep morale up while I suffer. . . . It was interesting, though, how some of my beta didn't really work for soloing. In this one undercling crack thing I buried my finger a lot deeper than I did when I was mini-tracking, and I struggled to get it back out. I also found that I didn't like making the long reach on the last pitch because it means getting way up on my toes, which didn't feel good without a rope. It's hard to be tuned in to all these nuances when I'm rehearsing the moves. The nice thing about soloing is that you're so focused, you don't feel your ankle at all. Or if you do, you don't care."

Jimmy touched down, and the look on his face was one of stunned relief, as if he had just soloed the route too. "I was so gripped," said Jimmy, pulling his camera case from around his neck. "I had my foot pasted on this little dish when Alex was climbing past me, and it was grinding off. And he was so close. I was trying to film, but at the same time looking at my foot and just being like 'Don't come off, don't come off.' I was so worried I would barn door and swing into him. I was totally overgripping all my gear, and I don't even remember pressing the record button. I was worried I forgot, but I didn't. I got the shot. I'm just never going to get used to that."

"Did you switch lenses?" asked Cheyne, who had also touched down.

"I totally chickened out," said Jimmy. "I didn't even reposition the whole time Alex was climbing." Jimmy saw me taking notes on my iPhone and added, "We are definitely way more gripped than Alex." Alex, a bemused smile on his face, just looked at Jimmy and shrugged.

THAT NIGHT ALEX invited me to go climbing the next day with him and Sanni. It rained overnight and the rock was still wet in the morning, so we made a plan to meet at two P.M. When I got to the van Alex was hanging from the Beastmaker by one arm and Sanni was sitting on the bed. Grunge metal played in the background. "What music is this?" I asked.

"Apocalyptica; it's cellos playing Metallica."

"Never heard of it. What else is on the playlist?"

"Tool, Nine Inch Nails." Alex grabbed a handful of M&M'S from a large bag on the counter and shoved them into his mouth.

"You need to take it easy on the sugar," Sanni said. Alex looked at her blankly. "He's been bingeing on M&M'S," Sanni said, catching my eyes.

"You know they have linked excess sugar consumption to migraines," I said to Alex. I've witnessed him suffer from debilitating headaches several times, including the one in Morocco that kept him in bed for most of a day.

"I've heard that," said Alex, "but I'm not sure it applies in my case. I've never noticed any kind of correlation."

It was three P.M. by the time we finally left the van. Alex and Sanni jumped on their bikes and said they'd meet me at the base of Lower Yosemite Falls. It took me a while to find a parking spot, and I figured they'd be waiting for me, but Alex and Sanni were just pulling up when I arrived. Sanni hopped off her bike shakily. She looked like she'd been in a fight since I'd last seen her ten minutes ago. Her black tights were ripped, her hair was askew, and she was limping.

"What the hell happened to you?"

"She swerved to get around a tourist and basically just ate it," said Alex, answering for her. "I'm afraid she's not a very good biker."

"I landed on my knee," said Sanni, pulling up her tights. Her knee was red and swollen and sported a golf ball–size knob.

"Wow, Sanni, if that was my leg I think I'd be going to the clinic," I said.

"I'm fine," she replied as she limped into the woods and hid her bike behind a tree. "Let's hike up to the base and I'll see how it feels."

I looked at Alex. "Some serious grit."

He raised his shoulders and gave me a smirk. "I know," he

replied. "Her attitude is awesome. It's probably the main reason we're still together."

By the time we got to the base of the climb ten minutes later, Sanni was slipping on her harness. I flaked out the rope, and Alex started whistling, soon joined by Sanni. The tune was vaguely familiar, but I couldn't quite place it. Were they consciously trying to entertain me, or was this just how they rolled?

"What song was that?" I asked, when they finished.

"The theme song for *Jurassic Park*," said Alex. "It's one of my favorite movie soundtracks. You know how much I love movie soundtracks, right? I've told you about that, haven't I? It's something I picked up from Peter Croft. He got me into it."

Before he set off, Alex teed up another song—"The Red" by a band called Chevelle—and shoved his iPhone in his hip pocket. As he scampered up a bushy corner, the grunge metal reverberated off the three-hundred-foot cliff.

"Place a piece, por favor," called up Sanni, when he was a hundred feet up without having put in any protection. Alex, heeding Sanni's request, threw a sling around a tree growing out of a crack and clipped his rope.

"Merci beaucoup," called Sanni.

WHEN ALEX HAD CLIMBED TWO hundred feet above the ground, Sanni and I began simul-climbing behind him. I was tied into the end of the rope, and Sanni was clipped into a knot—called a cow's tail—about twenty feet in front of me. The route was rated 5.10, a hike for Alex. As if to confirm this fact, Alex was wearing his approach shoes. For Sanni and me, this climb, called the Surprise, required careful execution. And since we were simul-climbing, we both had to match our movement to each other and to Alex. When he moved up, we moved up; when he stopped, we stopped. The difficulty with simul-climbing is that sometimes the leader will stop at an easy part to place a piece of protection, while the climber below is in the middle of a crux. Sometimes you have no choice but to keep moving, because you know you'll fall if you try to hang out for too long in the middle of a hard move. Since you're still moving, but the leader isn't, the rope slackens, which means if you do fall, you'll take a whipper, just like if you were leading. You can imagine what this would feel like for the person leading to whom your rope is tied. And if they happened to be a long way above their last piece, the resulting fall could be catastrophic. To prevent us from violently ripping him off the wall, Alex had fed his rope through a Mini Traxion that he attached to a solid piece just as we left the ground. It was the same tactic he had used in Morocco while climbing the Triple Crown with Tommy.

By the time Sanni and I got to the crux near the top of the route, Alex was in the woods, belaying us off a tree. I looked up and spotted what appeared to be a loose block on the slope above us. If I fell, I'd pluck Sanni off, and we'd both go flying across the face. The rope would rake across the slope above us, and if it snagged the television-size boulder sticking out of the sandy dirt, it could pry it loose. I'd seen this kind of thing happen. Once, while rappelling from the east face of Mount Babel in the Canadian Rockies, I had gone down the wrong way, and when I tried to swing over onto the correct line, my rope dislodged a melon-size rock that landed on my thigh, nearly breaking my leg. I knew from hard experience, and from studying the circumstances surrounding the fatal accidents that seemed to befall members of the climbing tribe every month or two, that most climbing accidents happen in an instant. One second, life is grand—the next, you are dying. I pictured what would happen if the rock came loose. It was roundish so it would roll easily. The slope below it was steep. If we both fell, the load would be more than three hundred pounds, which would elongate the rope, making it skinnier and, therefore, easier to sever. I remembered a time I was guiding on Cannon Cliff in New Hampshire, and my client had found himself in a similar situation. "Hey," I called down to him, "please be very careful, you're in a no-fall zone."

"Please don't say things like that to me," said the man, who was clearly irritated. "I would rather not know."

"If you want to hide from the danger, and not have your eyes wide-open, this probably isn't the right sport for you," I shot back. I don't know if he quit climbing, but I never heard from him again. I was pretty sure neither Alex nor Sanni saw this possibility for things to go badly wrong. This time I said nothing, but I climbed as if I was free soloing, hyperfocused, my fingers turning white as I overgripped the final set of tiny face holds leading up into the woods.

"ALEX KNOCKED ON MY FRONT DOOR," said Tommy. "It was shortly after you had all returned from Morocco. He walked in and he was kind of limping, which was a little strange. Then he started crying, which totally wigged me out because Alex just doesn't cry. He said he had fallen free soloing in Morocco. He lifted up his pants and his leg was all messed up. Then he pulled up his sleeve and a bone fell out onto my sofa. I was like, 'Dude, what are you doing here? You need to go to the hospital.' And then I started looking at all you guys and I got really mad. I woke up and I was like, *Wow, there's really something going on here that I hadn't let myself consciously digest.* It was an incredibly vivid dream."

It was nine thirty in the morning, and the valley was soaked from a downpour the night before. Tommy and I sat in camp chairs in one of the only dry spots we knew of beneath a fifteen-foot-tall egg-shaped rock called the MSG boulder. The overhanging face rising above the backs of our camp chairs proffered a difficult boulder problem that Tommy had climbed a few years ago. From where I sat I could finger the first hold, which was caked white with climber's chalk.

El Capitan, the granite monolith around which all our lives seemed to rotate, was visible through the widely spaced lodgepole pines that grew from the wet, loamy earth. The cliff was slicked with water, its sides gleaming. Mist rose from the meadow beneath it. Between El Cap and the Woodlot stood Ribbon Fall, which spills from an alcove on a 1,500-foot cliff just west of El Capitan. It was pumping from the recent rain, which filled the air with soothing white noise.

Tommy and his family were leaving Yosemite that afternoon, and I had asked him if we could chat about Alex. I was curious how he was feeling about our mutual friend's crazy plan now that he'd had more time to think about it.

The day that he fell on the Freeblast (the lower ten pitches of Freerider), Alex called Tommy to tell him what happened. They were supposed to meet up a few days later, but it didn't appear that Alex would be climbing with Tommy anytime soon. "When he called, the first thing I thought about was the dream," said Tommy. "I said to Alex, 'Whoa, I just had this crazy dream about you falling.' And then it hit me—this [Freerider] *is something he could very well die on.*"

"Did it make you feel like maybe you should be trying to talk him out of it?" I asked.

"I don't really feel like it's my role to talk him out of it. Part of me wants him to do this thing that's obviously very important to him. And if I was in his situation, I don't know if I could not try it. On the other hand, I think that him falling is a real possibility. And I hadn't let myself go there. I went and climbed the Freeblast the other day partly because I was just curious how it would feel to free solo it. Every time I have climbed that part of El Cap, I've kind of felt lucky to get through it. I'm like, 'Wow, I didn't slip.'"

"What do you think is driving him to do this?"

"I think he is driven by mastery. He listens to soundtracks of superhero movies and stuff like that," said Tommy, chuckling. "He likes to envision himself as this larger-than-life superhero. Which he kind of is."

"What about the film? Do you think it's putting pressure on him?"

"I grew up in this world where filming and publicizing things was very much looked down upon," replied Tommy. "It was supposed to be about the purity of the climber in the landscape, and you didn't want to project outside of that. But I have also grown up taking part in competitions and I understand the appeal. And I think each younger generation veers more towards being motivated by that side of things. Alex would be trying to free solo El Cap regardless of whether it was being filmed or not, but I'm sure that being filmed is a motivator for him, and quite possibly, a really positive motivator. It gets him excited because I think a lot of the appeal is wanting to look like a superhero to the masses—and that's not going to happen without a film. If you look at people like Peter Croft and the free soloists of the past, they did it under that old-school ethos. They didn't tell anybody about it, and the people in that world admired them for that, while people outside of that world didn't really care because they didn't know it was happening. I think Alex wants everybody to care."

"How do you think this ends? If he pulls this off, do you think he can be content with it as his ultimate climb and then maybe start winding things down?"

"It's hard to say this"—Tommy paused and looked down at the ground, then looked me in the eyes, wearing a grave expression—"but I think Alex will probably just continue doing this until he dies. If

I was younger I wouldn't say it like that, but I've seen that happen a lot in climbing. Everybody that I know that pushes it that hard in a really risky endeavor dies. I can't think of any exceptions to that, and he pushes it harder than anybody. I like to think that Alex is so good that it's not that dangerous, but I know that it's Russian roulette."

TOMMY MAY BE THE ONLY person who can keep up with Alex in the mountains, but there's one thing he won't do: climb without a rope. From an early age, his father drilled into him the family ethic of avoiding needlessly reckless pursuits. And by needlessly reckless he meant two specific types of climbing: Himalayan alpinism and free soloing.

"I'd be curious to know if there's any free soloist who has a family with a strong mountain background. It's almost easier to have a family that is oblivious to the whole thing," says Tommy.

The wisdom of his dad's edict has been borne out over the years. Tommy says he can think of at least ten times that he has fallen unexpectedly while climbing. Alex says he's never fallen unexpectedly, but Tommy points to several instances when he has done precisely that, including the last climb they did in Morocco. Alex was following Tommy's lead when he broke a hold on a 5.10 pitch and fell. When Tommy called him on it, Alex said, "If I was free soloing I would never have grabbed that hold."

"Maybe that's true," Tommy says, "but what if he didn't recognize that it's a loose hold? I once had a bad fall on El Capitan where the sole of my shoe just ripped off."

In 2014, while descending from a marathon linkup of seven peaks on Patagonia's Fitzroy massif, Tommy and Alex were discussing a familiar topic among all climbers: Were the risks worth the reward? Tommy told Alex that his risk calculus had changed since he became a father—he'd become more conservative as a climber. Alex replied bluntly that Tommy's family "would be fine without him." Tommy wasn't offended; Alex has no children, and he comes from a family that supposedly never used the "L word." Tommy understood the remark as perhaps reflecting Alex's own view of himself, that he wouldn't be unduly missed if he died soloing. Later, Tommy and Alex were crossing a glacier when Alex disappeared into a crevasse. For a few seconds, Tommy thought Alex might be lost somewhere in the bowels of the glacier. Then Alex climbed out of the hole and started giggling. "I was like, 'Hmmm,'" says Tommy. "Something's not quite right about this guy."

THE GROUND WAS STILL WET in Foresta the next morning, so I figured Alex would take the day off from climbing. But by mid-morning the sun was shining and the ground seemed to be dry. I was buzzing from multiple cups of coffee, and I got this strange feeling that I might be missing something important. I texted a couple of people, but no one responded. So I tried Jacob.

"Where are you guys?"

"Rostruming"

"Is he doing it?"

"Yes."

I frantically threw some climbing gear into my pack while Hampton got Tommy into his car seat. We arrived at the pull-off above the Rostrum on Highway 41 half an hour later. I climbed over the wall and wandered down a weathered slab, taking care to avoid the wet patches. The rock was pockmarked with nooks and crannies, most of which were filled with water. As the slab dropped away, the summit of the Rostrum came into view, where half a dozen people were tinkering with a giant camera crane perched at the lip of the cliff. Alex, wearing a bright red shirt, waved, as did a couple of the other guys. I worked my way toward the lip of a six-hundred-foot north-facing cliff that sits adjacent to the Rostrum, scoping for a place where I could watch the climb. From where I sat I could see most of the Excellent Adventure. Alex would climb all of the 5.11 North Face route (often just called the Regular Route or the Rostrum) as a warm-up leading to the 5.13 variation at the top. I couldn't see any of the Regular Route because it was hidden around a corner, but I knew it would take Alex only forty-five minutes or so to dispatch the lower six pitches.

Above the summit and a few miles to the northwest I could see the burned meadows of Foresta, and as I strained to spot our cabin, my eye was drawn to the thousands of orange ponderosa pines that lay scattered across the surrounding hills. The national forest service estimates that 66 million trees died across the Sierra Nevada as a result of the severe drought that plagued California from 2010 to 2016. A third of those trees had died just in the last year. Lack of groundwater dried out and weakened these majestic trees and left them susceptible to an infestation of pine beetles. I had just seen a bulletin about the pine beetle on a message board down in the village. It said that if the drought continued, every ponderosa in the Sierra Nevada would eventually die.

A FEW MINUTES LATER, Alex appeared silhouetted on the edge of the buttress, fifty feet below the Excellent Adventure. Before scrambling down to this vantage point, I had briefly debated not watching him at all. The Great Escape had been a distressing experience I didn't particularly want to repeat. But in the end I knew that as a reporter for *National Geographic* I needed to witness it. As soon as Alex came into view, it was obvious that today something was different. Perhaps it was my position, which offered a stunning bird's-eye perspective of a man laying down all his chips for the chance to tread on the razor's edge between life and death. It felt different to be watching from above rather than from below—where he'd land if anything went wrong. But there was something else, and as Alex stemmed up the overhanging corner below the roof, I realized what it was: The herky-jerky, gimpy-footed movement I had witnessed on the Great Escape was gone, replaced by a relaxed and proficient smoothness. Alex had found the flow, he was having fun, and the climbing appeared easy—despite the fact that it was anything but.

With his legs split wide, bridged between the pages of the granite open book, he made a long reach with his right hand to a horizontal flake above him. Every other climber who had scaled this route since the moves were first deciphered by Croft and Shultz seventeen years earlier had placed a camming device in the crack created by the flake to establish a fail-safe anchor point. Alex, unencumbered by such contrivances, would trust his continued existence to the four fingers on his right hand.

But if Alex was carrying the psychological weight of knowing that his life hung eight hundred feet in the air from a few bits of flesh and bone, he didn't show it. Instead, he dangled one-armed from the plate of rock, taking his time. Green forest painted the gap formed between his horizontal red-shirted body and the gray slab of rock from which his slender human form was suspended.

And then, in the middle of what may have been one of the boldest feats of athleticism ever, Alex did something that was surprising, casual, arrogant, and inspiring all at the same time. He reached down with his free hand to adjust his shirt where it had bunched up under the strap of his chalk bag. He hung there for far longer than was necessary, until finally, like a coiled spring, he surged over the ninety-degree lip of the roof to a fingertip edge that he latched with his left hand. With his arms stretched to his full ape index, he smoothly drew his legs over the lip like a cobra rising from a snake charmer's basket. Now there was nothing left but forty feet of heroic jamming up the final crack that sliced the gray shield of rock guarding the summit.

When he topped out, Alex stood at the cliff's edge, his heels inches from the void. He didn't yell or even speak, but his head bobbed up and down as if he was nodding affirmatively. I flashed back to a YouTube video of Dean Potter free soloing Heaven in 2006. When he pulled over the lip, Dean went ballistic. Fists balled, every muscle in his body flexed, he screamed at the top of his lungs like a Viking warrior filled with bloodlust. Alex, in contrast, just stood there silently. The only noticeable thing he did was hold his arms out in front of him, like a weight lifter admiring his muscles after a difficult set. It was something I'd seen him do many times, but I couldn't tell if it was vanity or if he was examining the thickness of the blood-gorged veins in his forearms as a way to gauge how pumped he had gotten, which is to say how hard he had pushed himself.

"You saw all that, right?" said Jimmy, slapping me a high five when I arrived on top a few minutes later.

"Uh, yeah," I replied, looking directly at Alex, who was sitting a few feet away. "It was only the sickest thing I've ever witnessed in my life." I took a step toward Alex and clasped his hand. "Nice work, my man."

"Thanks, dude." His brown eyes were wide open and twinkling. His mom has described them as "cow eyes," and they are that big, but a cow would never look at you the way Alex was looking at me right then. He was a man wide-open, stripped of all the protective layers we wear to shield us from the world. The smile he wore was so big and so genuine that it gave him an aura, a glow I had seen on him only a few times since I'd known him. Once was after he led the Emily pitch in Borneo, the other when he climbed the Rainbow Arch in Chad. And I'd seen it a third time, in the five-minute film of him soloing El Sendero Luminoso in Mexico. He was high on the wall, hanging from a fingertip edge, when he looked back over his shoulder at a cameraman hanging in the air above him. The look on his face—it's nothing more than the joy of knowing that life cannot be experienced more fully.

Peter Croft once explained the feeling you get from free soloing as

> a heightened type of perception. A little edge that you need to stand on looks huge—everything comes into high relief. That's just what happens to your body and your mind when you're focused intensely on the feedback you're getting from the environment and there are no other distractions. You become an instinctive animal rather than a person trying to do a hard climb, and that perception doesn't immediately go away when you get to the top. It dulls over time, but for a while it feels like you almost have super senses. Everything is more intense—the sounds of the swifts flying around or the colors of the sun going down. A lot of times I don't want to go down, I don't want it to end.

I had been reading a book I found in the Yosemite gift shop called *The Things They Carried*. In it, the author, Tim O'Brien, writes about his personal experience as a soldier in the Vietnam War.

After a firefight, there is always the immense pleasure of aliveness. The trees are alive. The grass, the soil—everything. All around you things are purely living, and you among them, and the aliveness makes you tremble. You feel an intense, out-of-the-skin awareness of your living self—your truest self, the human being you want to be and then become by the force of wanting it. . . . There is a kind of largeness to it, a kind of godliness.

"You weren't here when I topped out," said Alex. "But I was really fired up. I think that's the best solo I've ever done."

"Sort of the opposite of Morocco, huh?" I said.

"Yeah, totally. I felt really good on this one."

Maybe that's all any of us need to know. Maybe we're all guilty of ruthlessly overanalyzing Alex's motivations—like we do our own. Perhaps Alex is simply trying to "live deep and suck out all the marrow of life," as Henry David Thoreau wrote in *Walden*. Sebastian Junger, in his book *War,* which chronicles the fifteen months he spent embedded with a platoon in Afghanistan's Korengal Valley, explained it like this:

> For a nineteen-year-old at the working end of a .50 cal during a firefight that everyone comes out of okay, war is life multiplied by some number that no one has ever heard of. In some ways twenty minutes of combat is more life than you could scrape together in a lifetime of doing something else.

Jimmy and I looked at each other, and I knew we were both thinking that if Alex could free solo the Excellent Adventure and feel this good, he could—and he would—free solo Freerider.

Though no one said it, we sensed Alex would attempt his magnum opus—soon.

A few minutes later, Alex was sitting back from the edge gathering up his things. He looked tired now. The glow had already begun to fade from his face, and I was sure his ankle must have been throbbing. I wondered if he was still buzzing inside or if the high from the best free solo of his life had already dissolved. "I'll see you in a couple days," he said, throwing his shoes and chalk bag into a small daypack. He was off to Sacramento for a fundraising event for the Honnold Foundation.

As the crew packed up the crane, I asked Dave Allfrey if I could do some mini-tracking on the six-hundred-foot rope that the camera guys had used to film Alex's climb. "Of course," he said, giving me an earnest look, "but be careful down there. And text me when you're off the wall." Alex had just free soloed a 5.13, and Dave was worried about me on a 5.11 toprope.

Everyone was gone by the time I rappelled off. The North Face of the Rostrum overhangs from top to bottom and the rope dangled in the air beneath me. I couldn't see if it had a knot in the end, but I assumed it didn't—Dave would have taken it out so the rope wouldn't get caught behind a flake when he pulled it up. As I slid downward, I plugged camming devices into the cracks as directionals to pin the rope in place over the sections I wanted to climb. My plan was to climb the Regular Route, the same line Alex had just scrambled, sans the finish on the Excellent Adventure. Four hundred feet down, I swung onto a small ledge, clipped myself to a bolt anchor, and rigged up my Mini Traxions.

The first fifty feet went smoothly, but then the crack went from three inches wide to about eight. I knew that I needed to switch from a hand jam to an arm bar, so I slid my entire arm into the crack and pressed my palm against the cold stone. This created counterpressure against the back of my elbow, which in turn caused the inside of my biceps to grind against the outside edge of the crack. I held my entire weight with the arm bar and used my core muscles to lift my left leg as high as I could. I needed to slot my knee into the crack to hold myself in place, but it wouldn't quite fit. After five minutes of grinding my knee against the rock, I slipped out of the crack and slumped onto the Mini Traxions. As I hung there dangling on the rope hundreds of feet above the Merced River, I felt weak and impotent. The first time I had climbed this route, about ten years earlier, I had on-sighted it, no falls. My peak as a climber had come and gone. As I dangled on the rope contemplating the trajectory of my own climbing career—*it all went way faster than I could have imagined*—I remembered a conversation I'd recently had with Alex.

"You can't push the physical limits forever," he told me. "I've already begun my decline, so I won't be upping the ante forever. I'm training better and climbing better and smarter than I was five or six years ago, but physiologically I'll never have the body I did when I was twenty-four. That's just the biology of it."

I understood in that moment how brief Alex's window of opportunity was. The man I had just watched perform that godly feat was thirty-one years old. In a couple of years more, he might slip far enough down the back side of the climbing arc that Freerider would be a physical impossibility. But he couldn't have done it when he was twenty-four, twenty-five, or even twenty-eight, because he wasn't ready yet. I could see quite clearly how not completing this almost preordained conclusion to his career—the ultimate climb of the world's ultimate cliff, a free solo ascent of El Capitan—would dog him to the end of his days. Perhaps he needed this climb so he could quit the high-stakes free solo game. Maybe Tommy was wrong.

ALEX AND PETER CROFT, the Yosemite icon who was still climbing hard and regularly in the valley, sat in Alex's van on the edge of El Cap Meadow. Peter had arrived in the valley the day before to take a group of designers from the North Face product development team climbing for a few days. We'd all had dinner the night before, and the design team had showed us the new line of clothing they had been working on for fall 2017.

I was perched on the wooden fence between the parking area and the meadow, trying to stay out of the way, when Jimmy waved me over to one of the production vehicles. "Here, you should listen in," he said, handing me a headset. I slipped in the earpiece just in time to hear Alex say: "I would do the top pitches today if I had to." I had dropped into the middle of the conversation, but it sounded as though Alex was imagining himself on the final ten pitches of Freerider, including the Enduro Corner and the traverse to Round Table Ledge. This section of the wall is continuously overhanging and follows a laser-cut crack that hangs half a mile in the air over Yosemite Valley. The climbing is continuous at the 5.11 and 5.12 grades, but the jams are secure, and it's the type of climbing Alex excels at, especially without a rope. Cranking rope-less up this swath of immaculate stone was a huge part of why Alex wanted to free solo El Capitan. He knew exactly how good it was going to feel. "That part of the route is sick; it would be heroic," he said to Peter. "The feeling of going over the top would be so cool."

They chatted about some random stuff for the next few minutes, including a story I had heard before, about how Peter had idolized Tarzan when he was a kid. Peter said he actually wanted to move to Africa until he realized there is a lot of disease in the jungle.

I was trying to picture how scrappy Peter must have been as a feral kid running wild in the hills of British Columbia, when Alex said, "Do you think its douchey that I have a movie crew?"

A long pause followed before Peter answered. "People asked me if I would solo Astroman again [for the camera], but I didn't want to. It was so incredibly important to be doing it for the right reasons. It was just a matter of self-preservation, because I didn't want to risk being distracted. I've just always looked at soloing as something incredibly selfish. I don't mean it negatively, more just that it's not for anyone else."

"I think I'm doing it for the right reasons," said Alex. "But yeah, from the outside it looks bad."

On Thursday, November 10, Alex headed up to the top of El Cap to camp out for a couple of nights. Over the past week he had made two day-trips to the top, working his way down the route, rehearsing different sections with his Micro Traxion. He spent most of his time on the Enduro Corner and the Boulder Problem. At the end of each of these training forays, he rappelled to the ground. The mileage was putting a lot of wear and tear on his ankle, and he'd told me that the days were so grueling he had to take rest days afterward. Alex hates rest days.

"Come in quick," he said, when I knocked on the door of the van. "You're letting all the heat out." Alex had just gotten down from his camping trip and had texted me a little while earlier to invite Chris Sylvia and me for dinner. Sylvia was in the valley to climb with me for the weekend. Sanni was frying tortillas, cheese, and refried beans on the stove top. Alex was cutting up an avocado and some green peppers. The van smelled like a Mexican restaurant. I sat sideways in the driver's seat, which doesn't turn around, and Chris took the backward-facing passenger seat. Chris and I cracked beers, and Sanni poured herself a glass of red wine. Alex sipped from his water bottle. I noticed something I hadn't seen before, probably because I hadn't been in the van with the door shut. The inside of the door was covered in a piece of wood paneling decorated with an etching of El Capitan. The cliff's major features had been carved into the wood, including the Nose, the Heart, and a long continuous line denoting Freerider.

Alex saw me looking at it. "Mason carved that; pretty awesome, huh?"

"So how did it go up there?" I asked.

"I mean, nothing is a deal breaker so far. So we'll see."

"How does the Boulder Problem feel?"

"I've done it eleven or twelve times now without falling on it. I feel pretty good about it, but it's definitely something you have to get psyched up for. I mean, it's kind of the only spot on the whole route where you have to pull hard and be really, really precise."

"Do you have it completely dialed?"

"I used to do it differently, but I've sort of pioneered some new soloing beta that feels a little bit more secure."

ALEX WOULD LATER PANTOMIME EVERY move of the crux for me, which would have been comical if it wasn't so deadly serious. "Left foot into the little thumb-sprag crack thing. Right foot into this little dimple that you can toe in on pretty aggressively so it's opposing the left hand, then you can, like, zag over across to this flat, down-pointing crimp that's small but you can bite it pretty aggressively. I palm the wall a little bit so I can pop my foot up and then reach up to this upside-down thumb-sprag crimp thing."

"How big is that hold?" I had asked.

"It's the worst hold on the route. It's maybe this big." Alex held up his thumb and forefinger about an eighth of an inch apart. "It's really small. But you're pushing into it and you have a pretty good

311

foot, and so you get it with one thumb. You stand into it, flick your left foot out to this horrible sloping foothold thing that's, like, really bad. Surprisingly, my foot's never slipped off it, even though it looks like it's going to every time."

"What if it did slip?"

"For the first move it would kind of be okay because it's all op-position between the thumb press and the right foot, so the left foot's kind of a place holder at that point. Then you push into it. You unpeel one finger so you can leave room for your other thumb, and then you lean. Then the foot matters a little bit because you lean out to this hold out left. But even then, I don't know. If the foot blew you might still be able to hold it just between tension, between the right foot, the thumb, and the other hand. Anyway, you reach out to the sloping thing. You reach back to the crimp that you initially used, and then you bring your right foot through to this slopy dish thing. Left foot way over so you're lie-backing and then sag your hips over so you can match hands. You switch to this little undercling and you can get your palm over it. You put your right foot under this down-facing chip and then you karate kick into the corner."

"Wow."

"I know. It sounds fucked up. If you count hand moves, it's, what, one, two, three, four . . ."

"You've soloed stuff like that before, though, haven't you?"

"Kind of. I don't know if I've done moves quite like that."

"Because it's especially insecure?"

"Yeah. It's legitimately pretty hard."

Sanni handed plates of food to Chris and me and made a move toward the trash with the empty bag of shredded Mexican cheese.

"What are you doing?" said Alex.

"What does it look like I'm doing?" replied Sanni. "I'm throw-ing this away."

"But there's still some left in there," he said. Sanni held up the bag, and indeed, there was a tiny pinch of yellow cheese lining the seam along the bottom—enough to make a nice meal for a small mouse. Sanni rolled her eyes and put the bag in the minifridge.

"You guys sound like an old married couple," I said.

Sanni jumped up onto the bed and cuddled in next to Alex, who was propped up with a couple of pillows, his back against the side of the van.

"Looks like there's a storm coming in," I said. The forecast for Wednesday was 100 percent rain.

"Yeah," said Alex. "It's gonna wash all my tick marks off the route, and even if the route doesn't get that wet, I'll have to go up to the top to inspect it. Depending on how much precip we get, this could be the end of the season. So I'm thinking about maybe going for it on Tuesday. But we'll see. We'll see."

There was a burning question I wanted to ask, but I couldn't bring myself to do it. *Do you feel trapped by who you have become?* Maybe I could ask him when it was all said and done, but not right now. I didn't want to mess with his psyche, and my gut told me that it was too late for anyone, especially Alex, to be questioning his motives.

Moon-eyed Alex looked at me and said, "We'll see," one more time.

THE NEXT MORNING AT FOUR A.M., Alex set off with Brad Gobright to climb the Freeblast. Gobright, who was twenty-eight at the time, is an up-and-coming climber who began free soloing a few years ago after watching videos of Alex. The year before, he had fallen on a hard, dangerous route. He was wearing a rope, but his gear ripped out of the rock, and he landed on the ground, breaking his back. Just prior to this fall he turned heads, including

Alex's, when he free soloed a route in Colorado called Hairstyles and Attitudes, a slippery 5.12c that had never been climbed before without a rope. Since his fall he has not soloed anything hard.

The biggest problem Alex had run into so far while rehearsing the various sections of Freerider was the heat. Most days, by ten A.M. the rock was baking. Hot rock is not a climber's friend. It feels greasy, and it shreds your skin. But nature trends toward a state of equilibrium, and in a narrow corridor like Yosemite, heat that builds on the valley floor has only one place to go—up. These updrafts are a daily occurrence on a hot day in Yosemite, and for a climber high on the face of El Capitan, the cooling breeze is always most welcome. Alex was hoping to time his ascent such that he would be high on the wall by the time it got hot. The plan made sense on paper, but so far every day he had worked on the route, it had still felt uncomfortably hot. The thermals weren't enough to counteract the solar radiation being absorbed by El Cap's west face. The heat was such a conundrum that Alex had been speculating about whether he might be able to time the climb to take place in the unsettled weather right before a storm, similar to the day when he had fallen on the Freeblast two months earlier.

"But then I'm playing with the possibility that it could rain when I'm up there," he had said to me after coming down from one of his baking-hot training sessions on the route. "But, hey, I've got a camera team, so I could just call them over to rescue me." His almost sarcastic tone seemed to be his way of asking, *What do you think, would that be totally douchey?*

His solution was to start at four A.M., but this meant climbing the Freeblast, and the crux sixth pitch, on which he had now fallen twice, in the dark. So there was one last piece to the puzzle: to head up there before sunrise to see how it felt to climb it by headlamp.

We were all waiting in the meadow at nine A.M. when Alex and

Brad sauntered up, followed by Clair Popkin and Jim Hurst. "How'd it go?" I asked.

"It all felt good," said Alex. "I even pioneered some new beta." He detailed the new sequence for one of the slab sections.

"How was it climbing by headlamp?"

"It was fine. Not an issue."

The night before Jimmy had asked me if I could help hike a load of gear to the top. He planned to sleep up there with Cheyne, Mikey, and Jacob so they'd be in place to drop in on fixed ropes first thing in the morning. The plan was to position camera guys at key points along the route to film Alex as the historic climb unfolded.

A few minutes later I was shoving my pack full of extra batteries and camera lenses at the parking lot adjacent to a five-hundred-foot cliff called the Manure Pile. It's actually one of the most popular and classic climbing venues in the park, but because it sits adjacent and in the shadow of El Cap, it was long ago given this less than flattering name. The summit of El Cap looms 3,000 feet above the Manure Pile. While El Cap is by far the largest and most dramatic geologic feature in Yosemite, the summit is nondescript. Were it not for a large cairn marking the spot, you might wander on the indistinguishable slabs, littered with glacial erratics and wind-stunted juniper trees, trying to find the highest point of this mountain. I have climbed El Capitan twenty-three times, and not once have I even considered trying to find the actual summit. One thing is sure: There is no easy way to get to the top of this cliff.

Hikers have a few different options. From Tamarack Flat Campground on the Tioga Road, it's a fifteen-mile round-trip. Another option is the Yosemite Falls Trail, which has the advantage of starting right from the valley floor but the disadvantage of being so long that most people can't make the round trip in a day.

Climbers have access to what is probably the easiest way to get to the top, the East Ledges, El Cap's standard descent route. This is the route Alex had been taking and was the route we would follow this morning, as we labored to gain 3,000 feet of elevation in less than a mile of hiking.

As the heat began to rise, the five of us set off up a steep, dusty trail that dead-ended below a five-hundred-foot cliff—the East Ledges. Back when I used to climb El Capitan regularly, the East Ledges was used primarily as a descent route and there were no fixed ropes you could use to go up this way. If you wanted to use it as an ascent route, as we sometimes did, you had to climb it. That was before free climbing on El Capitan and practicing routes via mini-track had become de rigueur. Nowadays, most parties hoping to free climb Freerider will spend days, if not weeks and months, mini-tracking the moves on fixed ropes.

We took turns ascending the fixed ropes. At each station, we'd wait for the call that the person ahead was off the rope; then we'd ratchet our way up the vertical wall with ascenders and foot stirrups, our heavy packs threatening to pull us over backward. From the top of the fixed lines the East Ledges route follows narrow goat paths that tunnel through thick manzanita bushes until breaking clear onto a gently angled slab of rock littered with boulders and widely spaced pine trees. As we shuffled up these slabs, our feet bent inward by the slope, we passed the top outs for some of the routes I had climbed over the years—Zodiac, Zenyatta Mondatta, Native Son, Tangerine Trip, Pacific Ocean Wall, and the king daddy of them all, the Dawn Wall. All of these routes, and many others, incise El Capitan's southeast face, which stretched before us, a grand swath of vertical and overhanging granite bookended by the Nose, where the cliff turns a corner to the west. Along the way we passed numerous stone enclosures, bivouacs built by climbers camping on top after their ascents. I recognized many of them as places where I had slept over the years. We passed the Nose and the famous tree, the object both climbers on a team have to touch before stopping the clock on an attempt at the speed record. I climbed the Nose in a day twice. In 1994 it took me twenty-three and a half hours; then, with Greg Child in 2000, I did it in thirteen hours and forty-five minutes. (The current record, set by Alex and Tommy Caldwell on June 6, 2018, stands at a mind-boggling one hour, fifty-eight minutes, and seven seconds. Some have equated the sub-two-hour time to Roger Bannister's first sub-four-minute mile in 1954.)

Jimmy and Cheyne had gone ahead. Jacob and I were following Mikey, who stopped to point out a squat, ancient-looking tree with a trunk six feet in diameter. One side of the tree was melded to a car-size boulder. The tree must have been struck by lightning at some point, because its trunk was split open, with a hollow blackened chamber inside. Large dead limbs protruded from the trunk, but it still had green needles on a few of the branches. Jacob, who seemed to know a bit about trees, said it was a western juniper and probably eight hundred to a thousand years old.

Someone had constructed a snug bivouac shelter by piling up stones on the underside of the boulder. We had passed half a dozen of these structures on the way up, but for some reason, this one incensed Mikey. He threw down his pack and began aggressively dismantling it. "This is exactly the kind of thing that's going to lead to more climbing regulations," he said, kicking down one of the walls.

We found Jimmy and the other guys sitting on a sandy ledge about thirty feet above the top out for Freerider. Jimmy was eating gummy bears and had his shirt off and his pants unzipped. "Did you guys stop at the tree?" he asked. I nodded affirmatively as I plopped down a few feet in front of him. "Did you look inside?"

"No."

"Dean's urn is in there," said Jimmy. "We scattered his ashes off the top of Freerider after his memorial." Right then, as if on cue, a raven landed on a scraggly tree a few yards away. The raven was Dean's totem.

"Hey, Dean," said Mikey.

A few days later, Jimmy posted a picture to Instagram of a raven soaring above El Cap. The caption read: "Feathered friend that visited us everyday on top of El Cap #flyfree." I figured that only a handful of his 1.5 million followers would pick up on the hidden message to the climbing tribe.

PETER GWIN, the expeditions and adventure editor at *National Geographic* magazine, had arrived the day before to help me break the news of Alex's historic climb. That night we were ensconced at my cabin, hard at work on the story, which we planned to break within minutes of Alex topping out on Freerider. Alex's impending ascent had been one of the best-kept secrets in the history of the sport, but since *National Geographic* had the exclusive, and we'd all been working on this project for months, everyone was worried that someone might scoop us. I worried most about John Branch, a sports reporter for *The New York Times,* who won a Pulitzer in 2013 for his story about the deadly Tunnel Creek avalanche in Washington State. He also wrote a feature about the Dawn Wall, and he lives just a few hours from Yosemite in San Francisco. I knew he would be following Ondra's Dawn Wall attempt, which was all over social media, and it seemed like only a matter of time before one of his contacts in Yosemite spilled the beans about what Alex was up to.

By now, virtually all of the core Yosemite climbers knew that Alex was going to free solo Freerider. There were five different teams attempting to free climb the route, and it must have been obvious to them what was going on: Alex Honnold, being filmed by Jimmy Chin and Mikey Schaefer, rehearsing the crux pitches of Freerider, a route he had already done multiple times. Why else would he be doing that if not to prep for the free solo? It was well-known in the climbing community that Alex had been eyeing this prize for years.

The climb was scheduled to begin in less than twelve hours, and Peter and I, along with a few editors back at *National Geographic* headquarters in Washington, DC, were making our final edits to the piece, much like we had when breaking other outdoor industry news. But this was different.

I was sitting at the small kitchen table. Peter sat across from me on the couch, his computer in his lap. I knew it was coming.

"Hey, I hate to bring this up, but we need to talk about what we write if Alex falls," Gwin said.

The editors at *National Geographic* had discussed this gut-wrenching scenario at length and had even debated whether or not to cover Alex's attempt. Would it be seen in some quarters as promoting dangerous behavior? Could it be construed as ghoulish voyeurism? Ultimately, they concluded that—just as *National Geographic* had covered the first ascent of Mount Everest in 1953, which many at the time considered a suicidal endeavor, and many other dangerous climbing expeditions—if Alex was going to attempt to free solo El Capitan, *National Geographic* was going to cover it, whatever the outcome.

However, Peter and I hadn't really discussed exactly what we'd say if it turned out tragically. I had thought about it and had decided that trying to file a news story in the moments after watching a friend's death would be something I couldn't do. "I'm sorry, man, but I can't go there."

"It's okay," he said. "I wrote something on the plane." A minute later an invitation to a Google doc popped up in my e-mail. The first line read:

> YOSEMITE NATIONAL PARK—Renowned climber
> Alex Honnold died Tuesday after he fell while at-
> tempting to become the first person ever to scale
> the iconic 3,000-foot granite wall known as El Cap-
> itan without using any ropes or other safety gear.

I didn't read any further.

AT 2:57 A.M., I grabbed my phone off the bedside table and turned off the alarm three minutes before it was set to buzz me awake. Thoughts had been racing through my mind all night, and I had barely slept. Peter looked equally bleary-eyed and said he hadn't slept either. We made coffee and were in the car half an hour later. At 3:55 A.M., we pulled into the meadow, where half a dozen people were milling about. We were parked across the street from Alex's van. The light was on, and I could see him through the windshield in his orange jacket, doing something at the kitchen counter. There was no sign of Sanni, but I knew she was in there, probably still cuddled up in bed. Apart from the quick meeting in the meadow after he came down from the Freeblast, I hadn't seen Alex the day before. He and Sanni had spent most of the day hanging out in the van. Sanni later told me, "That jerk was planning to not tell me." He was being "really vague," but it was obvious, by the way he was talking with the crew, that something big was going down. "Tell me, I get it. I'm not dumb," she had said to Alex, who finally admitted that he was going for Freerider in the morning.

"I remember really trying not to totally let go. I just didn't even know what to feel. Yeah, I was freaked-out, but I also didn't know he felt ready, and I was still processing the fact that he wasn't going to tell me. If I did [cry], it was probably like a tear streaming down my face, while I'm just trying to hold a conversation. I know that I wouldn't be really upset in front of Alex. . . . I was scared. It was a big deal, but it's just not the time and place where you have a major breakdown . . . just a little baby breakdown."

Alex leaned over the bed and gave Sanni a kiss. She was sound asleep. She had tossed and turned all night and hadn't fallen asleep until three thirty A.M., when Alex was moving the van from Mike's driveway down to the El Cap Meadow. Alex had slept soundly, as usual. He exited the van, and a single camera guy emerged from the shadows. When I saw who it was—my friend Pablo Durana— I did a double take. He and I had been hanging out recently, and I had made a point not to tell him what I was working on in Yo- semite. And Pablo had been discreet enough not to ask, but he knew a lot of these guys and had filmed Alex on a climbing expe- dition to Angola the year before. Apparently, the production needed another hand and had recruited him. Pablo trailed a few feet behind Alex, who strolled off wearing a small backpack and his orange puffy.

We let them get a little ways ahead; then Peter and I fell in be- hind. The moon was almost full and so bright we didn't need our headlamps. The ponderosa pines lining the trail cast moon shad- ows, which we ducked in and out of like forest sprites. We were so stealthy that we startled a family of deer, which ran off into the woods. I felt like I did as a kid when I used to wait until my par- ents fell asleep and then climb out of my window to terrorize the neighborhood with my Wiffle bat tommy gun.

We found a log and sat down to wait about a hundred yards from the start of the route. Alex's headlight flickered through a thick scrub oak that stood between us and the spot where he was getting ready, putting on his shoes, cinching on his chalk bag, and taking one last glug of water. The nature of his quest was such that he couldn't carry anything but the clothes on his back, but he had stashed some water and energy bars in a few spots along the route. Every once in a while the bottom of the wall would light up when Alex panned it with his headlamp. Things got quiet. Time stood still. Had he started up? I couldn't see his light, but the moon was so bright that perhaps he had decided to climb without his headlamp.

Two climbers carrying a big wall rack and ropes walked past, within ten feet, but they didn't see us on the log. Peter and I said nothing. I was starting to wonder what was taking so long when Pablo emerged from the shadows. He had his headlamp off and carried a large camera in one hand. "Pssst." He looked up, surprised to find us sitting a few feet away.

"Hey," he said.

"What took him so long to get going?" I asked.

"He had to run off and take a nervous poo."

"How did he seem?"

"Casual. Just like normal. He was chatty, asking me how I was doing, stuff like that. Hey, I gotta run." As soon as he moved off, Alex's light appeared above the canopy, like a tiny ship setting forth from shore into a vertical ocean of rock.

ALEX DIPPED HIS RIGHT HAND into his chalk bag, gave it a shake to make sure it got a good coating of magnesium carbonate, then sank his thick fingers into the fissure with his thumb facing down. The rock felt like he thought it would, a little cold, but not frigid. The cold was never an issue for his fingers, but already he could tell that his toes felt squeezed. This was one of the problems that he couldn't seem to find a way around. If he chose a bigger pair of shoes, his feet would be more comfortable right now, but by the time he got to the Boulder Problem, they would probably feel sloppy. So he had gone with the smaller 41s. But the footwork-intensive slab cruxes on the Freeblast would still be cold. It was essential he get high performance from his shoes on these moves. His right shoe felt especially constricting. No wonder. His ankle was still swollen and his Achilles tendon felt stiff, its flexibility restricted from being bound within the bruised muscles of his ankle for more than a month.

The crack was slightly flared, but the size, which varied from half an inch to about an inch and a quarter, fit Alex's fingers like a glove. The jams were so secure that Alex knew both his feet could slip at the same time, and he'd easily be able to check the fall. The flared crack made for secure foot jams too. With his toes twisted into the same pods he used for his finger jams, the chance for a foot slip, even if his toes were slightly numb, was nil. The only problem was that the climbing was so easy, he couldn't yet tell how he was feeling. Was this a day like the one he had on University Wall, when he had power to waste? Or would today feel more like Rivières Pourpres, more like work? It was too soon to tell.

It took less than a minute for Alex to enter the death zone. Once you're one hundred feet above the ground, you might as well be a thousand—the fall will be equally fatal. There's a rule of thumb climbers use to calculate the odds of dying in a ground fall. Land badly (i.e., on your head) from ten feet above the ground, and the chance of it being fatal is 10 percent. At twenty feet, 20 percent. From thirty feet up, you'll hit the ground at thirty miles per hour. This would be like riding a bike at full speed into a brick wall. The equation is straightforward—the higher you get, the harder you hit that wall. That is, until you reach terminal velocity—about 122 miles per hour. Factoring in air resistance, it takes a falling body approximately twelve to fourteen seconds to reach this speed. This equates to a free fall of about 1,900 feet, or roughly the height of One World Trade Center, including the spire. But it's not necessary to reach terminal velocity for a fall to be fatal.

Göran Kropp—the Swedish adventurer who rode his bike to Everest in 1996, climbed the mountain without oxygen, and then rode home—died in 2002 after falling sixty feet and hitting a ledge at a small crag in Washington State. He slipped ten feet from the top of a 5.10a, and his highest piece of protection, a camming device, pulled out of the crack. The second-highest piece came unclipped from the rope. In 1989, Lynn Hill forgot to finish tying her knot at a crag called Buoux in France. At the top of the seventy-foot 5.11 warm-up, she called down for her partner to "take" and then sat back in her harness. Hill felt a slight tug as the rope pulled through and she went airborne. Witnesses say she windmilled her arms in the air to keep herself upright. She hit a branch of a large tree just above the ground and landed between two boulders. Miraculously, her only injuries were a broken ankle and a dislocated elbow. The snapping branch probably saved her life.

Alex reached the top of the second pitch, a 5.8 hand crack, seven minutes after leaving the ground. The third pitch starts with a rightward traverse under a roof. The climbing is thin and delicate and culminates with a rock over with the right foot onto a small chip. Even though he was already two hundred feet up, the roof marked the real "game on" point. Alex threw his foot onto the tiny hold. Before committing, he double-checked with his headlamp to make sure it was placed precisely where he wanted it. Since he wasn't warmed up, it was critically important that he execute the move precisely according to plan. He was less worried about moves higher on the wall because by then he'd be in the flow and would be able to trust himself to do the right thing instinctively. Alex bore down on a crimp with his left hand, crushing the hold as if he was climbing 5.14. The right foot held, and he reached through to an in-cut edge with his right hand. Stepping through to better holds, he exhaled and panned his light up the wall. Off to his right he heard voices. He had seen that a party was starting up the Nose at more or less the exact time he was beginning his quest up Freerider. The pair was yelling back and forth noisily, no doubt communicating about taking in and letting out rope. They sounded like Eastern Europeans. Alex's light was shielded from them by a bulge in the cliff. They had no idea what was happening 150 feet away.

The next two hundred feet involved straightforward finger jamming up discontinuous low-angle cracks. At the top of pitch 4, four hundred feet above the ground, Alex stopped to rest at a small stance. Above him rose the first of the back-to-back crux slab pitches. This wasn't the one he had fallen on earlier in the season, but it was probably a little harder than pitch 6. Alex stood on the tiny shelf and looked down at his feet. He wiggled his toes. *How do they feel?* he asked himself. *A little cold and numb.* He could stop and take off his shoes, rub his toes, but that would be dicey, and it would totally kill the flow he was trying to get into.

He looked down between his legs and saw two tiny lights at the base. *Mark and Peter on their iPhones?*

Alex looked up. At the top of the wall a beacon of light appeared. It had to be Mikey, who had surely spent a long, sleepless night on top. Everyone on the film crew knew that the money shot would be the Boulder Problem. It was thin, hard, and unforgiving, and at 2,100 feet above the valley floor, it could be framed from above in a way that would reveal the true grandeur and impossibility of what Alex was doing. And since Jimmy trusted Mikey more than anyone, it had long ago been decided that this would be Mikey's shot. It would be hours before Alex got to the Boulder Problem, but Mikey was leaving nothing to chance. When Alex arrived, Mikey would be ready. The rope would be rigged exactly where he wanted it, the anchors bombproof, his stance locked down, camera angles dialed, batteries charged, spare lenses at the ready.

"It wasn't an easy decision to take this job," Mikey had told me in Morocco. "Ultimately, I said yes because Alex guilted me into it. He truly wants me up there. And I do think I'm safer than a lot of other people. There are times when I'm five feet away from him filming, and if I slipped, I would kill him."

But there have been times when Alex has asked Mikey to film him soloing something, and Mikey has said no. "Just go do it for yourself," he would say.

Alex shined his light on the crack splitting the wall in front of him and located a small pod. He tucked the tips of his index and middle fingers on his right hand into the slot and twisted them to the right, pulling his elbow down toward the side of his chest. He tucked his right toe into a flare in the crack and reached high with his left hand to another pod. Years ago, before anyone had climbed this route, the crack was barely an eighth of an inch wide at its fattest, too small to fit anyone's fingers. To create a protection point, the first ascensionist had nailed the thinnest piton, called a knifeblade, into the crack. It bottomed out two inches in, half of its length sticking out. When his partner followed the pitch, he used his own hammer to knock the piton out, which meant banging it back and forth. In the process, the edges of the crack broke a little bit. After a few more ascents, the hole was big enough for the next-size piton, and then after a few more, the next size. This process continued until the early 1970s, when climbers realized that something had to be done about the scarring that was changing the face of Yosemite's cliffs. Thus began the dawn of a new era, the "clean climbing" revolution. The clean ethic relied on a new mode of protection called the nut. The first nuts were exactly that: nuts from the hardware store or scrounged from alongside railroad tracks. Climbers slotted these rudimentary chocks, slung with webbing, into constrictions in the cracks with their fingers, not a hammer, and with them they could now climb a route a thousand times without ever leaving a trace of their passage.

A good many of the free climbs in Yosemite, including this

section of Freerider, are possible (at anywhere near their current rating) only because of the artificial piton scars left behind as permanent reminders of the golden age. We love to celebrate the purity of our sport—communing with nature, living life on its simplest terms—but the truth is that it's all based on a haphazard short history full of human error and compromise.

Alex stepped over a small roof, where the crack petered out into a blank face. From here the route moves up and right past several bolts to the belay anchor about twenty feet above. He balanced on the last decent foothold before the first slab crux. The next move was unlike anything he had ever climbed without a rope—the "walking up glass" moves, as Alex had described them. At that moment, he would have gladly increased the difficulty rating in exchange for some holds. In Morocco, on Rivières Pourpres, he could overpower the moves because he had something to grip, but here, on the glacier-polished Yosemite granite, it was all about finesse.

"You have to make love to it," Alex once said, when describing this section of the climb.

The hardest moves ever climbed without a rope are three full number grades harder than this slab. In 2004, one of Germany's top rock climbers, Alexander Huber, free soloed a route called Kommunist, rated 5.14a. The crux is approximately thirty-three feet above the ground, but Huber intentionally avoided using bouldering crash pads that could have softened a potential fall. In an interview afterward he said, "I worked on the route until the moment I could perfectly control it under good conditions. I was convinced I wouldn't fall, but like anything in life, you never know 100 percent. This sliver of potential danger is the essence of alpinism and climbing." Of course, thirty feet off the deck there is also more than a sliver of hope that you won't die if you fall. Alex, on the other hand, was now six hundred feet above the valley floor. It was 4:54 A.M. and still pitch-black. He felt his own sliver of doubt, but not about what would happen if he slipped.

Alex shined his light down by his right knee onto the spot where he knew he had to put his right foot. The day before, when he came down from climbing this section by headlamp with Brad Gobright, he'd told a few people hanging outside his van, "Sometimes that kind of slab stuff is better in the dark because the shadows make the holds look bigger." This might be true if there's a bona fide imperfection in the rock, but the spot that now lay in the center of the yellowish halo cast by his headlamp had nothing to recommend it. There was no ripple, no depression in the rock; it was smooth, like a piece of gray construction paper. The reason it was *the* spot was not because there was something there to stand on. It was simply that it was in the right place, roughly in the zone where it would be possible to get over the right foot without having to hike his leg up too far. If he stepped too high, the weight transfer onto the smear would create too much downward pressure on his foot, which could cause it to slide out. What he needed right now was to use his body to push his foot *in* against the wall.

Alex has climbed more at night than most climbers have during the day, but nevertheless, it is still more difficult. Regardless of how well you can or can't see the holds among the shadows cast by your body and the myriad features of the rock, anyone who has climbed at night can attest that it *feels* different to climb in the dark, just like it feels different to hike in the dark. Perhaps it's our primal fear of what we can't see, of what might be lurking out there beyond the blinding glare of the campfire (or headlamp).

As he scanned the wall, his light glinted off the bolt situated about a foot to the right of his knee. But rather than providing security, as it has on the thousands of ascents the Freeblast has seen over the years, it now lurked with a tinge of menace in its conspicuous attachment to nothing. Alex looked up. One hundred and fifty feet above and to his left, Matt Irving, a new recruit to Jimmy's team, hung on a fixed rope, his camera pointed at Alex. Matt saw Alex staring at him. It was an awkward moment. Neither of them said anything—not yet. Alex was trying to get himself in the proper head space to make this move, but it was just like Peter Croft had said. The camera guys, the journalists at the base of the cliff, the distraught girlfriend back in the van—it was all a bit distracting.

"ROCK!!" A LOUD CRACKING SOUND filled the air—boulders tumbling downhill. My heart fluttered, but I quickly realized it was coming from farther up the west face. I checked my phone. It was 4:54. Alex had been climbing for about thirty minutes and appeared to have stopped on a small ledge. I assumed it was the stance at the top of pitch 4. Peter, sitting beside me, was texting with editors back in Washington, DC, who were adding in the details he was supplying to the Google doc. Alex looked down, and his light illuminated our hideout on the log. But instead of panning past, his headlamp stayed on us. Since we could see him, I guessed he could see us. "Hey, put your phone down," I said to Peter. "I think he's looking at us." *God, I hope we're not distracting him.* He stayed in the same spot for a few minutes, which I thought was odd. He wouldn't be tired yet, so why would he stop just when he was getting started?

I wondered if he was contemplating his chances. In Morocco, after he soloed Rivières Pourpres, we had discussed the probabilities. He said he wanted, needed, his odds to be at least 99 percent. But he recognized that somewhere in the ninetieth percentile might be more realistic. Anything less than 99 percent was not what he called "repeatable," but Alex had wondered aloud, as he had when hiking with Ueli Steck, if sometimes you just have to throw down all your chips and "take the chance." I remember learning, in my high school statistics class, about the exponential nature of probability. If there's a 99 percent chance that Alex won't fall on a difficult free solo, and he exposes himself to these odds one hundred times, the probability that he will survive to share these tales with his grandkids is .99 multiplied by itself one hundred times, or 0.99^{100}, which comes out to .366, or 36.6 percent. Flipped around, that's a nearly two-thirds chance of a bad outcome. This is a gross oversimplification, especially because Alex is probably several .9s past 99 percent on most of his solos. But the math does reveal an indisputable truth about risk: Keep on taking the risk, and the risk becomes greater.

He started moving again, but it was hard to see where he was exactly, relative to the two slab cruxes. Voices drifted down from above. I looked at Peter, but he was absorbed in his note taking. *That's odd,* I thought, keeping the idea to myself. *Why would Alex be talking to the cameraman?*

Alex's headlight lit up the bottom edge of the Half Dollar, but this time I could tell by how bright it was that he was in the crack system leading up to the flake. "He's done it," I whispered to Peter, gleefully rubbing my hands together. I sighed deeply. The tension that had tied my stomach muscles into ever-tighter knots over the past few days untwisted a few turns. Alex had thousands of feet of rock ahead of him, including numerous pitches of 5.12 and one pitch of 5.13a, but at that moment I believed he had the climb in the bag. "He's in cruiser territory for a while now," I said. "The sun will be up soon, so let's relocate to the meadow and get the spotting scope set up." It was 5:37 A.M.

As we packed up, Alex's light disappeared. I assumed he was somewhere up on Mammoth Terrace, a massive ledge system that marks the spot, a third of the way up El Capitan, where the lower slabs rear back into a 2,000-foot vertical and overhanging head-wall. I heard a noise and turned around to see Pablo, headlamp on, hustling up the trail.

"Hey, what's going on?" I called over as he scurried past, breathing hard. I had not expected to see him back up here.

"Alex is bailing," said Pablo. "He's on his way down."

"What? Why?"

"I don't know."

PETER AND I WERE PULLING out of the parking lot when Alex walked up. I wanted to check in with him, but the crew was filming, so I put the car in drive and did a U-turn. As we drove away, I saw Alex through the rearview mirror. He was looking in our direction, a frown on his face.

Sanni, I would later learn, was still sound asleep at that moment. She awoke when Alex opened the door to the van, having slept through the whole thing.

At 10:50 A.M., I was sipping coffee in the cafeteria with Gwin and Croft when a text came in from Alex. "Sorry about this morning. Let's hang tonight." It made me a little sad that Alex was apologizing for bailing. He was feeling beholden. That wasn't right.

I texted back:

"I was proud when I heard you were coming down.
U r the man. Yeah let's hang tonight. Let me know
what you guys end up doing."

I showed the text to the two Peters. Croft grimaced but didn't say anything. He had gone home a couple of days earlier after climbing the Freeblast with Alex. I had called him the night before to tell him that Alex was going for it. Croft had left his home in Bishop on the east side of the Sierra at four A.M. to be here in time to witness Alex's historic climb. Croft said he had just come from Mike Gauthier's and that Alex had "freaked out."

"Suddenly he jumped on his bike and rode away. He said he needed to clear his head and that he was going to free solo Astroman." Alex must have texted me somewhere along the way to Washington Column, the formation on the eastern end of the valley where Astroman is located.

Gwin and I headed off to do some climbing of our own. When we got back to the ground, there was a text inviting us to dinner at the production house in Foresta. "Bring some wine or beer if you can!"

We arrived a bit late. A dozen or so people, including Alex and Sanni, were seated around a big dining room table. I grabbed a plate of food and found a seat next to Alex.

"Hey, I tried to come over and talk to you guys this morning," he said, "but you just drove away."

"Yeah, sorry about that. I thought you might want some space, so we just peaced out. How did it go up there?"

"I didn't feel that great. My shoes were too tight and my toes were a little numb. It felt scary. I got to the move where I have to rock over onto that sketchy foot, and I knew if it blew that I was going to die. If I had been on my own, I probably would have downclimbed to the nearest stance and tried to pull it together, but it just felt weird with the camera right there and all the people watching me."

"I'm so glad you made that call, dude," I said to Alex. I realized that it came off a bit patronizing, but I wanted him to know that I thought it probably took more courage to back down than to push through.

"Yeah, it just wasn't my day, you know," he said.

I WAS REMINDED OF WHAT happened to Henry Barber in 1976 when a film crew talked him into on-sight soloing a 5.10 hand and finger crack on a sea cliff in Wales. Barber consented only on the condition that the cameramen were ready at the appointed time and that they didn't speak to him or distract him in any way while he was climbing. They agreed, but when the time came, the director told Barber to wait because the light wasn't right. Barber was tense and annoyed, and the cliff was blazing in the afternoon sun when they finally told him he could climb—four hours later. A few moves off the ground, a cameraman asked him to climb back down and start over.

"I started to climb and it seemed that everything was working against me," recounts Barber in his autobiography. "I felt the cameras and all of America watching me. . . . I just kept thinking, *Man, this is not where I want to be.*"

The climb quickly turned into a desperate battle. After lay-backing through the crux sixty feet up, Barber realized he couldn't reverse the moves he had just done, and, worse, that he no longer had the heart for what he was doing. In the film, which aired on ABC's *American Sportsmen,* you can see Barber shudder as he tries for a move, then backs off, realizing he doesn't have it. He looks tight. His characteristic flow on the rock is gone. A friend of Barber's who was at the base of the cliff became so unnerved that she had to leave. He considered calling for one of the cameramen to drop him a rope, but he knew that if he did, it would ruin the film. *Why am I doing this?* Barber asked himself. *Is this for my ego or so someone can make a successful film, or am I doing this for myself?*

When he finally topped out into a grassy meadow an hour and half after setting off, a different cameraman asked him to climb back down so he could film him topping out a second time. Barber obliged, but he now had tears in his eyes. When they finally turned off the cameras, he took off his shoes and threw them as far as he could. "I was beaten," he recounts in the book. "I wouldn't do anything like it again."

DIFFERENT TIME, different circumstances. Same conundrum. With the inherent pressure to make a good film, how does the free soloist venture right up to the boundary of his limits, when there is zero margin for overconfidence? When I was Alex's age, we called it "Kodak courage"—the tendency for people to push beyond their limits when performing for the camera. Nowadays, in a world where fatal wingsuit accidents are captured by blinking, helmet-mounted GoPros, we might more aptly call it "GoPro bravado." Even more insidious is the way social media has made it possible for people to feel pressure to perform, even when they're alone. "Engaging in risky behavior so that others will notice us is not a new concept that has only emerged with this generation," says Jerry Isaak, an associate professor of expeditionary studies at SUNY Plattsburgh. "What is new, however, is the nearly constant 'virtual presence' of the others we are trying to impress. With the development of social media and related technology, 'other people nearby' has been simultaneously expanded to a potentially worldwide audience and shrunk to the size and portability of a smartphone."

Some people thrive under the pressure of knowing their every move is being recorded for posterity, but there are others—and I think Alex Honnold and Henry Barber are in this category—who don't feel comfortable performing in front of a camera, at least not when they're operating near their limit. In these situations, rather than fomenting bravado, the camera creates feelings of stress and anxiety.

In 2014, while filming a commercial with Jimmy Chin in Yosemite, Alex was on his second solo lap on Heaven, the route Dean Potter first soloed in 2006 (in 2011, Alex had one-upped Potter, again, by "flashing" the route free solo). A few feet below the top, Alex made a long reach with his right hand, which he tried to fish into a fist jam. But he couldn't quite find the sweet spot, so he dropped back to the sloping shelf, where he dangled by his outstretched arms thousands of feet above the valley floor. Three more times he tried the move, each time coming up a little shorter. My old friend from Crazy Kids, Rob Frost, was assisting Jimmy that day, and he says he could see Alex battling to hold it together. A few seconds later, Alex called for a rope. Jimmy and Rob were too far away to assist, but luckily there were two other cameramen operating a crane a few feet above Alex. They lowered him a line, and Alex used it to pull himself over the lip. He would later admit that "technically" he *was* rescued, but he was quick to qualify it, saying that if he was alone, he would have just chalked up a bunch and gone for it—and he's confident he would have stuck it. He also says he never would have found himself in that position to begin with if he hadn't been performing for the cameras.

Snapping back to the present, I turned to Alex. "What about Astroman? How did that go?"

"I haven't been on it in seven years, and it felt hard," he said. "I almost fell on the Boulder Problem."

"What? You seriously almost fell?"

"Yeah. I got three moves in and my foot slipped, and I kind of sketched. So I downclimbed to the ledge, regrouped, and then I went for it. The move getting into the Harding Slot was really hard. I was like, 'Oh boy, it's game on.' I did the route in an hour thirteen, which was probably the speed record."

I looked around to see if anyone else was listening. They weren't. I had the feeling Alex hadn't told anyone else about this close call.

The Boulder Problem (not to be confused with the section of the same on Freerider) is the technical crux of Astroman, a very thin crack at the start of pitch 3. It's rated 5.11c, a grade and a half easier than the Boulder Problem on Freerider. A fall on either would mean the same thing. The only difference was how long you'd be in the air before the lights went out.

AFTER DINNER, Croft, Gwin, and I headed back to my cabin. We opened a bottle of wine Croft had in his milk crate of provisions, and the three of us slumped on the couch.

"Did Alex tell you he almost fell on the Boulder Problem?" I asked Croft.

"No," he said, "I'm really sorry to hear that. I would love to hear him say he was rock solid. The hardest stuff I've done, I just felt locked in. But you know, it's not that surprising. . . . [After the aborted attempt] he honestly looked like a caged animal. This whole movie thing just doesn't add up in terms of putting Alex in the proper head space to get this done. It's like one plus one equals three."

Croft took a sip of his wine, pursed his lips, and then started in on a story about the time he made the first free solo ascent of the Regular Route on the Rostrum. He was six hundred feet up the route when he arrived at a traverse across a steep face. It was the only section on the entire climb where he couldn't firmly jam his hands and feet into a crack, and as such it meant stepping out of his comfort zone. As he hung from the last good jam, psyching himself up for the move, he noticed an old piton off to his right with a sling tied through its eye. Croft reached over and moved the sling over to the left, so that it would be closer to his hands when he made the move. If he slipped, he might be able to grab it as he was falling off the mountain.

"As I was finishing off the last pitches, I knew I'd screwed up," he told us. "I figured, well, maybe I'm just being weird. But the longer I waited the worse it got." The next day, he went back and did it again, and in that same spot, he grabbed the sling again, but this time he pushed it around a corner, so there was no possible way he could grab it. "It sounds stupid," he went on, "but it seemed really important to me at the time, like I had to do it the right way."

"What year was that?" asked Gwin.

"I don't know. I'm really bad with numbers. Some people like Hans Florine know exactly how many times they've climbed the Nose, but I have no clue how many times I've climbed El Cap. I don't even know what year I started climbing."

We all had a good laugh at Croft's expense. "That was kind of classic the other day when Alex asked if you thought it was lame that he has a movie crew," I said. "He really looks up to you, and I think your response kind of threw him for a loop."

"I wasn't trying to be ethically pure or anything like that," said Croft, "I just always wanted the experience to be all mine, to drink it all in completely. I didn't want any distractions. I always felt self-conscious when there were cameras around, and you want all your focus to be on what you're doing. I always felt like even if nobody ever found out about what I was doing, it was still the coolest thing I could imagine. And it's really important that you're doing it for the right reasons."

"Do you remember a long time ago when you were on that panel about free soloing with Alex at the Banff Film Festival?" I asked. "You and I were hanging out in Red Rocks a few months later, and you told me that he was kind of acting a bit arrogant. I remember him back then, and it seemed like he often intentionally tried to make people feel uncomfortable."

"It might have been a certain amount of insecurity," replied Croft. "It was kind of like he thought that being arrogant was cool.

Or maybe he was trying to get a reaction because he didn't want to have another boring conversation. He was still fun to be around, but every once in a while he'd say something, and I'd look at him and be like, 'You need to get a little more real, Alex.' He reminded me of Spock in *Star Trek*, like he was part Vulcan. 'Well that's not logical,'" said Croft, impersonating Leonard Nimoy. "But the way he's evolved, he's become more human. I look up to the guy, for sure. I've got a ton of respect for him. He's kind of a hero now."

It was Monday of Thanksgiving week, and the sky was covered in gray canvas. A cold misting rain drizzled out of the sky. When I got to the base of Cookie Cliff, Alex and Sanni were mini-tracking a classic hand crack called Outer Limits. Sanni was about twenty feet off the deck, with Alex attached to the rope a few feet below her. "You're too close," she screeched.

"We're fine," replied Alex calmly.

"It's not fine," snapped Sanni. "I'm about to fall, and if I land on you, you're gonna say that I ruined your season." The way she phrased it made me think this was a topic they had covered before.

"Is it safe to have just one device?" she called down to me. Her voice was cracking, and she appeared to be on the verge of tears.

"Personally, I always use two," I told her. "It's possible, though Alex doesn't believe it, for the ratchet to disengage if you push against it in the wrong way."

"You told me about that in Morocco," said Alex, hanging from a hand jam, "but I tested it a bit afterwards, and if you actually fall, the rope sliding through the device always causes the cam to engage."

Arguing with Alex on points like this can be enjoyable, but I figured this wasn't the time or the place. So I didn't say: *Sure, but is the cam on the Mini Traxion strong enough to hold a shock load? Personally, I wouldn't want to bet my life on it.*

"I'm not into this," said Sanni. A few minutes later she and Alex rappelled to the ground. Most of the climbs were wet, so I put Alex on belay and he set off up an overhanging bolted route called Cookie Monster, rated 5.12a. Alex belayed me while I took a burn on toprope; then I handed the rope to Sanni and moved over to mini-track Outer Limits.

I was halfway up when I heard Alex say, "I think I'm going to do Cookie Monster again."

"Okay," replied Sanni, "lead or toprope?"

"By my onesie."

From my perch ninety feet above the ground, I enjoyed a bird's-eye view of the climb. Alex flowed up the rock, but he stopped every few moves, let go with one arm, and opened his hand, which suggested that lactic acid was building up in his forearms. At the top, he hung from the final jug hold with his right hand and brushed the back of his left against the chains hanging from the anchor bolts—the apparatus that every other climber who had ever done Cookie Monster used to lower off. It reminded me of a kid ringing the bell after climbing the greased pole at the fair—a tiny reveal of what it meant for Alex Honnold to free solo a route properly. Then he dropped back on his arms, downclimbed a few feet, and traversed across an overhanging face onto an adjacent route called Twilight Zone. He was back on the ground less than ten minutes after he set off.

"Do you think anyone has ever soloed Cookie Monster before?" he asked me.

"I doubt it. Will that go in your black book?"

"Yeah, definitely. Not necessarily tonight, but I get everything recorded every two or three days."

We didn't realize it at the time, but at that very moment, Adam

Ondra was topping out on the Dawn Wall, eight days after he had set off from the base. The world's best sport climber had spent about a month working the route and then redpointing it. Ondra had indeed one-upped Caldwell and Jorgeson, and the climbing press would hype this fact to no end. But Ondra could never have done what he did if Caldwell and Jorgeson had not spent years unlocking the secrets of the route. In the press coverage that followed, I was annoyed that this simple fact was not emphasized. Many of the reports didn't even mention it.

Ondra's timing was impeccable. The extended forecast called for rain and snow, off and on, for the next two weeks. I'd seen the season shut down like this before in November. "This was supposed to be the one good day this week," commented Alex as we sat on a sloped boulder at the base of Cookie Monster and watched the drizzle build into steady rain. "It's just gross. I think Sanni and I are going to bail. I'm pretty burnt. It's time to head south and hang in the sun."

"Where will you go?" I asked.

"Sanni has some relatives in San Diego, so we'll head there for Thanksgiving. We might come back in like ten days if the weather improves, but probably not."

"It does seem like the season is over," I said.

"Will you come back in the spring?" Alex asked.

"I will if you'll have me."

"Yeah, of course. You were low-key, and it was good to hang."

"We'll miss hanging out with you," said Sanni, giving me a warm hug.

I WAS ON THE ROAD the next morning at five A.M., en route to Fresno, where I planned to catch a flight home. On my way out of Foresta, I stopped at the Dumpsters to drop off my trash. The temperature was below freezing. A brisk wind gave the air a bite I felt on the end of my nose. The sky was filled with twinkling stars, reminding me of the night one week earlier when Alex had set off up Freerider. For some reason, the nip in the air brought me back to some of the inhospitable places climbing had taken me over the years. Type-two fun, as someone had once described it—god-awful while it's happening, sublime when it's over. In a strange way, it felt like that to be heading home. A sense of relief that it was over, that Alex was still alive, but also, a tinge of disappointment. A part of me didn't want to return to the humdrum of normal, everyday life.

When my plane took off from Fresno, Alex was sitting in El Cap Meadow, staring up at Freerider with one of his black books in his lap. He was reminding himself of everything he had learned about Freerider over the past two months—the tiny ripple on pitch 5 that gave him something to balance his hand on while he rocked over the sketchy foot; the way the karate kick at the end of the Boulder Problem felt slightly better when he sagged his hips before throwing it; the importance of getting the perfect pair of shoes—not too tight and not too loose. But most of all, he thought about how there weren't any showstopper moves. His dream was doable.

It just had to be the right day.

CHAPTER TWELVE

Fun

It was hot and stuffy in the van, but Alex didn't seem bothered. He sat sideways in the rear-facing passenger seat, his left leg propped on the driver's-side seat back. His size 12½ foot hung in the air, toes splayed, like a giant eagle talon. Considering the millions of feet of rock the guy has climbed in his life, and that his go-to climbing shoe size is 8½, his toes appeared surprisingly ungnarled—apart from the grape-size corn on his big toe.

I perched on his bed, feet dangling above the floor, admiring some photos pinned high on the wall above the galley. "Sanni printed those out and put them up over the winter," said Alex. One of them was a shot I recognized, a silhouette of Alex clinging to a wall high above the Gulf of Oman as the sun set over the Musandam Peninsula.

A college-ruled composition book with a geometric pattern of black and white triangles on its cover sat on the countertop to my left. A random name—Cody Quackenbush—was handwritten on its front. I later found out that Cody was a student of Alex's mom's at American River College. I wondered if Cody knew that Alex Honnold was using his notebook for his list of things to do before free soloing El Capitan.

"There's no ventilation in here, huh?" I said.

"Naw," said Alex. "If I open the door or a window the van will get filled with mosquitoes, and they'll keep me up all night buzzing around my head. That's a total rookie maneuver."

The door was sealed tight, and the windows were filled with pieces of foil-backed foam. It was dusk, and hardly any light leaked in through the chinks. I could see why Alex calls it "the box." The air felt heavy.

I hadn't seen Alex since that day in November when we parted ways at the Cookie Cliff. Over the winter, we had spoken a few times by phone, and in early March he texted me that he was buying a three-bedroom, two-and-a-half-bath house in a subdivision on the outskirts of Las Vegas. He said he wanted to diversify his investments and his financial adviser told him he would save a lot of money in taxes if he shifted his residence from California to Nevada. It would also give him and Sanni a home base and allow him to finally have his mail sent somewhere other than to his mother. I called him shortly after he closed on the sale to get a tour via FaceTime. Alex walked me through the house, which was bright and airy, with a lofted walkway on the second story, hardwood floors, and a small yard. But it was completely empty. Alex said Sanni was in charge of finding the furniture and appliances and that he had spent a lot of time over the past week trying to sort out homeowners insurance. I found it hard to picture him feeling at home in such a place, and indeed Alex was still living in the van, in the driveway. He said he was in no rush to move indoors.

His plans for the spring sounded like they were up in the air. Yeah, he was planning to head back to the valley, but he didn't sound 100 percent committed to the project. Then he mentioned, casually, that he might just go and solo Freerider on his own— without the camera crew. As I had predicted, he had been thinking a lot about his aborted attempt. "I don't really mind having somebody around if I think the climbing's all easy and I'm just charging," he would later tell me. "But I never really want people around when it's actually hard." Freerider was actually hard, to say the least.

"How's Sanni?" I asked, changing the subject.

"She's great," he replied. "But things are going so well with us that it kind of makes me a little worried. I have no angst." Some of his biggest solos, like the Rainbow Wall in Red Rocks, just up the road from his new home, were completed after breakups with his last girlfriend, Stacey Pearson. Alex, by his own admission, has done a lot of angst soloing, but there's one story he doesn't talk about much. It was February 2013, and he and Stacey had broken up for the umpteenth time. They often stayed with Chris Weidner when they were in Las Vegas, and since neither of them had anywhere else to go, they were both still staying at his house—Alex in the driveway in his van, Stacey on the couch. One morning, Alex tried to get in to use the bathroom, but the door was locked. He went over to the window above the couch to see if Stacey would let him in, but when he looked down, she wasn't there. He went back and knocked on the door. Weidner let him in.

"Where's Stacey?" demanded Alex.

"Ummm," replied Weidner. At that moment, she was upstairs in bed with one of Alex's friends, who was also staying at the house. Weidner says Alex looked up the stairway leading to the second floor. He could see Alex's heart sinking. Alex and Stacey were officially broken up, and she was now free to date whomever she wanted, but Alex still loved her, and apparently, he wasn't quite ready to move on.

"Seriously?" said Alex. "Wow, that was fast." He walked out, got in his van, and drove straight to Zion, where he on-sight soloed Shune's Buttress, an eight-hundred-foot 5.11+ that had never been climbed without a rope. The forecast called for snow in the afternoon, but Alex figured it was only an eight-pitch route and that he'd be long done by the time the weather moved in. The climbing was difficult, though, and it was snowing by the time he topped out on the buttress. What he hadn't realized is that there's another 1,500 feet of steep scrambling between the top of the climb and the summit of the mountain. Soon Alex found himself clawing his way up icy, snow-covered rock in a blizzard. At one point, he broke a hold and fell about eight feet through the branches of a small tree. He landed with a smack on a tiny pedestal of rock, inches away from having gone the distance to the ground.

SANNI AND I SPOKE a few days after I got the house tour from Alex. She told me that after celebrating Thanksgiving in Southern California with her family, she and Alex had driven to Vegas, where they climbed by day and camped in random parking lots each night. They'd been living together in the box for months. Sanni was burned-out on climbing, and like Alex, she was still trying to process what had happened up on El Cap. Alex's dream had not gone as planned, and morale was low.

Sanni was accustomed to living in tight quarters. For the past five years she'd been living in Seattle in a small house with four roommates. But Alex wasn't coping well with the constant engagement, and he didn't know how to tell Sanni that he needed space. One day, while they were parked outside a strip mall, it boiled over. Sanni stormed off, telling Alex as she got out of the van, "You need to figure out what you want, because I can't read your mind." She found her way to a coffee shop, where she realized that she had left her wallet in the van. Starving and dying for a cup of coffee, but too mad to call Alex, Sanni killed the afternoon and evening wandering from one closing Starbucks to the next. Somewhere along the way, she decided she'd had enough. The next day she would jump on a plane and fly back to her old life in Seattle. Around eight P.M., she finally called Alex, who came and picked her up. "I need to backtrack," he said, when she told him she was leaving. "I really want you to stay."

"You're so good at physical self-care," Sanni replied. "The second you get down from the wall, you take off your shoes, you drink water, and you start thinking about how to rest your body. But you're so bad at emotional self-care. Tell me what you need. Tell me what you want, because I'm not going take it personally, and probably I need it too." What he wanted, he said, was to be in a relationship with Sanni, but he needed some space. So they worked out a plan for how to give him an hour or two alone each day.

After the fight, things were different. "It made us stronger," she said. "Since then he has been a lot more open about his affection and a lot more willing to say how he's feeling."

"Did he go so far as to use the L word?" I asked Sanni. Sanni had already told me that she loved Alex, and always had.

"Of course he has, 100 percent," said Sanni, now laughing. "And I genuinely think he felt it, too. It was not under duress."

According to Sanni, Alex was vacillating about whether he would try El Cap again in the spring. One day he would talk about other climbing goals he had in Yosemite and Sanni would think, with more than a tinge of relief, *Okay, maybe he's done with it.* But then a few days later, he would say something like, "Yeah, I'm going to the valley, this is going to happen, it's going to be great, and then I will move on with my life."

What is it like to love someone who has a guillotine hanging over his head? I didn't have to ask the question.

"Everybody thinks I'm thinking about it all the time, but I'm not," she volunteered. "This morning was the first time in a really long time that I was actually like, 'Oh my gosh.' . . . It makes me want to cry to think about it. But I would never tell him that, because if somebody is about to go do something really hard, you don't want to be the person that's like, 'This is a terrible idea' . . . because that just doesn't help. Him doing this has to be his decision and come from his heart. I just don't want to be part of that decision."

But there was one thing she did tell Alex after the fight, knowing that he had often harnessed relationship turmoil to create the proper mind-set for free soloing: "You don't have to be suffering to succeed," she said. "You can have it all."

"I ERASED ALL MY SOCIAL MEDIA," said Alex, gesturing toward his beat-up iPhone sitting on the van's countertop. "I don't want the distraction in these final days, and I'm a little worried about what all the scrolling on my phone might be doing to my brain. I'm kind of nostalgic for the old days before I had a smartphone. I used to do a lot of quality thinking in the box back then."

I had similar concerns. To limit how much Internet I consumed each day, I had been playing recently with an IQ app. Alex's eyes opened wide when I told him about it. He sat up straight, grabbed his iPhone, and pulled up the App Store. "Which one did you download?" he asked, scrolling down the list and reading the names off to me. "What are the questions like?"

"Scrambled words, detecting patterns, math problems, stuff like that. It's a good way to use parts of your brain that might not see a lot of action, since you probably don't spend much time thinking in those ways. I know you did a lot of math and science when you were a kid, so think about how much of your brain is sitting unused nowadays."

"It's funny you mention that. I've actually been making a conscious effort to reassign all the neural pathways I used to use for math for memorizing beta."

The beta for Freerider could fill a book.

"Is that what you think about when you shut yourself up in the box?"

"Yeah, pretty much."

"Does it ever get boring?"

"No way, I love it. I could sit in here for hours by myself and just get totally lost in my head."

We both sat quietly for a bit.

"Hey, so I just finished reading this book that I think you'd really like," said Alex. "It's called *Sapiens*." He explained that the central premise of the book is that humans became the most dominant species on earth because we have the ability to cooperate flexibly in large groups. What gives us this unique ability to cooperate and work together in societies is our belief in shared myths—stories that illustrate universal truths of the human condition. The part Alex thought I would be most interested in was the end, where the book turns from the past to the future and explores what the coming decades may hold for our species. The author, Yuval Noah Harari, speculates that the presently unfolding scientific revolution in technologies like artificial intelligence and bioengineering is leading to a brave new world in which humans may become "amortal." The difference between an amortal and an immortal is that an amortal can still die—but only in an accident.

"You know the singularity is supposed to occur in the 2040s, right?" I said.

Alex, still looking for the best IQ app, rolled his eyes. He knew exactly what I was referring to, because I had talked his ear off over the years about the singularity, the name for the point in time at which computers become more intelligent than humans. One of the potential offshoots of a technological singularity is the possibility of curing illnesses like heart disease and cancer—and maybe even turning off aging altogether. This was an idea I had a hard time reconciling, because I had spent my whole life shaping a philosophy around the idea that my life-span was finite. As a young climber, I had decided that since I was going to die, even if I took it easy and didn't take any risks, I might as well try to squeeze every last bit of juice out of life. "Remembering that you are going to die is the best way I know to avoid the trap of thinking you have something to lose," said Steve Jobs, in a commencement address at Stanford in 2005. "You are already naked. There is no reason not to follow your heart."

Bachar was thinking along the same lines when he told that guy at the Tuolumne gas station, "You're soloing right now."

"I don't disagree with the hypothesis, just the time line," said Alex. "We've been talking about this tech revolution for decades, but it's not happening nearly as fast as everyone thought it would. Besides, you're too old anyway. You're going to miss the singularity." He said it in his typical deadpan fashion, but the way he dropped his eyelids ever so slightly, I knew he was poking me. Still, I decided not to ask the question that had been on my mind: *If you knew that you could only die in an accident—and not from old age or disease—would you still want to "go big"?*

I didn't want to do anything that might psyche Alex out, and for that reason, I didn't offer my condolences for the loss of his friend Ueli Steck. Less than three weeks earlier, the Swiss Machine had fallen off a 25,800-foot mountain called Nuptse, which lies next to Everest. Steck was climbing solo and moving fast, as he always did. He was acclimatizing for an attempt on Everest's seldom-climbed Hornbein Couloir, which he planned to solo and then link with a traverse to Lhotse, the world's fourth-highest mountain. Had he succeeded, it would have been the greatest enchainment in the history of Himalayan climbing. No one knows what happened, but the 3,000-foot fall was witnessed by several Sherpas and Everest climbers in Camps 1 and 2. Presumably, Steck had simply slipped.

I stood up and made a move toward the door of the van. It was eight P.M., Alex's bedtime. And that's when he locked me with his big brown eyes and said, "Sanni's coming back in a few days. She'll be here for about a week; then she leaves again on June second. I leave for Alaska on the twelfth, so that will give me about eight days to get it done." I stared back at him, waiting for the qualifier, the "we'll see, we'll see," which he always tacked on whenever we talked about Freerider. But he just looked at me earnestly and said nothing more. And it struck me that this was probably yet another step in the process he had laid out for himself years ago—the part where he tells someone, without being explicit, that he's made a decision. He was going for it on or around June 3. And I knew that somewhere, maybe in the Cody Quackenbush notebook, he would have this written down—noted simply as "EC" (El Cap).

A FEW DAYS LATER, I woke up in the second-floor apartment I was renting in Foresta. The wind was buffeting the house, and I could see a bank of gray clouds through the smoky sliding glass door on the other side of the room. My first thought was the same one I'd been having for weeks now. *Thank god I'm not Alex. Thank god I'm not free soloing El Cap.* I wasn't the one doing the climb, but I still woke up every day with a dark cloud hovering over me. More than the doing of the deed itself, it was the years of anticipation and preparation leading up to it that seemed to me the most impressive thing about this whole endeavor. I imagined that I was Alex and that I had set myself a nearly impossible task—something I absolutely did not have to do. I could walk away. But I didn't. Instead, I dug in—hard. I broke the inconceivable thing down into bite-size pieces, and every day, I worked on one of them, never worrying about the next, or how they would all eventually fit together.

Colin Haley, one of America's leading alpinists and a partner of

Alex's, once told me that he climbs because it satisfies a primal desire to have intensity in his life. He said he doesn't overthink the risks he takes as a climber because the experiences he finds in the mountains are "worth everything." Warren Harding, when asked by a reporter why he climbed, famously quipped, "We're insane. Can't be any other reason." After Alex's first attempt on Freerider, Peter Croft put it like this: "The great thing about a climbing hero is that they're doing something for no good reason at all. To put that much on the line, to work so hard for something that doesn't have any quantifiable value, it's just this wonderful, crazy, uniquely human thing."

Jimmy had texted me the night before to tell me that Alex needed a partner. I was watching an episode of *Prison Break* and sipping on a glass of vodka. I texted him back: "Absolutely!" But now, in the harsh light of day, the vodka vapors still swirling in my head, I regretted it. Alex would want to climb simultaneously, which would necessitate my matching his pace up the wall. In the past six months, I had barely touched rock. Instead, I had been sitting behind my computer, writing, and changing Tommy's diapers. What if I fell and pulled him off? What if I hurt him? What if I was responsible for stopping him from doing his dream climb?

Jimmy said that if I was interested, I should let Alex know. But as I lay in bed feeling weak, I decided that I wouldn't call or text him. I'd sit tight and hopefully in the interim he would find someone else. But if he did call, I would fake an injury. A few years earlier, I had offered to take a friend from Philadelphia up the Nose. On the first pitch, when Dan's feet were a body length above the ground, he let go and slumped onto the rope. "Did you hear that?" he said. "Did you hear that pop? I think I might have dislocated my shoulder." Dan had come down with an acute case of "Elcapitis." And now I had it too. I had herniated a disk right after leaving Yosemite in the fall, so I decided that when, or if, Alex called, I would fake a back injury. I even said it aloud to myself, to see how it sounded.

A few hours later, Alex called. "Hey, man, how's it going? I just soloed Easy Rider."

"How was it?" Easy Rider is the U-shaped linkup Dean Potter pioneered in 2011 that climbs the top six pitches of Freerider.

"It was soooo good," said Alex. "Uhh, we're breaking up, let me call you right back."

My phone rang a minute later. "Sorry about that. I jumped the gun. I know the phone doesn't work until I get to the tree at the top of the Nose, but I thought I'd try it a little early. I should be good now." I could hear scuffling and wind. He was on the move, hoofing down the summit slabs of El Cap. Always the multitasker, Alex usually calls someone when hiking down from El Cap. And he always times himself. Despite talking to me, he would set his record that day, making it from the top of Freerider to Mike's house in a little more than an hour, a factoid Alex would scribe into his notebook that evening.

"Hey, so do you want to go up the Freeblast with me tomorrow?" he asked.

I hesitated for a few seconds, realizing my back-injury story wasn't going to roll off my tongue as easily as I'd hoped. Then I just blurted out the truth. "I do, but I'm really worried that I'm going to hold you back and that I could fall and pull you off."

"No way, don't worry," he said. "I have a plan. We'll use Mini Traxions and you'll be fine. And it will be fun to get up on the Captain together."

"Are you sure?"

"Totally."

At 5:45 the next morning I was standing at the base of El Cap with Alex. Jimmy and Cheyne, who were planning to do some filming, had already headed up some fixed ropes. Alex reached into his black vinyl-coated pack and pulled out a ratty orange-and-white-flecked rope. The sheath was covered in little nicks, and the end had unraveled, with strands of white core sticking out messily.

"That's our rope?"

"Yeah, what's wrong with it?"

"It looks like it's been through a war."

"Whatever," said Alex, looking mildly annoyed. "This is actually the best rope I own. It's fine."

Alex had cut the bottoms of the legs off the black nylon pants he always wore, turning them into capris. But instead of carefully marking where on the cuff he wanted to shorten them and using a pair of scissors to make a clean cut, it looked like he'd hacked them off with a sharp rock. The legs were different lengths, the new hemline festooned with tatty triangles of fabric. He looked like a *Flintstones* character or maybe Huck Finn.

"Solo up to that ledge and put me on belay up there," said Alex, pointing to a shelf of rock forty feet above our heads. I must have looked incredulous, because he then added, "It's only 5.7." Without waiting to hear if I was comfortable starting our day with some free soloing, Alex took off. He was halfway up the first pitch when I got to the ledge. I pulled the rest of the rope up and tied into the end as it whipped off the shelf like pot warp reeling off the deck of a crab-fishing boat. I barely had time to dip my hands into my chalk bag before the rope came tight on my harness. Time to move.

My job was to make sure the rope never tugged on my harness. Each time it did, it meant Alex couldn't move up. The guy is generally unflappable, but if you want to test his patience, try simul-climbing with him and continuously bringing him up short. Jimmy once likened Alex to a racehorse: "You can't hold him back once you let him out of the gate." In that same conversation,

Jimmy also told me that Alex had "fired" him because he moved too slow one day when they were simul-climbing on the Freeblast. I had known this was going to hurt, but I had underestimated how much. I felt like I was at a track meet. One minute I was standing around waiting for my heat, the next I was going all out and looking for a place behind the bleachers where I could go vomit.

But there was something else I hadn't anticipated: how fun it would be. Alex was running it out fifty to a hundred feet between protection points, so there was hardly anything for me to do besides climb. And while he had an anvil (me) hanging off his harness, I had the opposite: the rope pulling me up from above like some magic beanstalk. Moving so fast over so much stone, I wondered whether it's how a bird feels when it flies, or a monkey as it swings through the canopy—a joy so deeply rooted in your soul that it makes you feel like you're doing exactly what you're supposed to be doing. Tom Frost, one of the Salathé Wall's first ascensionists, described this feeling as a religious experience: "The whole route felt like the Creator made it just for traditional climbers who would feel the love and fall in love in return."

I couldn't see Alex—a bulge in the rock was blocking my view of him—but I could see the mighty bulk of El Capitan hanging above me like some Gothic cathedral. Climbing, even on some little rock in the woods, is a joyful experience, but doing it on the side of a geologic marvel like El Capitan feels like a spiritual awakening. I felt like Stuart Little would if he walked into Notre Dame.

On the fifth pitch, the rope hung limply in front of me, which was not how I wanted it. I wanted it tight, like guitar-string tight, because at that moment, I wasn't sure how I was still stuck on. My toes were bent backward on the seventy-degree rock, making a deep crease in the leather on the top of my shoe. My fingers were pressed against blank rock on either side of my shoulders. There was nothing to grip, but my skin must have been adhering to something, because I knew that if I let go with either hand, I would slip off.

By this point, Alex was belaying me from the anchor at the top of pitch 6. I could yell, "Up rope" or "Take," telling him to reel in slack, but then I thought, *You're climbing with the Hon, Mark. That's kind of weak sauce.* I wondered if he was keeping the rope slack on purpose. I looked up and left. Jimmy was hanging on a fixed line, his camera trained right on me. He didn't say anything. If I was to avoid being that guy who fell in his film, I needed to keep moving before my feet melted out from under me. I could feel them slowly oozing off the smears. But I already had a loop of slack in front of me, and if I moved up and Alex didn't reel it in, I could slide ten to fifteen feet before the rope would snap tight on my harness.

"Up rope," I finally yelled. A few seconds passed: nothing. A few more. At the exact moment the rope came tight, my left foot skated out from under me. My fingertips bent backward, but somehow I didn't slide off the wall. I took a few deep breaths to center myself and then my left foot skated out from under me a second time. Again, I didn't fall, but I felt improbably adhered to the rock, as if I were cheating the laws of physics. At that moment I thought of myself in this position without a rope. My guts quivered.

Higher up, Alex directed me off right onto one of his variations that followed a series of small ledges cut like stairs into the rock. The staircase ended at a horizontal band of calcite thirty feet below the ledge where Alex was belaying. He coached me through the moves, which turned out to be even harder than the ones I'd just done. The handholds were on the left, footholds on the right, which forced me into an unfamiliar yoga-like contortion.

"Stick your left toe in the divot," said Alex. I looked out left and saw a triangle-shaped hole that resembled a snake eye. It was big enough for the pea-size chunk of rubber on the front of my shoe. I rocked over it like it was a ledge, committing my entire weight to it, knowing I just had to trust it because there was no other way to do this move—which is fine when there's a guy thirty feet above holding your rope.

"Nice job," said Alex, when I met him at anchor. It had been close, but I hadn't fallen on any of the pitches.

"How'd it go for you?" I asked.

"I'm grumpy," he replied.

"How come? Because of me? Because I was so slow?"

"Kind of. You did fine, but I had to wait for you in the middle of the first crux, a place where you want to just quickly move through, and so I fell. I wanted it to feel easy and it wasn't. I'm going to head back down and check it out a little more."

"Do you want a belay?"

"No, I think it will be easier if I just self-belay with my Grigri."

Alex had told me it was going to be hot on the wall, and it probably would be later in the day, but in the shade, with the stiff breeze, I was cold. I pulled up the hood on my shirt, and as I huddled on the ledge eating some jerky, I noticed an old bolt sticking out of the wall about five feet to the left of the main anchor. It was ancient, a rusted, brownish blob with an iron ring fastened through the eye of its hanger. I assumed it was one of the original bolts from the first ascent in 1961. There aren't many of these old bolts in Yosemite anymore. Most of them have been ripped out or been replaced with beefy stainless steel bolts by the American Safe Climbing Association (ASCA). I used to own one, a memento of the fifty-foot fall I took when I ripped it out of the Northwest Face of Half Dome on my first big wall in 1990. The ASCA sometimes leaves an old one here and there as a historical relic. This particular one undoubtedly had a story to tell.

The Salathé Wall was the second route on El Capitan. The first ascensionists, Royal Robbins, Chuck Pratt, and Tom Frost, had decided to up the ante on Warren Harding by climbing it in alpine style. Whereas Harding had spent a year and half sieging the Nose with half-inch hemp ropes (he later switched to nylon when one of them snapped) and a wheeled cart for hauling supplies, like coal in a mine, Robbins, Pratt, and Frost simply walked up to the base of the cliff and started up. I wondered if this ledge was where they spent their first night. Perhaps they had drilled the bolt so they had something secure to clip into as they bedded down right where I was sitting. What would they think about Honnold climbing this wall fifty-six years later, without a rope? Tom Frost was the only one still alive. Robbins had died in March. Pratt died in 2000. When asked by *Outside* magazine which climbers he respected from the new generation, Robbins had called out Honnold and Tommy Caldwell: "Many of the things that are being done today were clearly impossible in our day. And they're doing them."

Quietly jolted back from history to my immediate present, I noticed something strange that I hadn't seen at first. To the left of the main anchor, someone had chipped the word "slave" into the rock. It looked as though it had been pecked in with the pointy end of a wall hammer. An odd thing, considering that defacing the rock is one of the strongest taboos in climbing. I wondered who had done it and why.

My mind wandered back to Alex and the fact that he'd just fallen again on the slab. In October, Alex had told me that he had climbed the Freeblast twenty or so times. And he'd fallen twice— 10 percent of his attempts. I wasn't sure how many more times he had climbed it since, but even if he had doubled his previous tally, his ratio was now three out of forty: 7.5 percent. Sure, there were extenuating circumstances, like old silverbacks who forced him to stall out in the middle of the crux, shoes that were too loose or too tight, or just not being focused enough. But what struck me was that the odds seemed to have this weird way of staying consistent. The orange rope clipped to the anchor in front of me kept coming tight and then limp, as Alex went up and down. He wasn't giving up. But this slab was getting into his head.

I realized then and there that he would never have this slab section dialed in to his satisfaction—no matter how many times he rehearsed the moves. And he must have known it too; the climbing was just too insecure for him to ever feel the degree of certainty he sought for free solos. I remembered the story he'd told me about the slab move at the top of Half Dome, how his subconscious mind simply would not allow him to make the move. The same thing had happened the previous fall in this same spot on his first attempt.

What would happen this time? I wondered. Would he just roll the dice, as Ueli Steck had done on the South Face of Annapurna? Alex had said this climb was so singularly special that it might be worth just saying fuck it and rolling the dice. The question was: Could he override his instinct, which seemed to know, as only our primal selves can, that pulling this slab move without a rope was a very bad idea? *Was Tommy right,* I wondered, *when he said that this whole business was just a game of Russian roulette?*

"Well?" I asked, when he pulled back onto the ledge.

"I'm just kind of bummed," he replied. "I was so excited that I had maybe found a way around the slabs, but these variations just aren't noticeably better. That move is really insecure. I don't like it."

We stood side by side for a minute or two.

"What do you want to do?" said Alex finally. "Do you want to keep going, or do you want to bail?"

"I'm easy," I replied. "I'm here to support you, so whatever you want to do is fine."

"I'm not really bothered to keep going," said Alex, "but I'm also not stoked to deal with all these people either." Looking down the wall, we could see two parties on their way up. We would have to rappel past them, and invariably, they would want to know what we were doing, if they didn't already know. For the past month, Alex had again been all over Freerider, working various sections on almost a daily basis. All the climbers in Yosemite, it seemed, were being respectful and discreet, but with each passing day, word of Alex's spring campaign was spreading exponentially. He didn't say so, but I suspected he bore extra psychological weight now that his secret was going viral. It all added up to a whole lot of people, most of whom Alex didn't know, who had expectations of him.

"Let's chill for a few minutes," said Alex, plopping down onto the ledge and pulling up the hood on his shirt. He reached into his pack and pulled out an apple, took a big bite, and held it out to me. I took a chunk out of the other side and handed it back. Passing it back and forth, we quickly took it down to the core.

"Is it cool if I toss this?" I asked.

"Actually, give it to me." I handed it over, and he dropped it into his pack. "I do chuck them sometimes, but there are people down there, so let's just bring it down with us."

The normal way to descend a cliff is to feed the rope through a set of rappel rings, jam the two strands through a tubular friction plate, then slide down to the next anchor one at a time. This, of course, is not how Alex does it. His preferred method is called simul-rappelling, which entails a person on each end of the rope, sliding down at the same time. It requires careful coordination because if one person forgets that he's counterbalancing his partner and unclips, the other goes flying. It was in this manner that Alex and I ended up hanging on either side of a bearded young man who looked like he was about to slip off the side of the mountain.

"If you want, you can just step on that bolt," said Alex, "and from there you can reach this hold."

The guy looked bewildered. He didn't acknowledge that he knew it was Alex Honnold coaching him. But he knew. Everyone knows Alex. These days, there probably isn't a climber anywhere who wouldn't recognize him. Between his long neck, doe eyes, big ears, and uniform—the black pants and red shirt—he's memorable. The guy looked like I did when I climbed this section, but maybe worse, because he had a bad case of "sewing-machine leg"—which is exactly what it sounds like. Alex, sensing that his student was about to go airborne, swung in closer and started pointing out every possible hold. Following Alex's detailed instructions, the guy squeaked out the sequence, but he must have still been spooked, because when he got to the next bolt he hooked his finger through the hanger.

"Hey, man, you don't want to do that. If you slip, you're going to break your finger. It's better to pinch it like this," said Alex, holding up his fingers like how you'd grab someone's earlobe.

"Just a little unsolicited advice," I offered, hopping into the conversation. The guy hadn't said a word, so I wanted to give him an opening to say, "Yeah, thanks, I'll figure it out," in case he felt that Alex was oversharing. Some climbers don't appreciate being sprayed with beta.

The whole scene struck me as bizarre, considering that a few minutes earlier, Alex had told me he was dreading having to interact with these people. I expected Alex to be tight-lipped, but instead he was eager—a tad too eager, at least to my mind—to help a complete stranger.

THE NEXT DAY, I sat on a rock underneath a scrub oak watching the sky turn gray and enjoying the cool mist from Yosemite Falls. It would be dark in a few minutes, but I was in no rush to get back down to the valley floor. I wanted to think a little bit more about the route beneath me, a four-hundred-foot 5.6 called Munginella. Was I up for soloing it?

I'd been thinking so much about free soloing over the past year that it had gotten under my skin. In some ways, I found myself in a position similar to where Alex was in 2004. I was spending most of my time researching, studying, and writing about the great free soloists who had operated during my lifetime—Barber, Bachar, Croft, Potter, and Honnold. The deeper I got into the subject, the more it seemed to take hold of me. I kept asking myself what I might be capable of if I shelved my fear.

I had been talking and e-mailing with J. B. MacKinnon, the writer who arranged Alex's brain scan. He told me that after his trip to South Carolina with Alex, he had returned to his home in Vancouver "ready to push the limits" of his own brain. The reward he walked away with from working with Alex was the knowledge that we all have it within us to work a "little bit of Honnold's magic," as he said. We might not be able to shut down our fears on command, but as MacKinnon wrote in *Nautilus* magazine, "with conscious effort and gradual, repeated exposure to what we fear, any one of us might muster courage that we didn't know we had." MacKinnon hadn't free soloed in years, but a few days after he got home he went and soloed a couple of 5.7 routes at a local cliff, "just to remember the feeling." And the feeling must have been heady, because I talked to him again shortly after I arrived in Yosemite, and he told me that he was still soloing and had brought the grade up to 5.9. The Honnold magic held some allure for me, too. The more I thought about free soloing, the more I wanted to do it myself.

That spring, I was entering my thirty-second year of climbing, and while I wouldn't call myself a free soloist, I do consider soloing to be a requisite component of the game. I typically solo my home cliff, the five-hundred-foot Cathedral Ledge, a time or two each season, and in the winter I usually solo a few ice climbs. When I used to guide a lot, one of my weaknesses was spacing my protection points so widely that I might as well have been free soloing. My examiners at the American Mountain Guides Association gave me marginal scores for "running it out," but I kept doing it, almost compulsively.

Over the winter, I had decided that since I wasn't going to have a partner in Yosemite, or a lot of time to climb, I should do some free soloing. I had even written up a list of routes, some of which I had soloed before. Munginella was on the list. It was the only route on the list I had never climbed. I had just spent the past couple of hours rope soloing the route, which is different from mini-tracking. I led the route from the bottom, self-belaying myself with a Grigri on a skinny, eight-millimeter rope that I tied to an anchor at the base of each pitch. At the end of each lead, I'd rappel off, take out the gear, and then mini-track back up. This meant climbing the wall twice, which was good, because I was rehearsing it for the solo—like Alex on Freerider, just seven grades easier.

When I mentioned to Alex that I was thinking about free soloing Munginella, he had told me to just go for it, even though I'd never done it. He's not shy about pressing other people to push their limits. But I was glad I hadn't, because near the top, some three hundred feet off the deck, I encountered a move that was hard and committing for a 5.6. I hadn't expected the route to have a roof move. The only decent hold on this crux was a hand jam in the ceiling over my head. I slotted my hand into the fissure, touched the tip of my thumb to the base of my pinky, and flexed my fingers to hold it in place. It was a good jam, but it was behind my head, and as I pulled my feet up onto some small nubs on the wall in front of me, my body went inverted. I was surprised to find myself hanging nearly horizontal.

Looking over my right shoulder to take in the exposure, I

imagined how this move would feel without the rope. My last piece of protection was about twenty feet below me. If I fell, I would go twice that distance, plus rope stretch, which, on an eight-millimeter rope, is significant. So I was looking at a fifty-foot fall, minimum, and I would hit a ledge or two along the way. I'd suffer major, quite possibly fatal, bodily trauma—an unthinkable fall, really. But, no matter how run out I was, that strand of nylon, thinner than my pinky, profoundly altered my perception of the situation. It pushed the certainty of death around the corner, out of plain sight. However illusory, the rope provided an essential psychological buffer that allowed me to calmly hang my life from one hand stuffed in a crack, a dizzying height above the ground.

This is exactly what makes free-solo rock climbing so different from other extreme sports. If a big-wave surfer or an extreme skier falls, he could die. But he might not. When you fall free-solo rock climbing, there is no uncertainty. Though I can't possibly know how it would feel to plummet helplessly through the air from some horrific height, it nevertheless has for me a terrifying, visceral reality. I've had the falling-to-my-death nightmare many times. Psychologists have reported that it's one of the most common recurring dreams. Falling to one's death has to be right up there on the list of primal fears, alongside getting eaten by a shark and being buried alive. So what the hell was I thinking? Why would I choose to do this without the rope? Well, I was thinking I could do it and not fall. And that I'd get some kind of psychological payback from confronting one of my primal fears.

So I sat on that rock at the top of Munginella, and I tried to calculate my odds. On a toprope, I figured I could climb it a thousand times in a row without falling. With the security of a rope overhead, on terrain that's far below my maximum grade, it's easy to climb well, to be in the zone, smooth yet precise and focused with my movement. If I could climb the route a thousand times on a rope and not fall, I'd estimate my odds of success would be better than 99.9 percent.

But without a rope? What if in the middle of the roof I panicked, even a little? Would I lose the .9? And if I did get scared, was it possible I could freeze up, or maybe even do something wantonly self-destructive?

In the summer of 1987, I was sitting on a guardrail by the side of the road outside Sullivan Stadium in Foxboro, Massachusetts, having just emerged from a Grateful Dead concert. A young woman pulled out of the parking lot, and as she drove by me, I got a close look at her. She leaned over the wheel blinking repeatedly, as if she was having trouble seeing. Her face was red and streaming with tears. Whatever substances she was on, she was definitely in no shape to be driving. She made a left turn. A police cruiser was coming the other way. I was watching her closely, curious to see how she'd react to the cop, when she yanked the wheel to the side and drove head-on into him. Neither car was going that fast, so she didn't get badly hurt, but she was so hysterical afterward that they strapped her to a gurney and took her away in an ambulance. The reason I never forgot it was because I had seen her yank the wheel, as if she had done it on purpose.

It reminded me of the classic scene from the movie *Annie Hall*, in which Duane (played by Christopher Walken) says to Alvy Singer (played by Woody Allen):

> Sometimes when I'm driving . . . on the road at night . . . I see two headlights coming toward me. Fast. I have this sudden impulse to turn the wheel quickly, head-on into the oncoming car. I can anticipate the explosion. The sound of shattering glass. The . . . flames rising out of the flowing gasoline.

Alvy responds, "Right. Well, I have to . . . I have to go now, Duane, because I, I'm due back on the planet Earth."

Have you ever stood near the edge of a high place, like a rooftop, or a cliff-side overlook, and felt a strange compulsion to step off the edge, almost like the abyss was calling to you, beckoning you to take that leap into the void? If there was nothing between you and oblivion but one hand clinging to a rock, can you say with 100 percent certainty that you wouldn't just let go? As I asked myself this question and tried to quantify things that are probably unquantifiable, I wondered if this fear of a kind of suicide, the fear that perhaps we're not actually in control of our actions and thoughts, lies at the heart of why people react so viscerally to free soloing.

There was no way for me to know if some demon would make me let go of the hand jam in the roof without putting myself out there. And wasn't that part of the Honnold magic? But I also knew that the real essence of the lesson to be learned from Alex was having the courage not just to face down one's fears but also to follow the process with conscientiousness and premeditation. That's why I was scoping Munginella instead of just going for it. And it's why I was listening to the little voice inside my head, the one that tells me what's okay and what's not, the one that has kept me alive all these years. And that little voice was telling me that the overhanging hand jam was on the wrong side of the fence.

TOMMY CALDWELL SHOWED UP OVER Memorial Day weekend for a quick visit. Alex seized the opportunity and dragged him up Freerider in five and a half hours, a new speed record for the route. "Alex was on fire," Tommy told me the next day, as we hiked up to the start of the Dawn Wall. He said that while he was up on Freerider he had tried to imagine free soloing the route himself. "Honestly, I really can't fathom it."

"Did you guys talk about it?"

"I'm really hesitant to say anything at this point. Before, I was expressing a lot of doubt, telling him how I felt about it all. Now, I'm a little bit more like, 'He's going to do it no matter what,' so the best thing I can do is try and up his chances of success. And for me that means trying not to mentally rattle him. I don't want him up there having doubts because other people are having doubts."

We had found our way to a giant concavity in the southeast face called the Alcove. It marks the start for the Dawn Wall and several other famous routes, including the Reticent Wall, Mescalito, and South Seas; I had set off from here on all of them. Tommy and I found a flat place to sit down with our backs to the cliff. The Dawn Wall is so overhanging that we could see it rising in front of us. A portaledge covered in a red rainfly was hanging about 1,200 feet up.

"That's the camp where I spent months of my life," said Tommy. "The crux pitches are right above it." We could see one guy on the wall above the portaledge. The other one was probably belaying him from inside the ledge. They were aid climbers and had already been on the wall for several days.

I asked Tommy how he was feeling about Alex's odds. "Do you think it's less than 1 percent that he will fall?"

"No way," he replied. "I think it's like 10 percent, if I had to put a number on it."

"That high?"

"Well, I know you've done the math. If he's done the Freeblast thirty times and fallen three, that's 10 percent right there. And it's not like that's the only hard, insecure climbing on the route. If I were to go free solo it right now, I would be way less worried about the slabs than some of the stuff up high. I've actually never fallen on the Freeblast, and I've climbed it fifteen to twenty times. But

I've always felt real lucky to get through the Boulder Problem, and yesterday I fell on it. Alex was right above me, coaching me through the moves, but I missed when I threw the karate kick."

"Why do you think he's fallen on it as much as he has? Is he not a slab master?"

"Maybe not. Then again, I feel like Alex has climbed twice as much rock as anybody in the world . . . ever. Seems like maybe it's gotten in his head." He didn't say anything for a bit, then added, "I think I'm okay that I'm not going to be here. It's not really the kind of thing I want to spectate."

Tommy started to whistle. I wondered if he'd picked up the habit from Alex, or vice versa. They're the only two guys I know who whistle.

In the back of El Cap Meadow, there's a certain oak tree that sits on the bank of the Merced River. The trunk is about four or five feet across, which would make it about two hundred years old. Its dense canopy throws shade over the lush green grass, but in a couple of spots, where people like to sit, the grass is thinner and matted down. With your back against its trunk, you can take in the entirety of El Capitan, from the west face on its left side, around the Nose, and all the way up the southeast face to Horsetail Fall and the East Buttress. From the San Francisco beatniks in the fifties to the hippies of the sixties, the Stonemasters, the Chongo Nation, and the Stone Monkeys, the tree has always been the place for people to sit and get high and admire the grandeur of a magnificent cliff. It's a special tree for climbers, and not just because some of Dean Potter's ashes were scattered at its base.

The river, pumping with spring runoff, had partially flooded the meadow, but I found a dry spot under the tree, where I set up my spotting scope and then plopped down into my camp chair. Starting at the rim, I ran the scope down the wall until I found Alex and

Cheyne Lempe hanging on the anchor above the Boulder Problem. When Alex left the valley in the fall, he had climbed the Boulder Problem, Freerider's technical crux, about fifteen times in a row without falling a single time. I knew he'd done it a few more times this spring, including the two times he had climbed the route from top to bottom, and as far as I knew, he'd hadn't fallen on it yet.

You can try a climb a hundred times and fail on the same move a hundred times. But succeed on that move once, and you may be able to do it every time from then on. Why is that? And what caused the mental block that prevented you from doing it in the first place, when clearly you were capable of sticking the move all along? On climbing moves that are at or near your limit, there's a hard-to-define warrior spirit, a ferocity you must tap into when going for that next hold. Without that little extra bit of oomph, your fingers can hit the hold over and over but never latch. Sometimes, it can feel as though you're coming up short intentionally. This is such a well-known phenomenon in climbing that we even have a term for it: "punting."

But once you've proven to yourself that you can do a move or even an entire route, it's like a tiny door opens inside your mind, and the belief that you can do it, that you *will* succeed, creates a powerful positive visualization. Golfers are famous for using this technique with their putting. Visualize the ball rolling into the cup and there is a far better chance it will actually go in. The actor Jim Carrey tells the story of using positive visualization to find career success. In 1987, before he was famous, he wrote himself a check for 10 million dollars and on the memo line wrote "for acting services rendered." The story goes that he carried it around in his wallet until he finally found his breakout role in 1994.

In a way, it's what Alex was doing on Freerider. All the time he spent rehearsing the route was partly to memorize sequences and learn the intricacies of movement that would give him the greatest margin for error when executing the moves without a rope. But every time he succeeded on a crux move, he was also adding a few rings of chain mail to the mental armor he would wear when he set off on his ultimate climb.

So I had to blink to make sure my eyes weren't deceiving me when I saw Alex swing off the rock near the top of the Boulder Problem. I wasn't watching closely enough to see which move he slipped on, but one second he was on and the next he was dangling on the rope. He hung in his harness for a few seconds, then pulled back on and climbed up to the anchor. A few minutes later, he and Cheyne continued simul-rappelling down the wall.

As he neared the bottom of the cliff, I packed up my stuff and hiked to the base to meet him. I was holding a tree branch I had grabbed from the woods to use as a walking stick on the hike up.

"You look like some kind of Boy Scout troop leader," said Alex, chuckling. "And, hey, cool shirt, have you been to Mont Saint-Michel?"

"I haven't. I got this from my son Will, who just did a French exchange program with his high school. He said it was his favorite spot in France. He brought me back this shirt and some special Mont Saint-Michel salt that apparently they have in these sheds free for the taking."

"That's so funny," said Alex. "Because I can picture that. I was there as a kid and I remember my parents buying me this little toy crossbow."

"How old were you?"

"Like, four."

"And you remember it?"

"I do. Isn't that weird?"

And it was, kind of, because Alex had told me on other occasions that he remembers almost nothing from his youth.

On the hike out, Alex stopped to look at his phone. I thought he was texting until he said, "Wow, Trump just pulled us out of the Paris accord. That is so depressing." The news had just broken that minute. Alex looked dejected.

"You knew he was going to do it, didn't you?"

"I know they were saying so, but I was still hoping."

Alex doesn't talk much about his environmentalism, but it's one of his most deeply held convictions. Ted Hesser, the guy who shared his energy reports with Alex and now works for the Honnold Foundation, told me that Alex had recently written a 50,000-dollar check to help jump-start a grassroots solar-power initiative in Ethiopia. This was the first I'd heard about it. If I hadn't gone climbing with Ted, I never would have known. There were no press releases, no posts on Alex's social media.

"So how'd it go up there?"

"It went well," said Alex. Either he had forgotten about falling on the Boulder Problem, or he was choosing to put it out of his mind. "The route's in good shape. All my tick marks are still there, and it's totally dry. Conditions are pretty much perfect, and I think that's it. I don't think I'm going back up."

He sounded relieved to finally be done prepping the route, but the endless trips up and down El Cap over the past year had taken a toll on him physically. His eyes were glassy, and the crow's-feet on their edges looked deeper than I remembered them. A few days earlier, while I sat in the passenger seat as he did yet another hangboard session, he admitted that he was profoundly tired. "Every time I hike to the top of El Cap my legs just feel dead." He said he felt tired all winter and that there were many days when he wasn't happy with how he was climbing. But he did have one week of "total transcendence." All along, I had been wondering how he could time this so that he goes for it on a day when he's feeling transcendent. For every athlete who has a personal best at the Olympics, there are a dozen more who don't peak right when they need to. But for Alex, there was more on the line than the chance to win an Olympic medal. What he was endeavoring to do would be like going for the world record long jump between two skyscrapers spaced twenty-nine and a half feet apart.

As we strolled down the trail, El Cap at our back, it hit home for me, perhaps more poignantly than it ever had before, that the guy in front of me was more like the rest of us than we like to admit. He gets migraines and has a wicked sweet tooth. Sometimes he feels like he's wearing lead shoes. Once in a while, though he's loath to admit it, he falls unexpectedly.

"Is Sanni still here?" I asked.

"No, she left yesterday. Went back to our place in Vegas. I basically asked her to leave and she was totally cool about it."

I had somehow missed Sanni entirely this round. A few days earlier, I was chatting with Jimmy in his van when I saw her walking up the road. I was about to jump out and say hello when she stepped into Alex's van, which was parked a few feet away, and slid the door shut behind her. When the two of them are in the box, I don't like to bother them.

"How did the slabs feel?" I asked Alex.

"Really insecure. I still always feel like my feet could slip. But at the same time, I'm like, well, it's worked every time."

I didn't say what I was thinking. *Actually, it hasn't worked every time.*

When we got to my car we could see Tom Evans and a few other people sitting under a tree on the east side of the meadow with a giant spotting scope trained on the wall. Undoubtedly, they had just watched Alex rappel Freerider. Tom, who's in his seventies and has climbed El Capitan five times, runs a website called the ElCap Report, which chronicles the doings on El Cap with photos and daily blogs. He's a friend of Alex's and has been in the meadow observing and recording almost everything Alex has done on El

Capitan since he first showed up in the valley more than a decade ago. Alex told me that Tom knew about the plan and had asked if Alex would give him a heads-up before he went for it so he could photograph the ascent.

"How does he know?" I asked.

"Because he's not stupid," replied Alex.

I started climbing on El Cap before the Tom Evans days. When the Report started, I hated knowing that someone was watching me when I was up there, and writing about it on a website. I knew Tom enjoyed broad support, and I couldn't figure out why other people didn't feel like I did, that it was like letting a stranger into your bedroom. Something about knowing I was being watched killed part of the magic of being up on El Cap. I was so unsupportive of his mission that I never once checked out the website. It was only recently that I finally did, and I saw the disclaimer on the home page saying that if you didn't want to be photographed, just let him know, and he'd leave you alone. The fact that I was now doing the exact same thing as Tom was not lost on me.

When we pulled into Mike's, a small blue hatchback was parked next to Alex's van. "Oh wow, my mom's here," said Alex, looking a bit taken aback.

We found her on the front porch eating lunch with two friends. Alex and I gave his mom a hug and then she introduced us to her companions, who were visiting from France. Dierdre Wolownick (she changed back to her maiden name after the divorce) is tall and thin, and, like her son, she has distinctive-looking fingers. But they're not fat like Alex's. They're long and thin, with knobby knuckles. I remembered Alex once telling me that his mom is a lifelong piano player. I first met her in 2013 when she came to New Hampshire to do some rock climbing. Before the trip she sent out an e-mail to members of the American Alpine Club. It started out: "This is Alex Honnold's mom. Also a climber. I'll be climbing in the northeast this summer and I'm hoping to find some partners."

In November, a few days before Alex made his first attempt on Freerider, I went climbing with Dierdre. It was a bit surreal because she had no idea what her son was planning, and I didn't mention it. The night before our climb, she told me the story about the first and only time she had watched her son free solo. She and Alex were road-tripping on the East Coast, on their way to a family reunion, when Alex, who was seventeen at the time, asked if they could stop in the Shawangunks, a popular climbing area in the Catskills outside New York City. They were hiking under a famous cliff called the Near Trapps when Alex disappeared. Dierdre looked up and down the trail, wondering where he could have gone. Then she finally looked up and saw him clinging to the side of a cliff overhead. "Get down here," she yelled. "I'm fine, Mom," replied Alex.

"How did that feel to watch him being up off the ground without a rope?" I asked Dierdre.

"Well, I had to force myself to trust his judgment, because I didn't have any judgment in this type of situation. I'm thinking, 'Well, he obviously knows what he's doing, let him do it.'"

In the years since that first solo, as Alex slowly developed into an unparalleled climber, he never once told his mom before he went big. Dierdre always heard about his climbs afterward, of course, and she meticulously collected clippings from newspapers, magazines, and the Internet about her son's exploits. The scrapbooks, which Alex's friends call his Hall of Fame, can still be found to this day on the coffee table in her living room in Carmichael. What goes through a parent's mind, I wondered, when they hear that their child has just scaled a 2,000-foot sheer cliff without a rope?

"A sigh of relief, you know, that kind of thing," she said. "And, 'Wow! My son did that?' There's that side of it too. He's done these outstanding, outrageous things that nobody else can do. That's an honor, you know. But also, I wish he wouldn't."

I TOOK A GROUP PHOTO of the four of them. Alex and Dierdre were speaking in French. Mine is rusty, but it sounded like Dierdre was asking Alex if he would go on a hike with them. "Oui, oui," he replied. Alex didn't say anything about what he had up his sleeve, and his mom didn't ask. But she did give me an inquisitive look as I bid them all adieu. A few days earlier, Jimmy had told me that Dierdre had finally figured it out. She knew.

Poor woman, I thought as I jumped back in my rental car, leaving Alex to entertain his mom and her friends.

THE PROPERTY where I was staying in Foresta was hosting a music festival, so I had to move out the next day because the band was staying in my apartment. I called the reservations number for the park to see if by some miracle there were any campsites, tent cabins, or hotel rooms open, but, of course, there was nothing. It was Friday, June 2, and the park was thronged with tourists. Reservations in Yosemite open six months in advance, and to get one, you have to speed-dial the number the minute registration goes live. I decided I had only one option, which was to move back into a cave where I'd often slept in my younger days.

I was loading my pack with my sleeping bag and pillow when my phone dinged.

"Looks like it is on. I'm headed up in an hour or so," read the text from Jimmy. Alex had gone bouldering that morning, and then hiking in the afternoon with his mom and her friends. He had told me he was going to take two full rest days before he went for the climb. And his mom was still in the valley. I had assumed he wouldn't go for it until she left because, like Sanni's, his mom's presence carried a psychological weight—a weight that I didn't think he'd want on his shoulders when he set off. *Maybe he's just sick of waiting,* I thought.

One thing was sure: Now I really didn't want to sleep under a rock. With my luck, I'd get caught and kicked out of the park. On a whim, I called a hotel in El Portal, just outside the park boundary. They'd had a cancellation. It was 210 dollars for one night. The old Mark—the one who once lived an entire season in Yosemite off 107 dollars—cringed when I said, "I'll take it."

Half an hour later, I was parked at a pullout on the west side of El Cap Meadow, near the spot where I planned to watch the climb in the morning. I stood outside the driver's side with the door open and cracked a can of beer. "If You Leave Me Now" by Chicago played on the car's radio as I watched the last rays of sun slowly creep up the west face of El Capitan. I traced the line of Freerider from where it appeared just above the trees and spotted a party of climbers on Mammoth Terrace setting up their portaledge for the night. On dozens of nights in portaledges on the side of El Cap, a can of malt liquor in my chalk-stained hand, back against the wall, I've felt the heat from the stone radiating like a fireplace hearth. We used to drag along a boom box, which we padded with duct tape and foam from an old blown-out sleeping pad. All day long we'd listen to 104.1 the Hawk—the same station I was listening to now. I wondered if people still did that, if maybe the folks up on Mammoth—the ones who were going to wake up to the equivalent of an alien sighting in the morning—were listening to Chicago right now.

I tried to picture Alex up on the wall, but my mind didn't want to go there. Instead, it kept conjuring up a different image. *Alex trots out of the woods near the base of the Manure Pile. His face is glowing. He comes over to where I'm waiting and gives me a hug.* I looked around; there was no one nearby. I leaned on my forearms. Tears dripped off my cheeks and puddled on the roof of the rental car.

IT WAS PITCH-BLACK IN THE BOX when Alex awoke on the morning of June 3, 2017. *Okay, let's do this.* But when he picked up his phone, he saw to his disappointment that it was still only two thirty A.M. He rolled over and fell right back asleep. Two hours later his alarm jolted him awake. He swung his legs off the edge of the bed and hopped down onto his feet. Once standing upright, he realized that he didn't feel so great. He had gone to bed with a headache, and it lingered. Might have been from watching *The Hobbit* the afternoon before. For some reason watching movies during the day often gave him headaches. Or it could have been the multiple hours of speaking French on the hikes with his mom and her friends the past two days.

He flipped on the galley light and his breakfast was sitting on the countertop, premade the night before—a bowl of muesli topped with chia seeds, flax, and blueberries. He grabbed a carton of hemp milk from the minifridge and poured it over the top, then sat in the passenger seat holding the bowl in his lap. The muesli was a stash that he had been saving for this morning. The past few days he had been eating a different variety sold in the Yosemite grocery store, and he didn't like it as much. So he was surprised when he lost his appetite halfway through the bowl—he usually devoured his breakfast.

Alex slipped behind the wheel of the ProMaster and backed out slowly onto Lost Arrow Road. He took a right turn down Oak Lane, slowing as he crossed the two speed bumps outside the Yosemite preschool. A minute later he was rolling down the loop road toward El Capitan.

At the trailhead, it was still dark, so he threw on a headlamp. He carried a small black backpack with his shoes, a chalk bag, a water bottle, and a chocolate chip Clif Zbar. He wore a pair of tattered approach shoes, his Huck Finn pants, a red T-shirt, and a thin fleece hoodie. Near the base of the cliff, he heard a commotion and looked up to see a bear thrashing through the bushes toward the fixed lines coming down from the Nose. Alex looked up at the 3,000-foot vertical wall above him. *That's a big cliff,* he said to himself. Then he sat down and slipped on his climbing shoes. A few minutes later, he fastened his chalk bag around his waist, teed up his favorite playlist of "gnarly hate rock" on his iPhone, found his first toehold, and began inching his way upward.

He was barely off the ground when he heard jangling in the woods. Three climbers emerged from under the trees and looked up the wall. There was a guy on the first pitch of the Freeblast wearing scrappy cutoff black pants and a red T-shirt. And he wasn't attached to a rope.

"Oh my god," said one of them. "It's happening."

AT 5:35 A.M., a tiny dot appeared just above the forest. I plopped into my camp chair, feeling thankful for my puffy coat, hat, and gloves. According to the thermometer in the rental car, it was fifty-eight degrees, but it felt colder sitting in the mist that had settled over the meadow. The tall grass was covered in dew, and my legs were soaked from the knees down. It was too early for any tourists to be out, and the road was quiet. The only sound was a faint rustle of wind high overhead, up in the ether into which Alex was climbing. I pulled up my hood and tried to ignore the buzzing swarm of mosquitoes around my head as I looked for Alex through the eyepiece of my spotting scope. When I found him in the viewfinder, he was already 150 feet off the ground—well into the death zone. He was moving steadily upward, and I had to constantly adjust the angle of the spotting scope to keep him in the frame, which covered about a hundred feet of cliff.

There was a small red bundle on the back of his left hip—his hoodie, which he had rolled up and tied around his waist. I thought it was odd that he wouldn't either wear it or leave it behind. The sky had been gray on the drive up from El Portal, like it always is at dawn, but it had stayed gray. A high scud blocked the sun.

Twelve minutes later, Alex hauled himself up onto a small pedestal at the top of pitch 4. He reached down, unlaced his left shoe, and slipped the heel off the back of his foot, then did the same with his right. Above him rose the first of the crux slab pitches. The move that had caused him to abort in the fall was about fifty feet above him. Alex looked down and stared directly into the lens of the spotting scope. I doubted he could see me, but I was gazing right into his eyes. As usual, they were wide open. I texted this detail to Peter Gwin, who was back at *National Geographic*'s headquarters in DC updating that same Google doc. As I returned to my scope to find Alex, Trango came back to me. All these years later and I was still trying to share what makes climbing such a singular experience—only now I was on the other side of the lens. We say that we climb for our souls, but the truth is that most of us need to share the experience with others to make it meaningful.

Mikey was standing next to me, wearing a blue cotton hoodie and filming with a large camera set on a tripod. He had blown his knee out skiing a few weeks earlier and was walking with a limp, which meant he couldn't work with the crew on the wall.

After Alex's experience in the fall, and a lot of soul searching, he had decided not to have any camera guys on the crux pitches. Jimmy and Alex had been discussing these details over the past few weeks, and they had recently agreed that Jimmy and Cheyne would film only the top of the route—the section that Alex had never fallen on. Of course, close-up footage of Alex on the slabs and the Boulder Problem was critical for the film, so they agreed on a compromise. Jimmy would capture these shots with remotely operated cameras that he would strap to the wall. For most of the climb, including all of the most difficult sections, the camera team would be invisible to Alex. Still, I wondered whether he could block out the virtual presence that was hovering in the air all around him. Could he find the Zen that would allow him to enter that all-important flow state? He would have preferred that we weren't down here, or anywhere near El Cap, at all; he had mentioned this to me a few different times: after his first attempt, over the winter, and then a week earlier when we were hanging out in his van. Even in the abstract, knowing we were watching his every move was a distraction.

Alex was caught in a classic catch-22. Filming this climb had been his idea, after all. And he still wanted the greatest achievement of his life to be captured for posterity. It was also a little late in the game to walk away and leave Jimmy hanging.

It felt as though he stood on that ledge for half an hour, but when he pulled his shoes back on, I looked at my phone and only two minutes had elapsed. It was going to be a long morning. Alex set off, pulled over a small roof, and smeared his way up into the crux.

"I can't watch this," said Mikey, stepping away from his camera.

IT WAS OKAY. He always felt this way at the beginning of a big solo. It took time to find the flow state, that old friend that allowed him to surrender, to trust that he was going to climb to the best of his ability. If he slipped? That was just the cost of doing business. On every other big solo, he had compensated for the tightness by over-gripping. His fingers were so strong that he sometimes had to be careful he didn't rip the holds right off the mountain. And therein lay the problem he now faced: There were no handholds. He had no choice but to trust his feet.

But there was a tiny crust in the rock, which he had discovered in the fall. A crease no bigger than a perforation in a piece of notebook paper. It was a non-hold, almost like a tick mark—a thing that showed you where to put your hand. He had been glad when he found it, because even if he couldn't actually hold on to it, it was comforting to know there was *something* underneath his fingers. And there it was, right in front of him. But he didn't put his hand there. Instead, he reached up and pinched his fingers through the shiny steel hanger, his forefinger touching the tip of his thumb as if he was making the okay sign. He was careful not to let his fingers touch the metal. As long as he didn't grab the hanger, he reasoned, it wasn't cheating. Alex had decided to make this compromise a few days earlier, after we had climbed the slabs together and he had lowered back down to do the moves again. He didn't mention it to me until we were hiking out. "I tried this new thing on the first slab crux on pitch 5," he had said. "I pinched my finger through the hanger on that one sketchy foot move, the one I backed off on in the fall. I can do it without touching the hanger."

"Cool. Sort of like what you did on Half Dome with the carabiner, huh?"

"Yeah, exactly. I mean, if I fell I'm sure I'd break my finger."

"Well . . ."

"Yeah, it's a lot better than dying."

ALEX LOOKED UP AND FELT thankful there was no cameraman dangling above him. This time he was alone.

He rocked up onto the horrible foothold, his fingers hovering inside the hanger like he was playing the game Operation, trying to remove the patient's funny bone. He brought his left foot up, and for one or two seconds his body was splayed out, like a ski jumper doing a spread eagle. He shifted his weight onto his right foot, brought his left foot over to the same hold, and did a quick foot match. A second later he was through and onto good holds. The entire slab sequence had taken a total of twenty seconds. And for that brief moment in time, the equivalent of taking two deep breaths, there wasn't a person on the planet whose physical hold on the world was more tenuous. Had he so much as sneezed, it could have been the last move he ever made.

He quickly moved up through a swatch of vibrant lime green lichen and entered a serpentine band of calcite that stretched across the wall like a giant white snake. At the big step down on pitch 6, he grabbed the good hold with his left hand, then switched it to his right. Leaning out to the left, he slowly lowered himself downward, his left foot tapping against the rock, all herky-jerky, as he dropped into a crouch and his right knee bent like a blade closing on a jackknife.

"That can't be fun," I said quietly. Mikey stood a few feet away, still with his back to the wall. Even from half a mile away, it was obvious Alex was feeling tight. But he had made it through. In three minutes, he had put both the slab cruxes behind him, moves that had haunted him for years. He scrambled onto the ledge above, sat down, and spent the next two minutes loosening the lacing on his shoes. He didn't notice it, but just above his head was where someone had pecked the word "slave" into the rock.

FOREST ALTHERR WAS HAVING ONE of those dreams in which you think you've awoken, but you're still dreaming. He peered out of his sleeping bag and locked eyes with a climber sneaking past, his ropes pinning Forest and his partner Jeff to the wall. Just as the dream deepened, Forest woke up and saw a figure moving toward the ledge. *Oh shit, here it comes,* he thought.

Then he saw the red shirt and the black pants, and he knew exactly who it was. *Holy shit, it's Honnold.* Everyone had been talking about the upcoming free solo in Camp 4, but nothing could have prepared him for this moment.

"You guys look pooped," said Alex.

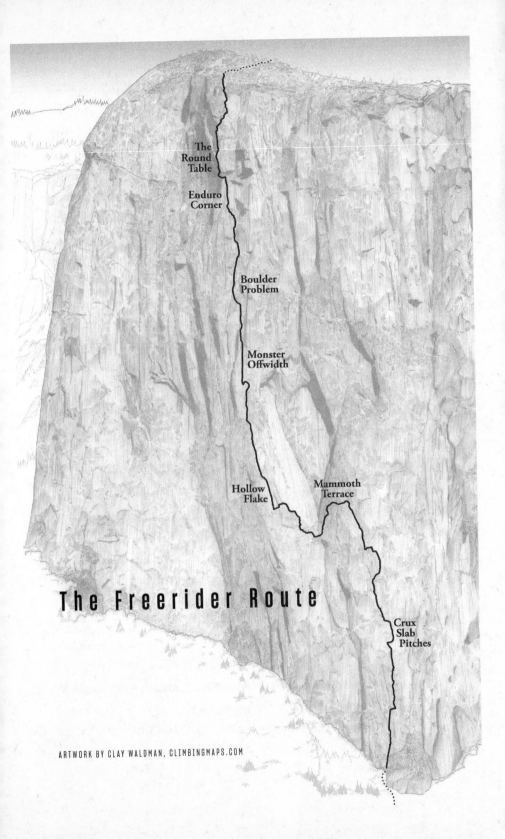

The Round
Table

Enduro
Corner

Boulder
Problem

Monster
Offwidth

Hollow
Flake

Mammoth
Terrace

The Freerider Route

Crux
Slab
Pitches

ARTWORK BY CLAY WALDMAN, CLIMBINGMAPS.COM

"No way, man," replied Forest defensively. "We didn't poop on the ledge. We have a poop tube."

It might have been that Forest was still half-asleep. It could have been the bad dream; or perhaps he just had poop on the brain. As an infectious disease epidemiologist, he'd been studying feces for years. His boss used to tag his progress reports with a pooping unicorn when his work was outstanding. It was an inside joke having to do with a viral Internet advertisement for a product called the Squatty Potty. The ad features a unicorn that poops rainbow-swirl ice cream. At the end, a bunch of smiling kids line up to get their poop cones. So when Forest came across a unicorn onesie on Amazon, he bought it. Ever since, he had been ticking off the FUA (First Unicorn Ascent) of classic routes around the country. He wore the onesie now, but Alex, focused as he was, didn't notice.

"No, sorry, I just meant that you guys look tired," said Alex.

The entire exchange lasted only a minute or two. Jeff would later recall that Alex didn't have a huge presence, that there was something casual about the way he carried himself, how he slumped his shoulders. "Had it been portrayed in a movie, they would have asked him to stand a little straighter and look more superheroish," he said.

As Alex moved past, Jeff wasn't sure what to say. *Have a nice day? Good luck? Take it easy?* None of these seemed appropriate, so he kept his mouth shut.

THE NORMAL METHOD FOR GETTING into the Hollow Flake is to have your partner lower you while you smear sideways across a slab. It's called a tension traverse, and it's similar to a pendulum, except that you don't swing back and forth. Both techniques are common on big walls and used for moving across blank sections between crack systems. Mark Hudon and Max Jones, the first climbers to try free climbing this section of El Capitan (they managed to free climb all but three hundred feet of the route in 1979, an inspired effort), found a way to avoid the tension traverse with a difficult climb down a thin crack. Alex had always found the pitch especially difficult because his fingers don't fit in the crack, especially near the bottom. Once, when climbing this pitch with Mason Earle, he had unexpectedly popped off.

Though free climbers don't like to admit it, it's easy to benefit from rope drag when traversing or downclimbing. If your partner is a little slow feeding the rope out, even a tiny bit of tension can prevent a slip.

It had famously happened to John Bachar in 1979 on a route called Clever Lever in Colorado's Eldorado Canyon. Bachar had just climbed the route, which features a 5.12 lunge to a jug hold at the lip of a roof twenty feet above the ground. He felt so solid on it that when he got back to the ground, he decided to free solo it. At the crux, he threw for the jug and easily latched it. Unfortunately, he had failed to notice when doing it the first time that the weight of the rope running through the protection had checked his outward swing. Now, without a rope, his legs swung out so far from the wall that his body went horizontal and his hand slipped off the jug. He hit the ground feet first, on the only flat spot in a garden of jagged boulders, and then tumbled another ninety feet down a slab. When he came to a rest, he popped up to a sitting position and thought, *Holy shit, I'm okay*, a second before a boulder he had dislodged on his way down the hill slammed into his back, knocking him out cold.

ON PAPER, THE MONSTER OFFWIDTH appears to be one of the easier pitches on Freerider. The topo shows a straight black line, and the grade is listed at 5.11a. But climbers familiar with this route know that the Monster got its name because it's been known to eat people alive. An off-width is the name for any crack that is too wide for standard jamming technique. A slotted hand or a sideways clenched fist will usually jam well in a crack up to four inches wide. Any wider, and you have to get creative with moves like hand stacks, arm bars, and chicken wings. The big difference between off-widths and regular cracks is that you often can't hang off one arm while moving the other up, which means you have to lock yourself into the crack between moves with your legs. Off-width climbing is like trying to run up a steep hill wearing a heavy pack. The beta for the Monster on Mountain Project, an online guidebook, recommends carrying enough protection so you can build a mini anchor in the crack to hang off when you vomit from overexertion.

Alex is lucky in that his size 12½ foot, crammed into a size 8½ shoe, fits perfectly when T-boned in the Monster. Climbers call this a "heel-toe jam." Over and over, he pulled his right foot as high as he could, stuck it sideways in the crack, and then stood up on it while pulling himself up with a left-hand arm bar. His left hip, without a harness to get in the way, slid smoothly up the fissure. Like a snake, he methodically slithered his way up until his butt found a tiny shelf in the left wall the size of a toilet seat. Alex took in the view and thought about the Boulder Problem, which was now just a few hundred feet above him.

At 7:53 A.M., he scrambled into the alcove below El Cap Spire, a flat-topped 150-foot-tall tower that juts like an upturned thumb from the side of the wall. He'd made it just in time because nature was calling. Behind the spire, he found an out-of-the-way spot and shat into a crack. He felt awful about it and hoped it would rain—hard—before the next party came up it. But it had to happen, because he couldn't risk shitting his pants on the crux.

ON THE LAST GOOD LEDGE below the Boulder Problem, Alex took off his shoes and shirt. For the second time of the day, he looked down directly into the lens of the spotting scope. Then he pulled down his pants, gave us what Mikey called "the full frontal," and took a leak. Afterward, he went and sat down and had a drink of water from a bottle he had previously stashed on the ledge. Seven minutes after he got there, he slipped his shoes and shirt back on, stood up, and shook his hands like a sprinter at the starting line of a hundred-meter dash. He slathered chalk onto the backs of his hands and looked poised to set off when he sat back down and took his shoes off again.

"I don't want to watch this," said Mikey for the second time.

Minutes later, Alex was standing on the last good footholds below Freerider's crux. Unlike every other difficult patch on the route, these moves are so tenuous that there's only one way to do them. Other sections of the route, like the slabs, for example, have multiple possibilities. Alex could screw up a sequence and still feel confident that he could get through the moves. On the Enduro Corner, there was a sequence for the jams—left hand thumb up, right hand thumb down—and he had ticked the holds accordingly. But he had also practiced the pitch "off-handed," as he called it, meaning he intentionally grabbed with the wrong hand. He had told me that it didn't even feel that much harder. There are thousands of individual moves on Freerider and, despite memorizing many of them, Alex trusted himself to figure a lot of them out on the fly. When he was in the flow state, his body sometimes knew what to do better than his mind did. This intuitive kinesthetic awareness was how he found a lot of the refinements to his sequences. But the Boulder Problem isn't like that. As Alex had explained to me in exquisite detail that day in Foresta, there is one way, and only one way, to do it. And he knew that if he screwed it up, if he pushed his thumb against the pencil-eraser hold in the wrong way, it would probably cause his feet to skate off the tiny nubs that were holding him up. And the handholds were so bad that if his foot slipped, there was no way he could check the fall.

After three hours of squinting with my left eye while I gazed through the scope with my right, I had developed a mild headache. I reached up to put my left hand over my eye, so I wouldn't have to scrunch it shut, and it felt wet on my face. My palms were sweating. The scope gave the illusion that I was watching Alex on a screen, like this was a YouTube video. But my pounding heart knew it was all too real. I must have looked away, because now I don't remember seeing him do the karate kick. What I do remember is next seeing Alex's left leg stuck out horizontally like a dancer's. He had nailed the Boulder Problem—the 5.13a crux, 2,100 feet in the air—that had spit him off two days earlier. A few seconds later, at 8:23 A.M., he pulled onto the ledge above the Boulder Problem, turned around, and held his hands over his head. It was a gesture somewhat out of character for Alex, but he was connecting with those of us who were witnessing the climb. He was sharing the joy.

THE FINAL PITCHES WERE LIKE a victory lap. By now Alex had spent so much time on Freerider that a lot of the holds felt like old friends. *I love this move*, he thought, over and over, as he karate-chopped his way up the perfect hand and finger cracks. As he joyfully reeled himself upward, the valley floor, half a mile down, was spread below like the tableau of a model train set. Old-growth black oak trees speckled El Cap Meadow like pieces of broccoli, the vehicles inching along the loop road like Matchbox cars. The sun-stippled Merced River sparkled as it lazily flowed downvalley alongside the meadow, which appeared to undulate as its tall golden grass swayed in the breeze. This was the section of the climb that had been playing on the highlight reel in Alex's mind for the past nine years. He felt like the hero in an action movie of his own making, which, in a way, he was. A few feet away, Jimmy dangled on the end of a rope, camera trained on Alex.

THERE WAS NO CHEERING CROWD when Alex pulled over the final block, no spraying of champagne, no gushing reporters asking him what it felt like to have just completed the greatest rock climb of all time. Alex walked a few feet back from the edge and took off his shirt and shoes. He was covered in chalk from the tips of his fingers all the way up his Popeye-like forearms. He stood on the rim, squinting into the bright morning sun, arms by his sides. It was 9:28 A.M. The first free solo ascent of El Capitan had taken three hours and fifty-six minutes.

Alex would later post a photo to Instagram of him and Jimmy hugging a few feet from the edge of the cliff. The caption reads, in part: "I was elated, @jimmychin was probably just relieved that his movie has a happy ending." Jimmy's got both arms around Alex. His eyes are shut, and his mouth is wide-open, like he's yelling. Alex, standing erect and almost a head taller than Jimmy, wears an enigmatic, toothy smile.

MY STORY BREAKING THE NEWS of Alex's historic ascent posted on *National Geographic*'s website at ten A.M. It immediately went viral.

Tommy Caldwell had given me a quote. He called the climb "the moon-landing of free soloing."

Peter Croft had said, "After this, I really don't see what's next. This is the big classic jump."

Later, *The New York Times* would write that Honnold's free solo of El Capitan should be celebrated "as one of the great athletic feats of any kind, ever."

But there were haters, too. The link to the story on *National Geographic*'s Facebook page racked up more than 2,000 comments, and I was shocked at how many of them were negative.

> Idiots like this fucker are why gym rats are climbing outside without helmets. I don't want to ruin my next climbing day carrying your brain dead asshat self off the cliff when you bash your skull in on a 20 foot whipper that you should walk away from.

> Had he fallen, who would have paid for his bodies recovery? His parents? Always irritates me to think of how much stupidity I pay for as a responsible tax payer.

> . . . I am getting rather tired of hearing athletes talk like anything they do benefits mankind in any way. While the feat itself is extremely impressive, it is ultimately meaningless and the world is no different today because of it. . . . Why don't you devote all that time and energy into doing something for someone else for a change?

There were also hundreds of comments from Alex's fans and supporters.

> Gotta love all the Debbie Downers here, pissing on this guy's Wheaties just because they envy

someone willing to take risks while they sit at home judging other people from the bottom of a bag of chips.

Alex never read any of them.

At 11:29 A.M. I heard a familiar whistle. A few seconds later, Alex emerged from the forest and trotted across the small meadow where I was waiting for him. The Huck Finn pants were covered in chalk, as was his shirt. On his head he wore a black baseball cap, his ears sticking out from underneath. It felt a little odd as he jogged across the meadow and I stood there waiting. But the awkward moment lasted only a few seconds before Alex locked me in the warmest embrace I've ever had from him. I slapped him on the shoulder and then stepped back to take in his expression. He was glowing. I was too. I might have cried, like I had at the end of *The Karate Kid,* when Daniel-san wins the tournament (I had watched it with my eleven-year-old daughter, who was getting into karate, right before I left for this trip), if I hadn't gotten it out of my system the night before. This scene was playing out exactly how I had pictured it in my mind beforehand. Weird.

Alex sat down on a rock, and I dropped into the dirt next to him. It was hot. Mosquitoes buzzed around us. I noticed a thin dark line on his upper lip, the faintest hint of a mustache. He's not a hairy dude, which made me wonder how long it had been since he had shaved. I looked down at his shoes. The laces, de-sheathed and broken, had been jury-rigged back together. Alex pulled an apple out of his pack and asked if I had any water. I gave him what was left in my bottle.

"So, did it go perfectly?" I asked.

"It went pretty much perfectly. I had to take a dump down behind the spire. I feel pretty bad about it. But it's just one of those things. I hope nobody's climbing Excalibur for a while. The idea of soloing the crux sort of loosened things up."

We sat a hundred yards off the trail to the Manure Pile Buttress. Climbers, carrying ropes and gear, were walking back and forth, looking in our direction. By now, news outlets all over the world were reporting Alex's feat, and climbers were reading about it on their phones. "Hey, Alex, glad you didn't die," yelled someone walking by on the trail.

In the background, a mob was swarming up the cliff's most popular offering—After Six. It's one of Yosemite's easiest multipitch routes, and it was on my list of solos. So far, I had ticked off exactly none of them.

I asked Alex if he had thought about anything other than the moves on his way up the climb. He said that on the easier sections, he was already thinking about his next goal, which was to climb the grade 9a (9a is a French grade, equivalent to 5.14d/5.15a on the Yosemite Decimal System), two ticks below the world standard of 9c. It struck me as slightly preposterous that, having just made the greatest climb of all time, Alex would be looking forward to becoming like the fiftieth best sport climber in the world. But 9a happens to be one notch harder than what Alex has climbed to date. It's something that he will have to accomplish with the use of a rope, of course. But greater climbing prowess would open the door to more free-solo projects as well. "Imagine what I could do if I was as strong as Adam Ondra," Alex said one day between burns on the Beastmaker.

"So it's still just game on?" I asked.

"It's kind of been a strategy the whole time I've worked on this—to look past it, to think what's beyond, what other stuff I'm excited about. So this just feels like a seminormal day. I want to eat some lunch, I want to get in the shade, and then I'm probably going to hangboard in a bit."

"A normal person would probably take the afternoon off after they free soloed El Cap," I replied.

"But I've been hangboarding every other day, and it's the other day."

AN HOUR LATER, I was sitting on an upside-down canoe outside the door of Alex's van, which was now parked back in Mike's driveway. Birds chirped and flitted among the branches of the oak trees overhead. Yosemite Falls roared in the background, so ever present it hardly registered. On Lost Arrow Road, there were no news trucks, no groupies, no rangers offering congratulations. It was just Alex and me. Sanni was on her way to the airport. She and Alex had spoken on the phone shortly after he topped out. Sanni cried. "The only reason I'm sad not to be there is because I wanted to see your smile, that big goofy grin that doesn't come out that often," she said. "But I can hear it through the phone."

So I sat there. And I watched Alex. Barefoot and bare-chested, wearing only a pair of bright red shorts, he hung two-handed from the Beastmaker. Because he had been hangboarding every other day. And today was the other day.

| Author's Note

The idea for this book grew out of an assignment for *National Geographic* magazine to cover Alex Honnold's free solo of El Capitan. At the time of this writing, that article is scheduled to be published in March 2019. Some of the material in this book is taken verbatim from that article—and vice versa.

I have also used other articles I've written over the years for *Climbing*, *Men's Journal*, *National Geographic*, and *Outside* as sources, and this book contains select passages that were taken verbatim from these earlier works.

Other sources for this book include films, YouTube videos, social media, online forums, podcasts, books, articles, news stories, and countless conversations and interviews. In many instances, the sources for information contained herein—be it a magazine, book, or individual—have been credited in the text. Some material that appears in quotes was sourced from the many articles that have been written about Alex over the years and are attributed in the text. One exception is on page 33, where Alex describes himself as a "ganglylooking" dude. This is quoted from Joseph Hooper's *Men's Journal* article, "The Radical Calm of Alex Honnold."

Some of the stories in this book took place many years ago. I re-created the tales of my youth in Chapter Two mostly from memory. These are stories I've been telling for decades, and I have endeavored, to the best of my ability, to recount them accurately. But memory can be a funny thing.

Sources for Chapter Three include John Long's *Stories from the Dirt*, Warren Harding's *Downward Bound*, Trip Gabriel's 1983 *Rolling Stone* magazine article "Valley Boys," Burr Snider's 1986 profile of Harding in the *San Francisco Examiner* entitled "The Life of Warren 'Batso' Harding," and *Men's Journal's* "The Legend of Dope Lake" by Greg Nichols. I am also indebted to Long and Dean Fidelman for sharing their recollections of Bachar and the Stonemasters. Their books— *The Stonemasters: California Rock Climbers in the Seventies* and *Yosemite in the Fifties*—are essential reads for anyone looking to learn more about Yosemite's climbing history. I also gleaned a lot of information from the various forums on SuperTopo, into which one can easily get lost.

In Chapter Four, I am deeply indebted to Alex Lowther's superb profile of Alex for *Alpinist* magazine entitled "Less and Less Alone," as well as Seth Heller's profile of Alex in *Rock and Ice*, "A View from the Top." The story of Alex's fall on Mount Tallac was sourced from him and his mother, Dierdre Wolownick, and I also referenced news articles written about the incident at the time. This chapter (not to mention this entire book) also benefitted greatly from Alex's autobiography, cowritten with David Roberts, *Alone on the Wall*. The journal entry Alex recorded after his fall on Mount Tallac ("Fell, broke hand . . . airlifted . . .") was sourced directly from Alex's book. Some of the dialogue in this book has been sourced from *Alone on the Wall*, including the exchange Alex had with the hiker on his way down from soloing Half Dome. *Alone on the Wall*, by the way, has been rereleased with three new chapters containing Alex's first-person account of his free solo of El Capitan.

The section on the early history of Yosemite, including the Mariposa Battalion, was sourced from Lafayette Bunnell's book *Discovery of the Yosemite*; Benjamin Madley's book *An American Genocide*; and Daniel Duane's *New York Times* article "What's in a Name?" I also spoke with

Madley and Duane and corresponded with Teenie Matlock, a professor at the University of California Merced, to fact-check this section.

Various articles written by Cedar Wright, James Lucas, and Duane Raleigh were valuable sources of information about Alex, John Bachar, and Michael Reardon. Wright's column for *Climbing* magazine, The Wright Stuff, was an important source of information on the Stone Monkeys.

In Chapter Five I was able to refer back to my journal from the Trango expedition, as well as a paper copy of the entire Quokka website, which my father printed while the trip was unfolding. I also benefitted from the article for *Climbing* magazine that I wrote at the time, as well as Jennifer Lowe-Anker's excellent book *Forget Me Not,* which covers, among many things, the Great Sail Peak and the Great Trango expeditions. Some of the dialogue in this chapter was pulled from the film we made, *Great Trango Tower: A Granite Mile High,* which can be found on YouTube.

Chapter Six was sourced from my journal of the Borneo expedition and the article I wrote for *Men's Journal,* "Borneo's Forbidden Chasm." Another important reference was the book *Descent into Chaos* by Richard Connaughton, as well as numerous news articles written at the time of the rescue.

Much of the reporting about Dean Potter came from extensive interviews with two of his best friends, Dean Fidelman and Jim Hurst. I also watched numerous YouTube videos of Dean, including *Eiger Jump,* which contains excellent footage of Potter's freeBASE of Deep Blue Sea. Matt Samet's excellent article for *Outside Online,* "How Dean Potter Became Everyone's Favorite Wingsuited Slacklining Speed Climber," is where I sourced the line "living like plankton" that appears on page 177.

Chapter Eight benefitted immensely from Joseph Hooper, who shared his notes with me from his reporting for his *Men's Journal* article "The Radical Calm of Alex Honnold." This material was critical for me in re-creating the story of Tommy Caldwell and

Kevin Jorgeson topping out the Dawn Wall. Other sources for the Dawn Wall section include Tommy's autobiography, *The Push;* Andrew Bisharat's reporting for *Rock and Ice* magazine and his website, EveningSends.com; John Branch's numerous articles about the climb that appeared in *The New York Times*; Burr Snider's Harding profile in the *San Francisco Examiner*; Harding's book, *Downward Bound*; and a CBS *Evening News* broadcast from November 1970.

My main source for Chapter Nine was the writer J. B. MacKinnon, who was extremely generous in helping me to understand the brain scan that Alex underwent at the Medical University of South Carolina. In re-creating this scene for the book, I relied heavily on interviews with JB and his article for *Nautilus* magazine, "The Strange Brain of the World's Greatest Solo Climber." I am also indebted to Dr. Jane Joseph and Joseph LeDoux, who spoke with me at length about this subject. For those who would like to learn more about the amygdala, LeDoux's book *Anxious* is an excellent source.

The more recent stories, including the trip to Morocco and the two trips to Yosemite, I reported in person with extensive note-taking. Much of the dialogue comes from recorded interviews and conversations. In some cases, where stories were recounted to me, I re-created dialogue based on what interviewees remembered of past conversations in which they had taken part. Some scenes in these three chapters recount situations in which I was not able to take notes or make recordings at the time—while climbing on El Capitan with Alex, for example. And there were many times when hanging out with Alex that I made a conscious decision not to take notes so as to preserve the authenticity of the scene. In these instances I took notes at the next available opportunity. In cases where I was unsure if I had it right, I fact-checked with the relevant parties. The quote on page 378, where the climbers show up while Alex is setting off and they say, "Oh my god, it's happening," was told to me secondhand and confirmed by Alex. It also appears in J. B. MacKinnon's piece for *The New Yorker,* "Alex Honnold's Perfect Climb."

| Acknowledgments

Out of all the people who helped bring these chapters to fruition, no one had a bigger impact than my friend and fellow Crazy Kid Jeff Chapman. If you enjoyed this story, please tip your hat to Jeff, because it's in large part due to the many hours he spent editing, analyzing, and providing feedback on the manuscript. His insights were at times of such genius that I found myself pumping my fist in the air, as if I had just topped out El Capitan without a rope. I can't thank you enough, Jeff, and I hope someday I can return the favor.

I am also extremely grateful to *National Geographic* magazine and my editor, Peter Gwin, for assigning me to report on Alex Honnold's historic free solo of El Capitan. Without *National Geographic's* support and belief in the importance of this story, the book that you are holding would not exist. By the same token, I am deeply indebted to Jimmy Chin, who collaborated with me on the article and invited me to be a part of his project. The film he codirected with his wife, Elizabeth Chai Vasarhelyi, about Alex's impossible climb will be of keen interest to anyone who has read this book.

There would have been no story to tell without Alex Honnold. Thank you, Alex, for your friendship, for being who you are, for your inspiration and support, and for trusting me to get this right. I owe the same thanks to Cassandra "Sanni" McCandless, who openly shared her story with me, climbed with me, and even babysat for my son Tommy. I'd also like to thank Alex's mom, Dierdre Wolownick, for sharing her many stories about Alex as a youth. (And congratulations, Dierdre, for becoming the oldest woman to climb El Capitan at age sixty-six!)

It was serendipitous that around the same time I was developing the proposal for this book I happened to sit on a panel alongside author Virginia Morell. I owe a huge debt to Virginia for introducing me to her literary agent, Gillian MacKenzie. Gillian turned out to be not only a kindred spirit but a brilliant agent who helped me to find the perfect editor and publisher for this book. I would also like to thank Gillian's business partner at MacKenzie Wolf, Kirsten Wolf, and their assistant, Allison Devereux.

I got very lucky when Gillian introduced me to Stephen Morrow at Dutton. He understood from the moment we first sat down together, even better than I did, what this book could be. His guiding hand and unwavering belief in this project kept me on track during the year and a half we worked together on the manuscript. Along the way, Stephen became a close friend, and I can say with certainty that this would be a far lesser work were it not for his expertise and passion. At Dutton, I would also like to thank John Parsley, Christine Ball, Amanda Walker, Madeline Newquist, LeeAnn Pemberton, Eileen Chetti, and everyone on the Penguin Random House sales force—you all made me feel like I was part of a team that was far stronger than the sum of its parts.

I am indebted to Tommy Caldwell, Peter Croft, John Long, Dean Fidelman, Mandi Finger, Ben Smalley, Chris Weidner, Maury Birdwell, Ted Hesser, Colin Haley, Mike Gauthier, Emily Harrington, Brad Gobright, Peter Mortimer, Nick Rosen, Jim Hurst, Mikey Schaefer, Pablo Durana, Matt Irving, Dave Allfrey,

Cheyne Lempe, Clair Popkin, Joseph LeDoux, Jane Joseph, Henry Barber, Nik Wallenda, Forest Altherr, and Jeff Ball, all of who generously gave of their time to help me better understand Alex Honnold and some of the other characters in this book.

And a huge thank-you to all the people who contributed visuals: Corey Rich, Austin Siadak, Dean Fidelman, Clayton Boyd, the Frost family, Phil Bard, Cameron Lawson, Jared Ogden, Tim Kemple, and Frank Hoover.

I owe a lot to the many editors I've worked with over the years. You taught me how to use the written word to tell stories and always made me look like a better writer than I am. They include: Duane Raleigh, Alison Osius, Mike Benge, Jeff Achey, Michael Kennedy, Matt Samet, Dougald MacDonald, Jonathan Thesenga, Brad Wieners, Grayson Schaffer, Kevin Haynes, John Birmingham, Alex Bhattacharji, Steve Byers, and Mike Benoist.

Greg Child, Jeff Achey, John Climaco, Shaun Pinkham, Jim Zellers, and my father-in-law, Alan Kew, reviewed the manuscript and provided critical feedback. Each one of you had a piece in making this book better than it would have been without your input. Thank you for your time and support.

I'd also like to thank all the members of the climbing tribe, especially those with whom I have roped up over the years. A few of you are (and I apologize in advance for anyone who should be on this list but is not): Simon Ahlgren, Baker Bent, Christian George, Ben Spiess, Rob Frost, Randy Rackliff, Tyler Hamilton, Chris Davenport, Pete Masterson, Jimmy Surette, Scott Lee, Freddie Wilkinson, Mark Richey, Dustin Cormier, Sean Lorway, Bruce Ostler, Charlie Townsend, Frank Carus, Tom Burt, Shaun Pinkham, Eli Simon, Warren Hollinger, Jerry Gore, Ed February, Andy de Klerk, David Hamlin, Jeff Achey, John Climaco, John Catto, Kit Deslauriers, Renan Ozturk, Hazel Findlay, James Pearson, Brady Robinson, Peter Croft, Kristoffer Erickson, Pete Athans,

Kasha Rigby, Hilaree Nelson, Rick Armstrong, Chris Figenshau, Heidi Wirtz, Sam Elias, Cameron Lawson, Pat Ament, Eugene Fisher, Steve Schneider, Mike Pennings, Jeff Hollenbaugh, Lance Lemkau, Brad Tomlin, Lee Smith, Brad Bond, Ted Hesser, Spencer Salovaara, and Bob Snover.

A few climbers in particular deserve special mention: Jared Ogden and Kevin Thaw, with whom I did the bulk of my expeditions, are the best partners I've ever had; Greg Child, a hero from my Crazy Kids days, who later became a mentor, partner, and friend; Conrad Anker, for opening the door for me to pursue climbing full-time, for his mentorship, and for suggesting that I bring Alex Honnold on that expedition to Borneo. Alex Lowe was my idol as a young climber, and despite our falling out on Great Trango Tower, I still consider it a great privilege to have roped up with him. His memory lives on through the Alex Lowe Charitable Foundation and the Khumbu Climbing Center.

My career as a climber would have followed a very different trajectory were it not for the support and encouragement I've received from the North Face over the past twenty-two years. Foremost, I thank Katie Ramage, Chris Sylvia, Maeve Sloane, Kevin Hogan, Andy Coutant, Landon Bassett, Mark Hyde, Bill Brown, Tom Herbst, Todd Spaletto, Steve Rendle, the entire athlete team; and most important, my great friend, the late Ann Krcik.

Thanks to my sister, Amy Synnott-D'Annibale, who set me on the path to becoming a writer when she helped me land my first official magazine assignment back in 1996. My mom, Suzanne Synnott, instilled in me at a young age that I was special and meant to do great things. My late father, William Synnott, gave me my drive, work ethic, and love for the outdoors. He would have done his best to hide it, but I know he would have been proud to hold this book in his hands.

ACKNOWLEDGMENTS

Thanks to all the writers whose work has been helpful to me in telling this story: David Roberts, Duane Raleigh, Andrew Bisharat, Alex Lowther, J. B. MacKinnon, Joseph Hooper, Daniel Duane, John Branch, Benjamin Madley, James Lucas, Julie Ellison, Seth Heller, Cedar Wright, Matt Samet, Trip Gabriel, and Burr Snider.

There's a saying among climbers that we are "living the dream." It's almost always said sarcastically, in acknowledgment of the fact that the climbing life is a tricky one, especially when we're not on the wall. No one understands this better than my family. Finding the right balance between my passion for climbing and the responsibilities of being a husband and father has been the greatest challenge of my life. And I'll readily admit that I haven't always gotten it right. But I hope this book might one day help my children—Will, Matt, Lilla, and Tommy—appreciate why this sport is so important to me.

Lastly, I thank my wife, Hampton, who is by far my biggest supporter and without whom I could not have completed this project. Her contribution as an editor, confidant, mom, athlete, adventurer, best friend, and moral rock cannot be overstated. I could not have a better partner for the climb through life.

| About the Author

Mark Synnott is a twenty-year member of the North Face Global Athlete Team. He is a frequent contributor to *National Geographic* magazine and has written for *Outside, Men's Journal, Skiing, Rock and Ice,* and *Climbing.* He is also an IFMGA-certified mountain guide and a trainer for the Pararescuemen of the United States Air Force.